Tanned Leather Hand-Made Bags

Handy Patterns with Marked Stitching Holes for Hand-stitching Included

By PIGPONG (Yoko Ganaha, Piggy Tsujioka)

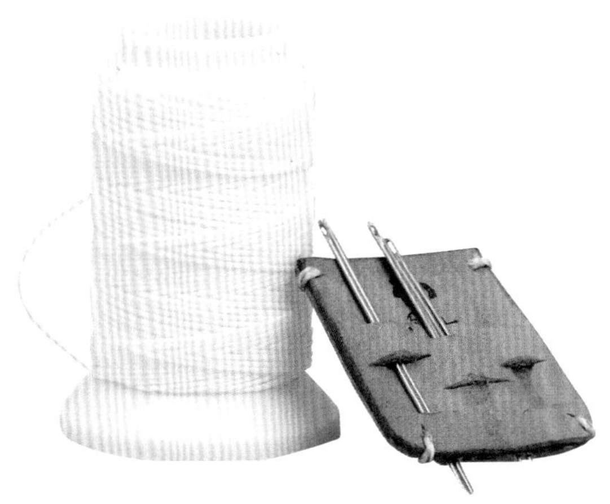

Welcome to our Studio

These are tanned leather bags and items produced with this book

Introduction

Leather is a material that is unexpectedly easy to handle.

When you make a bag using fabric you need to treat the cut edges or else they will become frayed. You could also double gore the edge and hide the seams. By contrast, it is okay to leave cut leather edges untreated. When compared to making a fabric bag, the process for making a leather bag is fairly simple.

Imagine the procedure you will use to be somewhere between paper crafts, which simply involve cutting and pasting, and fabric sewing. That might give you a better idea of what leathercraft is all about. You should also remember that, unlike a piece of paper, leather will stretch. So, making curves is actually easier than with paper crafts.

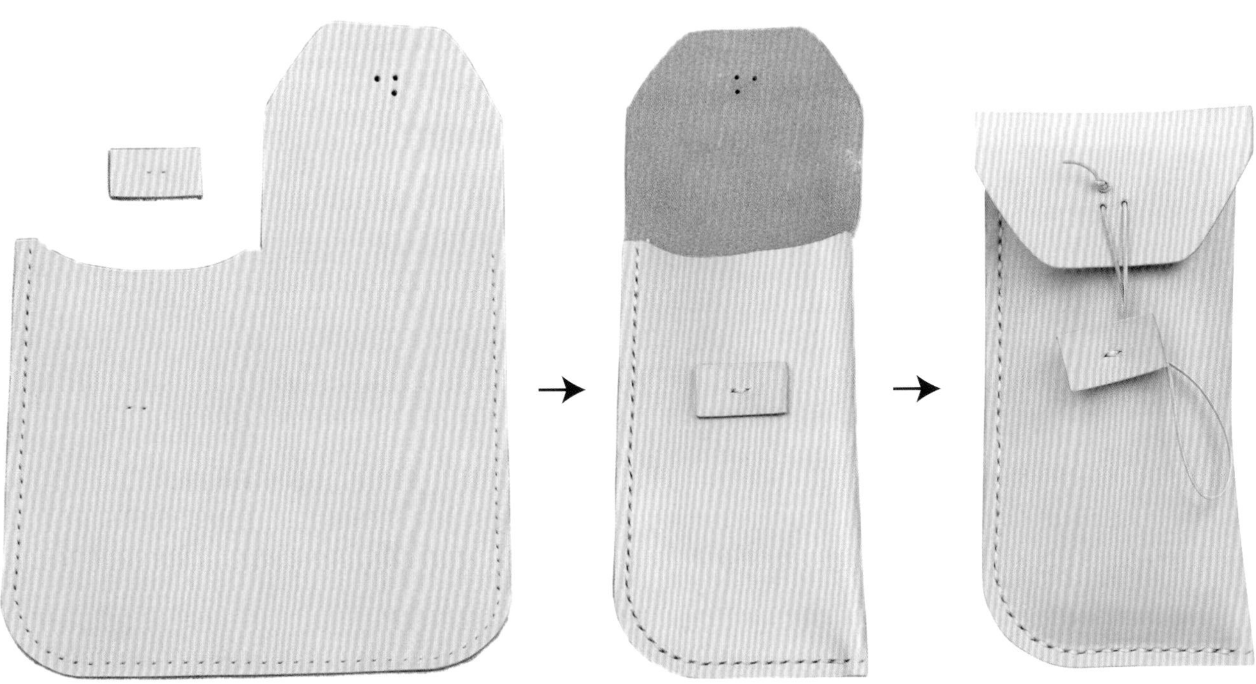

As an example, the pen case shown above was made by stitching folded leather. The leather was stretched after wetting it a little. That is how the case became "plump."

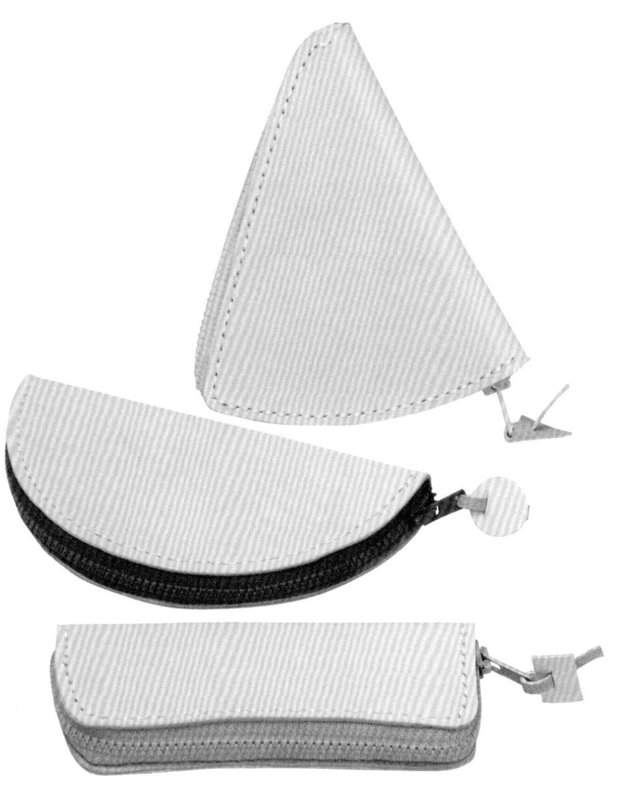

These cases can be made by cutting leather in a circular or triangular shape and then simply sewing on a zipper.

By gluing and sewing two pieces of leather together you get a bag.

Above, on the left, is a case for carrying compact disks. The larger one on the right allows you to even add a few vinyl records and carry them around.

The Production Method Used in This Book

This book is special because of the patterns attached at the end. These patterns even have the stitch-hole positions marked on them. In general, leather is stitched *after* piercing the stitching holes. Which is to say that, as far as hand-stitching is concerned, punching the stitching holes is the most important part of the procedure. As long as the number of stitching holes matches on both the front and backside, you just have to sew them together along the stitching holes to complete the stitching.

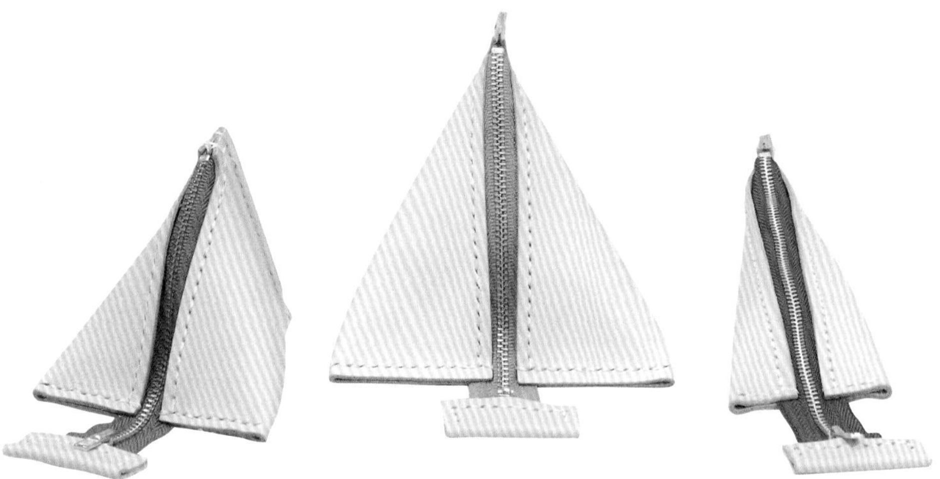

After sewing on a zipper, the case shown above was made by sewing a folded, rectangular-shaped piece of leather together.

Make a slit in the leather and then sew together. This creates the darts needed for the bulges.

In this book we use 1.8 mm to 2 mm (Đ in.) thick leather, which is easy for even beginners to handle. A great variety of bag structures are introduced here. These bags can all be made by leaving out the usual difficult procedures, such as skiving (partially shaving leather in order to make it thinner), etc.

Simple designs match up well with tanned leather.

An original bag can be made by changing the size of the bag or the design of the handles.

Example: The two bags shown on the left are the same cylindrical shape. However, the way the handles are attached completely changes the look of each bag.

Tanned leather gradually becomes soft.
Please be aware that, in this book, neither thick leather nor backing is used. So, the shape of each bag may be altered due to aging of the leather or due to heavy use.
Just think of this as part of the charm of an aged tanned leather bag.

Contents

Chapter 3 59

Practical Application of the Basic Methods

Chapter 4 137

Patterns

About Tanned Leather

As we all know, leather is just tanned animal skin. But there are different types of tanning. Representative methods include vegetable (tannin) tanning and chrome tanning.

Tannin is a natural substance that is found in black tea. Vegetable (tannin) tanning, which has been around for a very long time, is a method that uses chemicals contained in tree bark. Due to the primitive nature of this process, it is very time-consuming.

Among the various broadly termed "vegetable-tanned leathers," or simply "tanned leathers," this book specifically deals with cowhide – often called "natural vegetable-tanned leather" - that is closest to the hide's natural state (i.e., it is left untreated by any process, such as dying, etc.).
If worn-out vegetable-tanned leather is simply thrown away it will just gradually decompose into soil, which is similar to what happens with dead animals in the wilderness.

Chrome tanning is a tanning method that uses chemical agents. Since it takes fewer steps than vegetable tanning, and since the process can be industrialized, most commercially circulated leather products are chrome-tanned leather. This leather is often dyed or has some surface finishing.

Characteristics of Natural Vegetable-tanned Leather

Natural vegetable-tanned leather is durable and firm. However, it has the following negative characteristics: the surface is easily scratched, it tends to absorb moisture, it is easily stretched when wet, and the color changes easily due to oxidization. That being said, it is easy to process and to form shapes with this leather. In addition, it becomes soft, and more lustrous, when broken-in. Its shading changes gradually to a nice warm, amber color. Which is to say, natural vegetable-tanned leather embodies the authentic attraction of broken-in leather.

Since natural vegetable-tanned leather is not treated with surface finishing, the areas that contain scars and bug bites are clearly visible, and wrinkles and veins show up. Of course, this all just proves that the leather is from an authentic animal skin. If we remain unconcerned with such little scars, including some damaged areas, we can enjoy leather crafting and the use of leather crafted bags and everyday items that we ourselves have created.

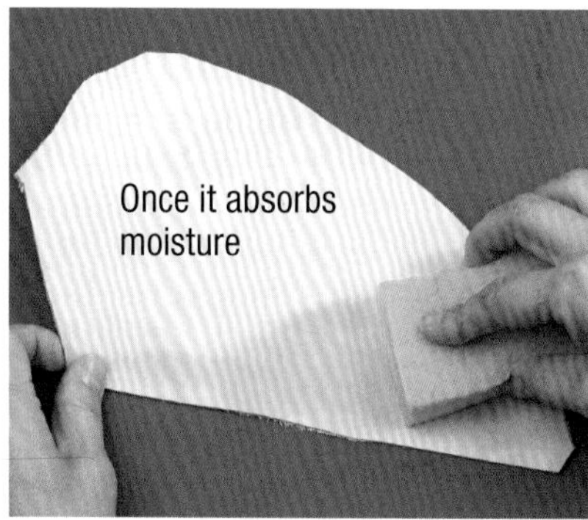

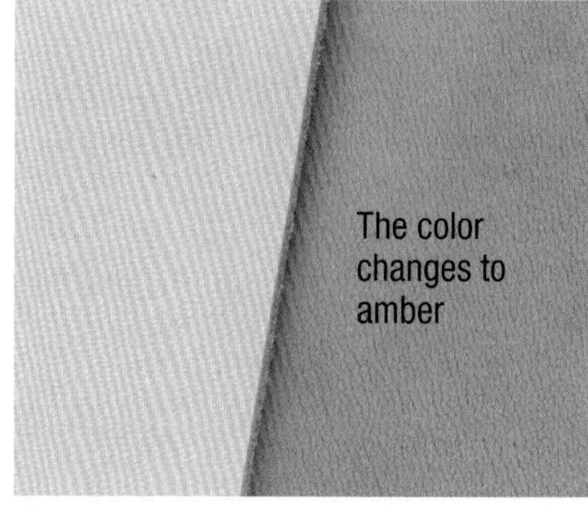

Things to Keep in Mind during Production

In leathercraft, the front-side of the leather is called the "grain-side" and the rear-side is called the "flesh-side."

Grain-side

Flesh-side

Edge

The grain-side of brand new tanned leather is pale beige. It is easily soiled and once stained it is very difficult to clean. Therefore, make sure you wash your hands before working with your leather. In addition, keep the working surface and vinyl cutting mat clean. Some people wear thin rubber gloves when hand-stitching to prevent their oily and sweaty hands from touching the leather.

The grain-side of the tanned leather is easily dented, even with just a little pressure. Even pushing down on the grain-side of the leather with a fingernail can leave marks.

Since hand-stitching thread is pre-waxed, it easily collects impurities. Removing excess wax is recommended. To do this, simply rub the thread in between two pieces of cloth.

When your leather project is finished you can protect the surface with oil, etc.

Brand-new item

Even if the leather on your project was stained by soiled hands while in production, once the finished product has been used for a while the stain will become far less obvious.
Also, if it is stained or scratched during daily use it isn't necessary to worry excessively because scratches and stains will become far less visible as the leather breaks in.

Nonetheless, I would recommend caring for your finished products with oil to prevent the grain-side of the leather from becoming frayed.

This particular item has been used for some time now

Leather Crafting Tools

Gluing Pattern

Glue Stick Use glue with low water content to prevent the pattern from wrinkling.

Drafting Tape

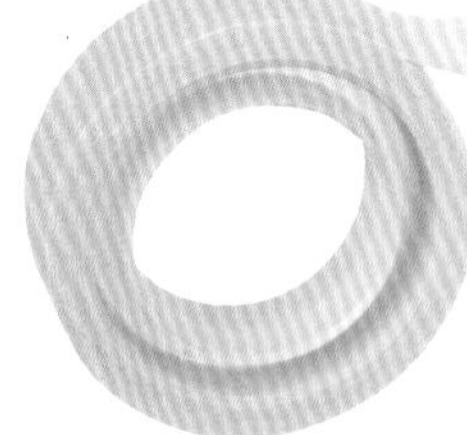

Drafting tape that can be easily removed after having been pasted on the grain-side of the leather.

Burnishing Leather

Tokonole (Tragacanth substitute)

Apply when burnishing the flesh-side or the edge of the leather.

Wood Slicker Used for slicking areas where Tokonole has been applied.

Dresser A file used to adjust and polish edges.

Gluing Leather

Adhesive Use a type of adhesive that requires application on both surfaces that need to be glued. Apply the adhesive and bond the leather together by applying pressure after the adhesive has dried.

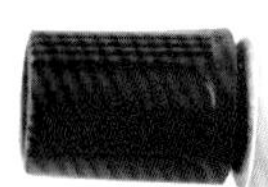

Cutting Leather

Vinyl Board A thick vinyl mat.
Place under the leather when cutting.

Large Utility Knife Use for cutting the leather.

Punching the Stitching Holes

Use 1.8 to 2 mm (⅛ in.) tanned leather.

Lacing Chisels

Instructions given in this book use 1.8 to 2 mm (1/8 in.) tanned leather and a 5 mm (¼ in.) wide, four-prong lacing chisel. The stitching holes marked on the patterns are set for 5 mm (¼ in.) wide, four-prong lacing chisels as well. If you use a different size lacing chisel, the stitching hole intervals will not match with the marks on the pattern so please be careful.

Use a four-prong chisel for a straight line and a two-prong chisel for curved lines.

Lacing Needle Used for punching individual stitching holes.

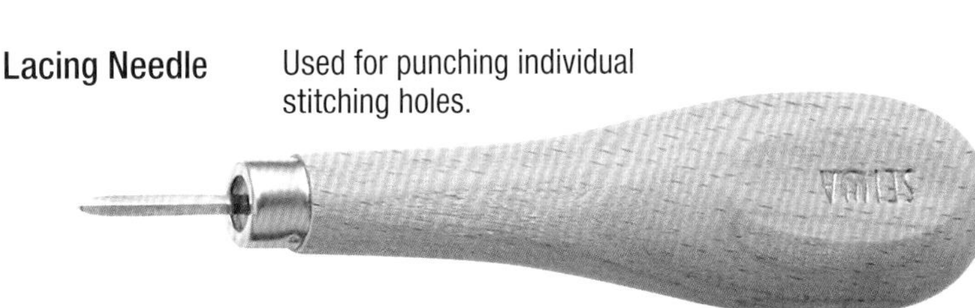

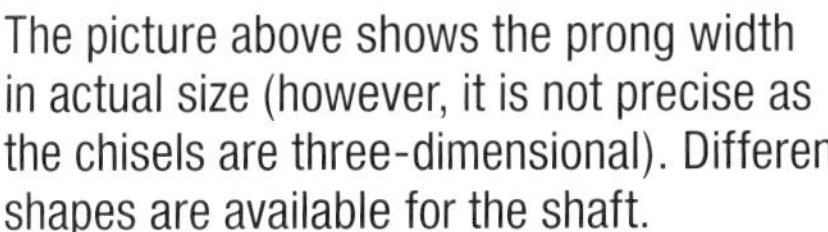

The picture above shows the prong width in actual size (however, it is not precise as the chisels are three-dimensional). Different shapes are available for the shaft.

Punching Round Holes

Single-hole Punch (Hole punch for grommets) Use for punching a round hole. Various sizes are available.

Marking

Scratch Awl Use this for marking positions or scoring lines.

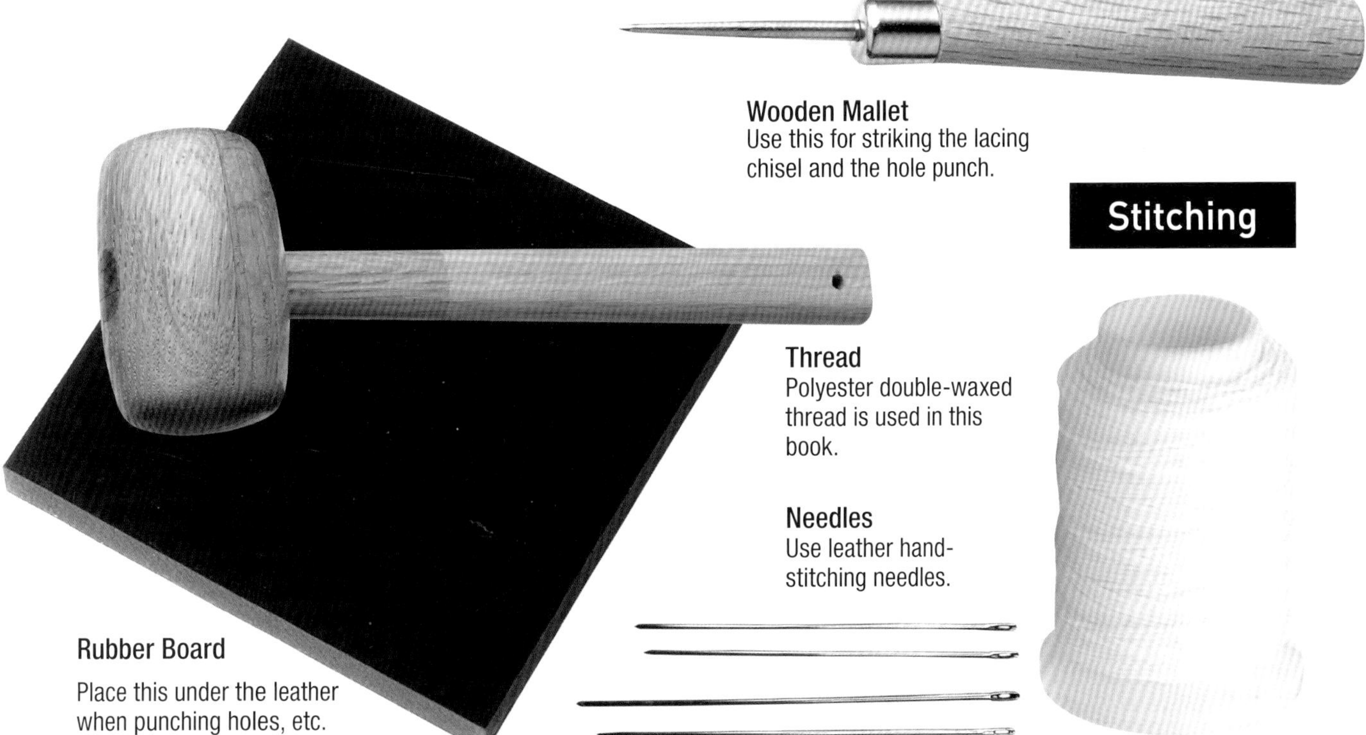

Wooden Mallet
Use this for striking the lacing chisel and the hole punch.

Rubber Board
Place this under the leather when punching holes, etc.

Stitching

Thread
Polyester double-waxed thread is used in this book.

Needles
Use leather hand-stitching needles.

Purchasing Leather

Leather can be purchased at leather specialty stores of course, but you can also find it at major fabric stores and online stores.

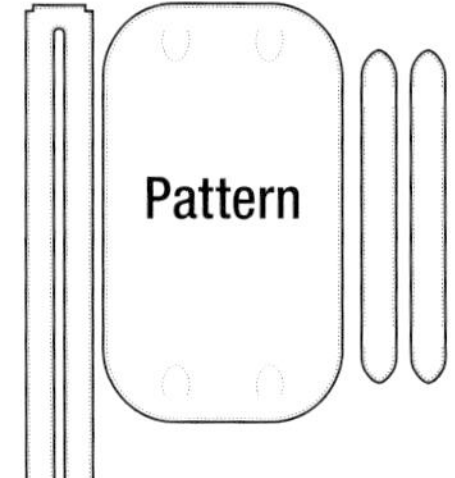

Leather is not square shaped like fabric. When you purchase leather, bring the actual sized patterns of all necessary pieces with you. Lay them on the leather to make sure it is sufficient in size. Even though the pattern includes seam allowances, I would recommend choosing leather that is larger than what is needed in order to compensate for cutting margins, bends in the leather, etc.

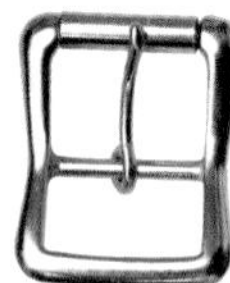

Leather from different parts of the animal tends to vary in thickness and characteristics. How the pattern is placed on the leather and how each item is cut becomes very important. If there are damaged areas or areas that can be easily stretched just check to see that they are usable or if it is possible to avoid these areas completely.

As for metal hardware, there are many varieties available. There may be a time when you cannot decide which metal hardware to use and you are not sure about which tool goes with the hardware. For choosing leather and hardware I would recommend that you confirm your choice with a knowledgeable sales clerk before making your purchase.

[Leather Measurement Units]

Each hide has a unique shape. Generally, leather is measured in square feet (sq. ft.). However, some patterns call for a certain number of yards.

1ds

10×10cm

Leathercraft supply floor (Photo: SEIWA)

[A Half Cowhide (cowhide split in half at the back)]

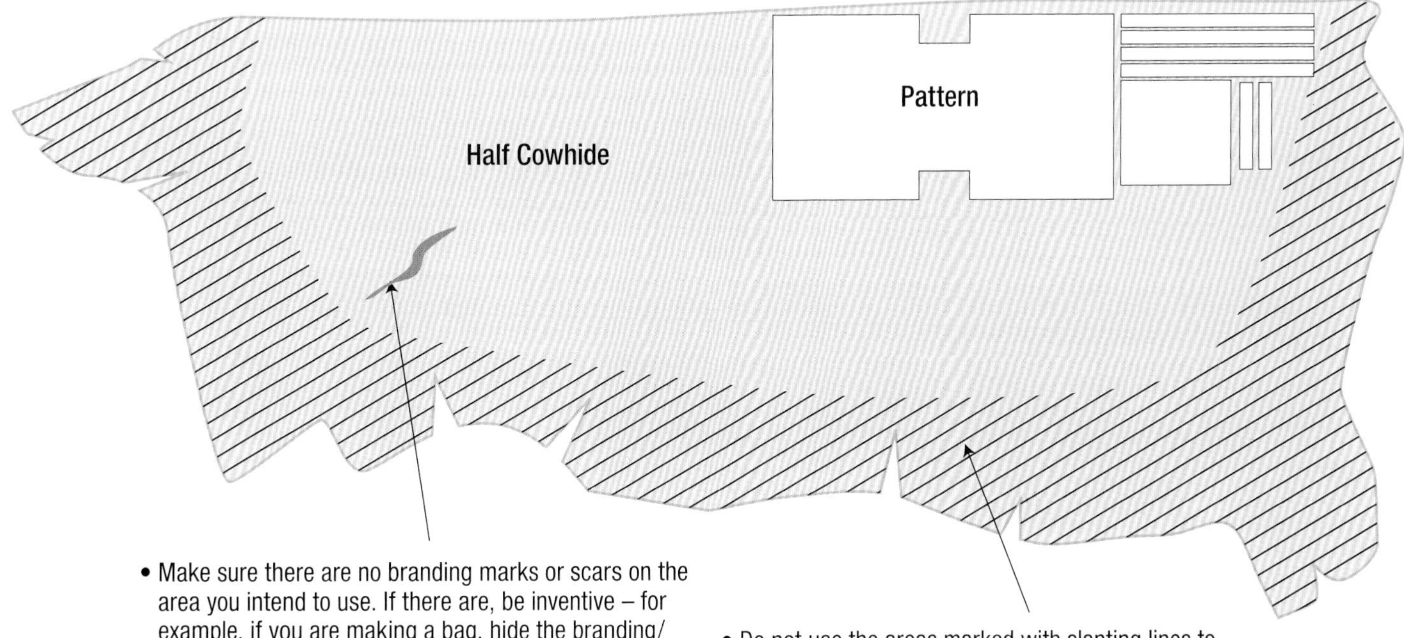

- Make sure there are no branding marks or scars on the area you intend to use. If there are, be inventive – for example, if you are making a bag, hide the branding/scar by attaching a pocket, etc.

- Do not use the areas marked with slanting lines to make the body of a bag or single-gore handles, as these areas have uneven thickness and are prone to stretching. Actually the slant-lined areas are most appropriate for making small items.

- When using remnant leather (like that marked with slanting lines) be aware of its uneven thickness and place your patterns to avoid areas that will wrinkle.

À LA CAMPAGNE

Chapter 1

Leathercraft Basics

Basic procedures for methods of cutting, stitching, etc., are introduced in this chapter. We will explain the basics for making a very simple pen case.

Basic Pen Case

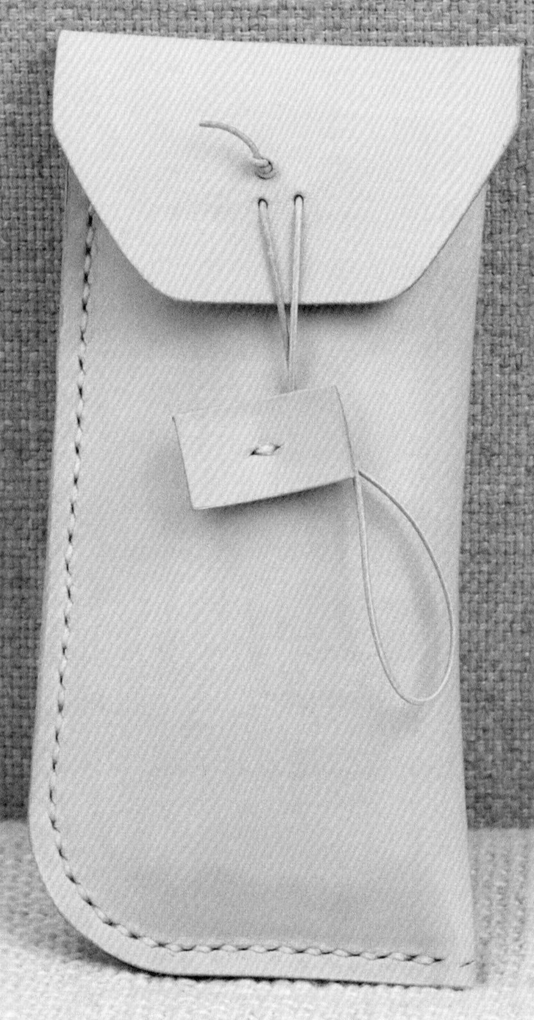

Shown above is a plain pen case made just by folding and sewing a single sheet of leather. We will follow the basic procedures of leathercraft in making the case.

Pattern

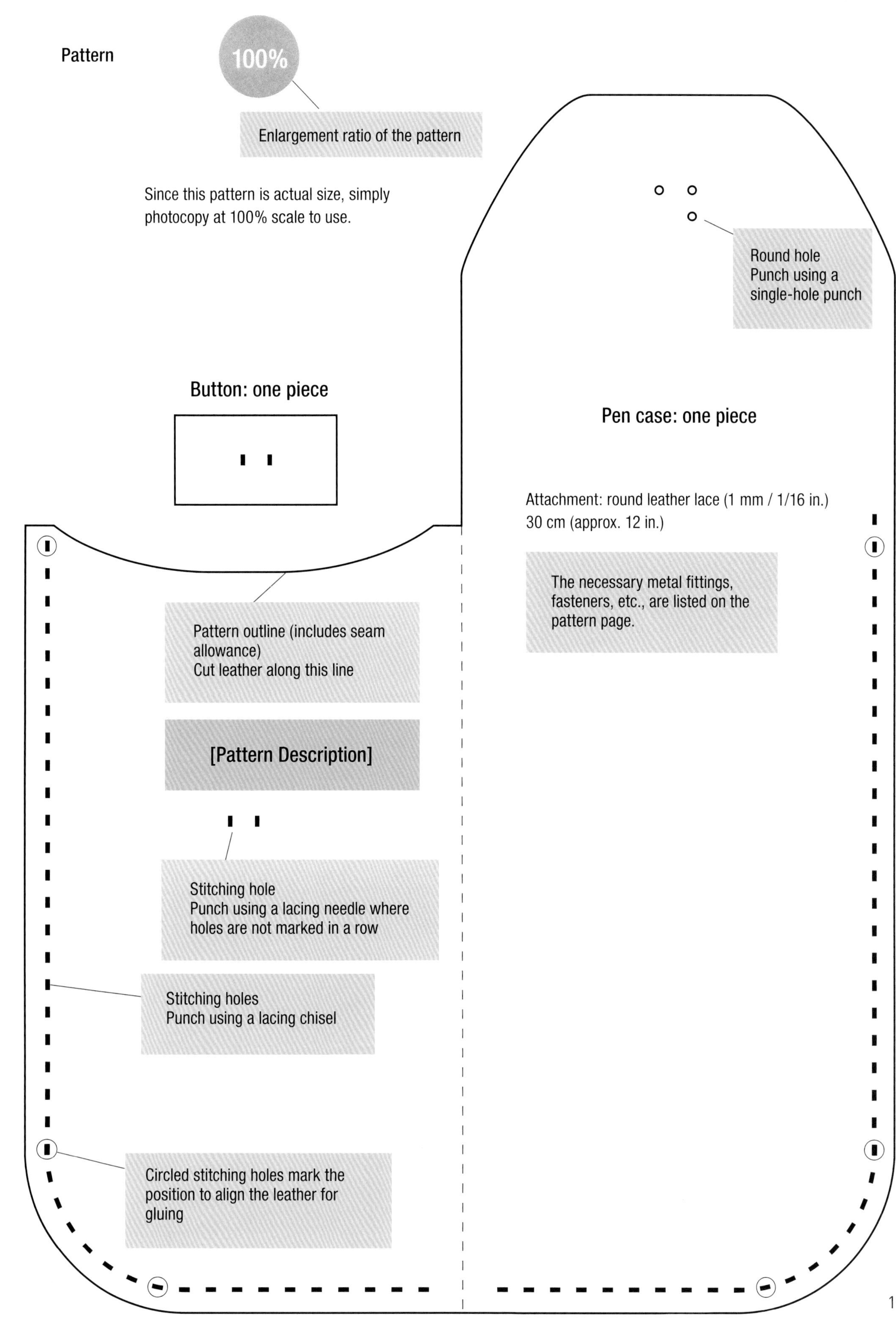

100%
Enlargement ratio of the pattern
Since this pattern is actual size, simply photocopy at 100% scale to use.
Round hole
Punch using a single-hole punch
Button: one piece
Pen case: one piece
Attachment: round leather lace (1 mm / 1/16 in.) 30 cm (approx. 12 in.)
The necessary metal fittings, fasteners, etc., are listed on the pattern page.
Pattern outline (includes seam allowance)
Cut leather along this line
[Pattern Description]
Stitching hole
Punch using a lacing needle where holes are not marked in a row
Stitching holes
Punch using a lacing chisel
Circled stitching holes mark the position to align the leather for gluing

The Basic Procedure

This describes the production flow. Detailed instructions for each procedure are given on the page number at the top right corner of each illustration.

For a project that has more items or requires three-dimensional stitching, the procedure after gluing differs slightly, but the production flow remains basically the same.

Preparation

Prepare the patterns P22

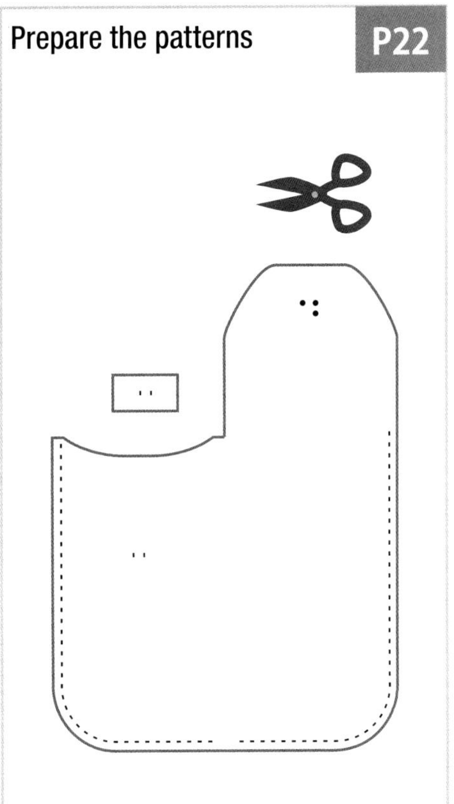

Tape the patterns on the leather P24

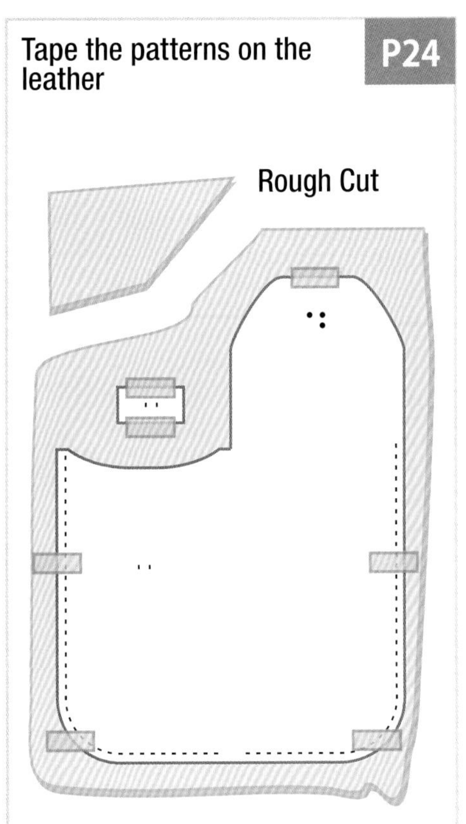

Preparation

Burnish the flesh-side P30

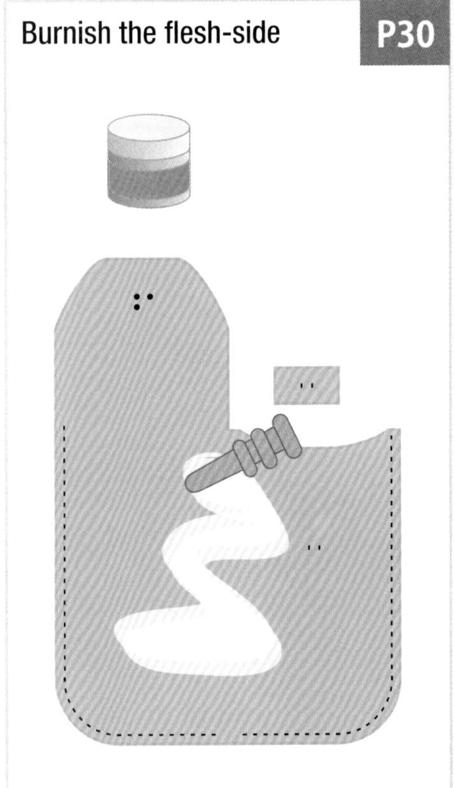

Burnish the edges P31

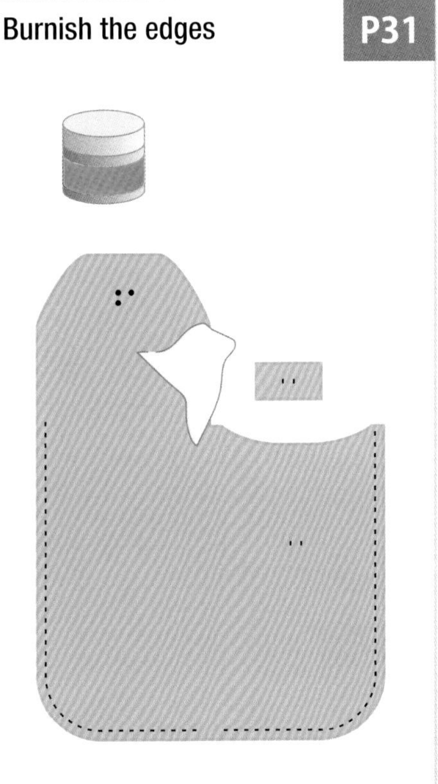

Glue

P32

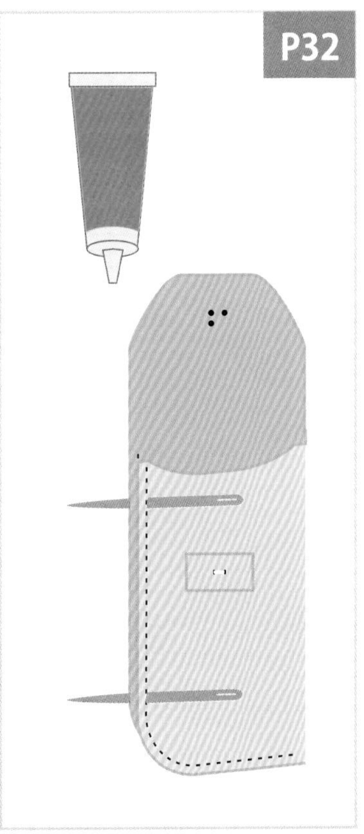

Transfer the patterns P25

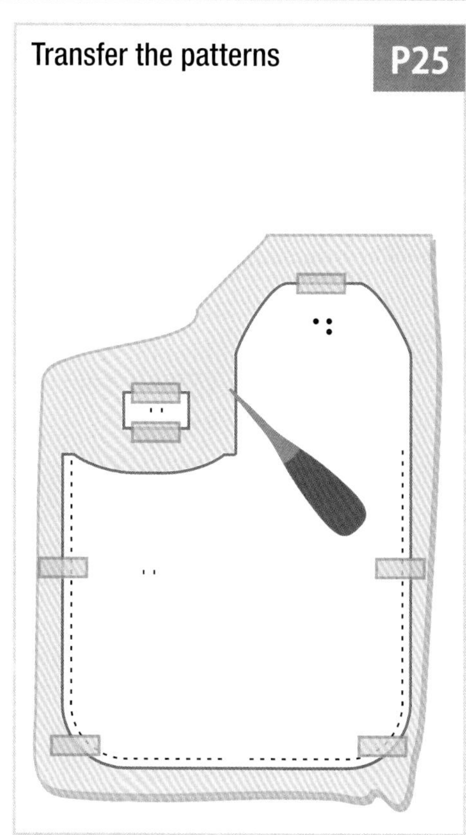

Punch the stitching holes P26

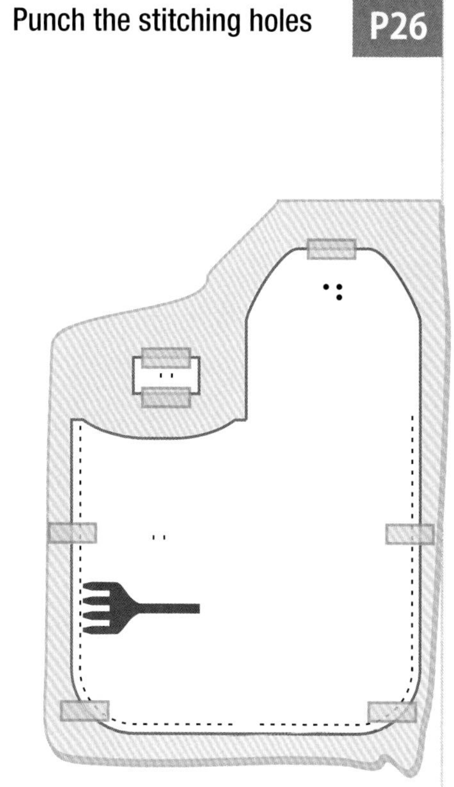

Cut the leather P28

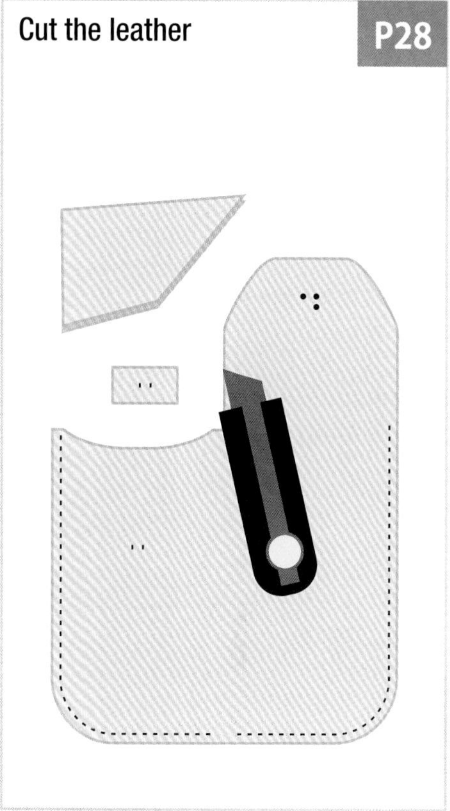

Stitch

Finishing touches

P34

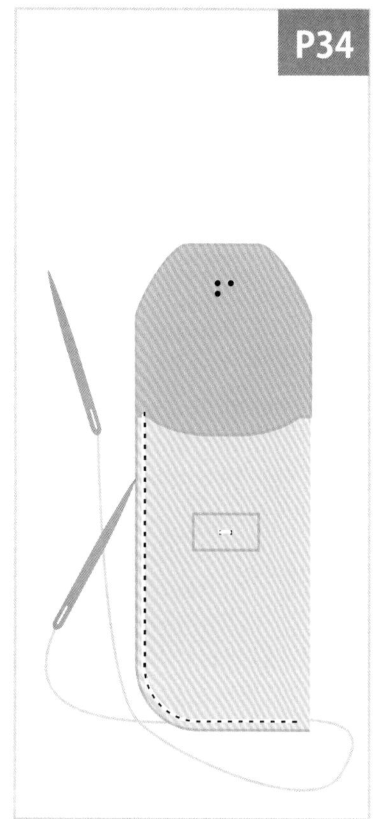

P43

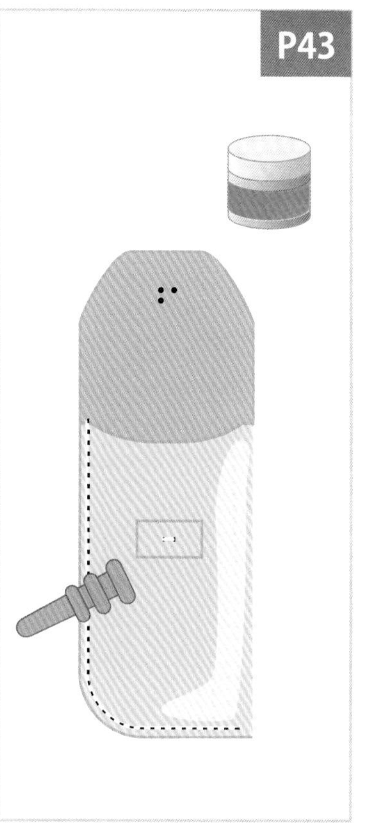

Complete

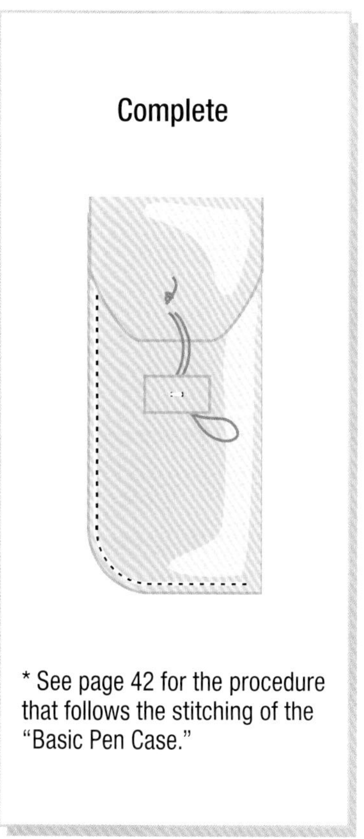

* See page 42 for the procedure that follows the stitching of the "Basic Pen Case."

Prepare the Patterns

Photocopy patterns that you will need. Make photocopies of the actual size patterns for the number of items required.

Using a glue stick, paste the patterns on a piece of thick copy paper or a sheet of "simili paper" (this is a large sized white sheet of paper available at stationary stores) to reinforce.

* Do not use glue with high water content as it will make the paper stretch.
Make sure the size of the photocopied pattern is correct and that the perpendicular and horizontal lines are aligned.

1 To prevent distortion be sure to make your photocopy of the pattern by firmly opening the pages.

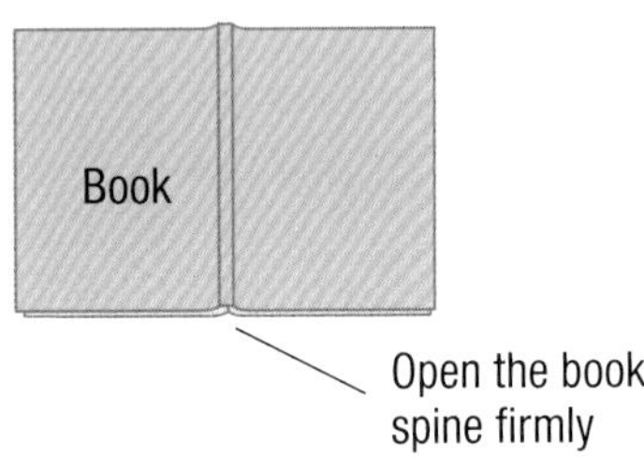

Make an enlarged photocopy for those patterns that are scaled-down.

After making an enlarged photocopy, make sure the gauge printed beside the pattern is 20 cm (7 7/8 in.) long.

When making photocopies at a copy center bring a ruler with you and make certain of the photocopied gauge length.

2 Roughly cut out the photocopy.

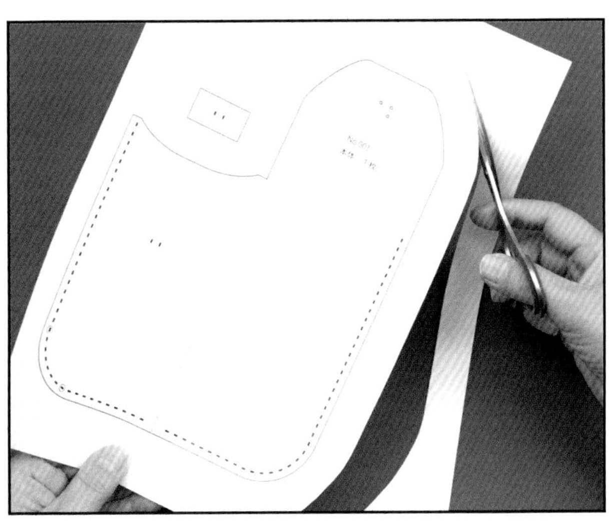

3 Paste on a sheet of simili paper or thick copy paper. Paste the seam allowance area of the pattern firmly to prevent it from falling off.

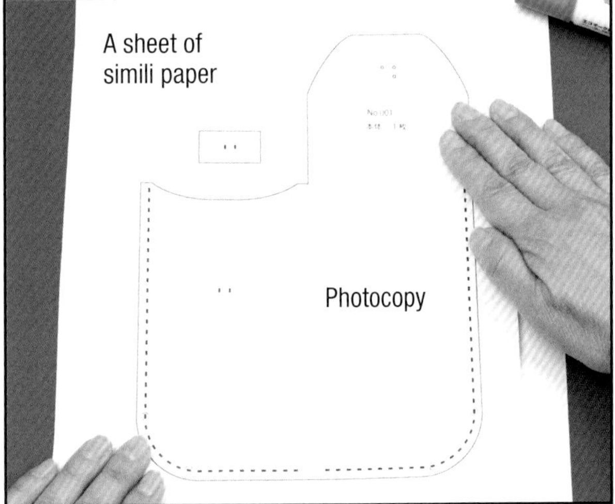

4 Cut along the outline.

[Large-size Pattern]

Large-sized patterns that do not fit on a single page are divided so that the pattern fits A3 (ledger) size paper. This makes enlarging the photocopy easier. Make as many photocopies as required.

1 Along with the outline and dotted line, be sure to cut the photocopied pattern orthogonally so that the edges of the simili paper easily align.

2 To prevent perpendicular and horizontal misalignment, paste the first piece by aligning at the corner of the simili paper. After that, match the ⊕ marks and paste the second piece while aligning the top side of the second piece and the simili paper.

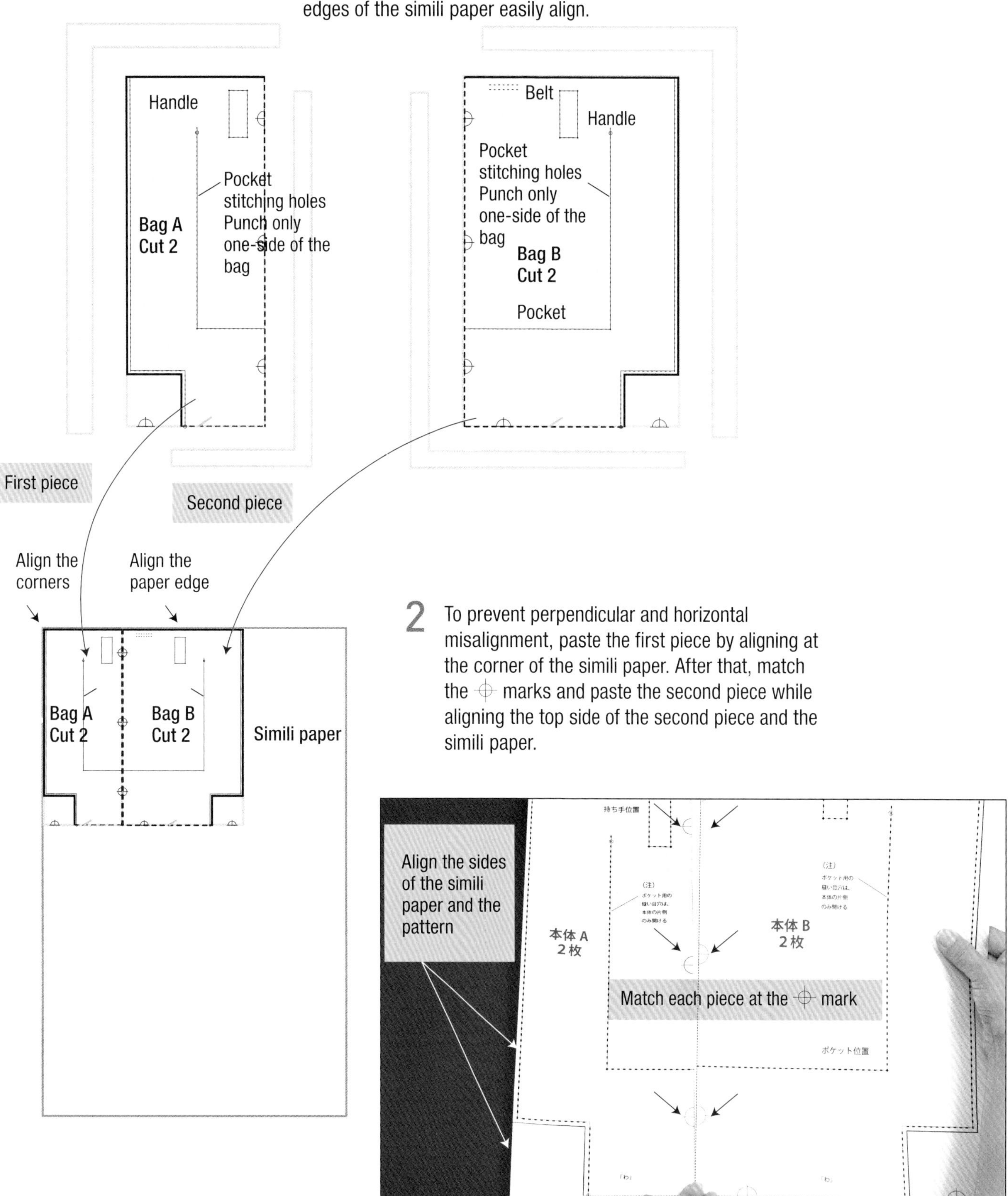

Taping Patterns onto Leather

Rough Cut

Place the patterns on the grain-side of the leather and secure using drafting tape (a type of tape you can paste and easily peel off).

In cases where the leather is warped, moisten the grain-side with a wet sponge and adjust to make it flat. After the leather has completely dried, tape the patterns on.

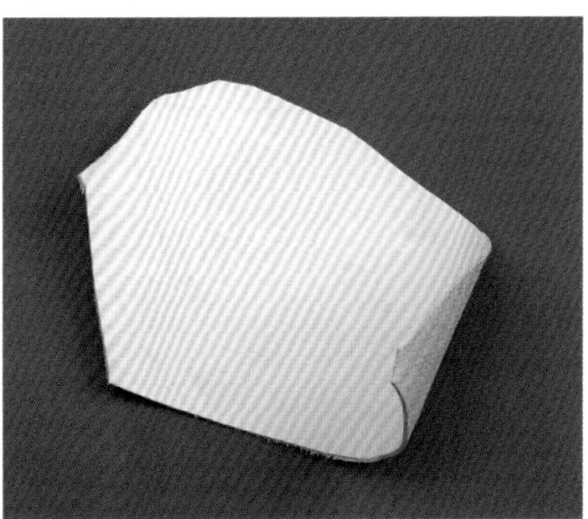

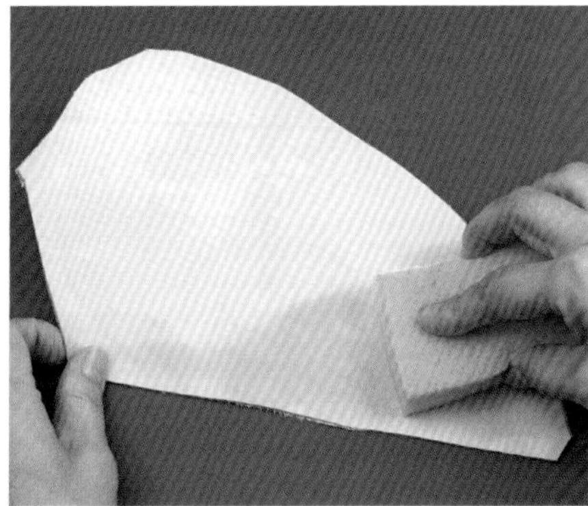

1 Place the pattern for each item on the grain-side of the leather, and then secure in several places using drafting tape.

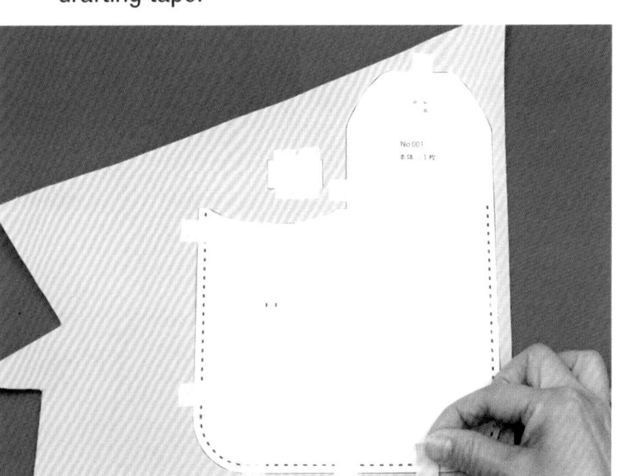

2 At the edge of the leather, secure the pattern by taping to the flesh-side.

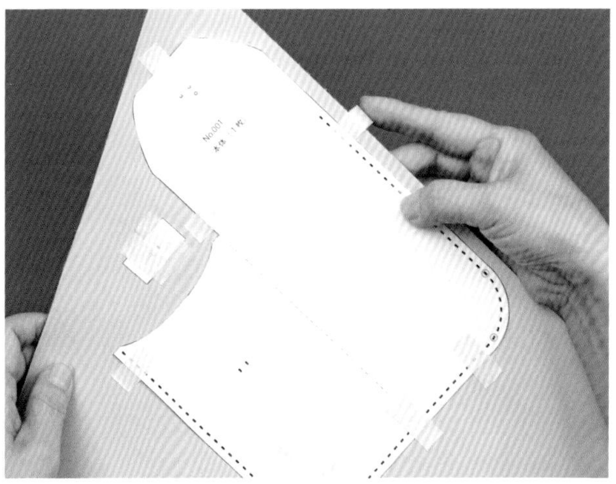

3 For larger sized leather, place a vinyl cutting board under it and cut out the leather roughly with a utility knife. Make sure to press down on the surface of the leather, not the pattern, when cutting the leather as the pattern will move easily. (Please refer to page 28 for cutting.)

Once you cut the leather, firmly secure the patterns alongside the cut edge by taping them over the flesh-side of the leather (in the same manner as step 2 above).

Transfer the pattern outline onto the grain-side of the leather using a scratch awl. Do not use the point of the scratch awl. Instead place the tip at an angle to score the line.

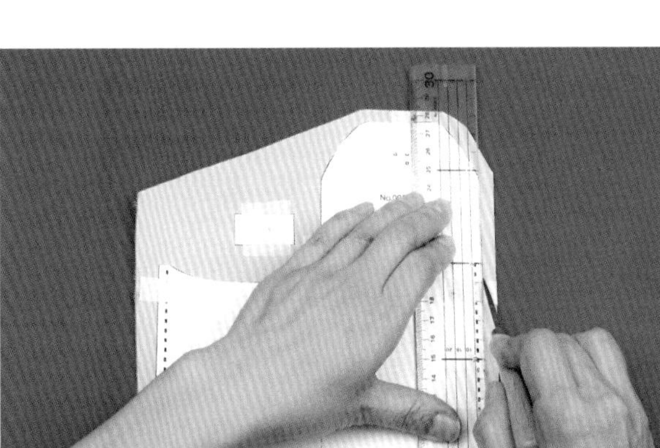

1

For straight lines, align a ruler with the edge of the pattern and then score. Do not mark over-top of the drafting tape as the awl tip will tear the tape.

After punching the stitching holes, and after peeling off the tape, connect the scored lines.

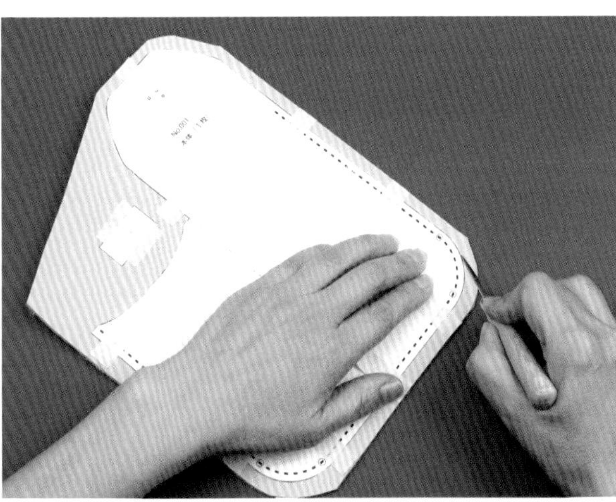

2

For curved lines, hold the pattern and then score a precise line by following alongside the pattern with the awl tip.

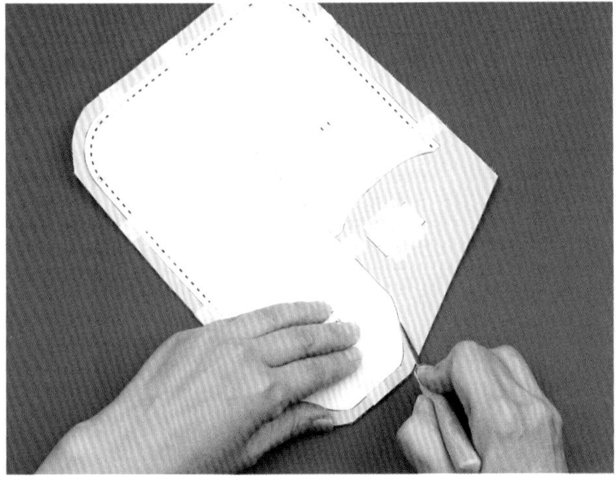

Punching Stitching Holes

To punch stitching holes marked on the pattern, use a 5 mm (¼ in.) wide, four-prong lacing chisel. The number of stitching holes is made to match with each seam. So, be very careful not to accidently change the number of stitching holes. A little practice is needed to be able to punch a neat hole straight down through to the back. For beginners I would recommend that you practice punching holes using a piece of scrap leather.

[Hole Punching Basics]
On a rubber board, place the leather so that the direction of the stitching holes is perpendicular to you. Place the lacing chisel perpendicular to the leather and then strike with a wooden mallet a couple of times to punch the holes. Make sure that the holes are punched all the way through.

Attention

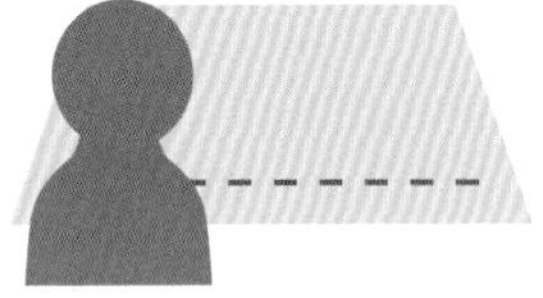

When the direction of the stitching holes is horizontal to you, the lacing chisel tends to slant.

The adhesive strength of drafting tape is fairly weak, so be sure that the pattern doesn't shift out of position.

Tools for punching holes, such as lacing chisels, are very sharp-edged so be sure to work with caution.

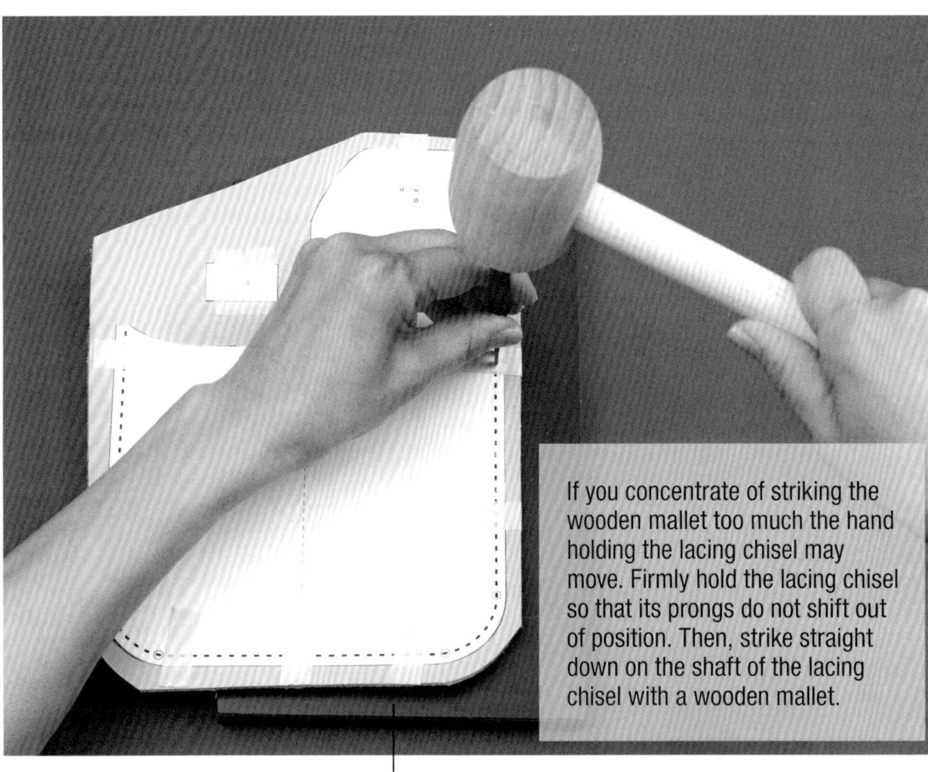

If you concentrate of striking the wooden mallet too much the hand holding the lacing chisel may move. Firmly hold the lacing chisel so that its prongs do not shift out of position. Then, strike straight down on the shaft of the lacing chisel with a wooden mallet.

Rubber board

[Straight Stitching Holes]

1 Use a four-prong lacing chisel. Place the prongs of the lacing chisel on the hole positions of the pattern.

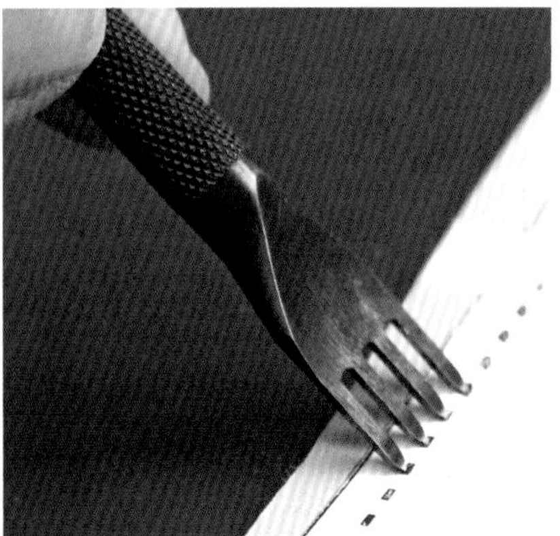

2 Place the lacing chisel perpendicular to the leather.

Hold the bottom part of the lacing chisel and make sure your hand touches the leather – this will stabilize the chisel and, as a result, the prongs will stay in position.

[Curved Line Stitching Holes]

Use a two-prong lacing chisel. Place the prong on the curve and punch holes in the same manner as the four-prong lacing chisel.

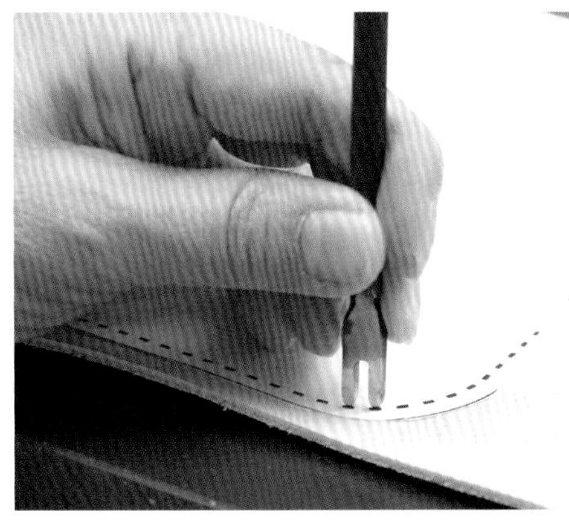

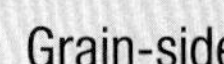

[Single Stitching Hole]

Pierce firmly with a lacing needle.

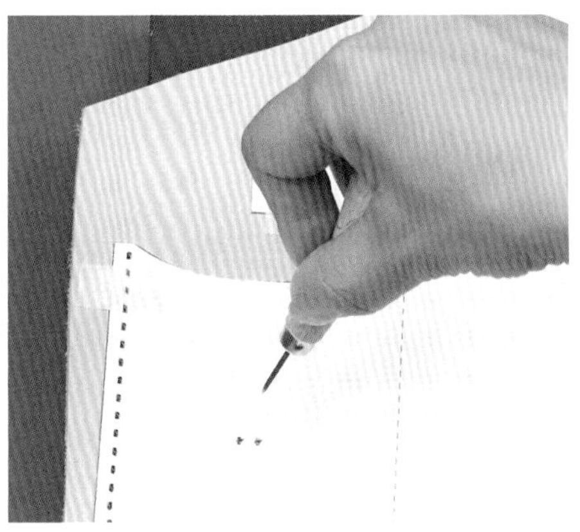

[Round Hole]

Hold the single-hole punch perpendicular to the leather and strike with a wooden mallet.

[Marking]

After punching all the holes, pierce the circled stitch holes with a scratch awl. Then, turn the leather over and mark the pierced position with a pencil from the flesh-side of the leather.

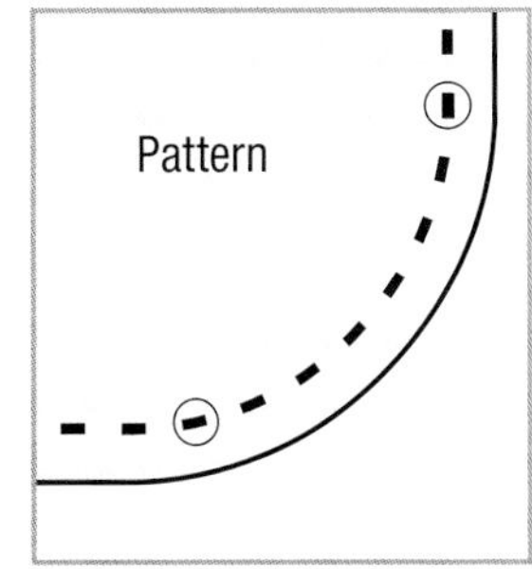

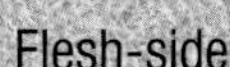

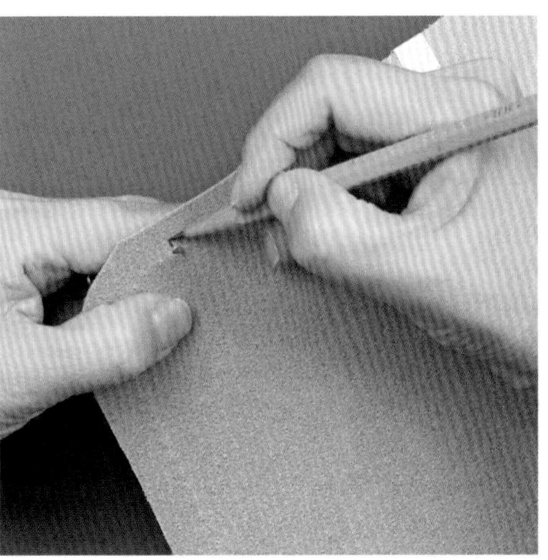

Cutting Leather

Put the leather on a vinyl board and then cut the leather using a large-size utility knife. Compared to materials of similar thickness, leather is easier to cut. However, it can be stretched and warped easily so you must carefully cut along the scored line with a scratch awl.

[Peel Off the Pattern]
For the taped areas, connect the outline marked in the previous step as you peel each piece of tape off.

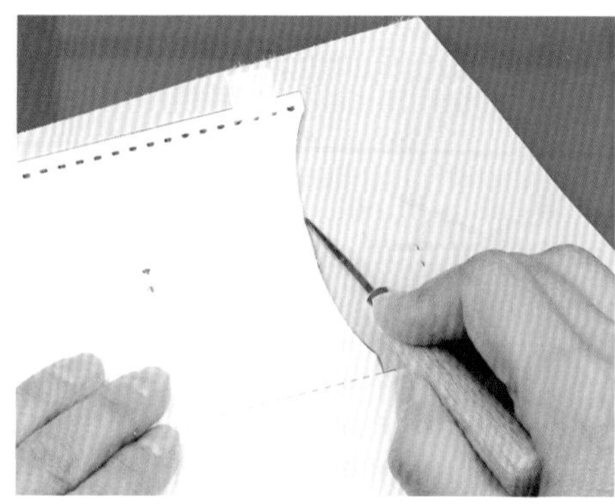

[Cautions for Cutting Leather]

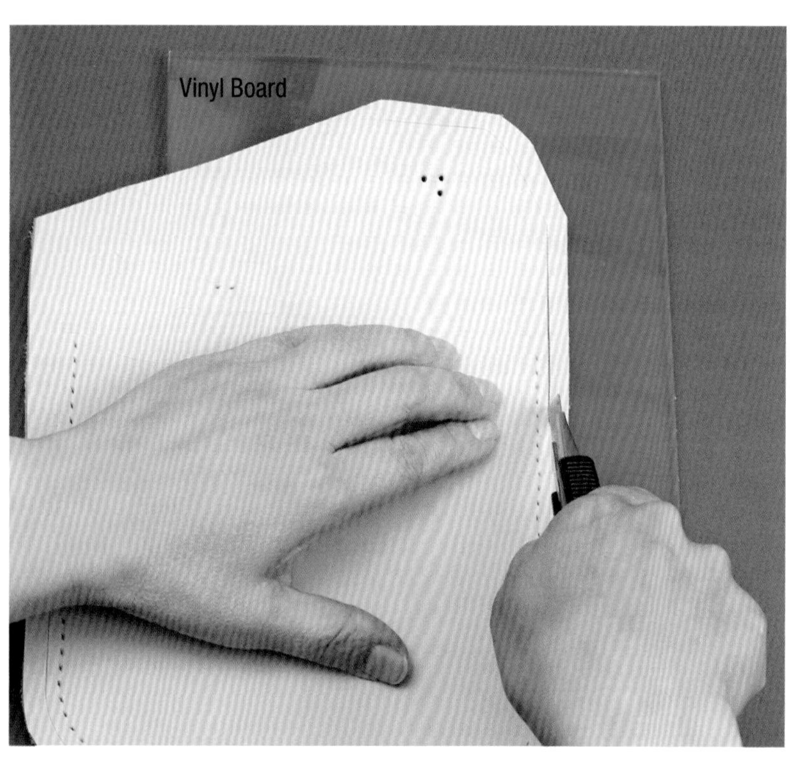

Remove the pattern from the leather. Place the vinyl board on a working surface and put the leather on top. Be sure that it is perpendicular to your body. Firmly press down on the leather and then slowly and carefully cut the leather along the scored line with a large-size utility knife.

Attention

If you cut the leather horizontal to your body the edge will end up slanted.

Do not use a ruler as a guideline as the leather is fairly slippery. Please be sure not to place your fingers in the direction of the utility knife as that can be quite dangerous.

Do not cut the leather if the pattern is still taped on top as patterns taped on leather tend to come off very easily.

[Blade Angle]

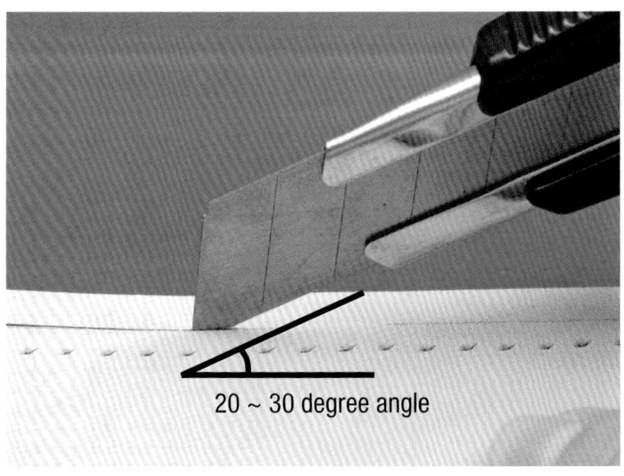

Cut the leather by holding the utility knife so the blade is angled at 20 ~ 30 degrees to the leather.

If the blade angles to the left or right, the cut edge will be slanted.
Please pay special attention when you cut thick leather.

Be sure to snap off the blade so you are always cutting with a fresh razor.

[Cutting a Corner]

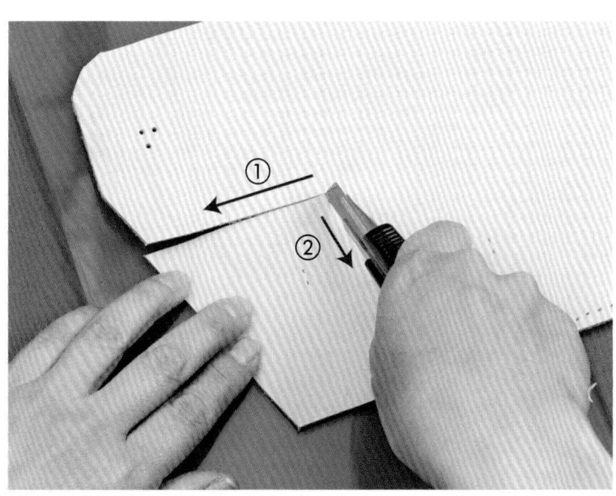

① Firmly place the blade at the intersection and then proceed to cut toward the exterior.

② Once again place the blade at the intersection and then cut steadily along the remaining line.

[Curved Lines]

Always keep the direction of cut perpendicular to your body by rotating the leather, and cut little by little.

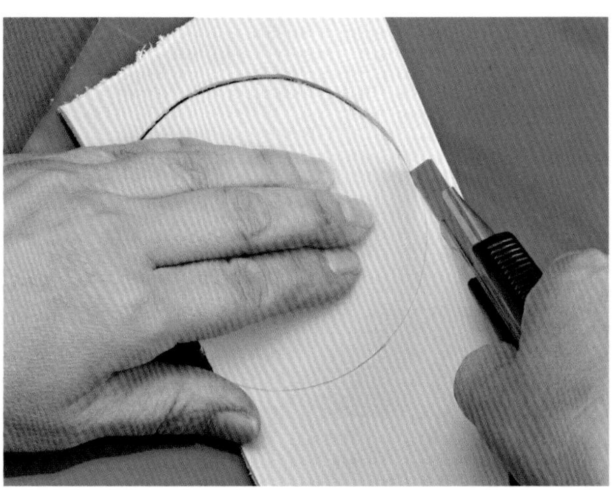

Cutting is complete.

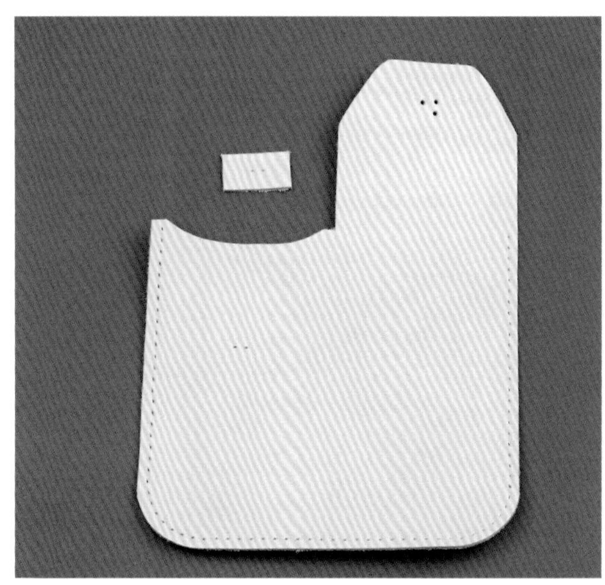

Burnishing the Flesh-side

On the flesh-side of the leather the fibers become grainy and come off as the leather breaks in. In order to prevent this, burnish the flesh-side by applying Tokonole (Tragacanth substitute). Do not burnish gluing areas as burnished surfaces hinder the adhesive action of glue.

Before burnishing

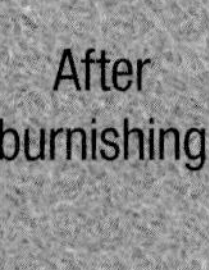

After burnishing

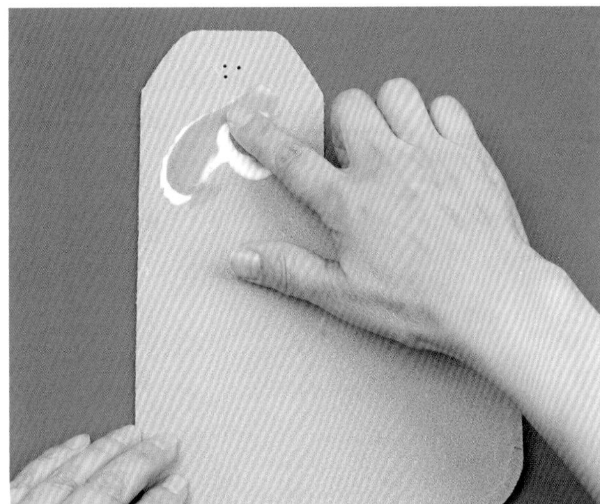

1

Take some Tokonole on the tip of your finger and spread it lightly onto the flesh-side of the leather. If Tokonole is spread all the way to the edge, it may spread to the grain-side of the leather. This will result in soiling of the grain-side, so avoid application near the edges of the leather.

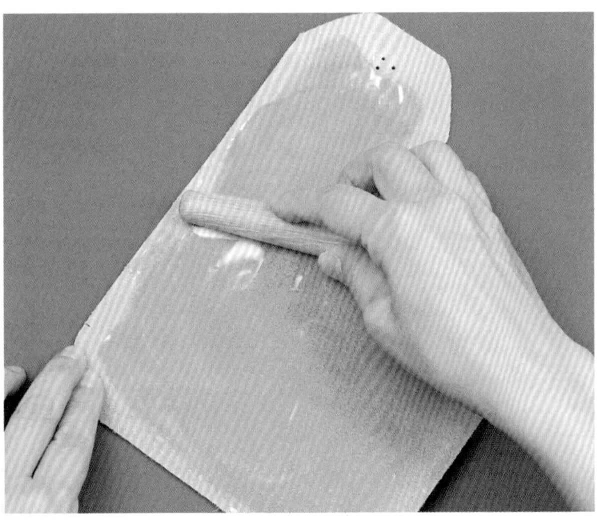

2

Spread the Tokonole out using a wood slicker, etc. Do not apply Tokonole on the seam allowance as these will need to be glued together (if Tokonole is applied on the stitching holes, it will not plug them). Repeat step 1 and 2 to apply Tokonole over the entirety of the leather.

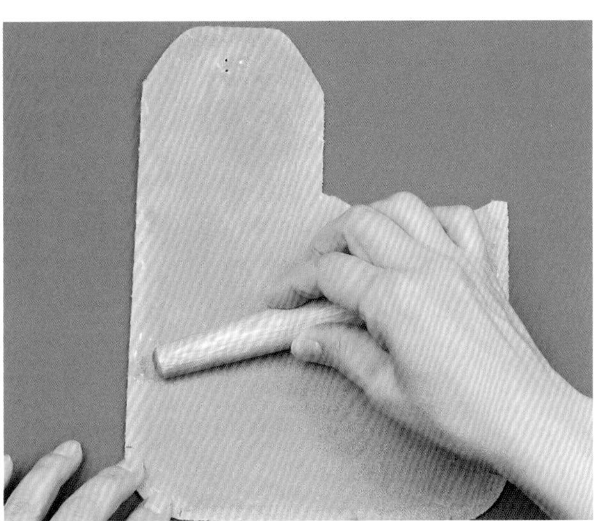

3

When Tokonole has pretty much dried (i.e., it does not feel tacky to the touch), burnish the flesh-side by sliding the slicker back and forth. Doing this will smooth the fibers of the flesh-side, which then becomes lustrous.

Burnishing Edges

Burnish the edge of the leather by applying Tokonole. Similar to burnishing the flesh-side, leather fibers on the edge will become smooth and lustrous. Burnish the edges of the seams after stitching. Contrarily, burnish items such as handles, pockets, straps, etc., before gluing them to the main piece.

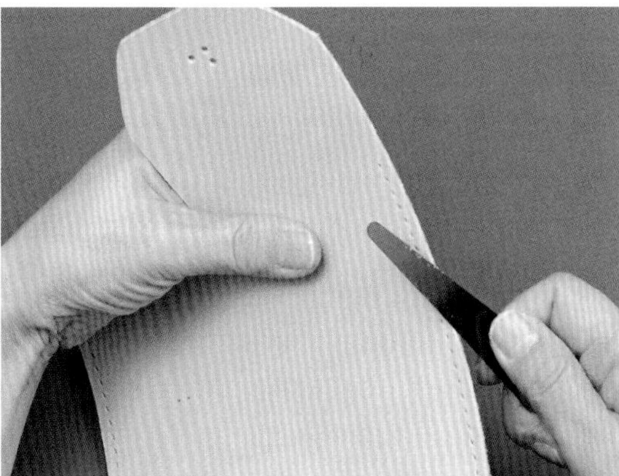

1

Since leather left untreated after cutting with a utility knife is difficult to burnish (because the grain-side is still sharp) you must gently file the grain-side down.

2

Take a small amount of Tokonole on a fingertip and then spread it alongside the cut edge, while being careful not to touch both sides of the leather.

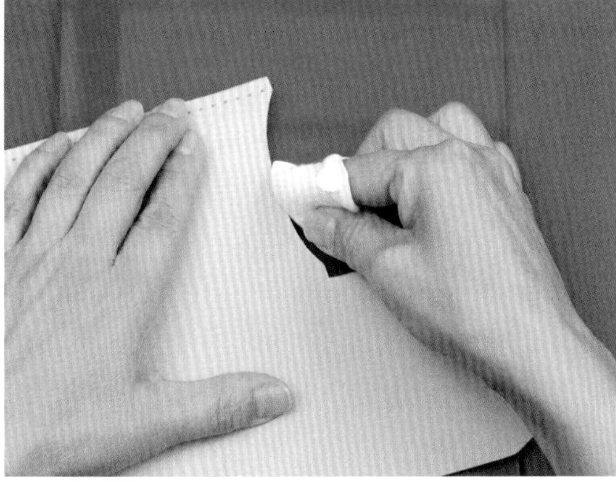

3

After the leather has pretty much dried you will be working with a single sheet of leather that is approximately 2 mm (1/16 in.) thick. Put a piece of cloth over the edge and rub both sides to burnish the edge.

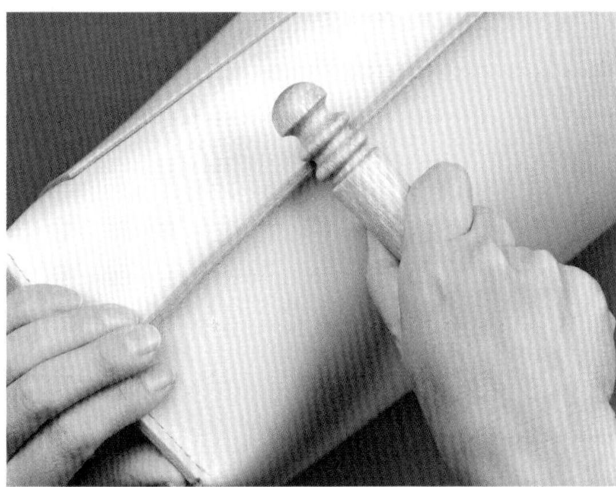

When you are working with thick leather, or a seam edge, burnish the edge using a slicker that has a groove that matches the thickness of the leather.

Before burnishing

Burnished

Gluing Leather

In this book, you will use a type of adhesive that requires application on both sides of the leather that you intend to glue together. Apply the adhesive to both sides and allow to dry. Then, bond each side by applying pressure.

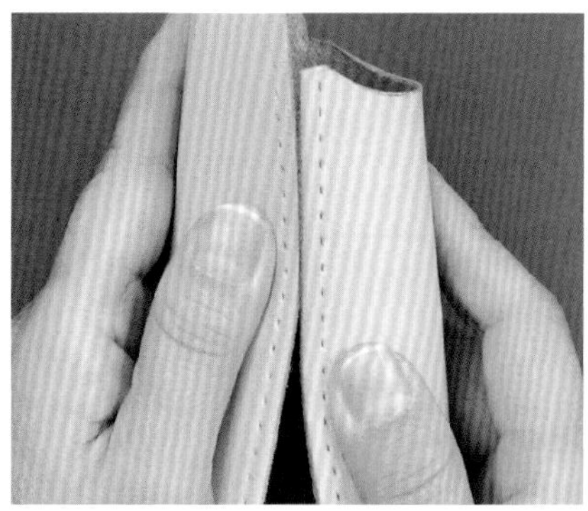

* For the basic pen case, glue the leather together after attaching the other required items. Refer page 42.

* For gluing large-sized leather products, such as a bag, please refer to page 76.

Before gluing, make sure that the number of stitching holes matches.

[Gluing by Matching Stitching Holes]

1 Apply adhesive on the seam allowance and spread it outward with a spatula. Be careful that the adhesive does not jut out to the grain-side of the leather.

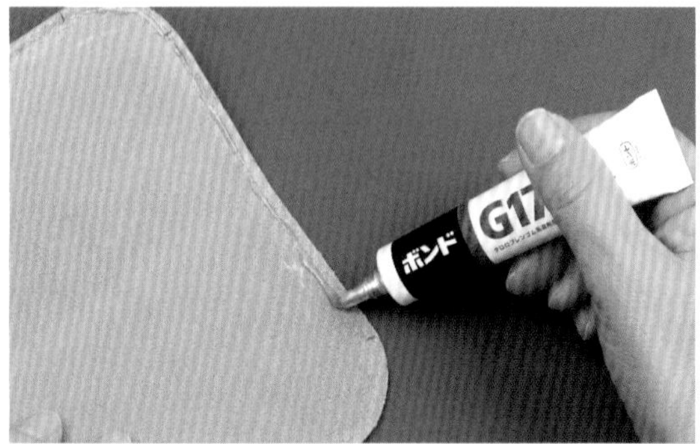

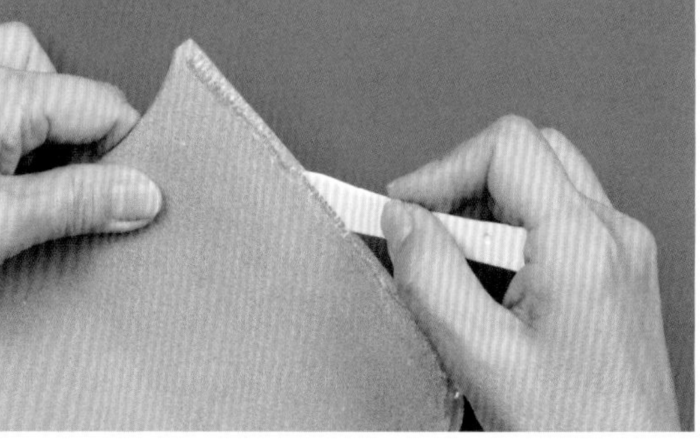

2 After the adhesive has dried, force a needle into one circled stitching hole and then feed the needle into the circled stitching hole on the opposite side.

3 In order to prevent the glued edges from becoming crooked, pierce the needle perpendicular and gently press the leather down to bond.

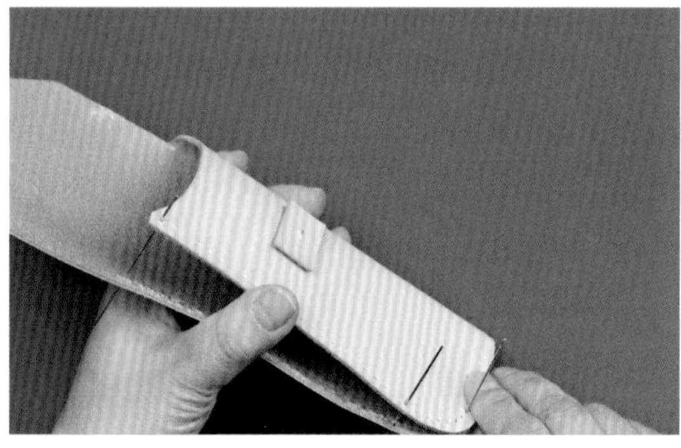

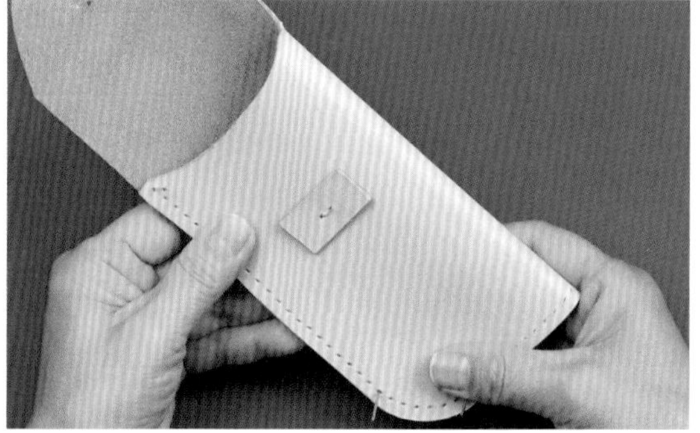

4 Every few stitches, make fine adjustments with an awl to align the position of the stitching holes. Doing this will make stitching the leather easier.

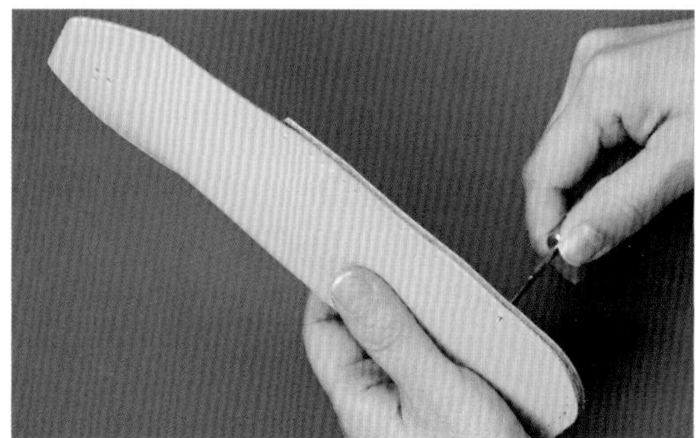

[Long-Narrow Strips of Leather] After gluing, cut a long and narrow strip of leather, like a bag's handle.

1 Prepare strips of leather. One should be the same size as the pattern and the other should be larger than the pattern. Apply adhesive on the flesh-side of both strips.

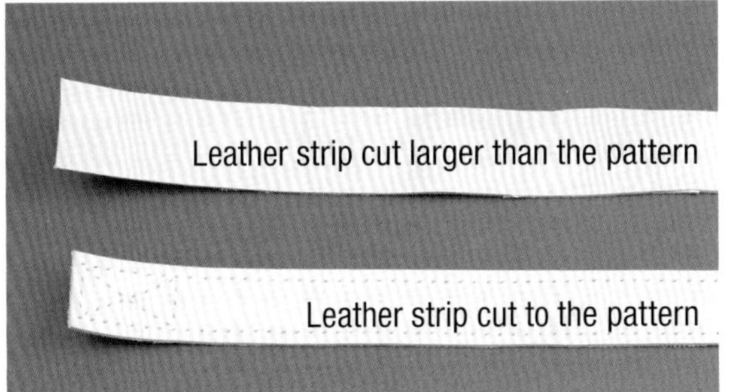

2 Glue them together.

3 Press down on the leather using a slicker, etc., to bond them.

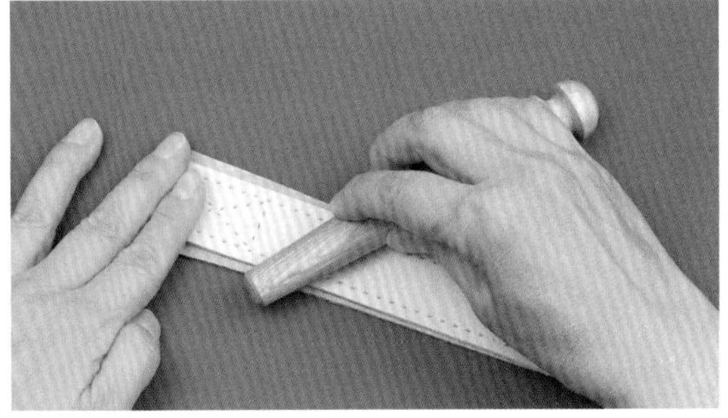

4 Place the pattern sized leather strip on the larger strip, facing leather-side up, and cut off the excess.

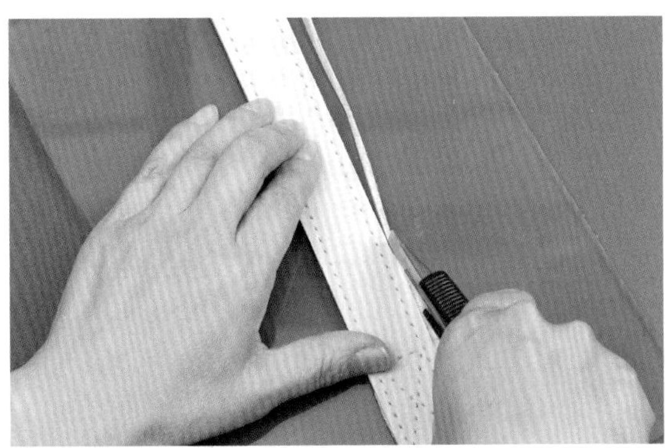

5 Once again punch the stitching holes out using a lacing chisel. If the punch does not go all the way through the leather, turn it over and punch out the holes from the back-side by using the punch mark traces.

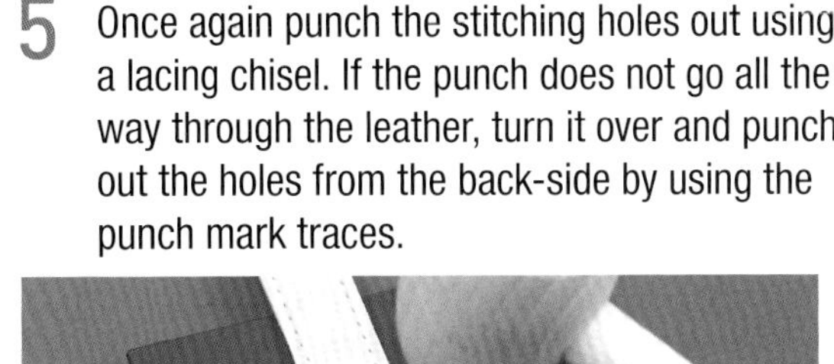

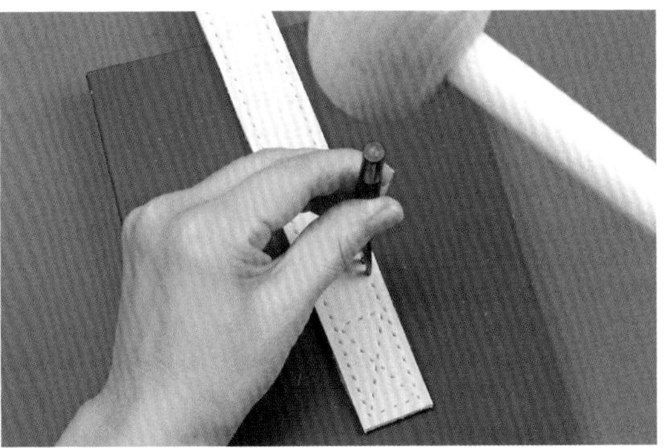

[The Grain-side and Flesh-side were Burnished with Tokonole]

Since the burnished grain-side and the burnished flesh-side are hard to bond, you must rough up the surface by scratching with a utility knife. Then apply adhesive.

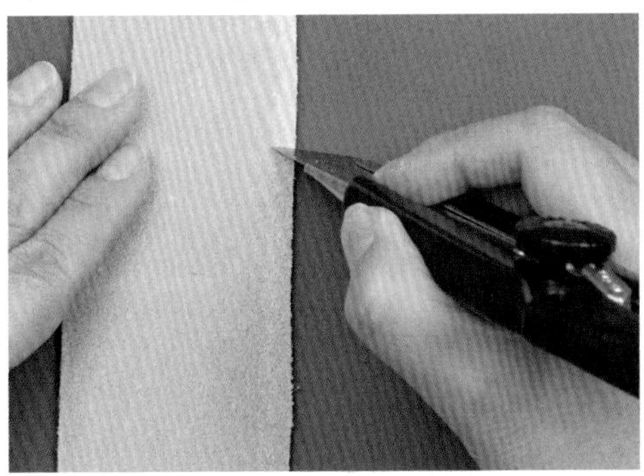

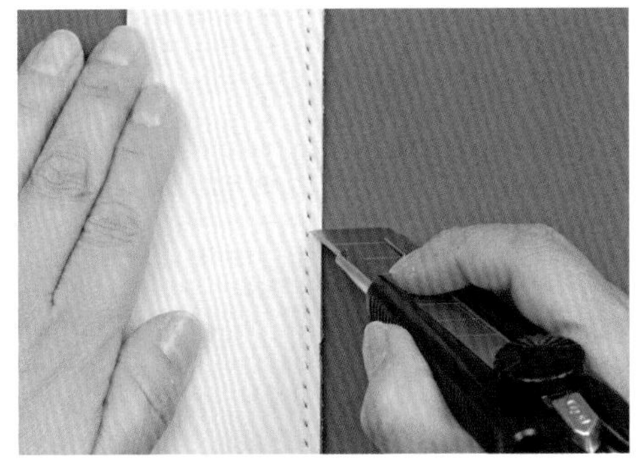

Prepare Thread and Needle

Leather sewing requires waxed thread so that the thread does not become thinner due to the large amount of friction. This book uses double-waxed polyester thread. Prior to sewing, place the thread on a piece of cloth, pinch it, and then pull to remove excess wax on the thread.

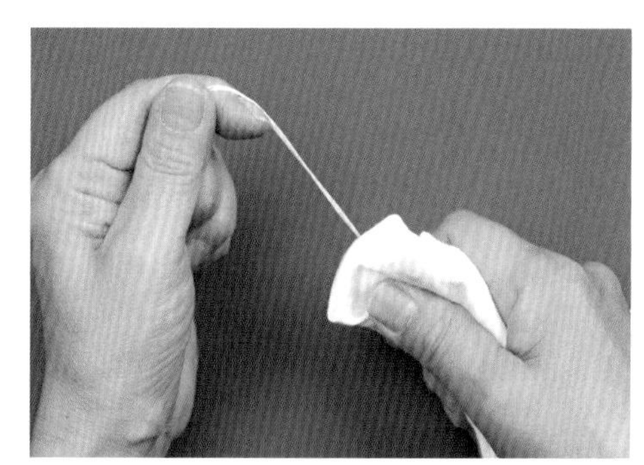

[Threading]

Since leather sewing requires one to continuously pull on the thread, you must use a special method to thread the needle so that the thread doesn't become loose.

1 Thread the needle.

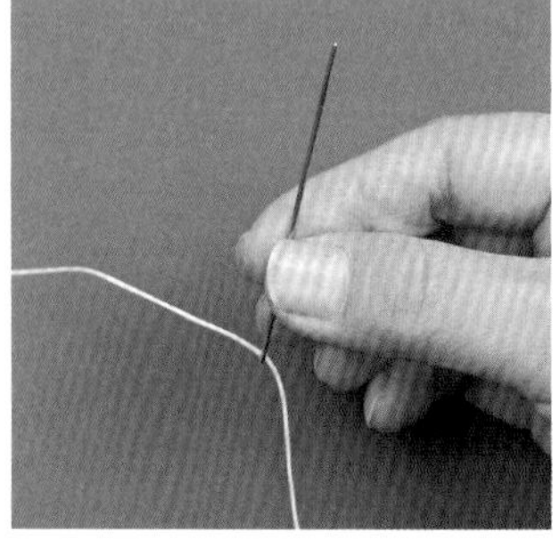

2 Hold the thread. Loosen the twine of the thread by twisting it backwards and then pierce the needle through the gaps a few times.

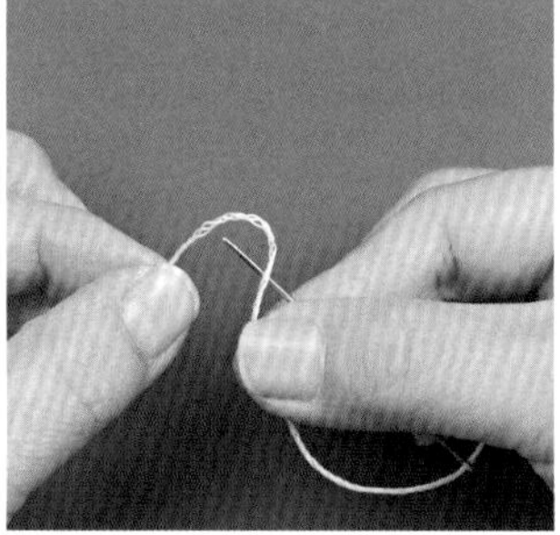

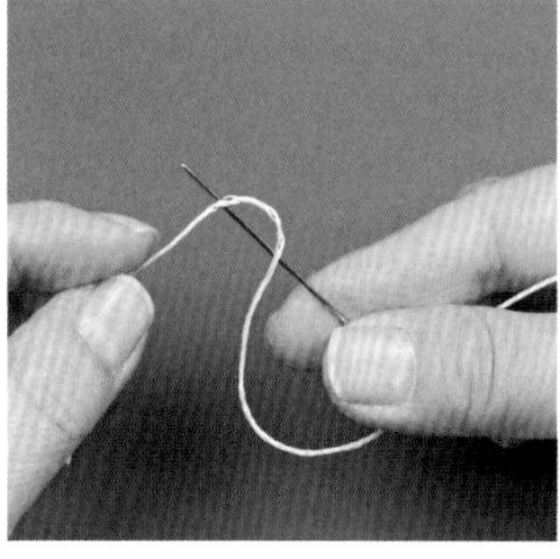

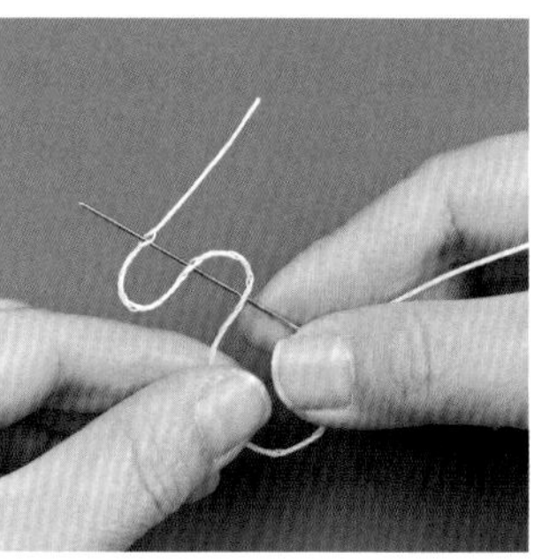

3 Push the point of the needle all the way through the thread.

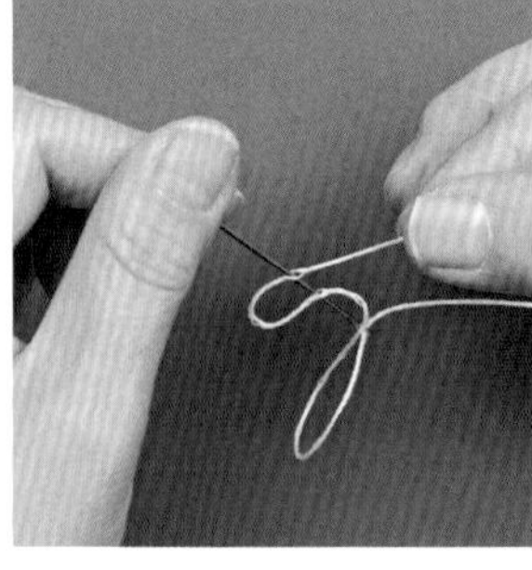

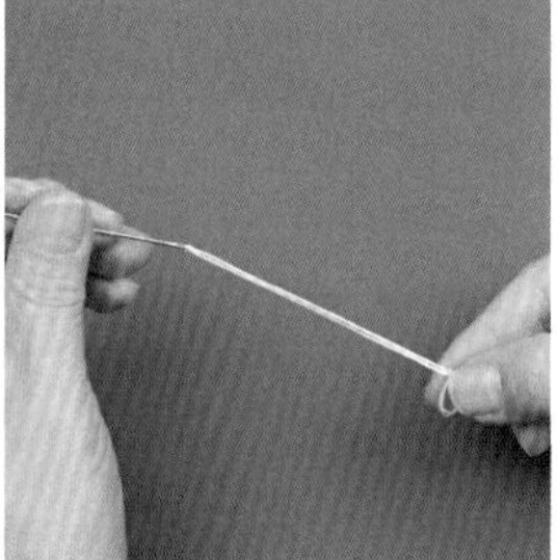

4 Hold the longer thread and pull.

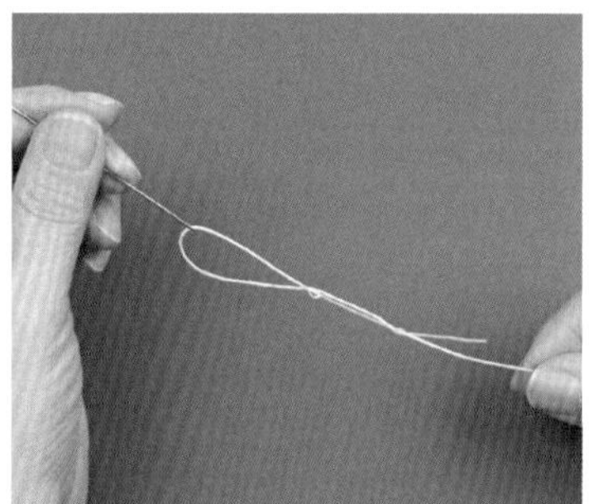

5 Adjust the thread.

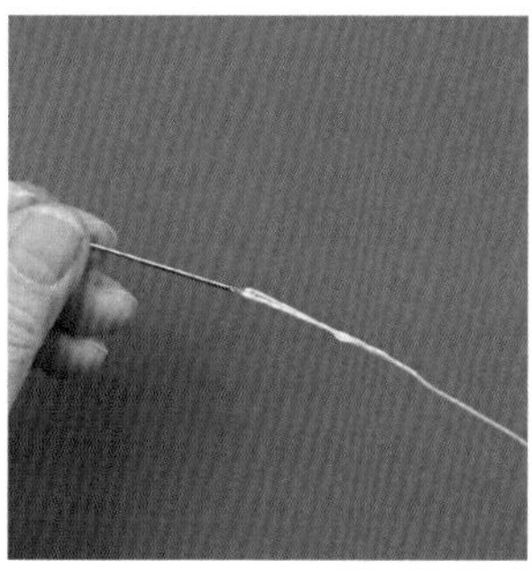

Begin Stitching

Decide where you will begin to stitch so that you finish at a point where disposing of the thread ends is easy.

For small items start stitching from the bottom so the stitch ends at the opening. That way it will be easy to get rid of the ends.

For long items where thread may run low while stitching (like handles, etc.), begin stitching from the middle.

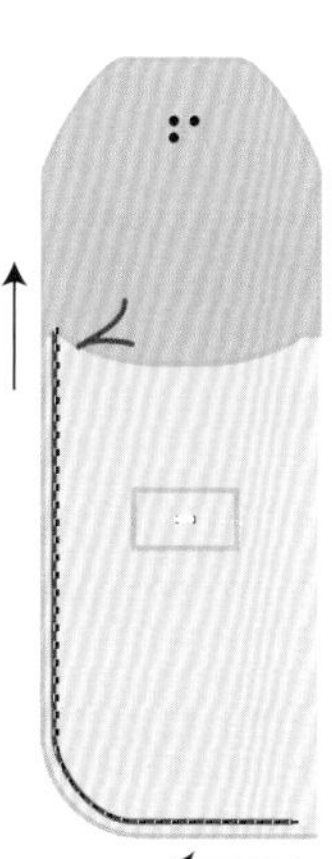

For small items, begin the stitch at the middle and come back to the middle.

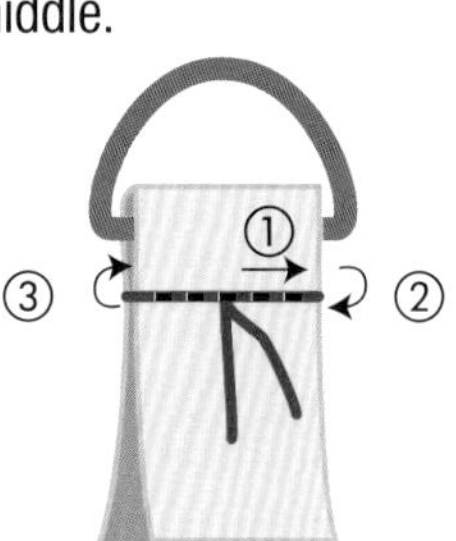

The First Stitch

There are several methods of stitching (see page 36 to 39). The length of thread required and the length of thread-tail varies depending on the stitching method.

★ If the thread is too long, it is hard to handle; thus, you should keep the length of thread that you pull through to the opposite side to a little less than 1 m (3.25 ft.).

Put the needle through the first stitching hole

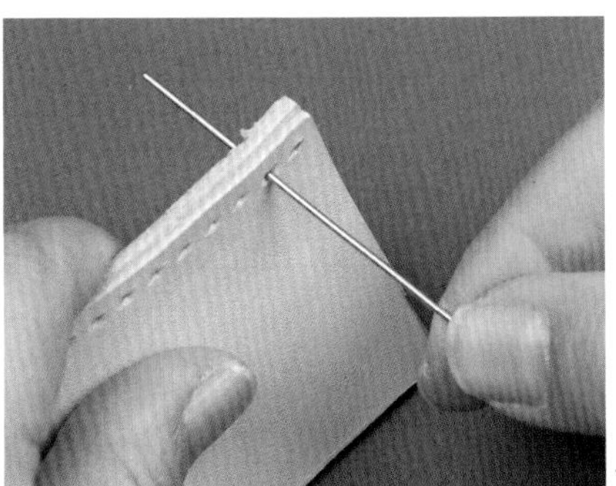

Saddle Stitch, Running Stitch

Thread Length: approx. four times as long as the stitching length

Adjust the thread so that the length of thread on the left and right sides matches

★ For saddle stitches you should thread one needle to each end

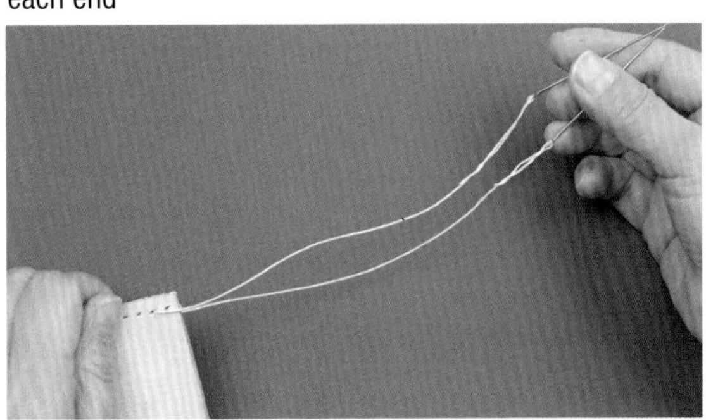

Backstitch

Thread Length: approx. three times as long as the stitching length

Start stitching from the back-side

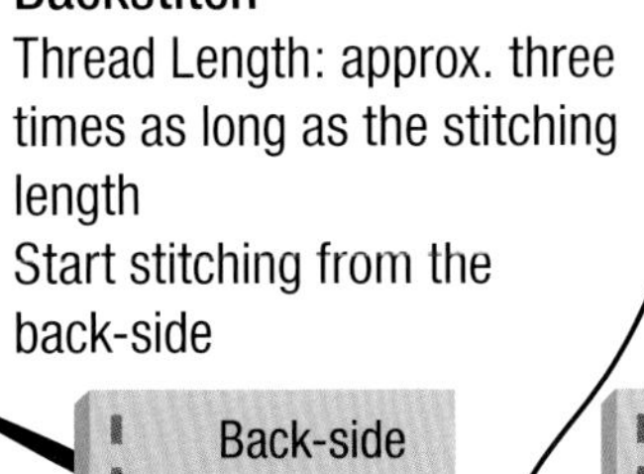

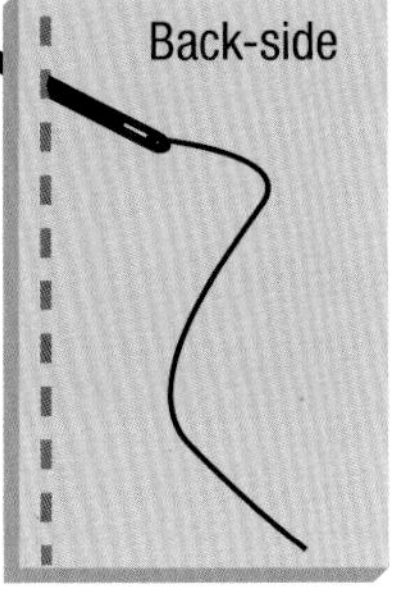

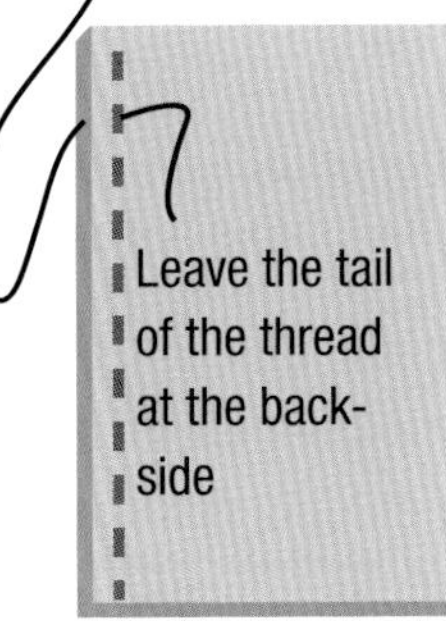

Sewing an Awl Stitch

Thread Length: approx. three times as long as the stitching length

Start stitching from the back-side

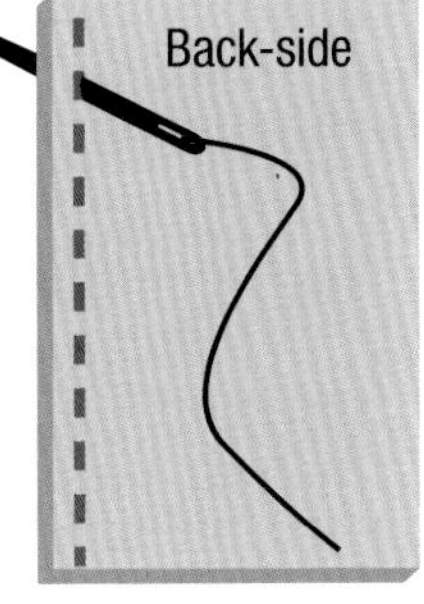

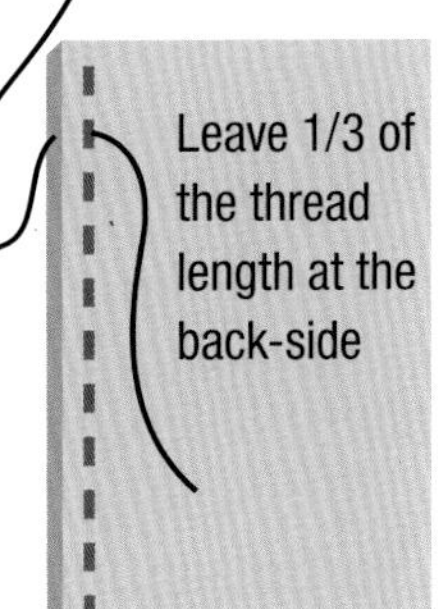

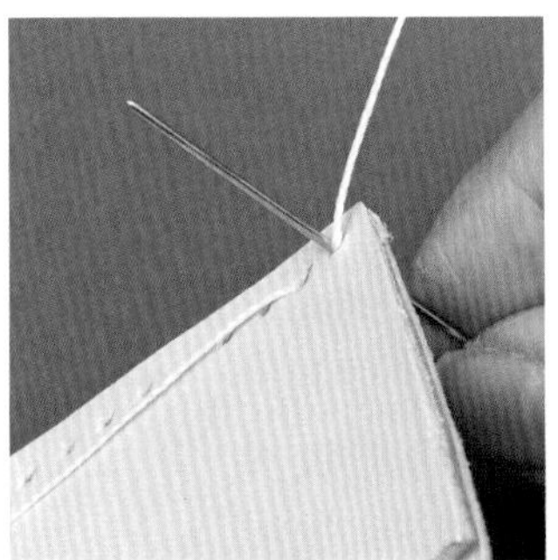

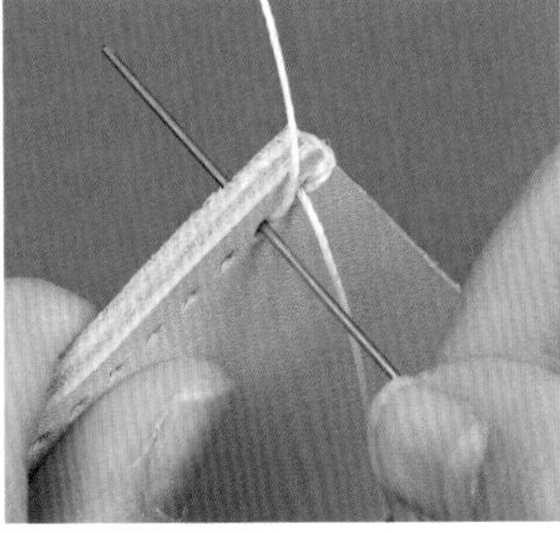

Since the openings of a bag or a pocket can easily become strained, double stitch them at the ends. Insert the needle a hole or two before the end and double stitch the end hole, then come back to where the stitch started.

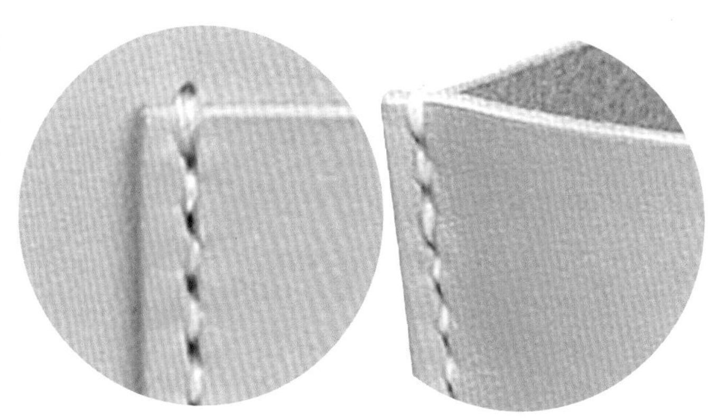

Saddle Stitch

This is the most common method of hand-stitching leather. While stitching using two needles, firmly tighten the thread for each hole. The seam does not become frayed, even if one thread is cut, because it is sewn from both sides.

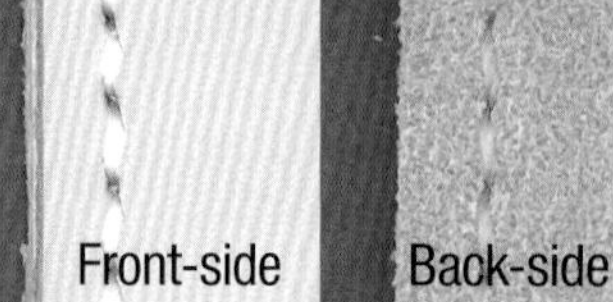

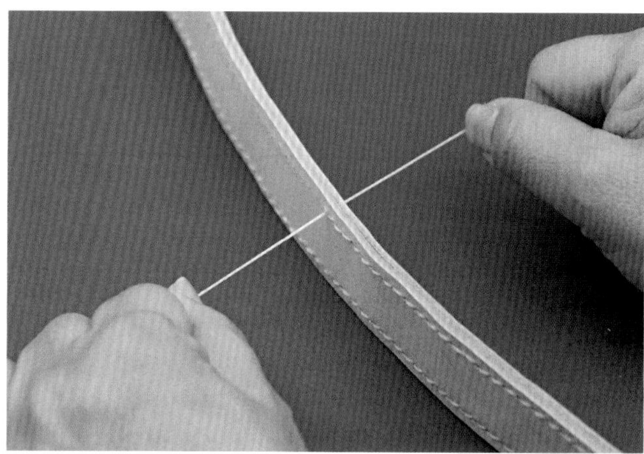

* The diagrams use different colored thread to illustrate the instructions. One thread of each color is used.

1 Always start with the needle at the back-side (red) first, and then insert the needle in the next hole.

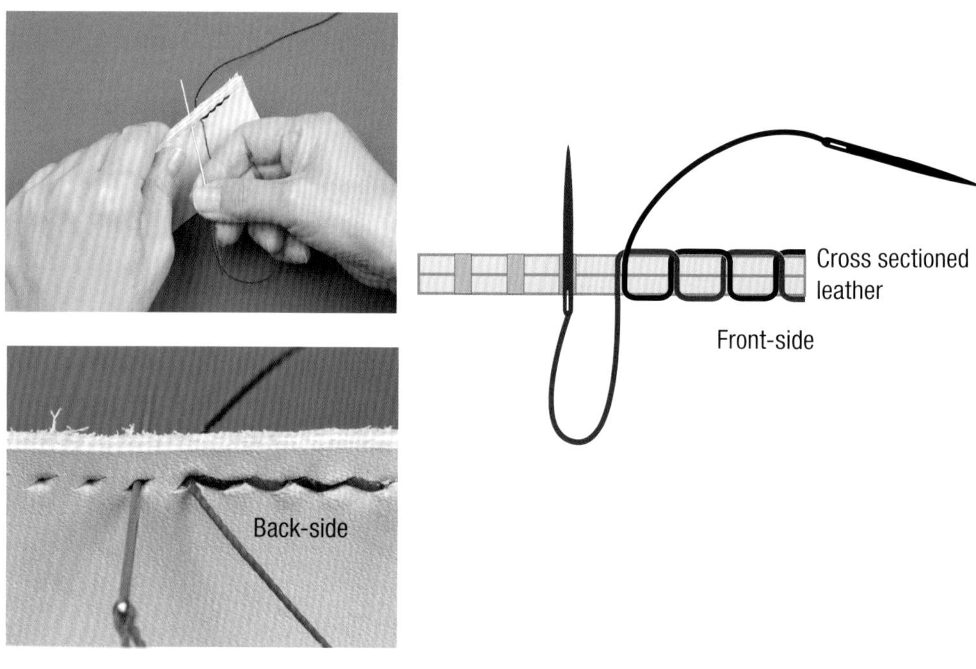

2 Pull the thread through at an angle (diagonally upward).

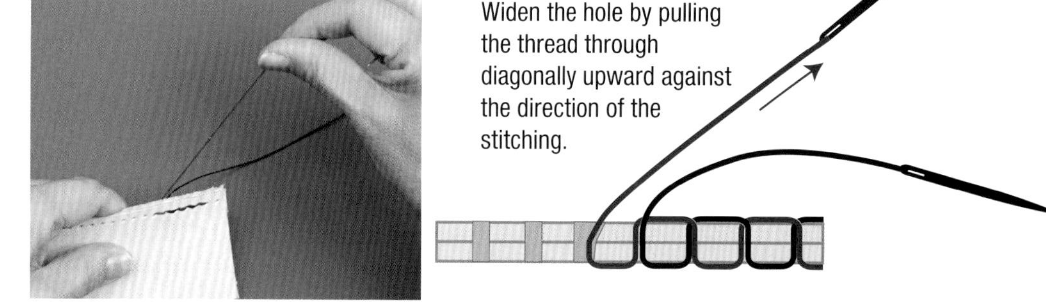

3 Insert the other needle (black) from the back-side into the same hole you just used.

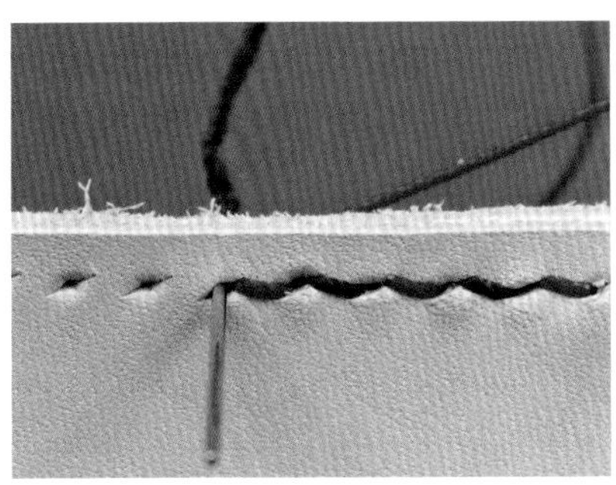

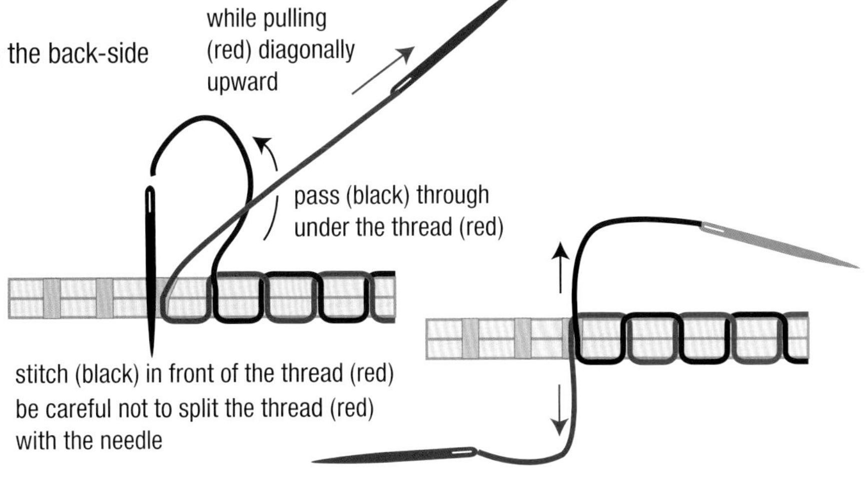

4 Pull both threads at the same time. For the next hole, insert the front-side needle into the hole and then, while pulling it diagonally upward, insert the back-side needle into the same hole. By doing so, the stitch finishes beautifully.

Running Stitch

When a running stitch is made on each side, it becomes a saddle stitch. Compared to a saddle stitch, the aesthetic of a running stitch is less appealing. However, it is suitable for sewing small items and thin leather (whose shape would be deformed by forcefully pulling thread from both sides).

* The diagrams use different colored thread to illustrate the instructions. One thread of each color is used.

1 Thread a needle. After inserting the needle through the starting hole, adjust the length of thread trailing from the front-side and back-side so that each side has the same length.
Refer to page 35 for stitching the start hole.

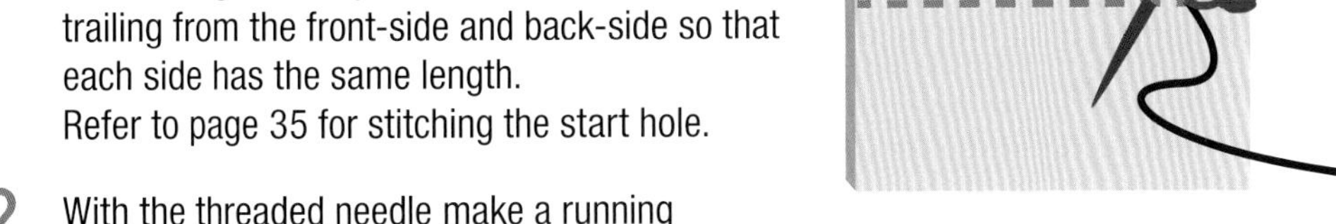

2 With the threaded needle make a running stitch all the way around.

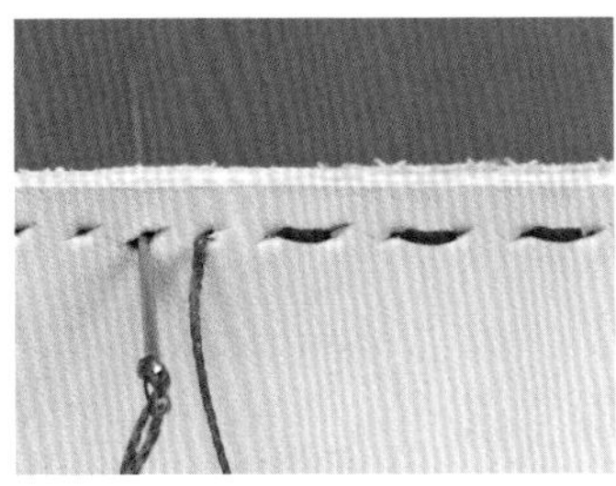

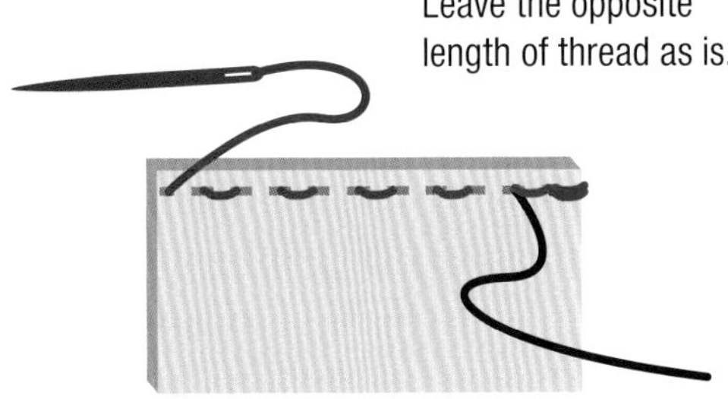

3 After coming back to the starting point, pull the needle through to the back-side and cut the thread off. Insert the tip of the opposite side thread through the needle. While being careful not to split the already stitched thread with the needle, put the needle through the gap in the stitching hole and perform a running stitch all the way around.

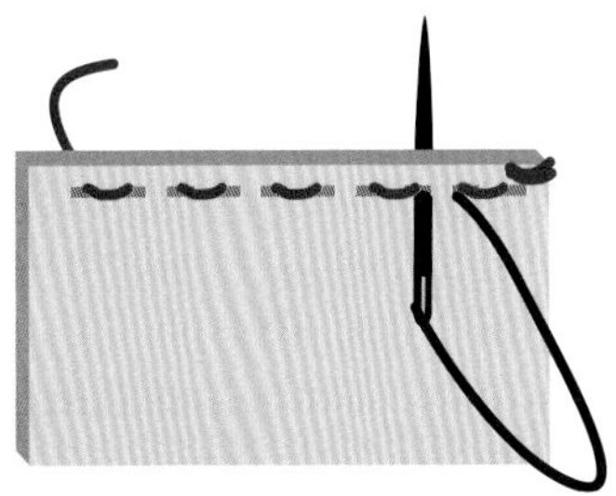

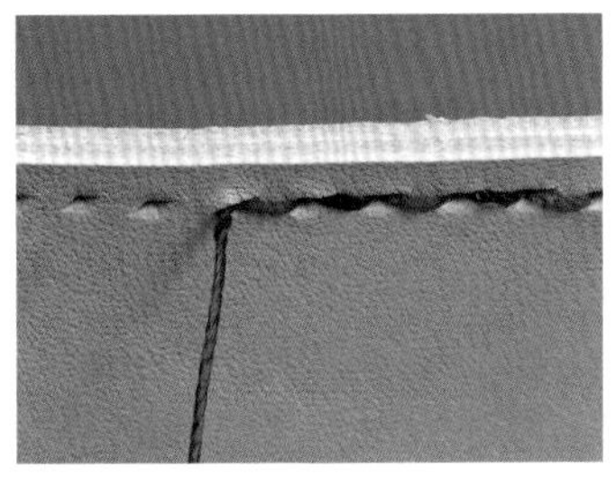

Backstitch

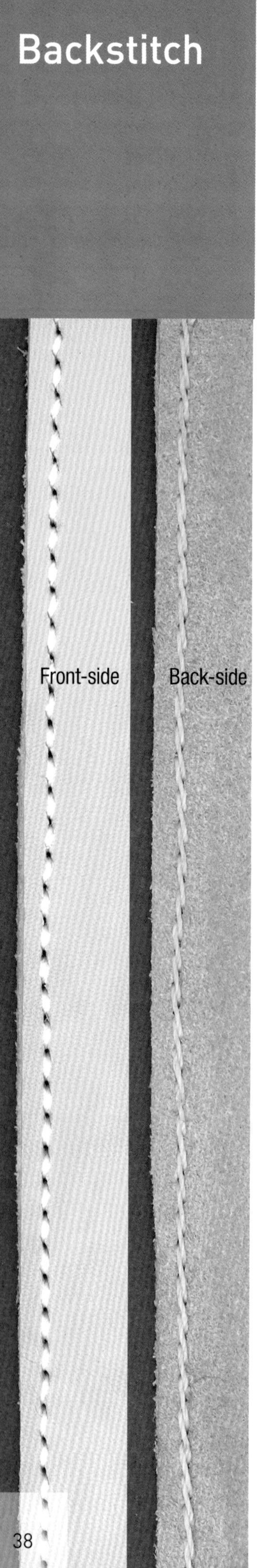

This stitch is suitable for use when you are not concerned about how the back-side looks (i.e., inside an item, etc.).

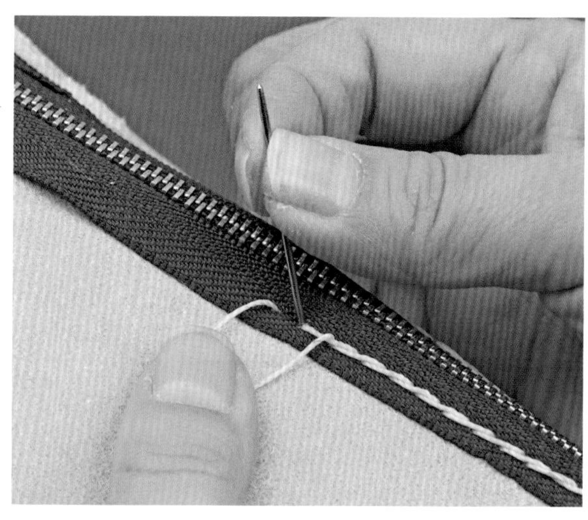

[Beginning of Stitch]

1 From the back-side, insert the needle a few stitches before the end stitch.

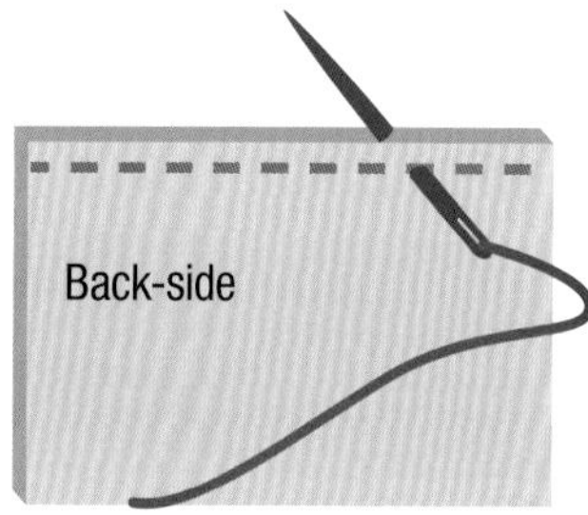

2 Refer to page 35 and sew the end stitch twice. Then insert the needle in the hole that is two stitches before the end stitch.

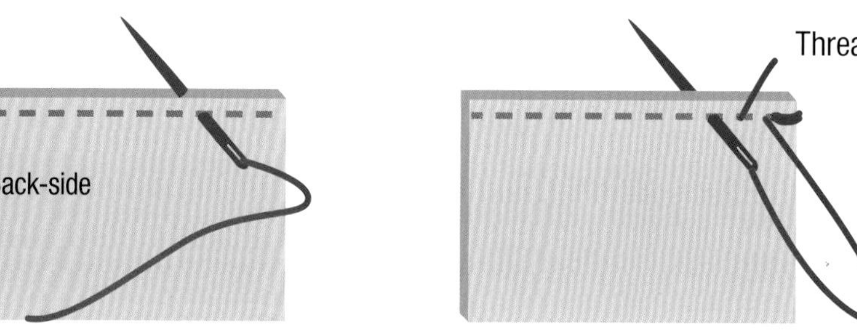

3 From the front-side, perform one backstitch and pull the needle through to the back-side.

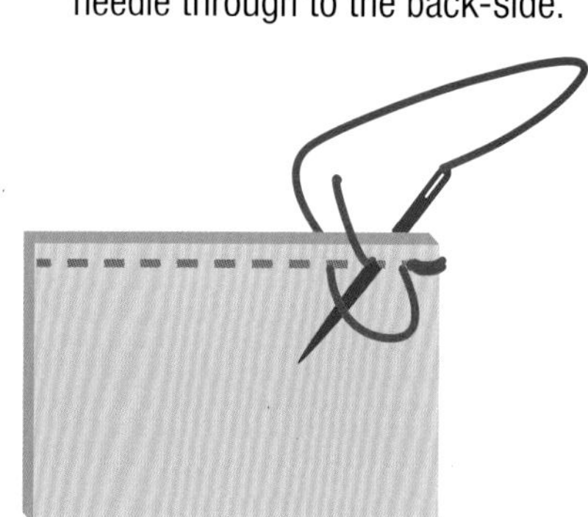

[How to Stitch the Thread]

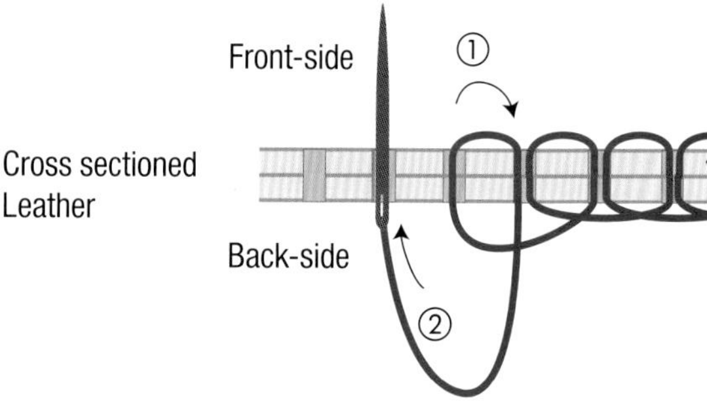

① From the front side, backstitch once and pull the needle through to the back side.

② From the back side, pull the needle through to the front-side two stitches forward. Repeat this process

Front-side

Back-side

Leave loose

In step ①, if you split the opposite side thread with the needle, the thread will tangle. Do not pull the thread taut. Rather leave it loose and pull the needle through while avoiding the thread.

Sewing an Awl Stitch

This is a stitch where the thread proceeds in the same manner as a sewing machine. It is a very quick way to stitch. This stitch will become frayed if it is cut in a particular spot. Thus, it lacks strength when compared to the saddle stitch. Since the thread is crossed *inside* the leather, this stitch is most suitable for thick leather.

This is a method that usually uses a tool called a speedy-stitcher. However, this section introduces a method for producing this stitch without using such a tool.

* Different colored threads are used to show the instructions clearly.

1 Thread the needle. Refer to page 35 and sew the starting stitch.

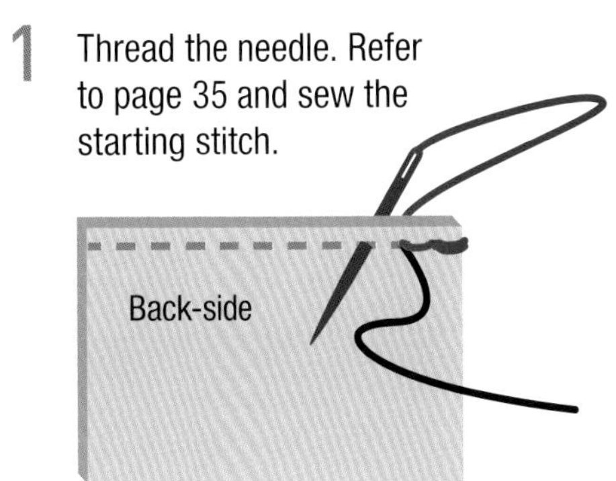

2 Push the needle through from the front-side and stitch over the back-side thread (there is no needle threaded). Then pull the needle through to the front-side again.

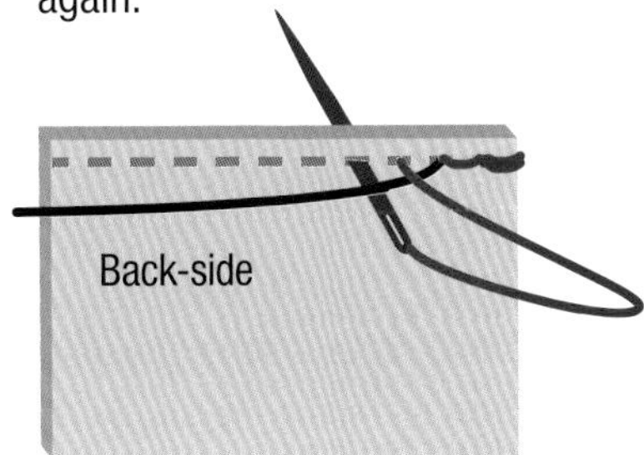

3 Firmly pull the thread on both sides while adjusting tautness so the thread that returns to the front-side is hidden inside of the thick leather.

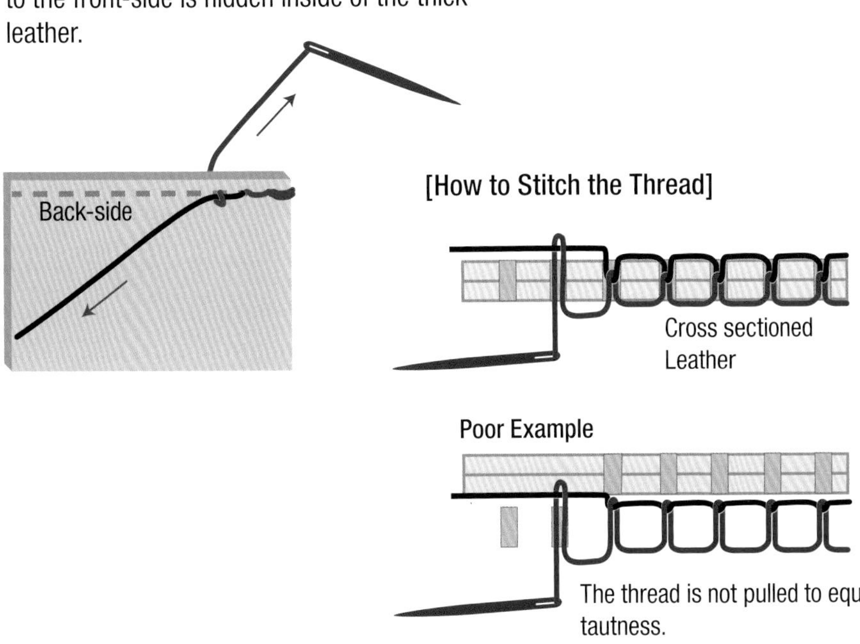

Poor Example
A crossed over thread is visible because the thread has not been pulled tightly.

Splicing Thread

1 When you run out of thread, backstitch once from the front-side and pull the thread through to the back-side and cut it. If you continue to stitch with very little thread it will become very difficult to properly dispose of the thread ends (see "Disposing of Thread Ends" on the next page).

2 Thread a needle with some new thread and push it through the same hole where you made your last stitch. Continue to sew.

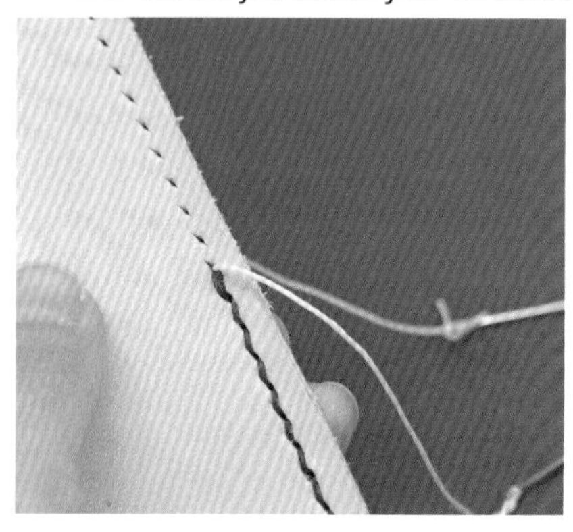

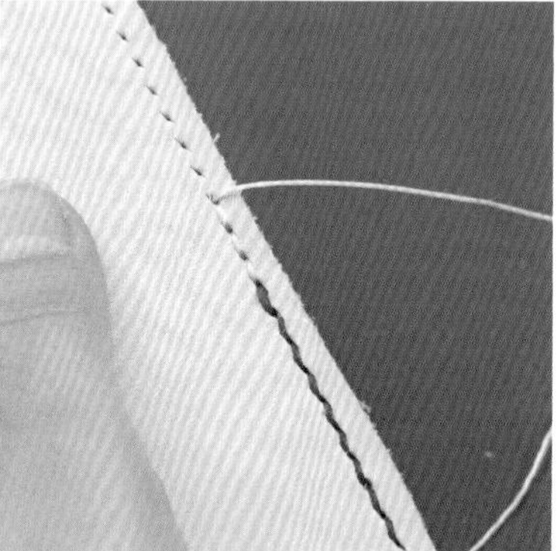

When performing a backstitch, put the needle with its new thread back into the same position where the thread ended on the back-side. Then, continue to backstitch.

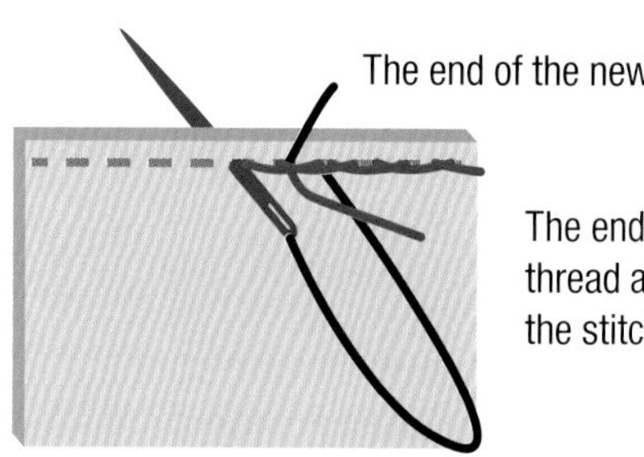

End of Stitching

1 A few stitches before the stitch ends, leave a tail of thread on the back-side, and then stitch using the other needle to the end.

2 Stitch twice at the end, and then stitch back to a few stitches behind the tail of the thread.

When performing a backstitch, change to a running stitch a few stitches before the end.

Stitch twice at the end, then stitch back to one hole prior to where you changed the stitch.

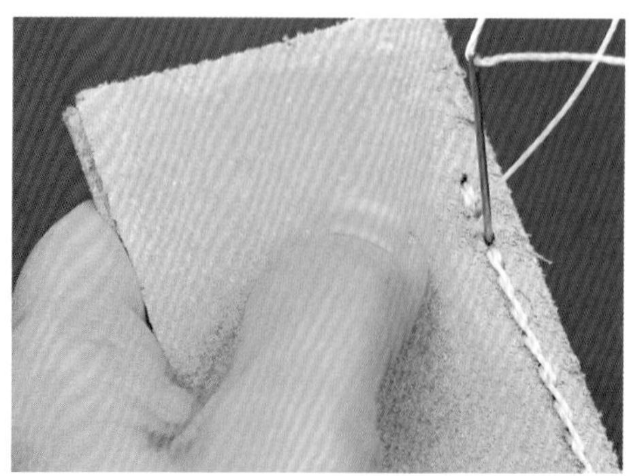

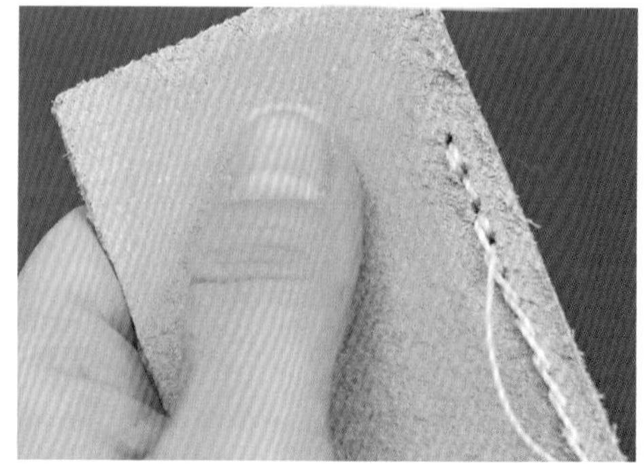

Disposing of Thread Ends

Dispose of thread ends where they will not be obviously noticed. For example, you can dispose of ends inside of a bag or on the back side of an item like a handle, etc. Please choose an appropriate method depending on the position of the end stitch.

[Tying]

This method is used when disposing of thread ends inside of a bag, etc., where the end of the thread or a visible knot is not a concern.

1 Loosely tie the thread. Apply woodworking adhesive over the holes so the stitches are closed.

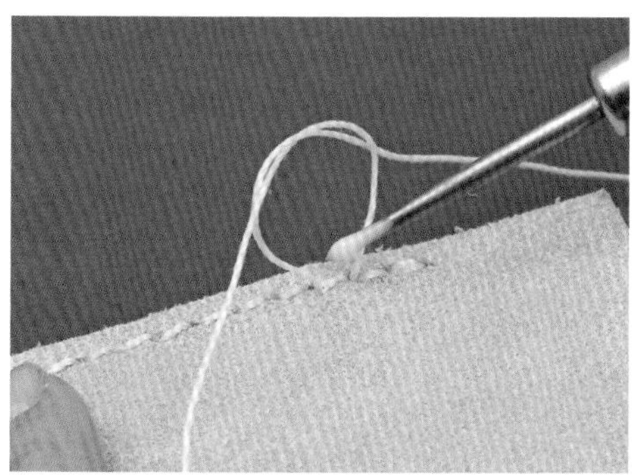

2 Again tie the thread firmly and pull the thread tight. With the head of an awl, press the knot down firmly.

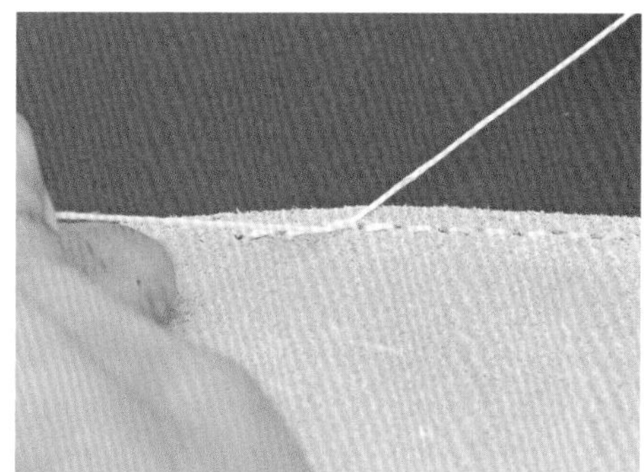

[Heating]

Polyester thread can be secured by melting the end with heat.

1 Leave 2 to 3 mm (approx. ⅛ in.) of thread out and then cut the thread. Melt the thread by heating the end with a lighter. Be very cautious that the fire does not spread.

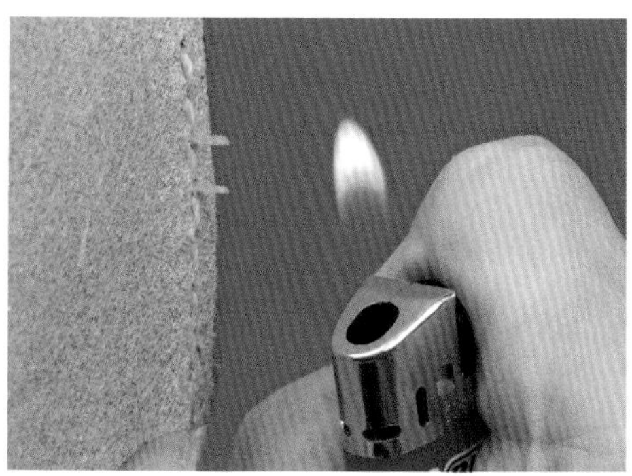

2 Quickly press the thread using the bottom of the lighter.

Since leather is not resistant to fire you should not heat it directly. For areas where it is difficult to use a lighter, such as the inside of a bag, use another method.

* Please be careful when using the lighter.

[Cutting]

Leave 2 to 3 mm (approx. ⅛ in.) of thread out and then cut the thread. Take some bonding agent and apply it over the stitch with the tip of an awl. Using the awl shaft, press the thread down firmly in order to close the stitch.

Putting Items Together

For bag-like projects, make each attached item *before* gluing it to the main item. Also, attach the items *after* burnishing the edges.

[Steps for Making Bags]

1 For straps and handles, stitch them by excluding the area that is going to be sewn onto the main piece. Burnish the edges.

Sew onto the bag

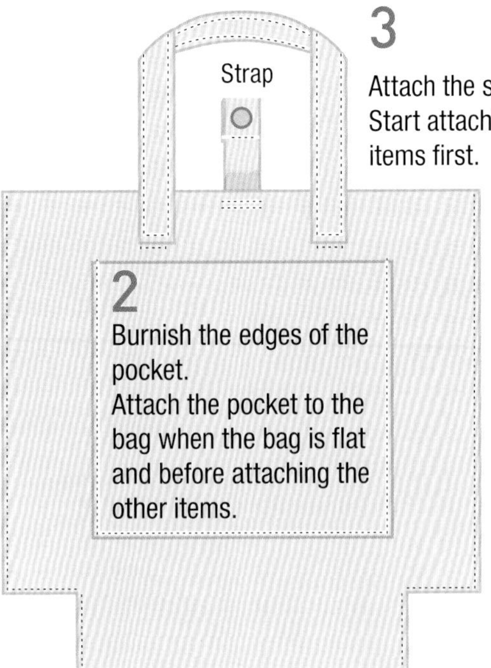

2 Burnish the edges of the pocket. Attach the pocket to the bag when the bag is flat and before attaching the other items.

3 Attach the strap. Start attaching small items first.

4 Attach the handle.

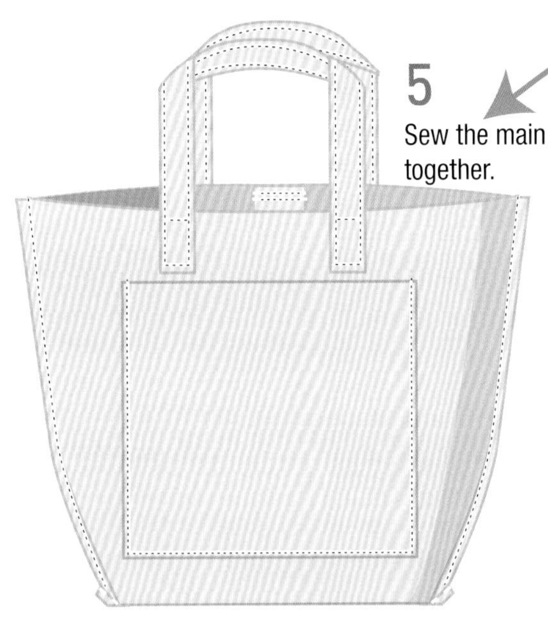

5 Sew the main piece together.

[Steps for Making a Basic Pen Case]

1 Before gluing, sew the item onto the main piece. Align the holes and "dispose of the thread" a few times on the back-side.

2 Align the marked stitching holes, glue, and then start stitching from the bottom corner.

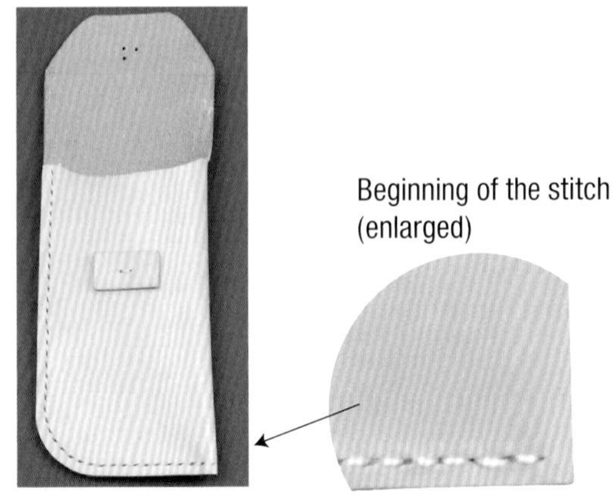

Beginning of the stitch (enlarged)

Finishing

Once stitching is finished, adjust the seam allowance along the seam. With a project that is flat, like the basic pen case, it becomes easier to insert items by inflating the shape.

[Adjusting the Edges]

1

Adjust the uneven edges of the seam, until they are even, by filing with a "dresser" (a file).

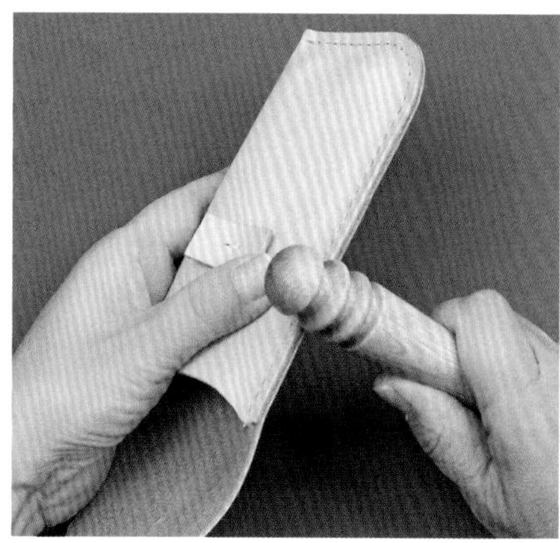

2

Apply Tokonole, then burnish using a slicker.

[Inflating]

1 Use a wet sponge to lightly moisten the grain-side (front-side) of the leather.

2 Rub the seam from the inside with a slicker to widen, or insert a folded piece of paper into the pen case. Make the bottom corners of the folded paper round so as not to stretch out the bottom of the case.

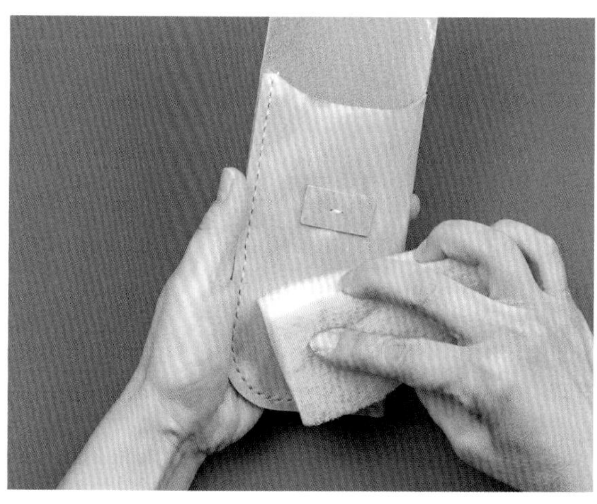

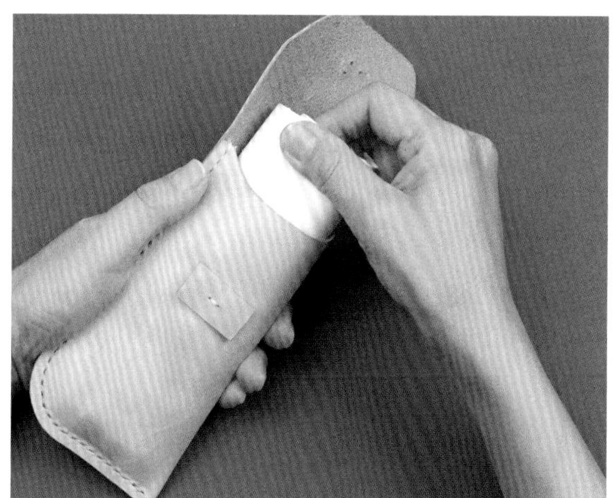

[Finishing the Basic Pen Case]

Finally, pass leather lacing through the holes to complete.

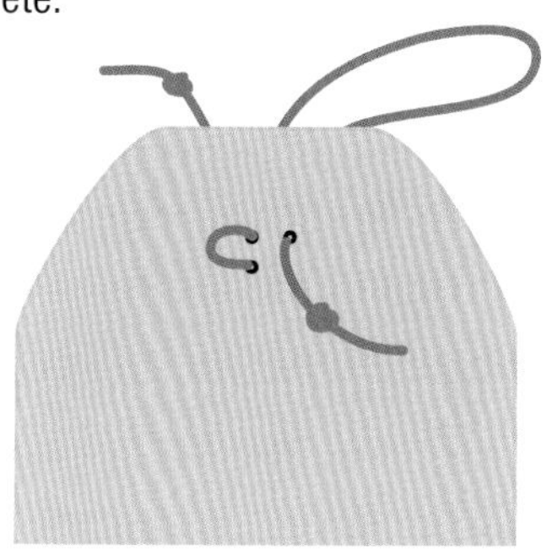

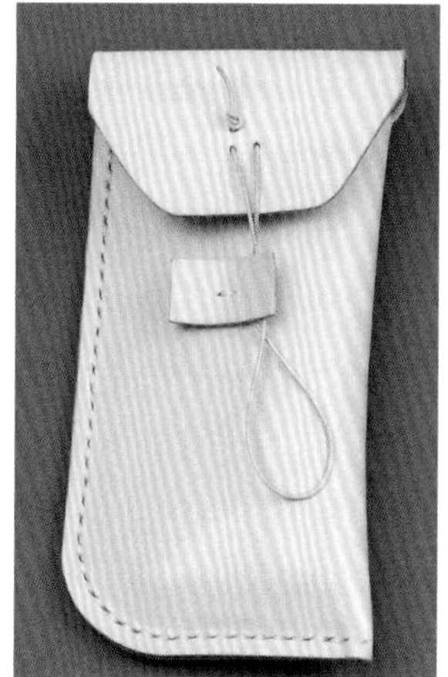

Applying leather oil can prevent the leather from mold and dirt so your project will last a long time.

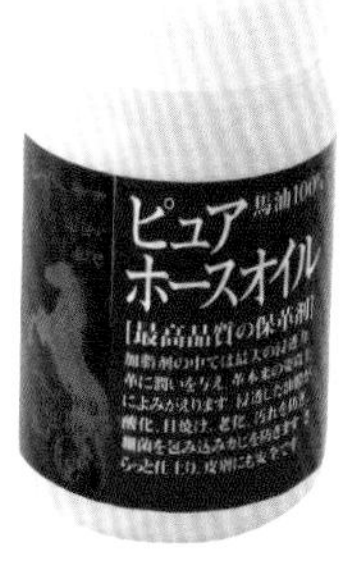

Above is a needle case that was introduced in the section on aging tanned leather. Since these pieces have metal fittings attached, they look like professional works of leathercraft. However, they are just simple items made by sewing two pieces of leather together. Refer to page 51 for instructions.

Chapter 2

Simple Bags and Items

In this chapter we introduce project design variations that you can make using methods introduced in chapter 1.

cutting pattern

An Envelope-shaped Case

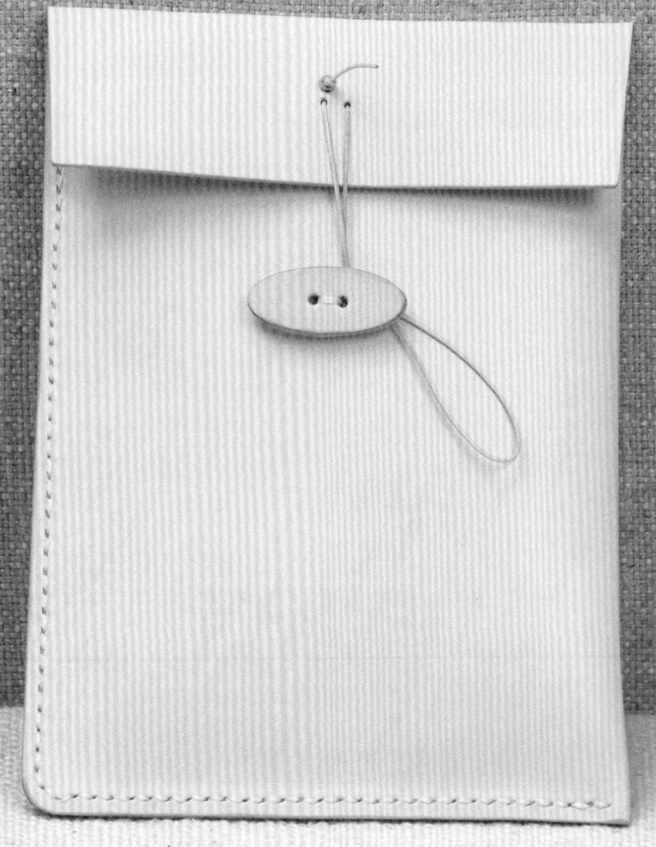

This is the same structure as the basic pen case. The only difference is its size.

how to make

1 Punch stitching holes and cut the leather according to the pattern. Burnish the flesh-side of the leather and the edges.

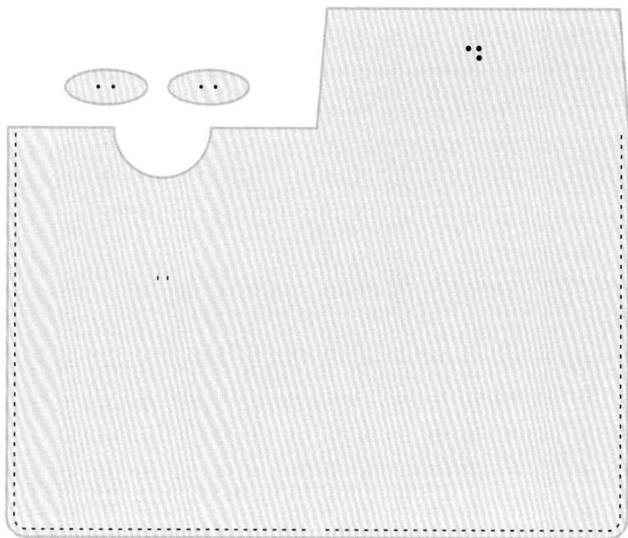

2 Put two pieces of the button leather together, with the flesh-side facing in, and glue them. Sew the button onto the case and tie the thread at the back.

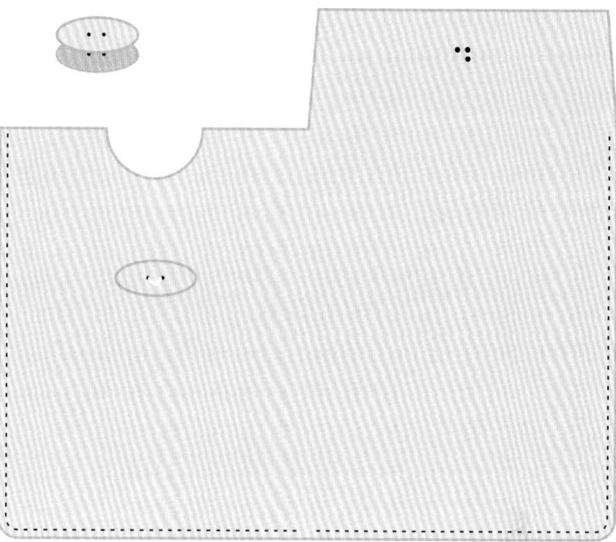

3 Align the marked stitching holes and glue together. Make fine adjustments to align the position of the holes by piercing the stitching holes, every few stitches, with an awl. This makes stitching easier.

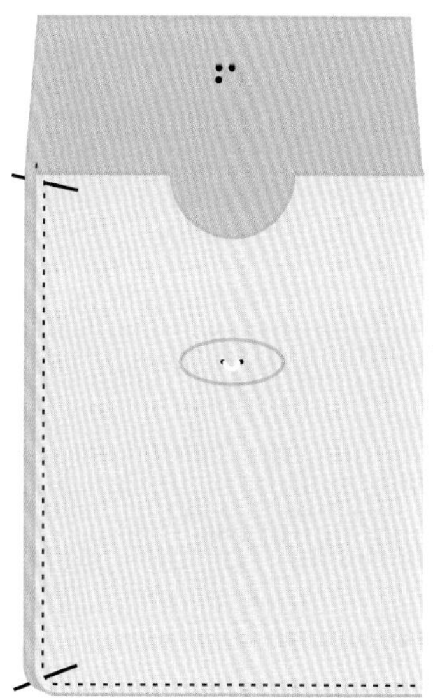

4 Begin stitching from the bottom corner.

5 Put leather lacing through the hole and tie the ends.

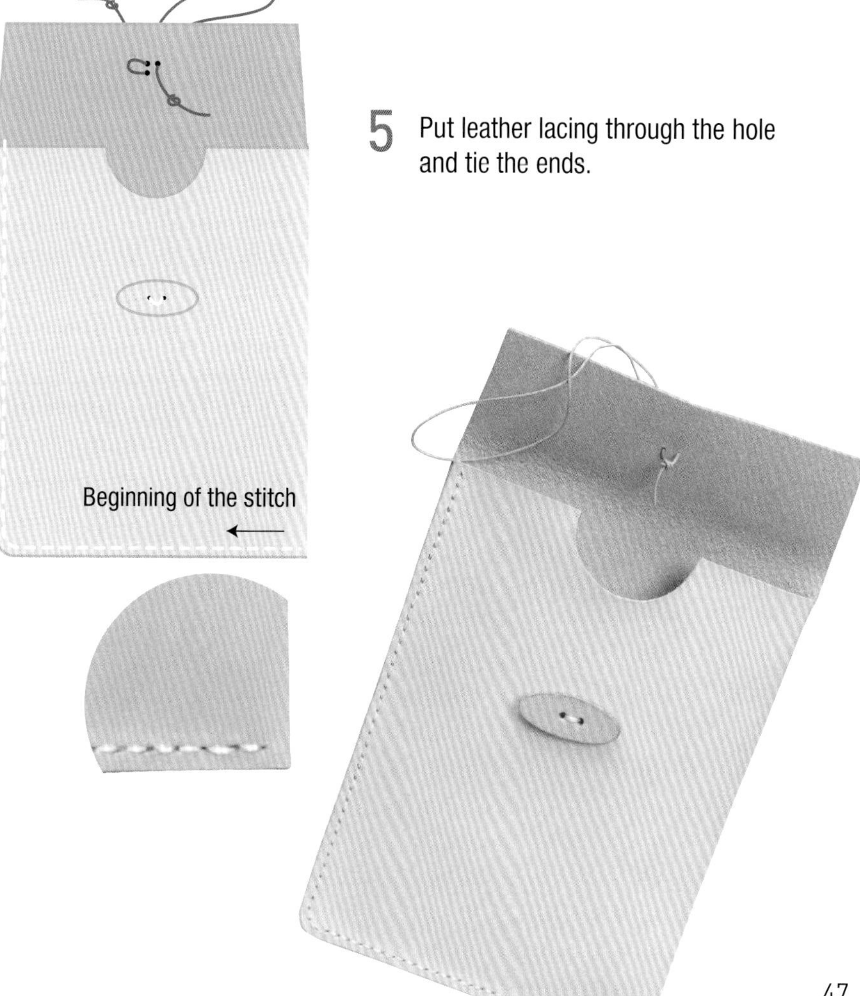

cutting pattern

Credit Card Case/ Luggage Tag and Business Card Holder

Sew together two pieces of leather that have been lain on top of each other. Similar to a coin purse, the opening closes by overlapping the knobs at the top. The credit card case/luggage tag opens by loosening the leather cord.

how to make

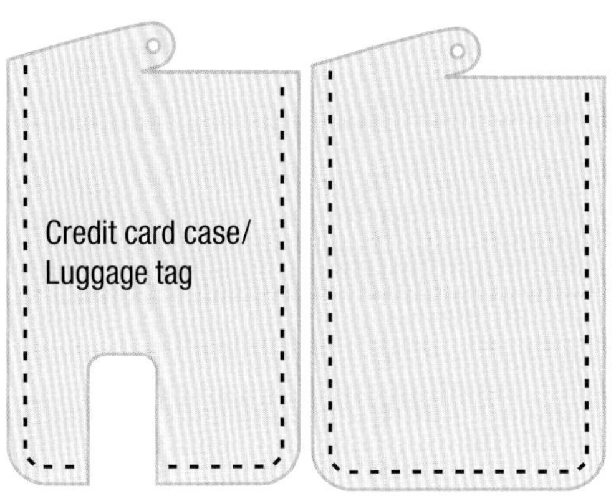

1 Punch the stitching holes and cut the leather according to the pattern. Burnish the flesh-side of the leather and the edges.

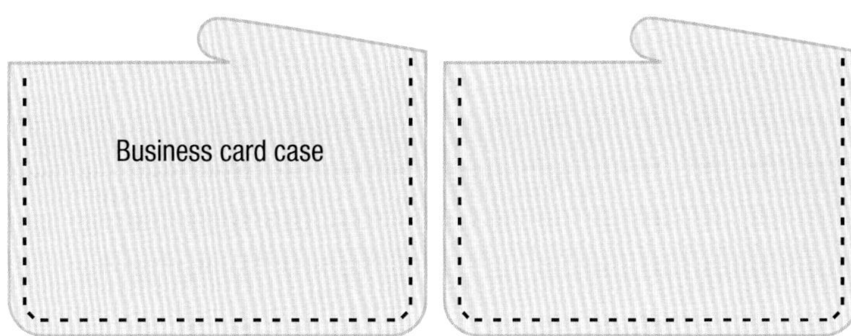

2 Align the marked stitching holes and glue the leather. Then stitch.

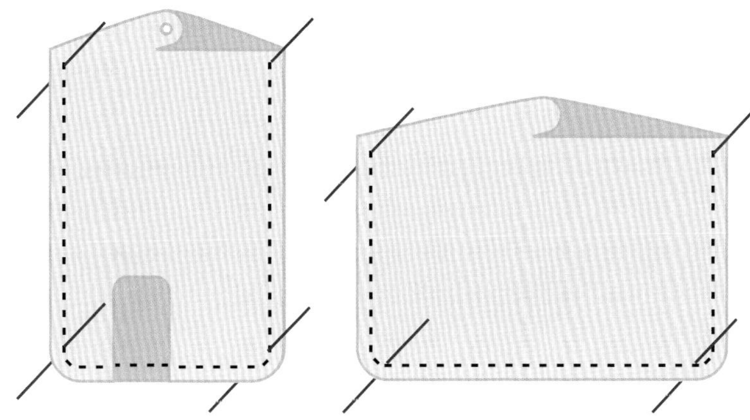

Thread the leather cord

detail

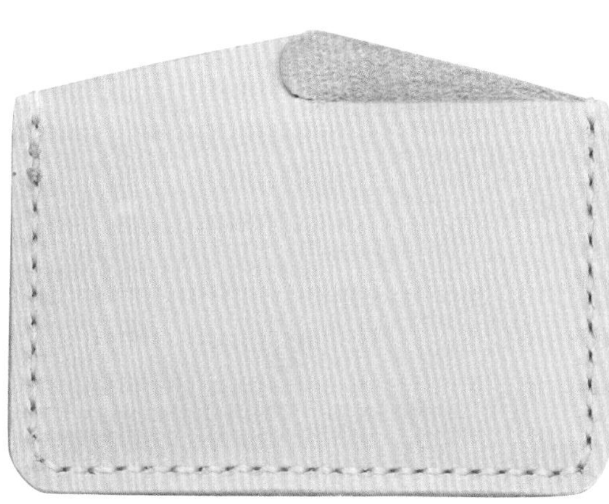

cutting pattern

A CD-sized Bag

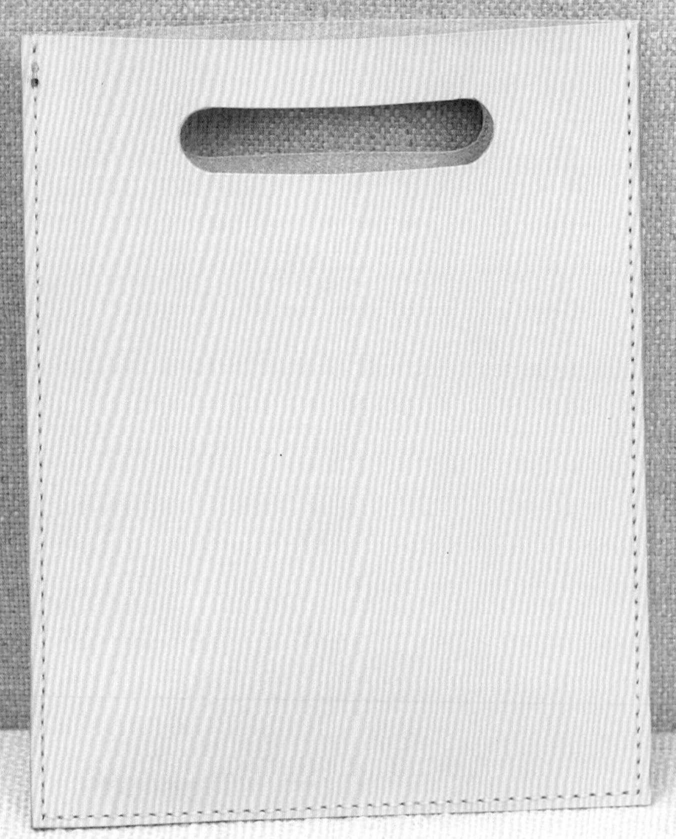

This is a small two-gored bag that can carry CD's.
One tip for a beautiful finish is burnishing the edge of the oval hand hole well.

how to make

A CD-sized Bag

1

Punch the stitching holes and cut the leather according to the pattern. Burnish the flesh-side of the leather and the edges.

2

Apply glue along the bottom of the bag. Place the flesh-sides inward and put the two pieces of leather together. In order to prevent unintentional gluing of leather, place a piece of paper in between the two pieces. Glue the leather as you align the stitching holes.

As you slide the paper along, every few holes glue the leather

Paper

Glue bottom

3

Similar to step 2, apply glue on one side and then bond each side separately. Then, stitch the leather.

Paper

Glue side

As you slide the paper along, every few holes glue the leather

Finish stitching

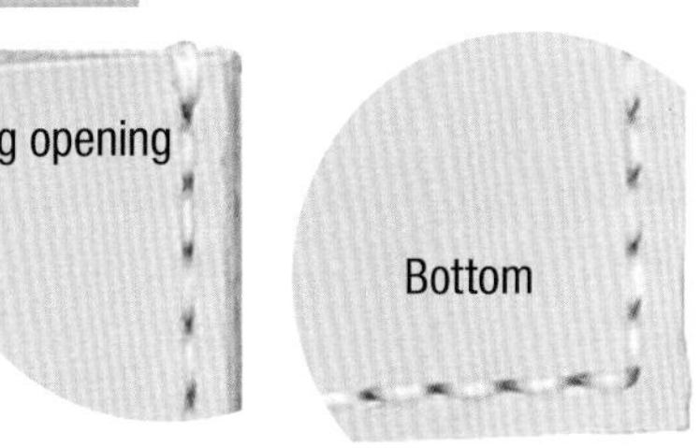

how to make

A Needle Case (P. 44)

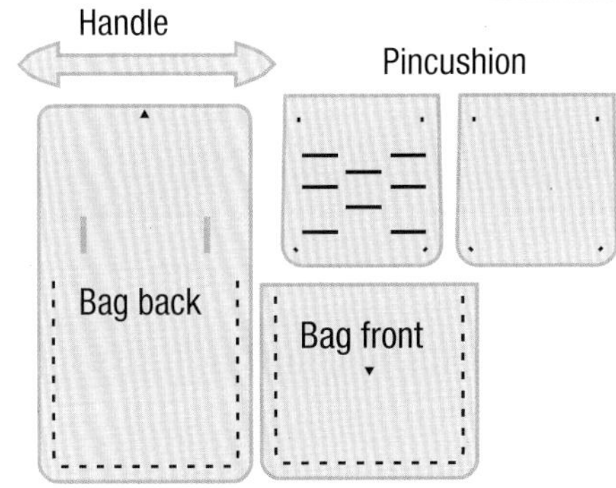

1 Punch the stitching holes and cut the leather according to the pattern. Burnish the flesh-side of the leather and the edges.

2 Attach a metal fitting (tuck lock clasps) by aligning with the center mark.

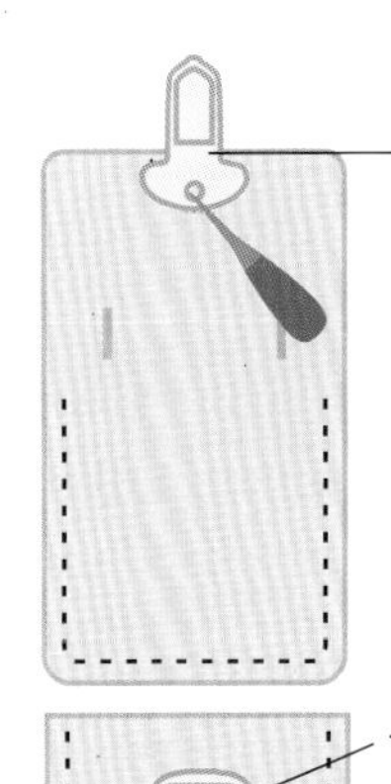

Put a metal fitting in place by pinching the leather in between the fitting's slit. Then secure the fitting with a rivet.

Make slits, and then bend the shaft of the fitting. This is same method as attaching a magnetic snap. Refer to page 87, step 5.

3 Place the two pieces of bag leather together with the flesh-sides facing each other. Align the marked stitching holes and glue. Then stitch the leather.

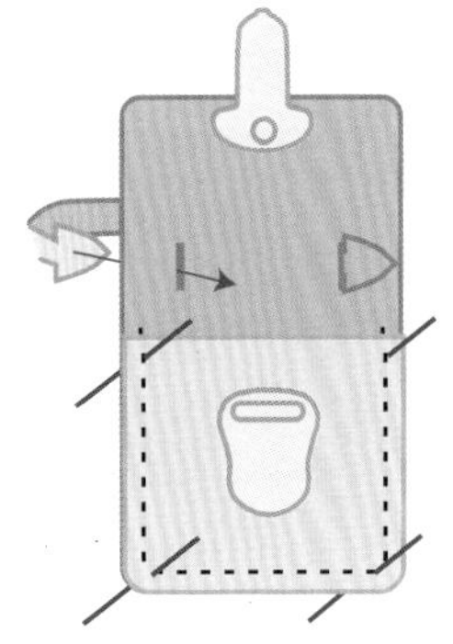

For the pincushion, apply glue along the sides and stitch the leather by aligning the stitching holes.

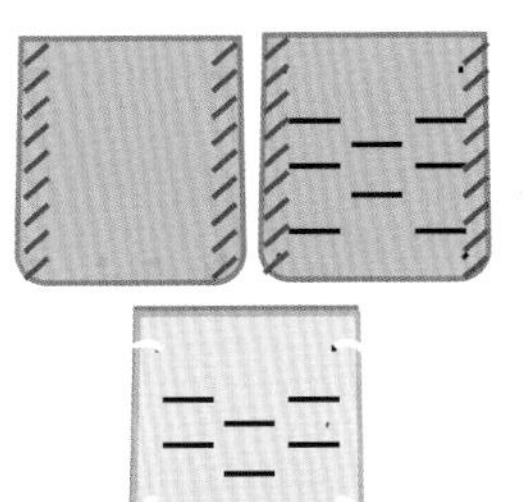

cutting pattern

A Vinyl Record-sized Bag

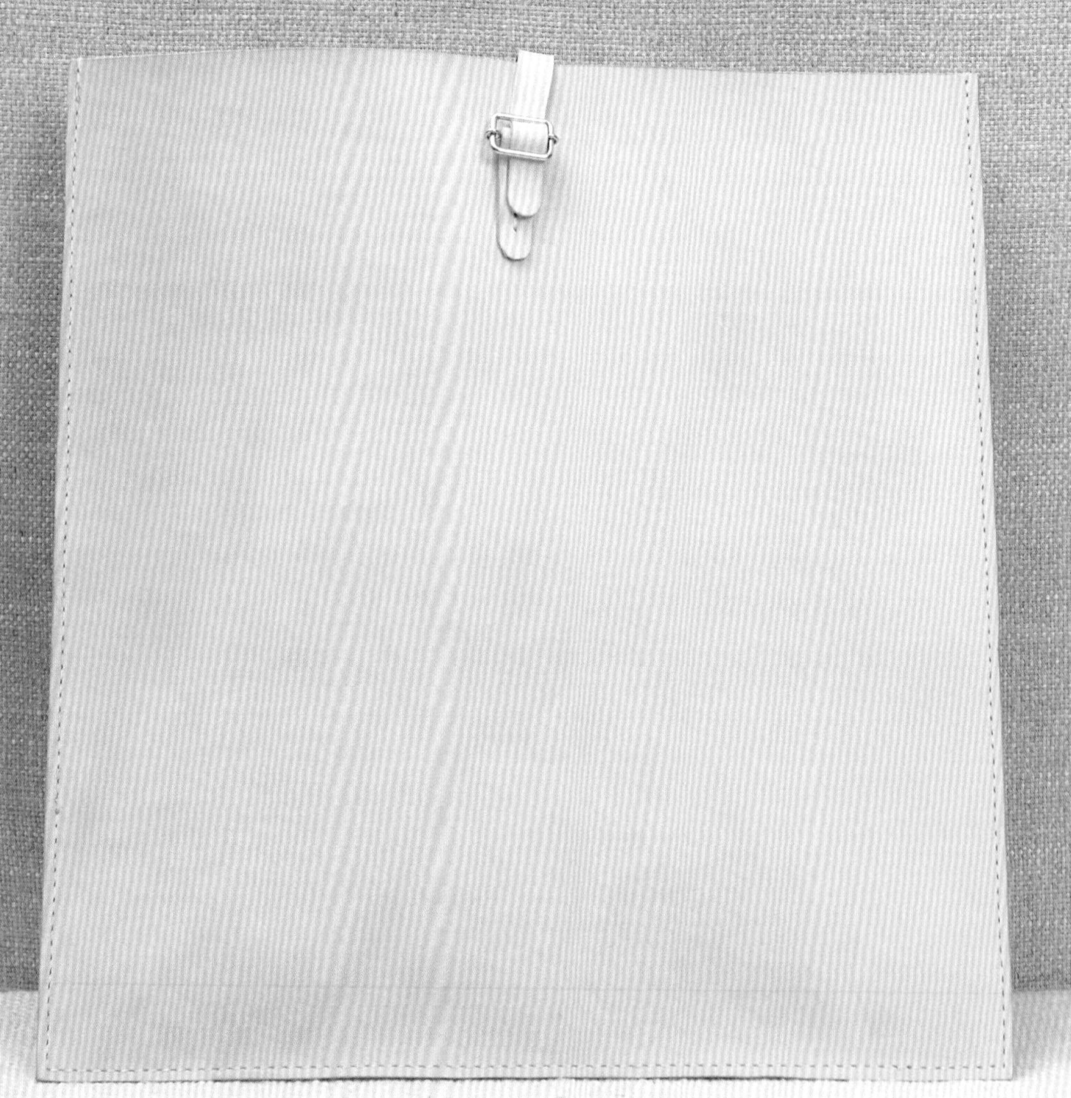

A vinyl record-sized bag made from a large leather sheet.
Attaching handles creates a totally different bag.

how to make

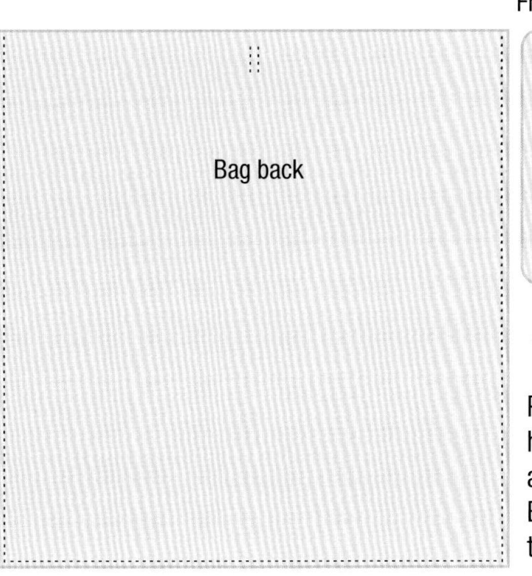

Belt

Front Back

1

Punch the stitching holes and cut the leather according to the pattern. Burnish the flesh-side of the leather and the edges.

2

Put the front-side belt leather through the bar of the buckle. Then, align the stitching holes and fold the leather in half to glue. Align the stitching holes and glue the leather together. Then stitch.

3

Glue the back-side of the belt leather onto the back of the bag leather by aligning the stitching holes. Then stitch.

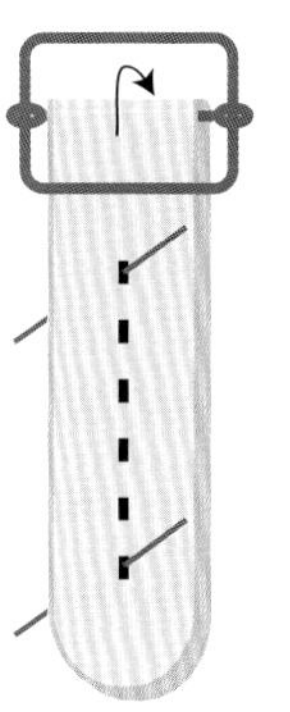

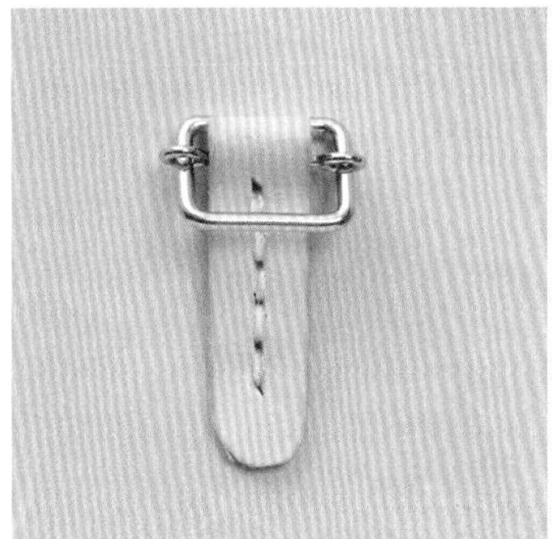

4

Apply glue along the bottom of the bag. Place the flesh-sides inward and put the two pieces together. In order to prevent unintentional gluing of leather, place a sheet of paper in between the two pieces. Glue the leather as you align the stitching holes. Next, glue each side separately in a same manner as the bottom and then stitch.

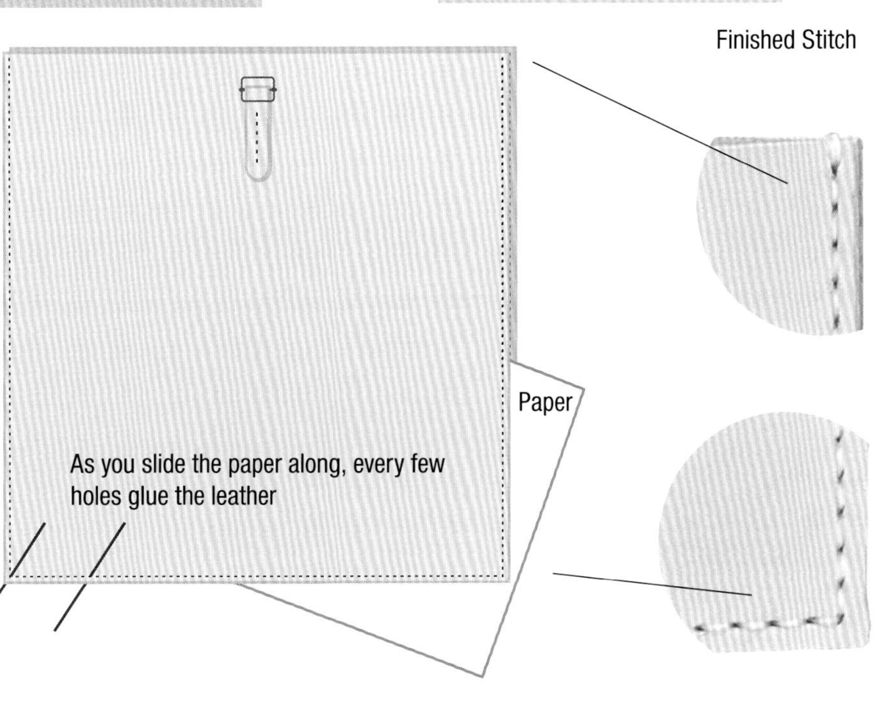

cutting pattern

A Journal Cover

A cover for paperback-sized journals or a notebook.

how to make

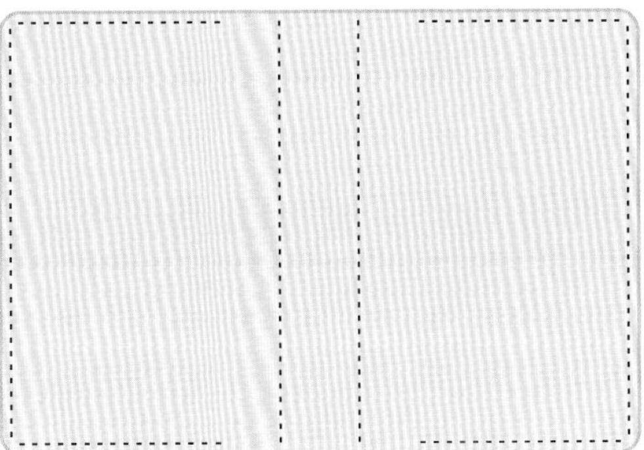

1 Punch the stitching holes and cut the leather according to the pattern. Burnish the flesh-side of the leather and the edges.

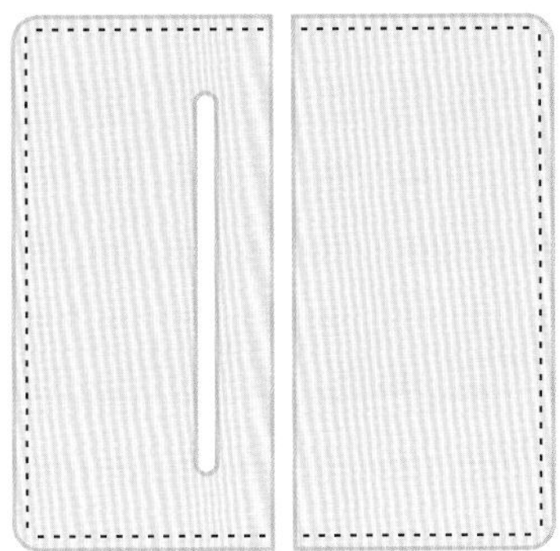

2 For each side, separately, place the two pieces of bag leather together with the flesh-sides facing each other and line up the stitching holes. Then stitch.

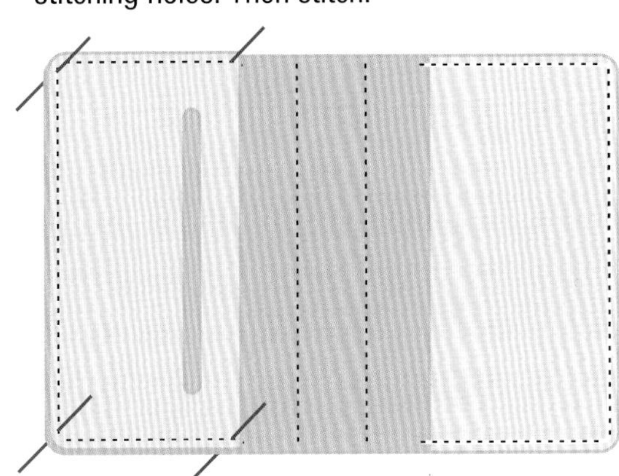

3 Moisten the leather and put folded paper in the pockets to stretch the leather so that the journal's covers can be easily inserted.

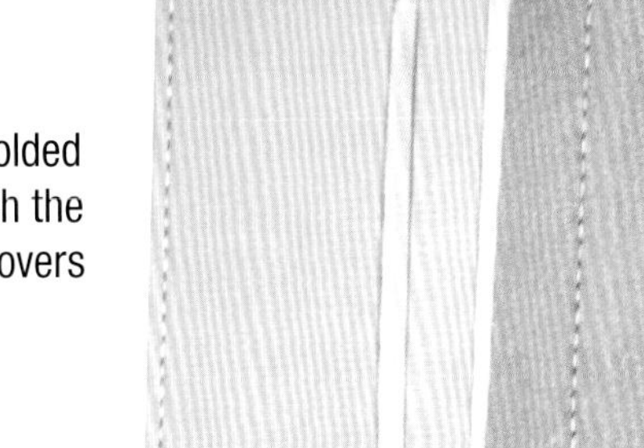

detail

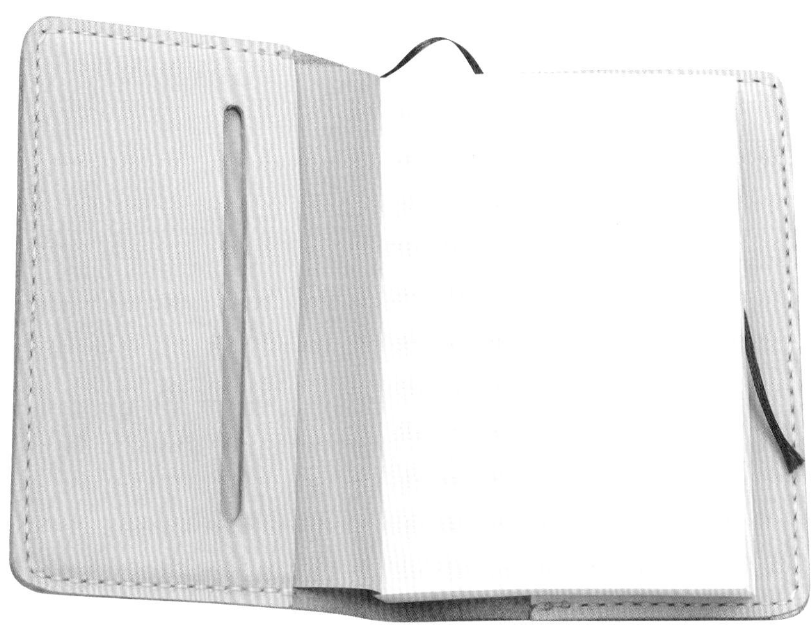

cutting pattern

A Tool Pouch

This is a tool pouch for use with a belt. Since tanned leather is used, it feels stiff in the beginning. However, it will gradually break in and adjust to the curve of the belt. Please alter the pattern according to the size of the tools that you intend to carry in the pouch.

how to make

1 Punch the stitching holes and cut the leather according to the pattern. Score a line along the folding lines using an awl. Burnish the flesh-side of the leather and the edges.

2 Fold the leather, in order, according to the folding lines

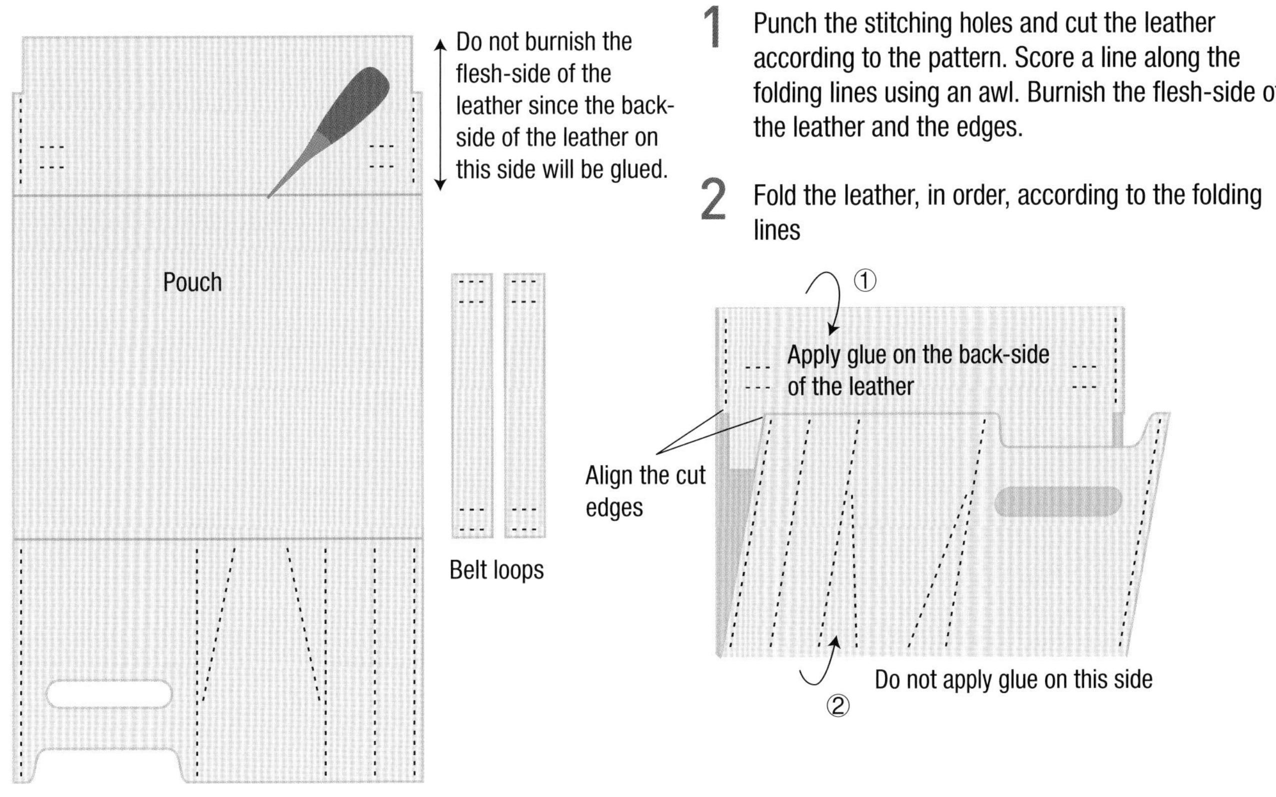

3 Punch the stitching holes with a lacing chisel according to the pattern. Punch the holes all the way through to the back. If the leather is too thick, punch out the traces seen on the back with a lacing chisel.

4 Stitch according to the stitching holes.

5 Align the stitching holes and fold the belt loop. Then glue and stitch.

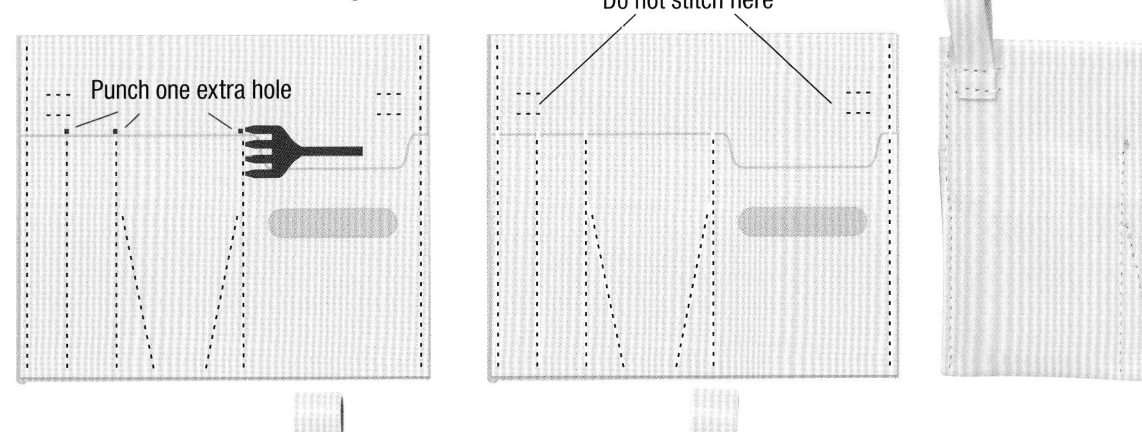

6 Moisten the leather and put folded paper or a pen in the pockets to stretch the leather in order to adjust the shape. This will make it more functional.

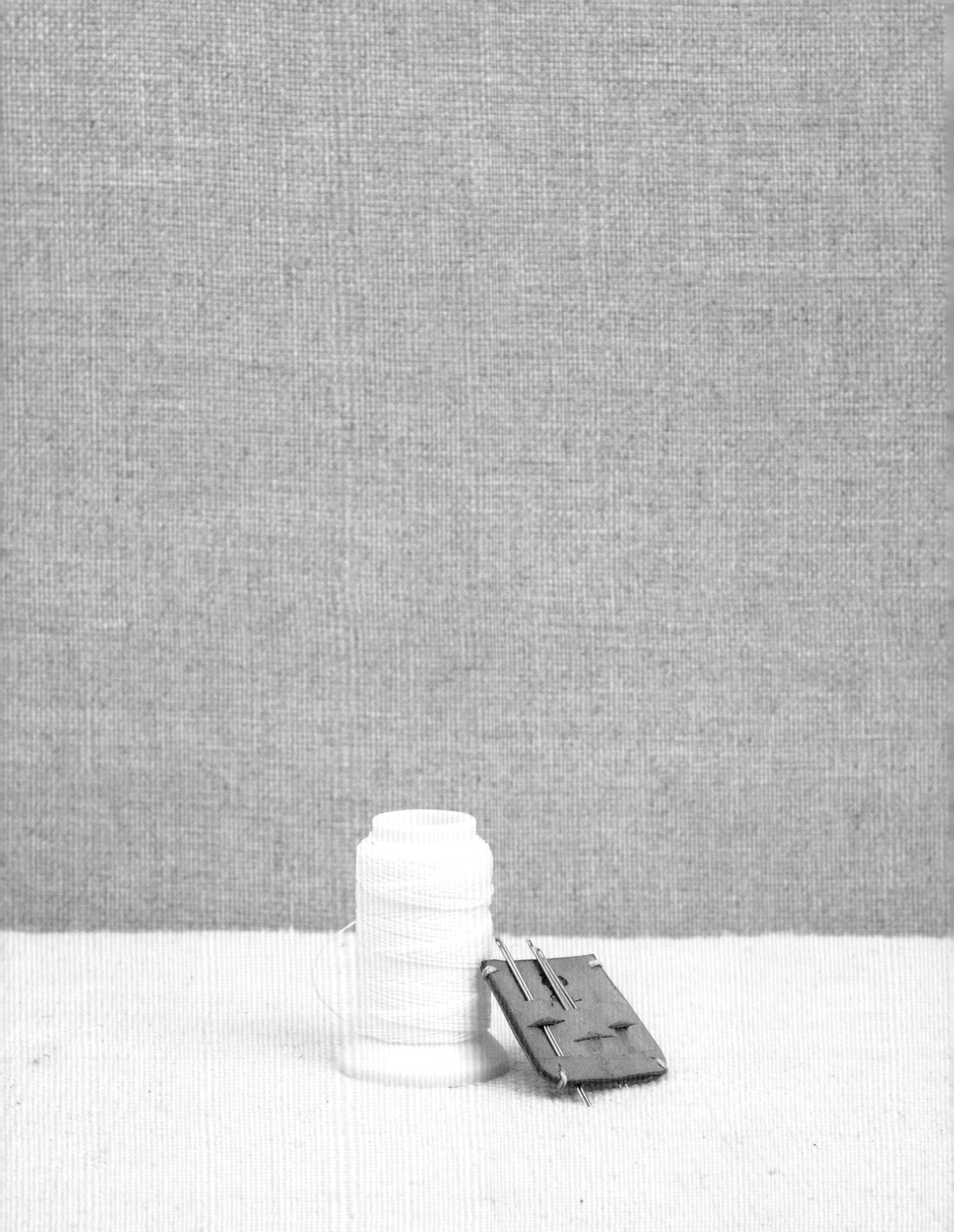

Chapter 3

Practical Application of the Basic Methods

This section introduces leather projects that essentially use the basic method explained in chapter 1. For projects that require multiple items, or ones that are sewn three-dimensionally, etc., specific design-based production points are listed below. As you progress through your project, please feel free to revisit chapter 1 in addition to following the points listed below.

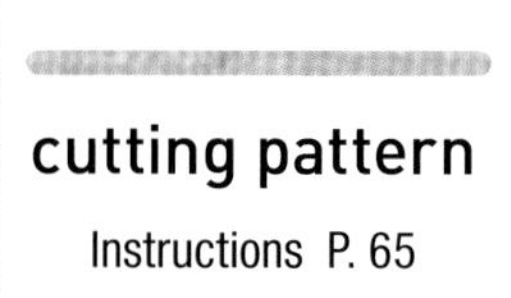

A Pen Case with a Zipper

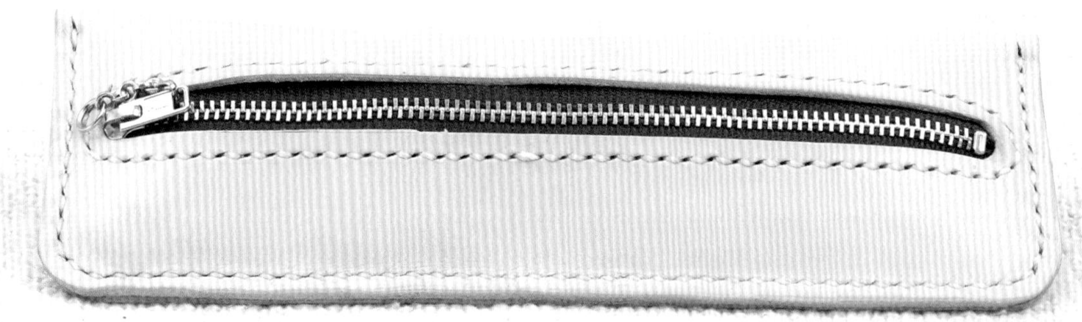

Sew the zipper on first and then fold the leather in half and stitch. This case requires just a few simple steps.

Sewing on a Zipper

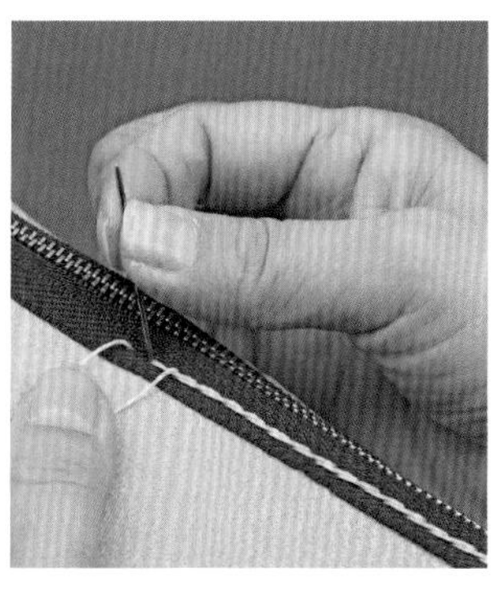

Glue zipper tape on the leather, and then sew it on. Since the punched stitching holes are not visible through the zipper tape you should punch a scratch awl or a needle through each stitching hole to mark its position. Then stitch as you confirm stitching hole positions.

[Sewing a Zipper onto Something Flat]

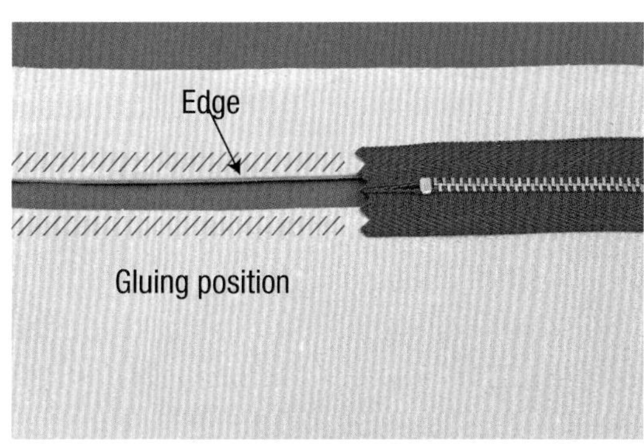

1 Put the zipper in the correct gluing position and then apply glue on the inside of the zipper tape. Be careful to apply glue so that it does not flow all the way to the edge of the leather.

2 Place the zipper flat and lay the leather on top.

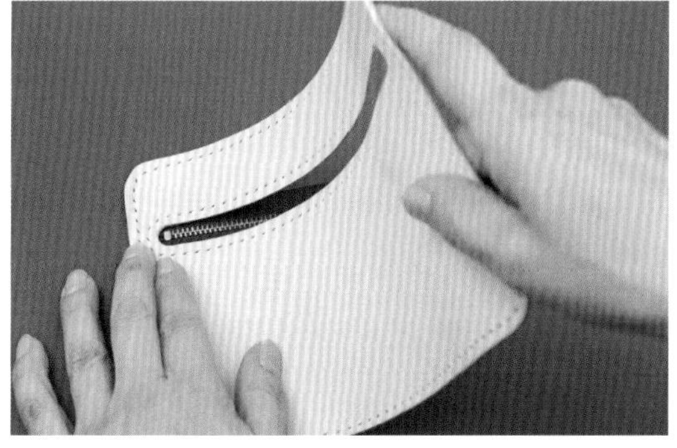

3 Fold the ends of zipper tape, glue them down, and then sew.

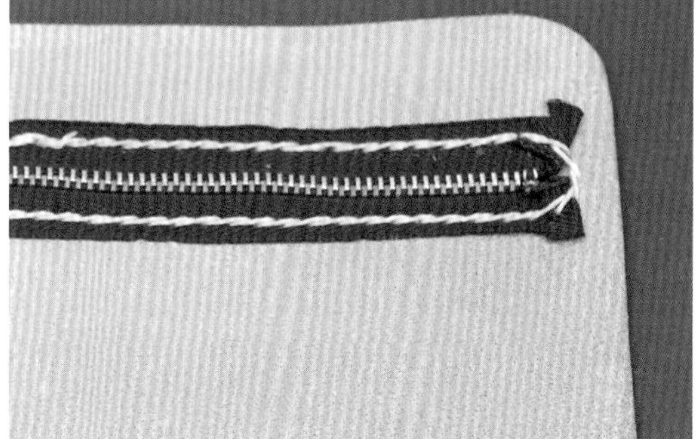

[Gluing on a Zipper by Folding Leather]

1 On one side of the leather, glue a zipper and mark both ends of the zipper on the zipper tape using a ruler. Sew this glued side first.

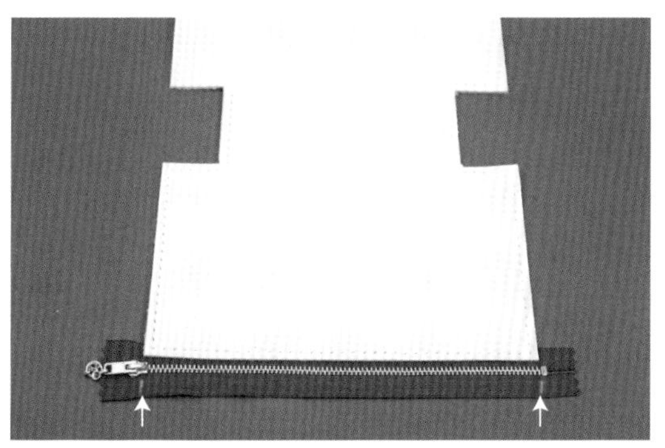

2 As for the other side, leave the zipper closed and align the leather with the marks on the tape and then glue. Open the zipper and sew it on.

cutting pattern

A Triangular Pouch

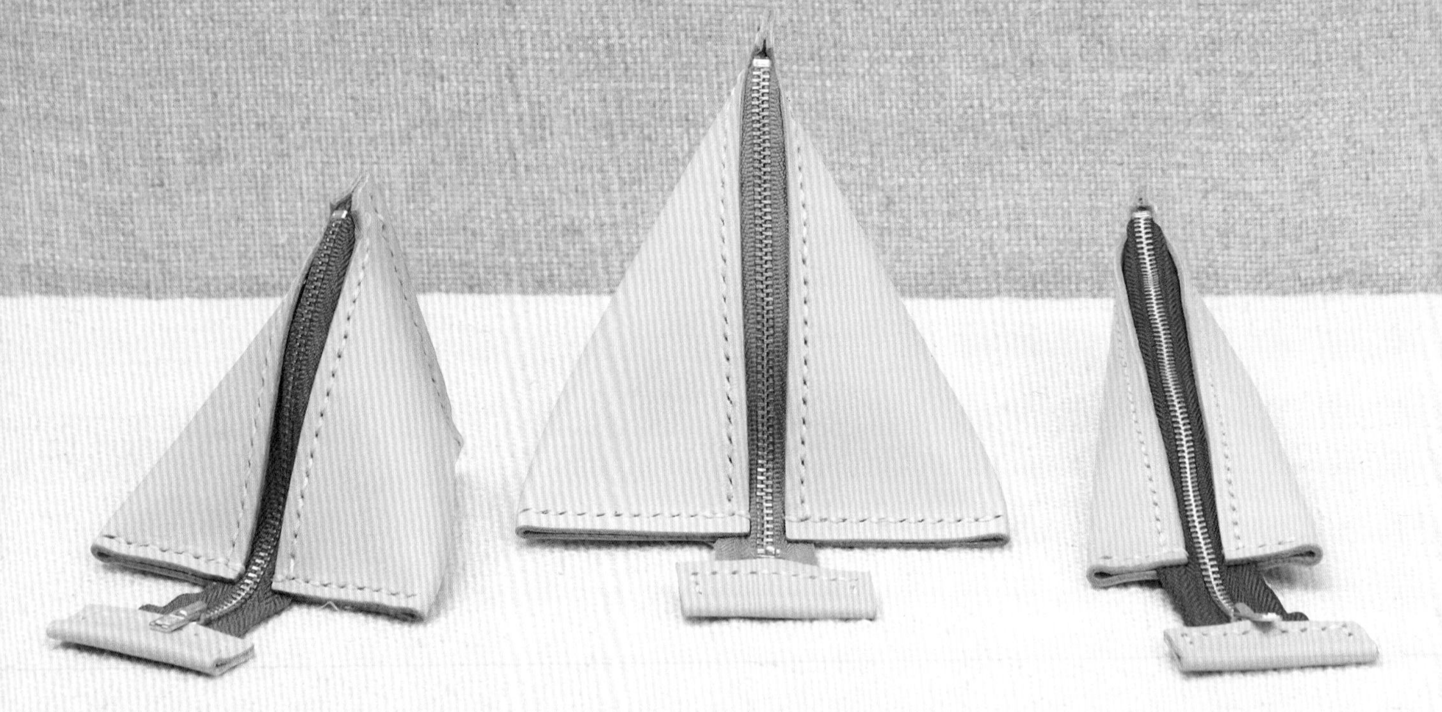

Make a cylindrical shape by bonding both sides of a sheet of leather. Close one opening horizontally and the other vertically so that it makes a shape like this.

how to make

1 Punch the stitching holes and cut out the leather according to the pattern. Burnish the flesh-side of the leather and the edges.

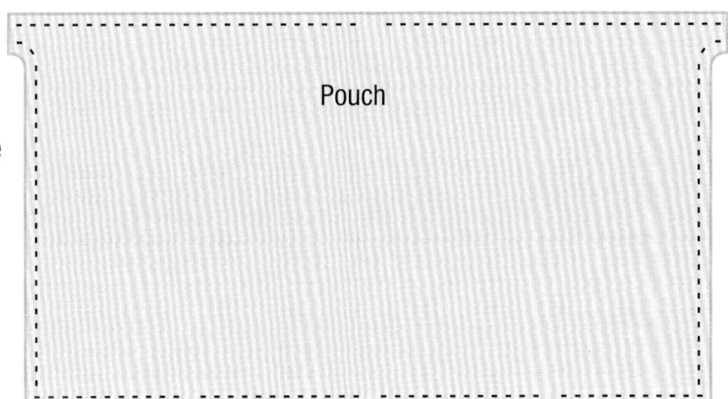

2 Glue the zipper on and then sew. Refer to page 61, "Sewing on a Zipper."

3 Align the marked stitching holes on one side and glue. Then sew.

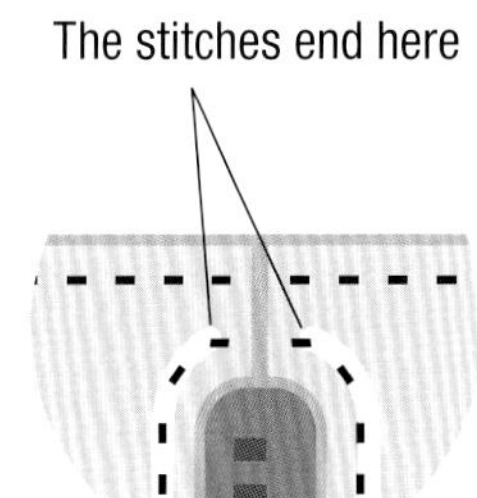

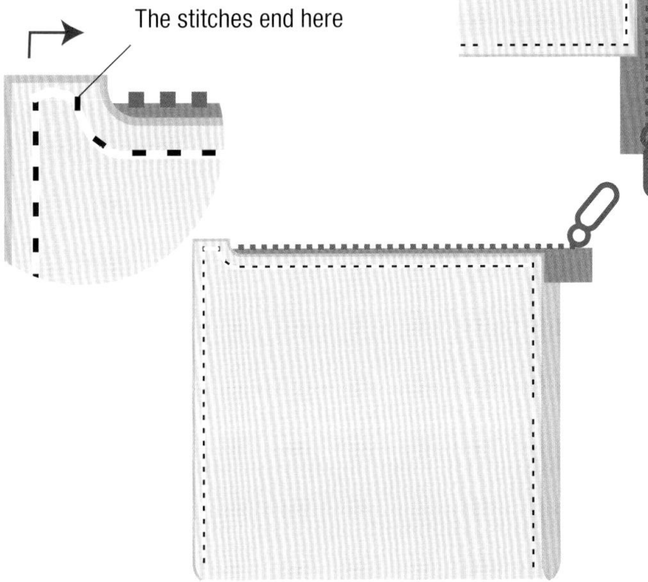

4 Align the marked stitching holes on the other side and glue. Then sew.

5 Apply glue on the zipper tag and then wrap it around the tape extension. Align the marked stitching holes. Then glue and sew.

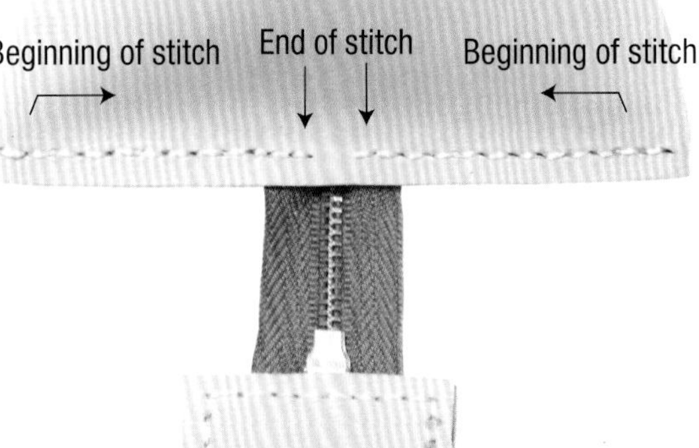

cutting pattern

Flat Cases

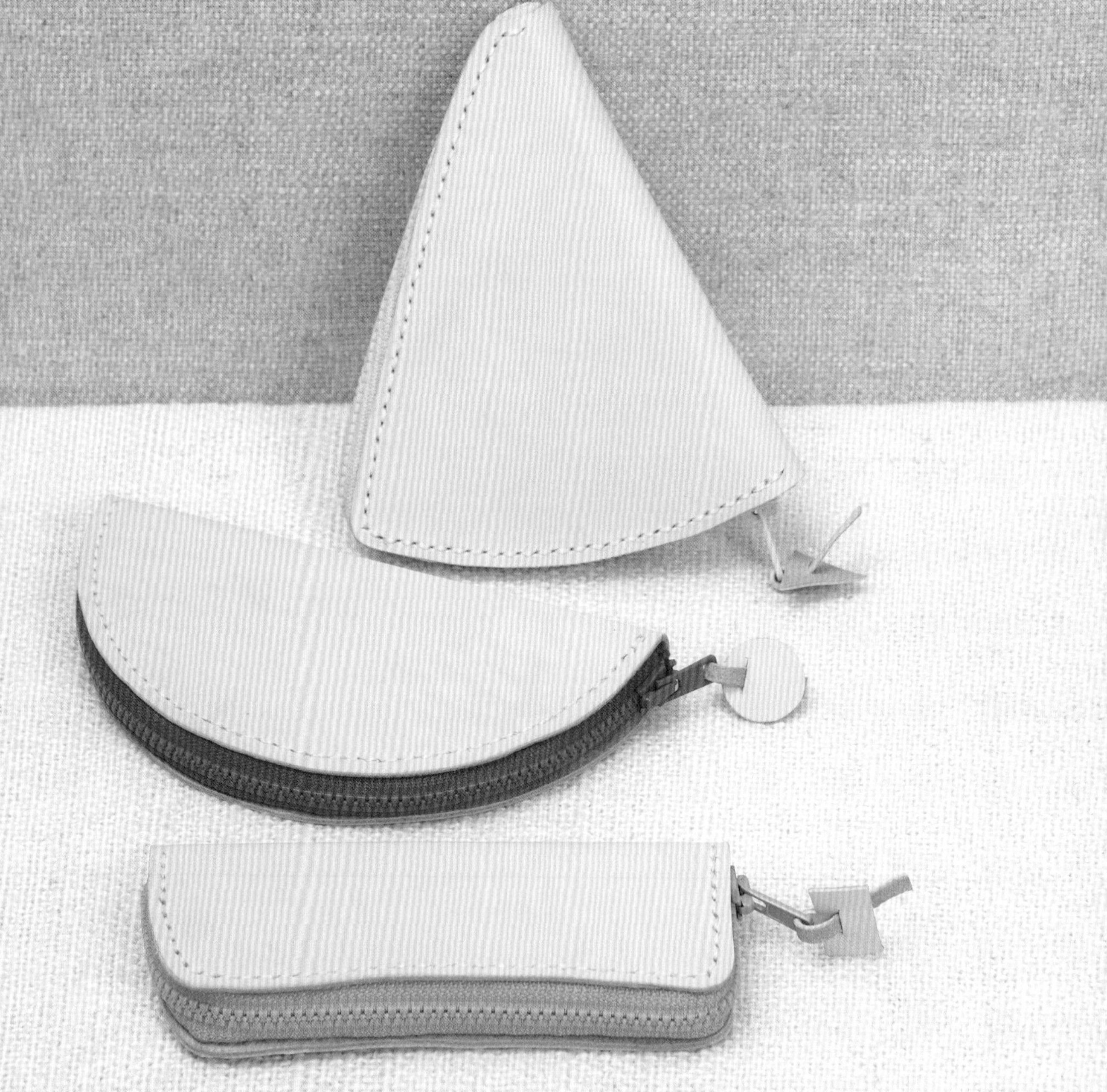

A vibrant colored zipper goes well with tanned leather.

how to make

A Flat Case

1 Punch the stitching holes and cut out the leather according to the pattern. Burnish the flesh-side of the leather and the edges.

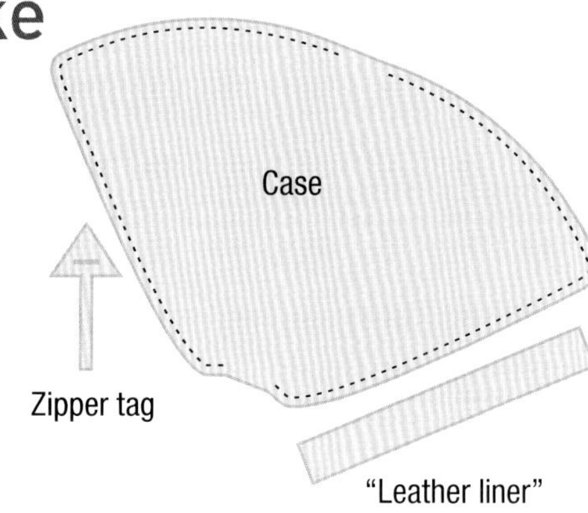

2 Glue on a zipper and then sew.
Refer to page 61, "Sewing on a Zipper."
Apply glue along the seam allowance on one side of the leather case. Tuck the zipper tape under to glue it down around the corner.

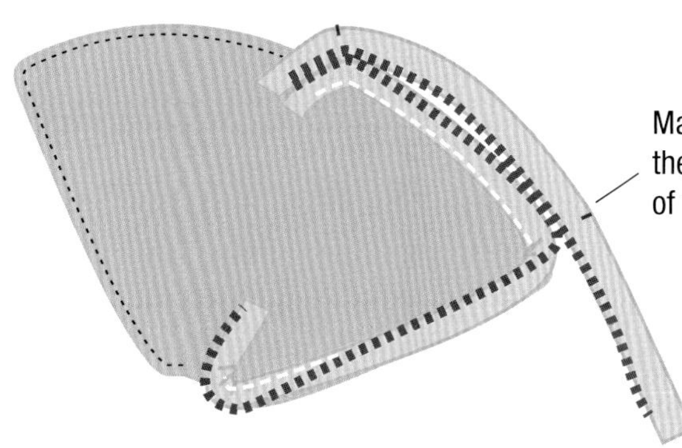

Mark the position of the corner on the back of the zipper tape.

3 For the other side, align the mark with the corner of the case and then glue it down and sew.

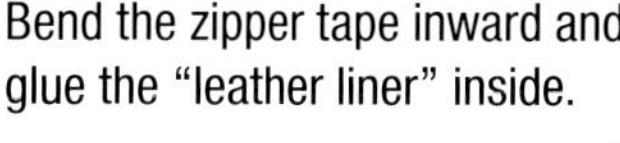

Bend the zipper tape inward and glue the "leather liner" inside.

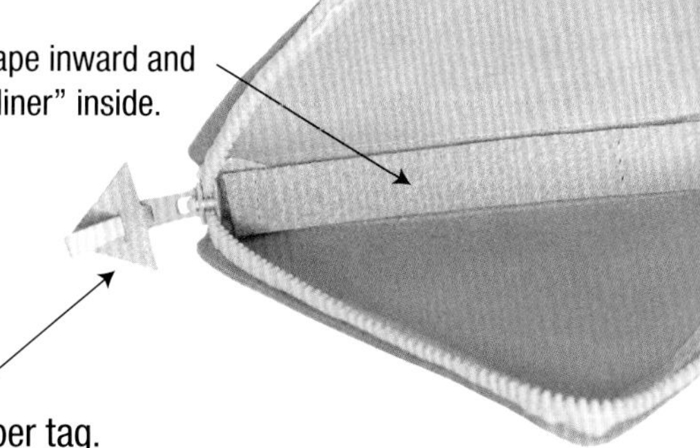

4 Attach a zipper tag.

how to make

A Pen Case with a Zipper P. 60

1 According to the pattern, punch the stitching holes and cut out the leather. Burnish the flesh-side of the leather and the edges.

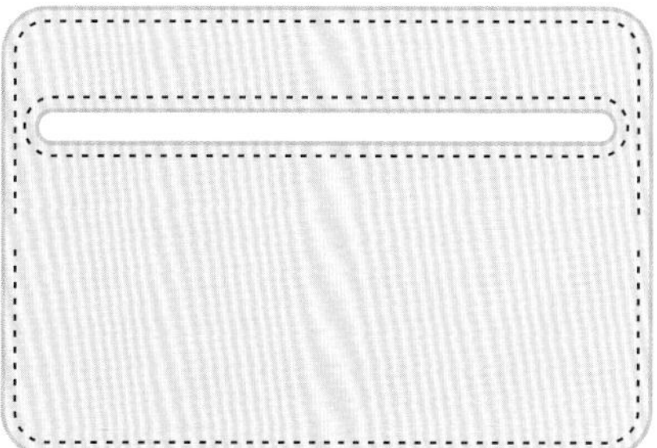

2 Glue on a zipper. Then sew.
Refer to page 61, "Sewing on a Zipper."

3 Glue while aligning the marked stitching holes, and then sew.

The stitching ends here

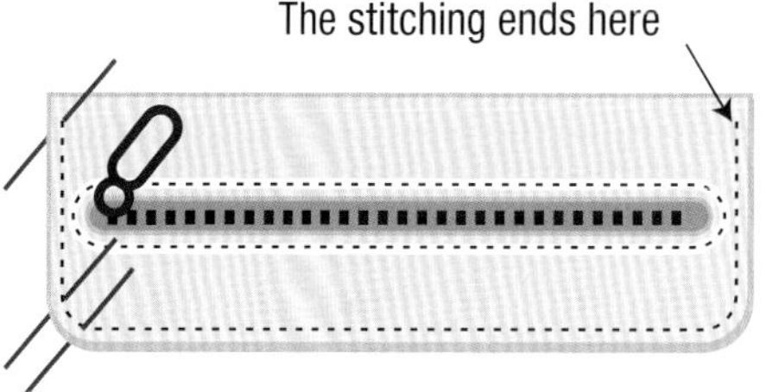

Stitch end

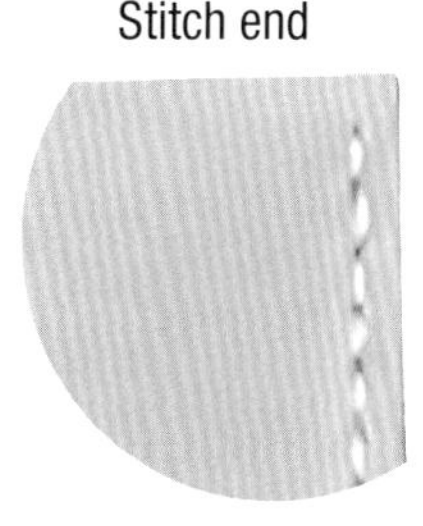

Instructions P. 68

Accessories Made Using Leather Fragments

Leather cords, buttons, tags. Do not throw out remnant leather.
It can be used in many different ways.

how to use

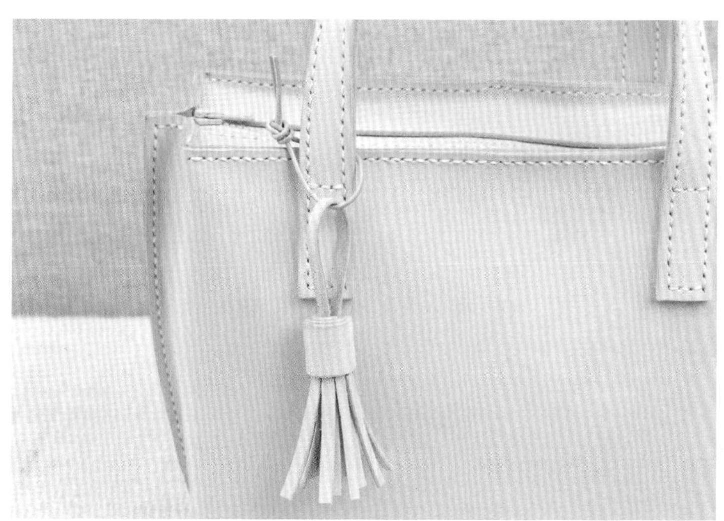

how to make

Accessories Made Using Leather Fragments

There are many leather remnants after making something like a bag. Let's try to use as many as possible. Small leather fragments and long-thin pieces of leather are easily stretched, so they are difficult to cut. Cut slightly larger sized leather remnants to make thin cords. Patterns are drawn using a black line. By photocopying at 160% scale, they will become the same size as those shown on page 66. However, in reality, there is no fixed size so you can make your items any size you want.

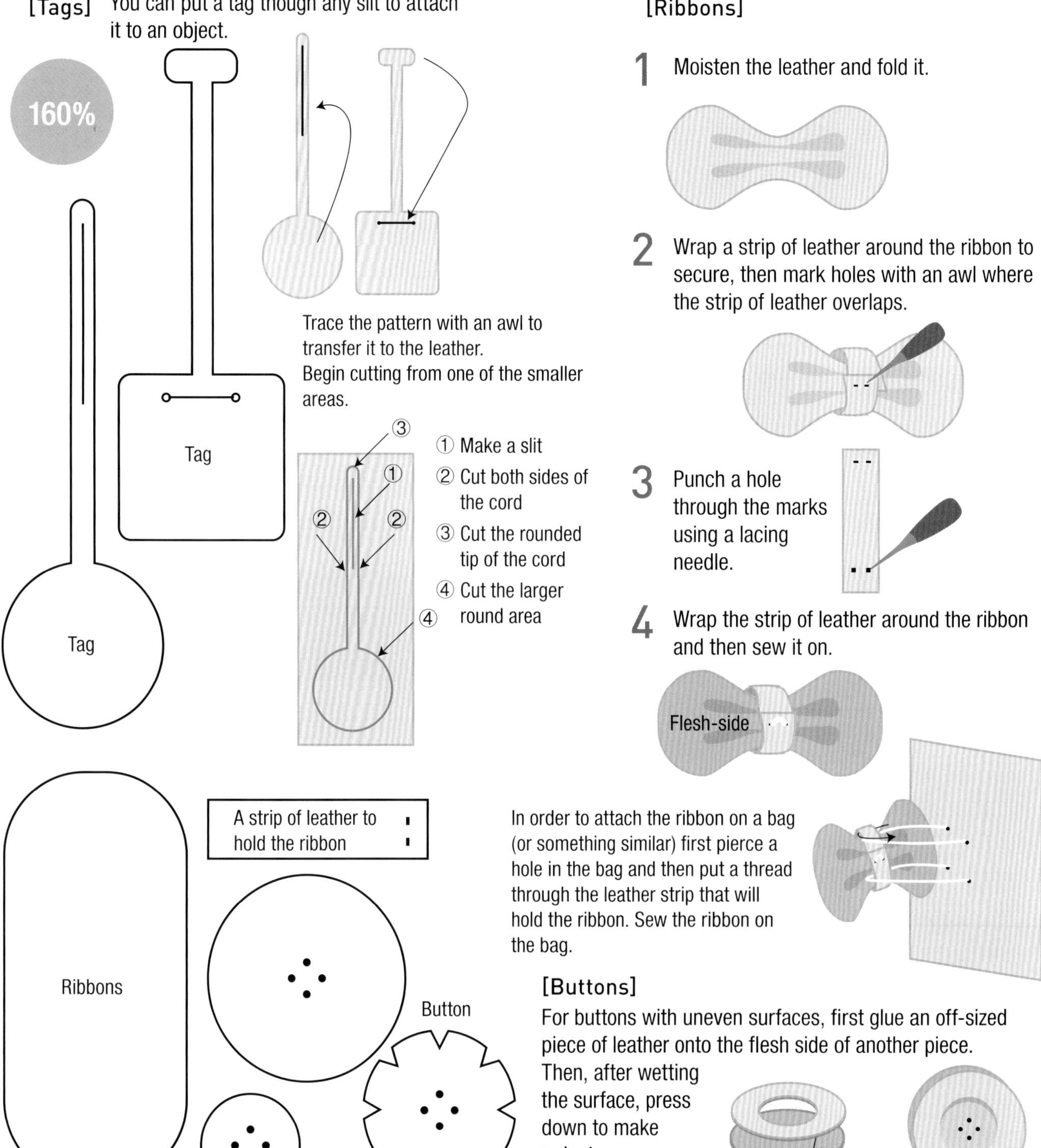

[Buttons]

For buttons with uneven surfaces, first glue an off-sized piece of leather onto the flesh side of another piece. Then, after wetting the surface, press down to make a dent.

Flesh-side

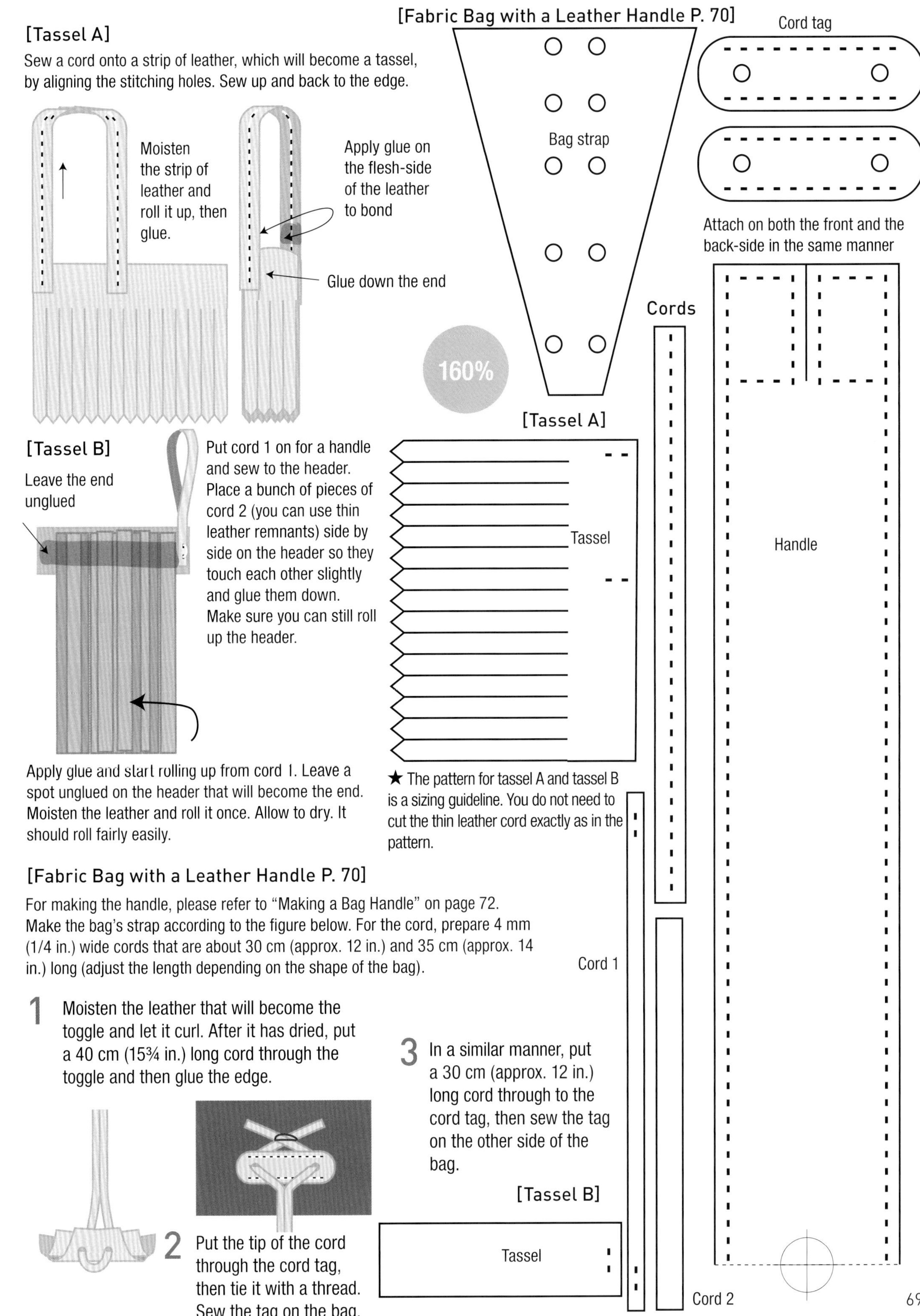

[Fabric Bag with a Leather Handle P. 70]

For making the handle, please refer to "Making a Bag Handle" on page 72. Make the bag's strap according to the figure below. For the cord, prepare 4 mm (1/4 in.) wide cords that are about 30 cm (approx. 12 in.) and 35 cm (approx. 14 in.) long (adjust the length depending on the shape of the bag).

1 Moisten the leather that will become the toggle and let it curl. After it has dried, put a 40 cm (15¾ in.) long cord through the toggle and then glue the edge.

2 Put the tip of the cord through the cord tag, then tie it with a thread. Sew the tag on the bag.

3 In a similar manner, put a 30 cm (approx. 12 in.) long cord through to the cord tag, then sew the tag on the other side of the bag.

cutting pattern

A Fabric Bag with a Leather Handle

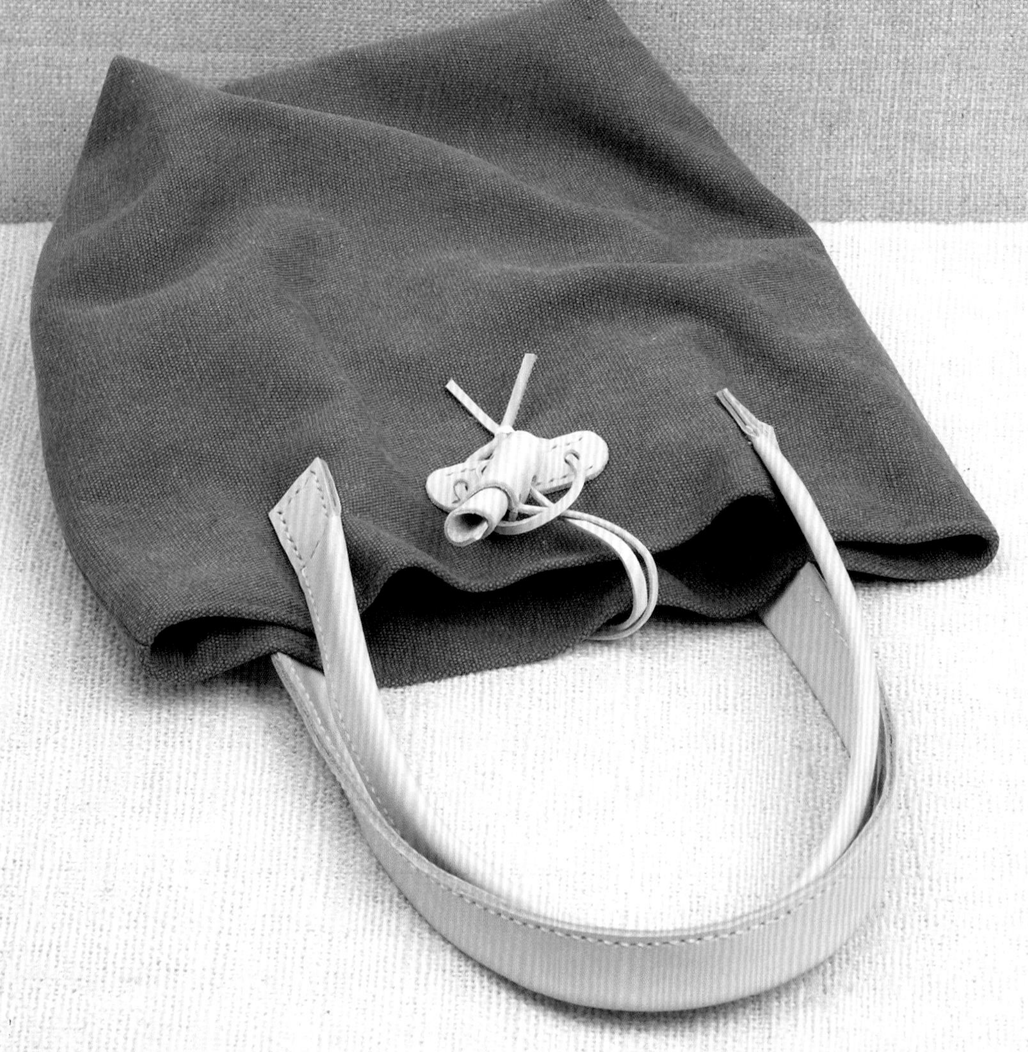

Would you like to change the handle of a cotton or canvas tote bag to a leather handle?

Changing a Bag Handle

Personal preferences for the width and length of a bag handle vary depending on whether it is carried on the arm or the shoulder. Please adjust the handle as instructed below.

[Changing Handle Type]

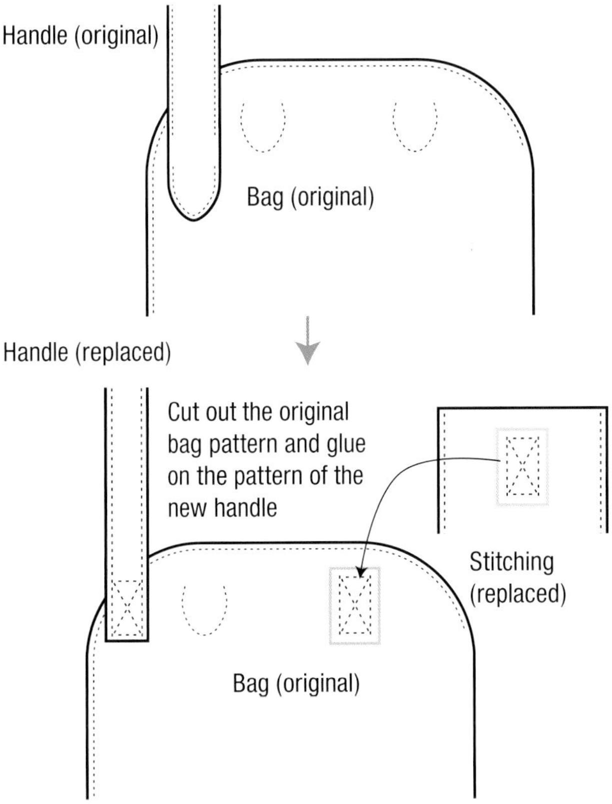

[Changing Handle Length]

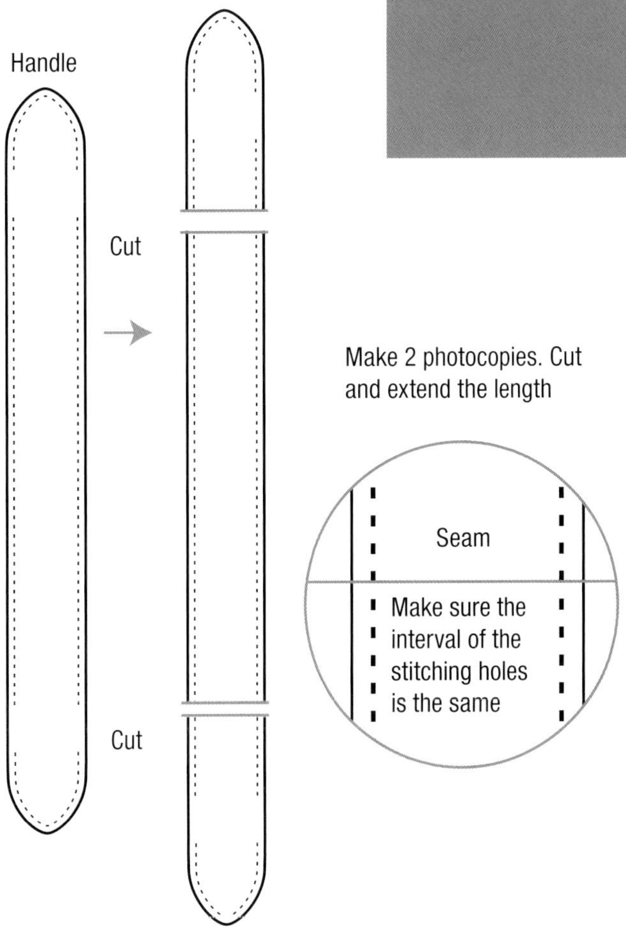

detail

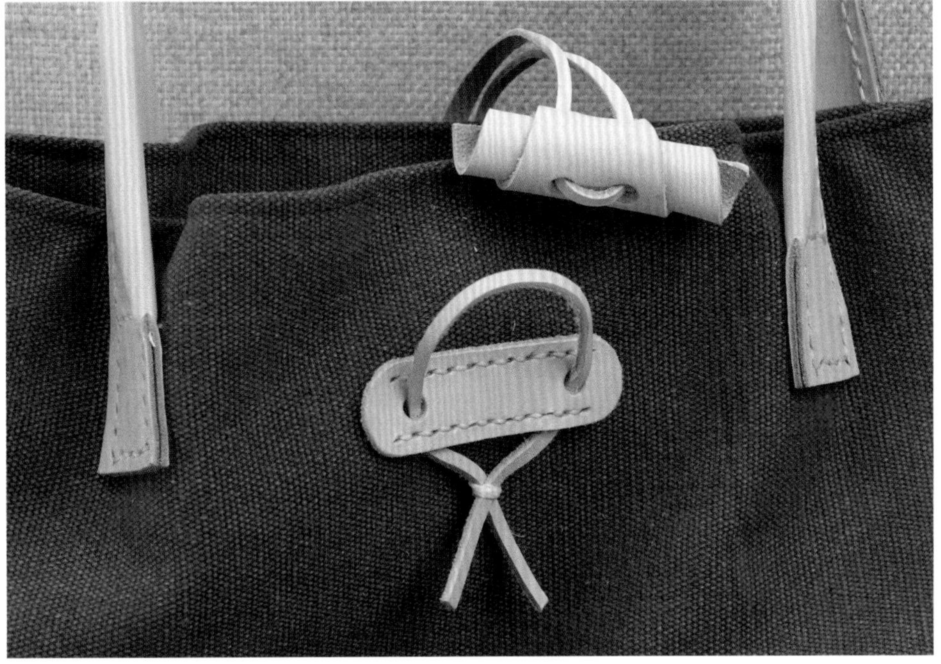

Making a Bag Handle

Three different handle structure types are introduced in this book. For each handle type, stitch them up except where they will be sewn onto a bag. Burnish the edges.

[Double-ply Handle]

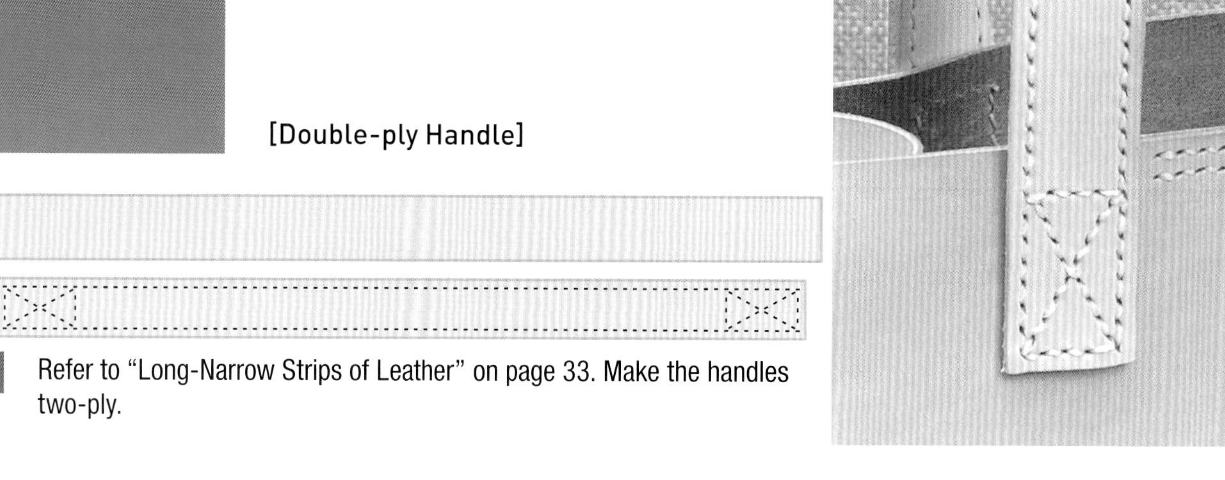

1 Refer to “Long-Narrow Strips of Leather” on page 33. Make the handles two-ply.

2 Stitch the leather, except where it will be sewn onto the bag.

[Folded Handle]

1 Punch the stitching holes and cut out the leather according to the pattern.

2 Align the stitching holes and fold the leather in half, then glue.
Put a piece of paper between the folded leather edges and put an awl or a needle in every few stitching holes in order to keep it aligned. Continue to glue.

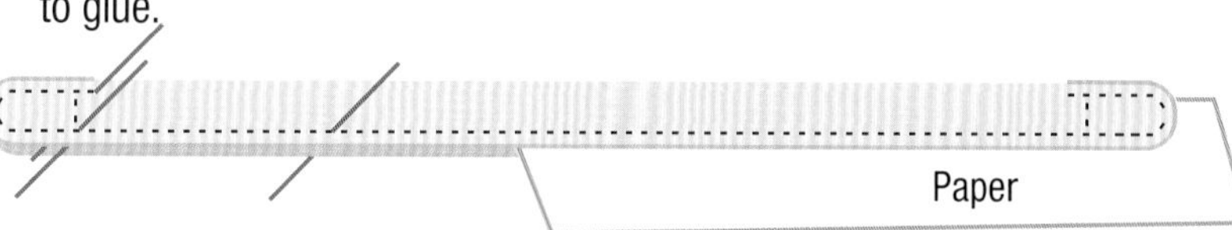

As shown in the picture on the right, when you sew a handle on a bag by inserting the bag in between the ends of the handle, you do not glue the ends together.

3 Stitch, except where it will be sewn onto the bag.

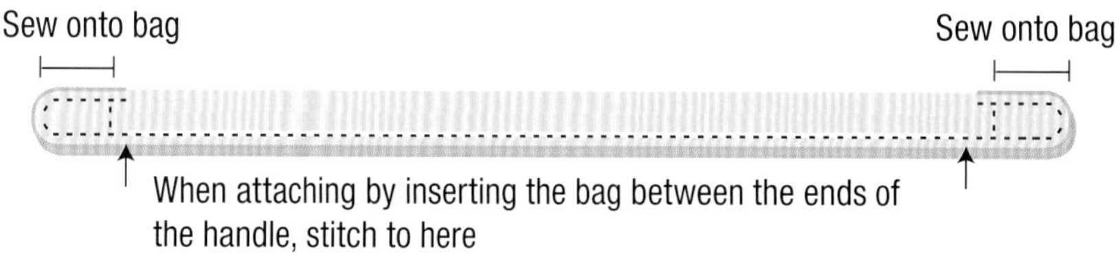

[Cored Handle]

1 Punch the stitching holes and cut out the leather according to the pattern.

2 Glue a cord, the same length as the central stitching holes, in the middle of the handle.

Flesh-side

Cord

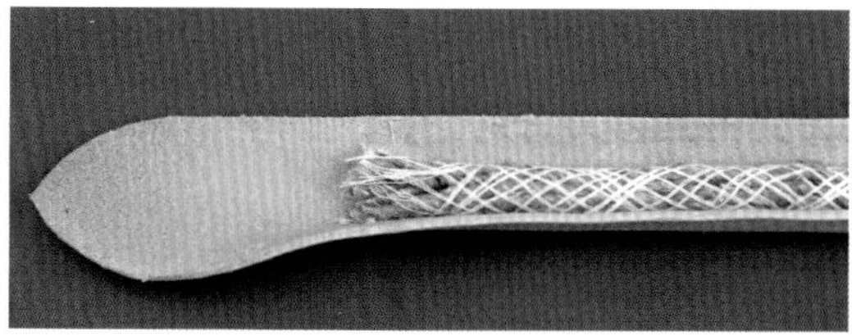

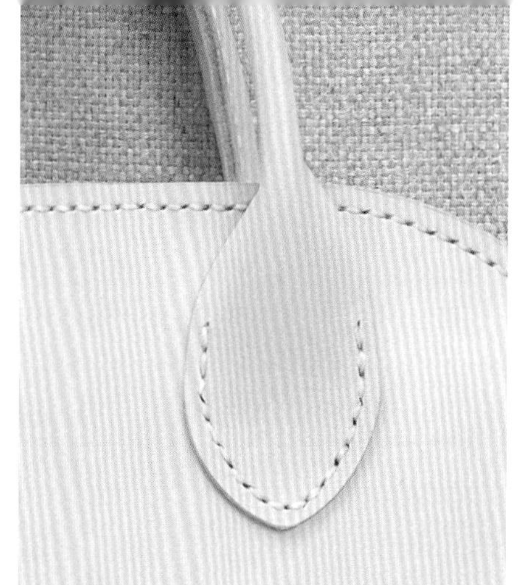

Sometimes items cover the base of the handle. This book does not use such items as the process for attaching them is quite complicated. Since there are no items at the base of the handle to add strength, please be sure to use the most durable part of the leather for your handle bases so they do not stretch.

3 Align the central stitching holes, fold the leather in half, and then glue.

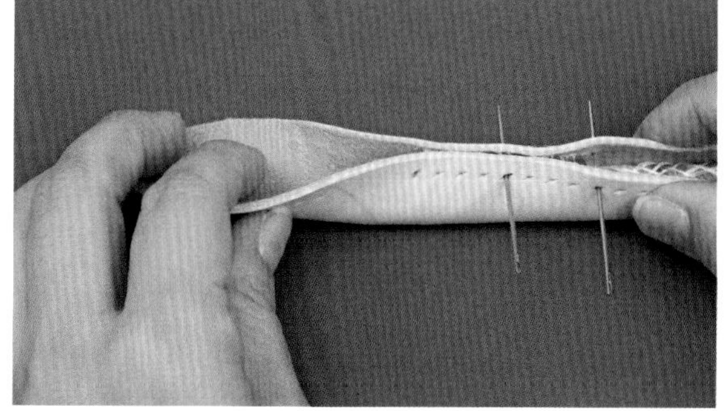

4 Stitch the straight core of the handle.

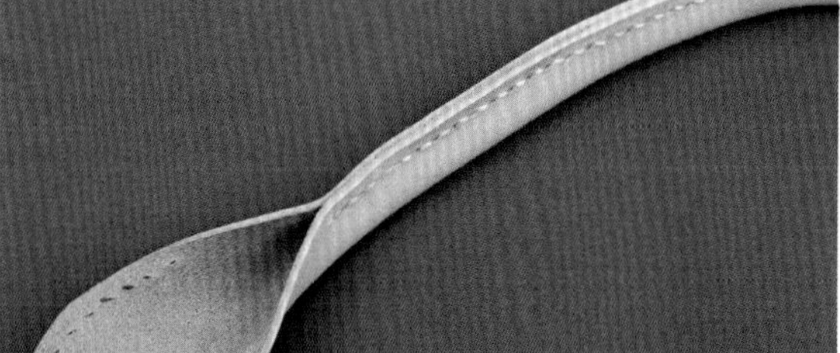

[Sewing on the Handle]

Burnish the edges. Align the stitching holes, then glue and sew. If the thread used to stitch the sides of the handle is long enough, just use the same thread to sew the handle on the bag.

Flat handle

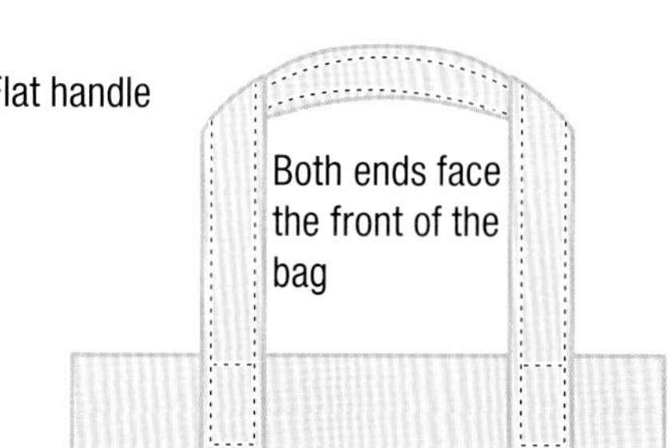

Folded handle

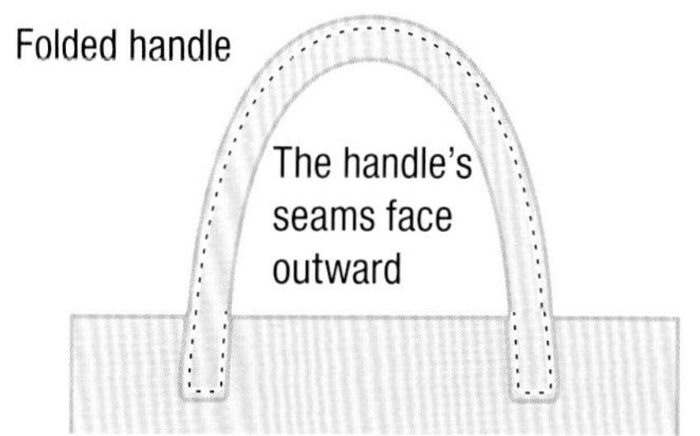

Lay on top

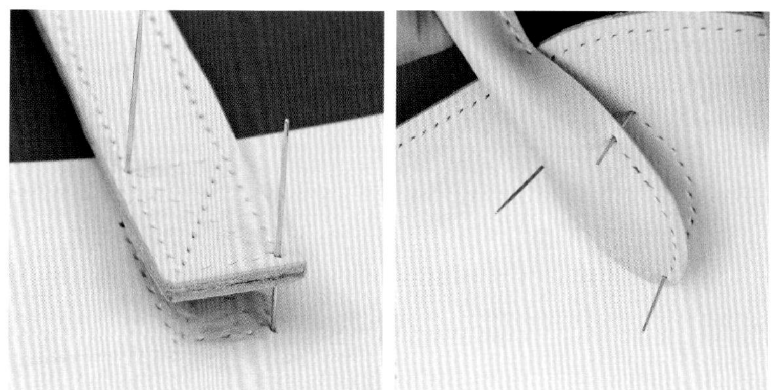

Insert the bag between the ends and attach

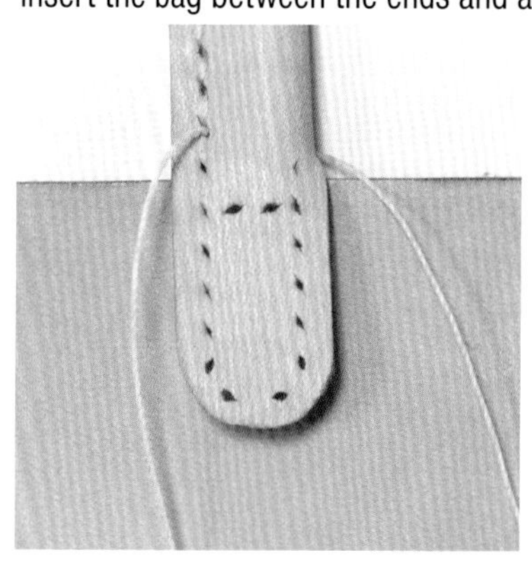

cutting pattern

A Three-gored Tall Bag

This is a tall bag in which a wine bottle can fit. After stitching the bag, sew on the handle.

how to make

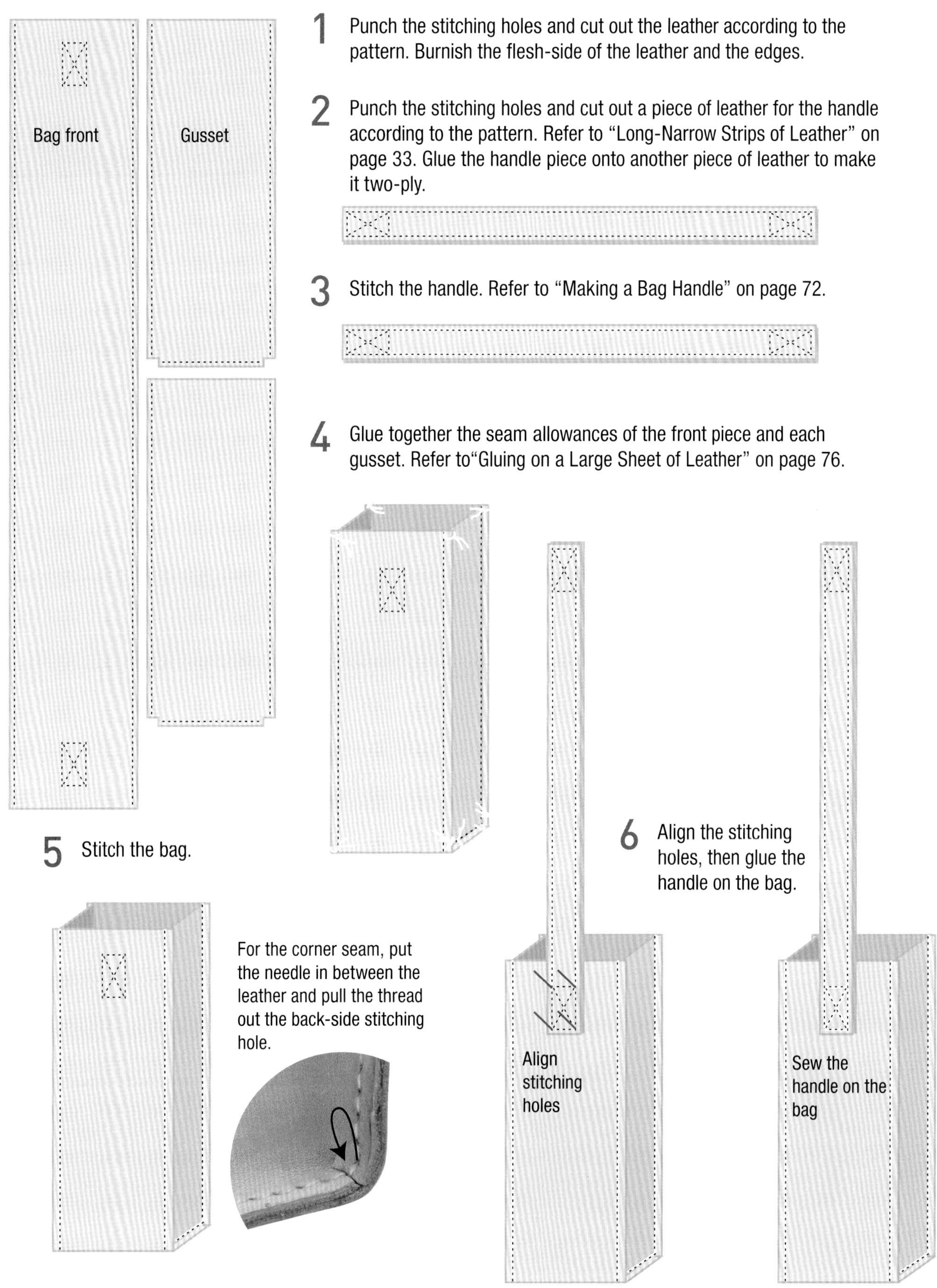

1 Punch the stitching holes and cut out the leather according to the pattern. Burnish the flesh-side of the leather and the edges.

2 Punch the stitching holes and cut out a piece of leather for the handle according to the pattern. Refer to "Long-Narrow Strips of Leather" on page 33. Glue the handle piece onto another piece of leather to make it two-ply.

3 Stitch the handle. Refer to "Making a Bag Handle" on page 72.

4 Glue together the seam allowances of the front piece and each gusset. Refer to"Gluing on a Large Sheet of Leather" on page 76.

5 Stitch the bag.

For the corner seam, put the needle in between the leather and pull the thread out the back-side stitching hole.

6 Align the stitching holes, then glue the handle on the bag.

After one side is attached, do the same on the other side.

Gluing on a Large Sheet of Leather

Since bag leather tends to be large, the stitching holes can easily fall out of alignment while gluing.
If the stitching holes are misaligned, the needles will not go through the stitching holes with ease and the finished bag shape will be unattractive.
Therefore, one extra step is necessary in order to align the stitching holes.

★ For areas that are glued three-dimensionally, the finish will be more beautiful if the leather is glued after you bend it.

★ Since the stitching holes are easily unaligned in these areas, temporarily secure them with thread.

[Bend by Moistening]

1 At first, lightly moisten the grain-side of the leather entirely with a wet sponge. Then, moisten the section you intend to bend again.

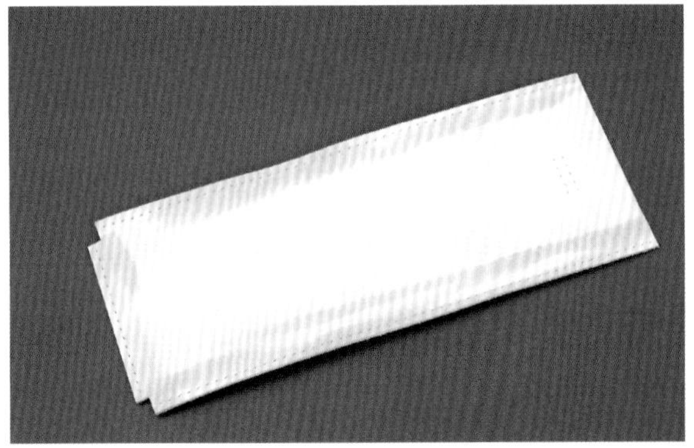

2 Bend the leather from slightly inside the stitching holes. Evenly bend the leather but do not warp or stretch it. Do not bend the leather too hard or it will leave a line. Dry the leather completely.

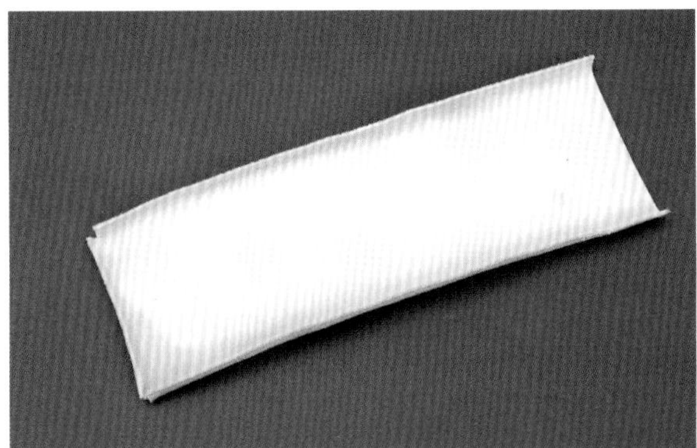

[Glue by Aligning the Stitching Holes]

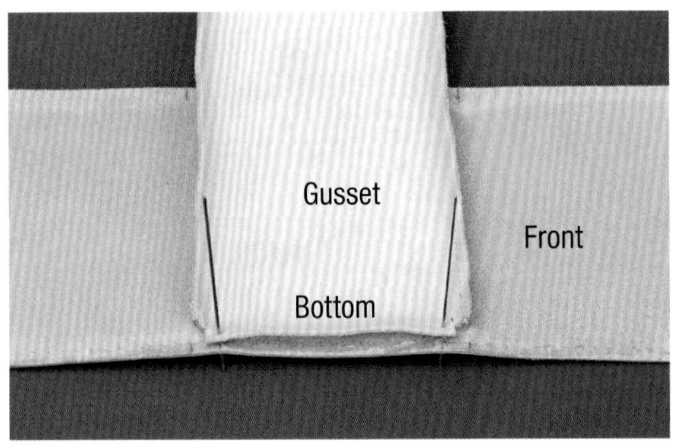

1 When gluing the leather, aligning the stitching holes is easier if you start gluing from the center of the longest seam. (In this case, the center is on the bottom.) After you have glued the center, apply glue alongside the seam allowance on the gusset piece and let the glue dry. Align the marked stitching holes.

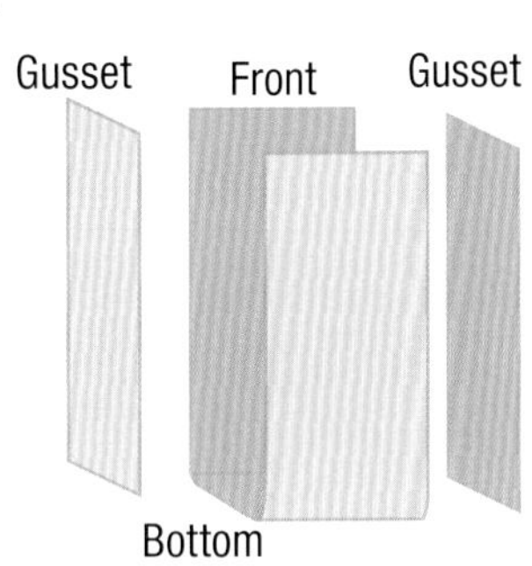

2 Bond the leather so the seam allowances match.
In order to prevent the bonding surface from falling out of position, temporarily secure the marked stitching holes by tying them with thread. Make just a single temporary stitch, as several temporary stitches will make it very difficult to pull the non-temporary thread all the way through.

Align seam allowance

Secure temporarily

Make fine adjustments to align the stitching holes by piercing an awl through every few stitches. This will make stitching the leather easier.

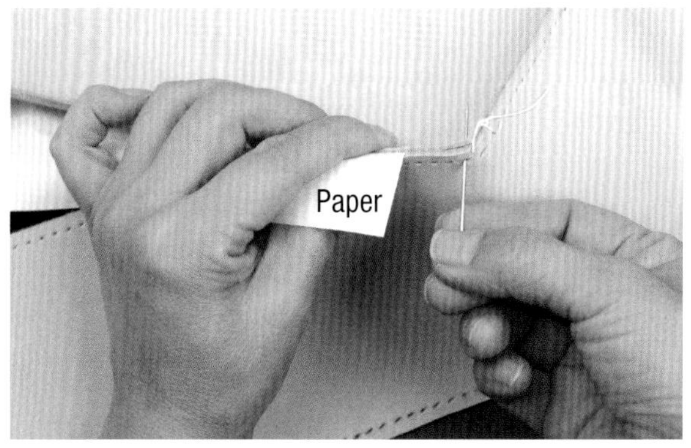

3 Gluing the corner.
Align the marked stitching holes, then glue. Put a piece of paper in between so as not to unintentionally glue other areas.

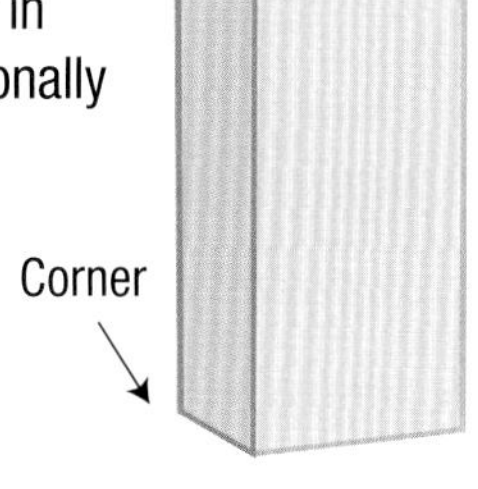

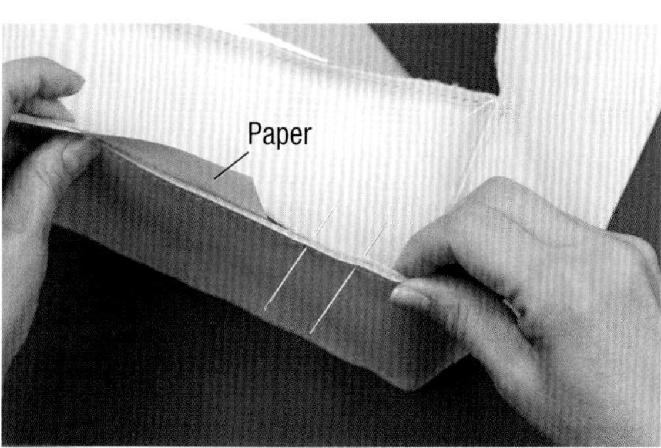

4 Gluing the gusset.
While sliding the piece of paper along, continue to glue as you align the stitching holes every few stitches.

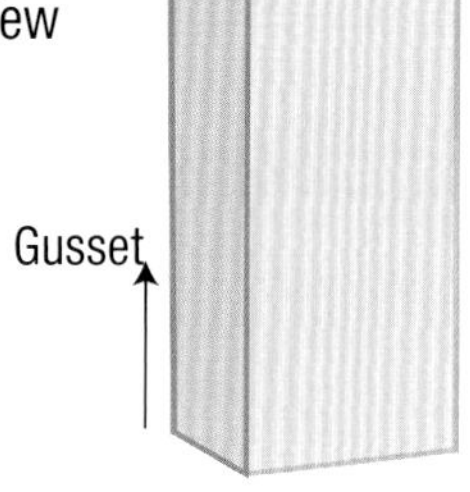

5 In order to keep the stitching holes aligned, temporarily secure the leather with thread at the necessary positions and bond both sides. Make fine adjustments to align the stitching holes by piercing a stitching hole with an awl every few stitches.

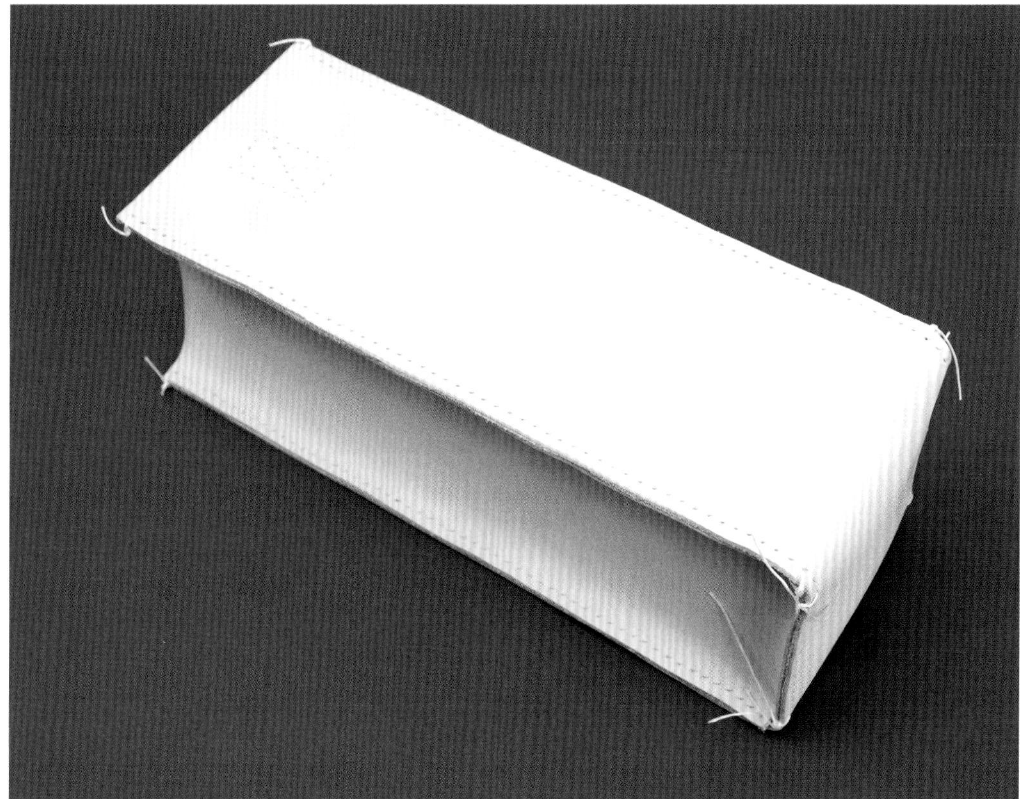

cutting pattern

A Three-gored Tote Bag

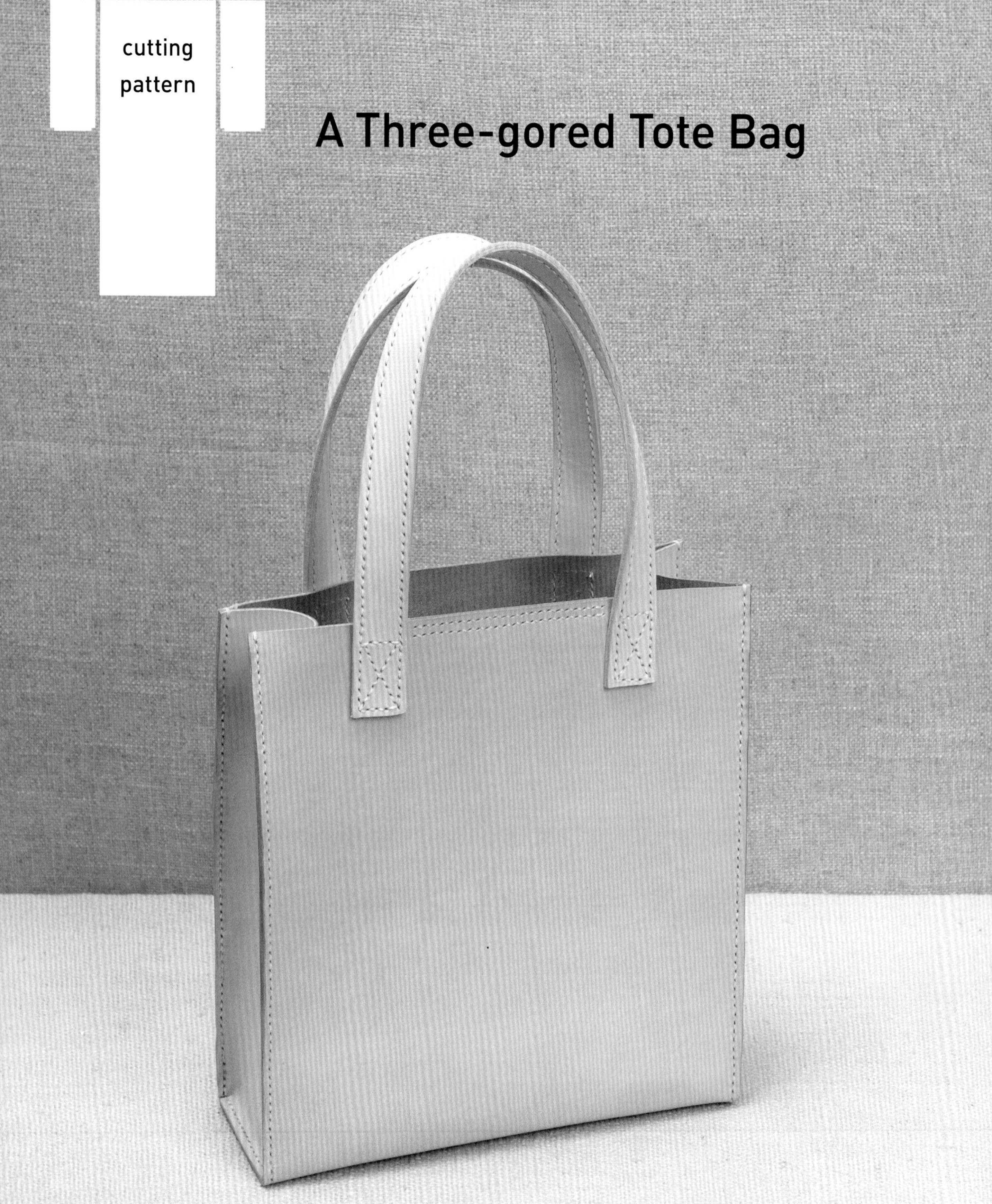

This uses the same structure as the three-gored tall bag (see P. 74), but it is a different size. A pocket is also attached inside.

how to make

1 For the bag and the pocket piece, punch the stitching holes and cut the leather according to the pattern.
Burnish the flesh-side of the leather and the edges.

2 For the two handle pieces, punch the stitching holes and cut the leather according to the pattern.
Refer to "Long-Narrow Strips of Leather" on page 33. Glue each handle piece onto another piece of leather to make it two-ply.

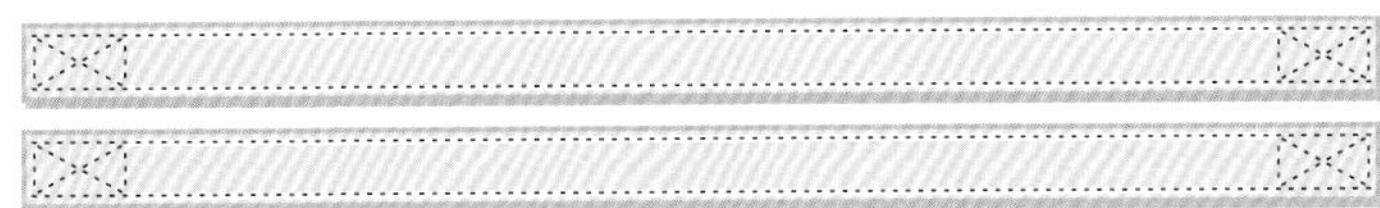

3 Stitch the handle. Refer to "Making a Bag Handle" on page 72.

4 Align the pocket with the mark on the bag front, then glue and sew.

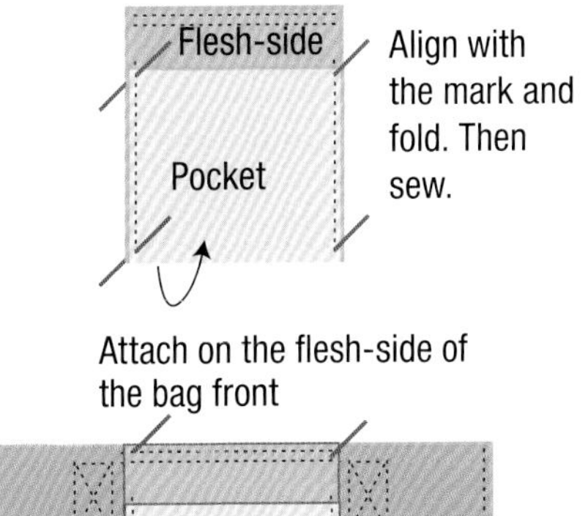

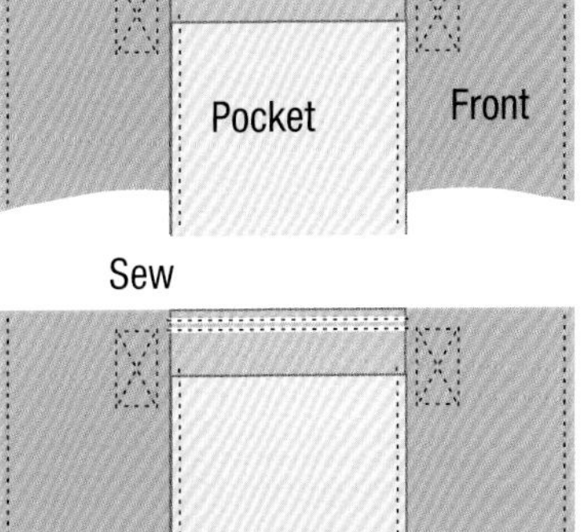

5 Align the handle with the mark on the bag front and glue. Then sew.

6 Glue the bag front and the gusset at the seam allowance. Refer to "Gluing on a Large Sheet of Leather" on page 76.

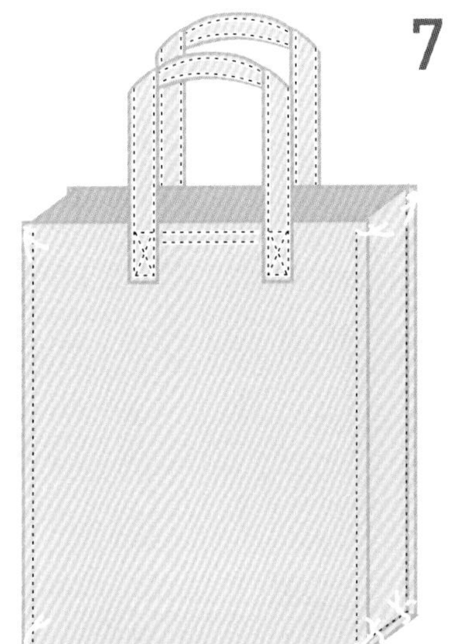

7 Sew the bag.

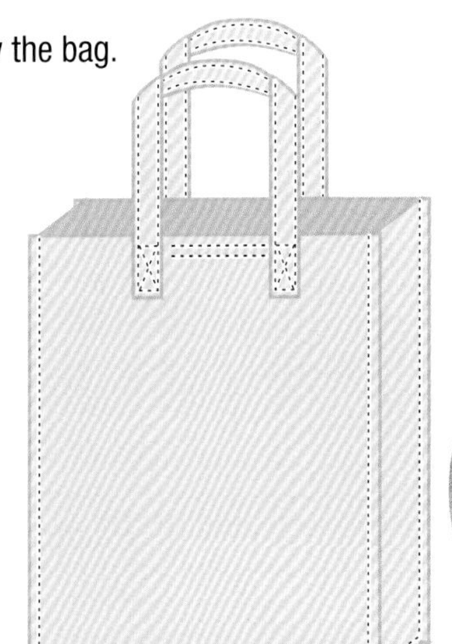

For the corner seams, put the needle in between the leather and pull the thread out the back-side stitching hole.

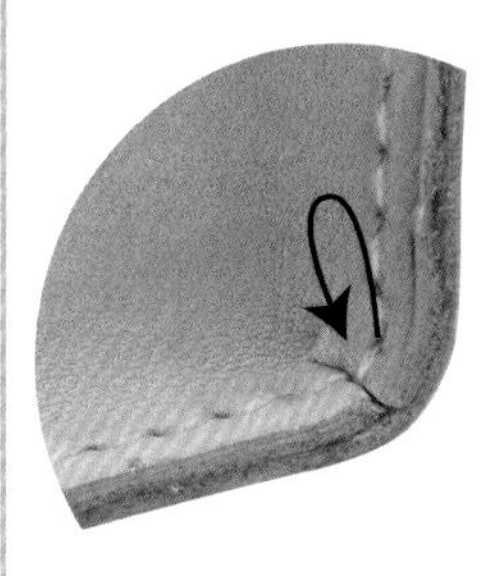

cutting pattern

A Zipper Pouch Using a Single Sheet of Leather

This item uses a single sheet of leather, folded at the bottom, to make the width of the pouch.

how to make

1. For the pouch, and the zipper tag piece, punch the stitching holes and cut according to the pattern. Burnish the flesh-side of the pouch leather and each edge.

2. Sew a zipper on the opening of the pouch. Refer to "Sewing on a Zipper" on page 61.

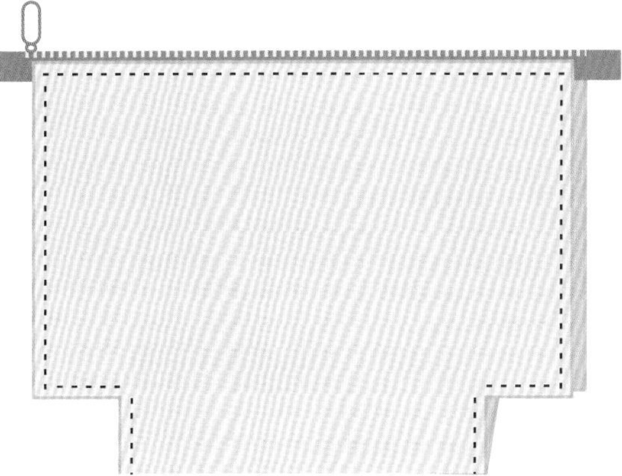

3. Align the marks on the pouch piece and glue along the seam allowance. Then sew. Refer to "Making a Bag Using a Single Sheet of Leather" on page 82.

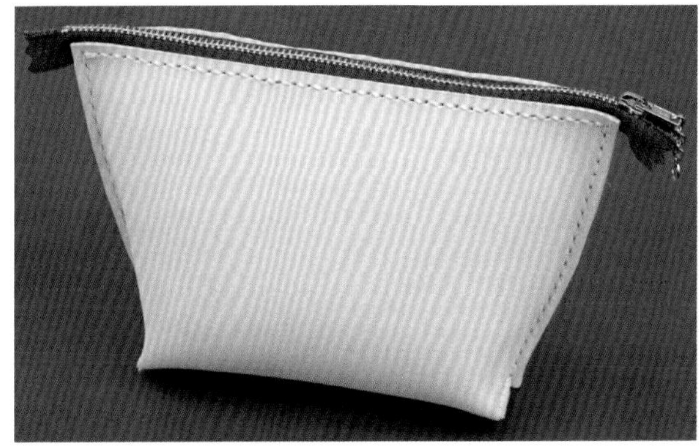

4. Apply glue to the zipper tag pieces. Cover the zipper end and align the tag piece with the mark and glue. Then sew.

detail

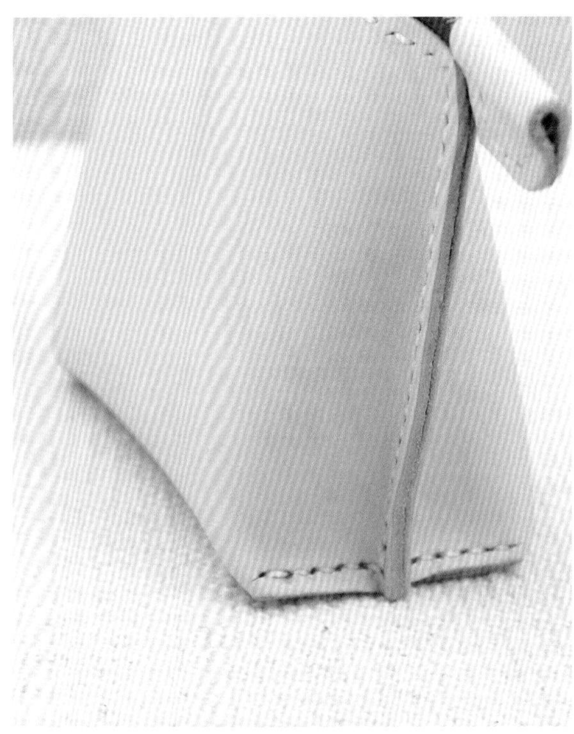

Making a Bag Using a Single Sheet of Leather

This sewing method for a single sheet of leather applies to the pouch with a zipper (P. 80), the tote bag (P. 84), the shoulder bag (P. 88), and the bag with a zipper (P. 94).

This section deals with making zipper pouches. Although, it should be noted that the method described applies to other bags as well.

[Stitching the Sides]

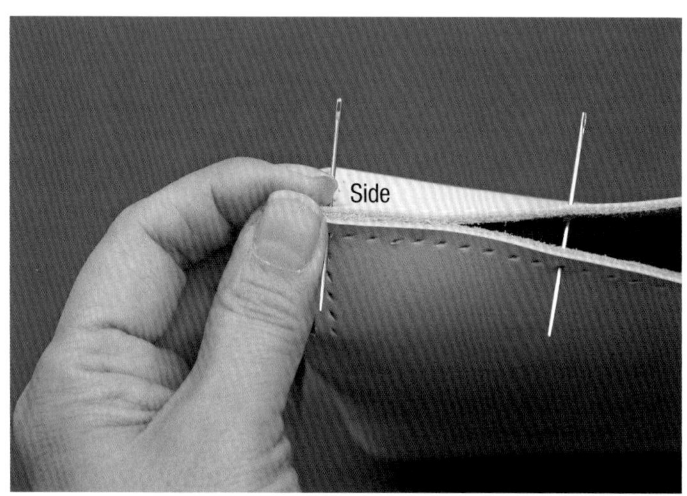

1 Glue both sides. Align the marked holes on each side. For large items, temporarily secure the leather with thread. Realign the stitching holes with an awl to make fine adjustments.

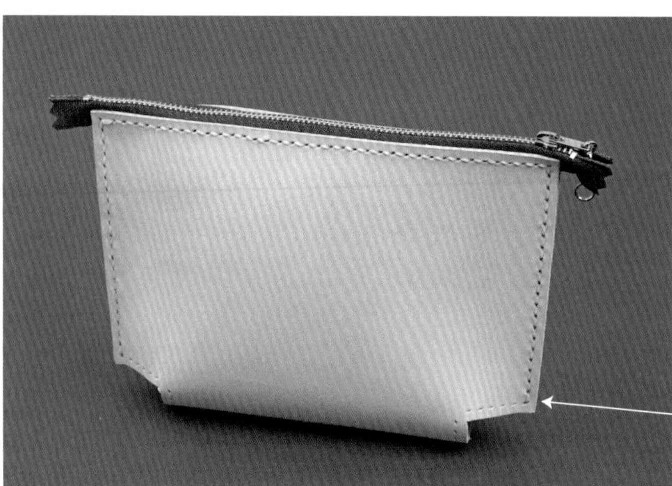

2 Stitch the sides.
For items that do not need a zipper, such as totes and shoulder bags, just stitch around the opening.

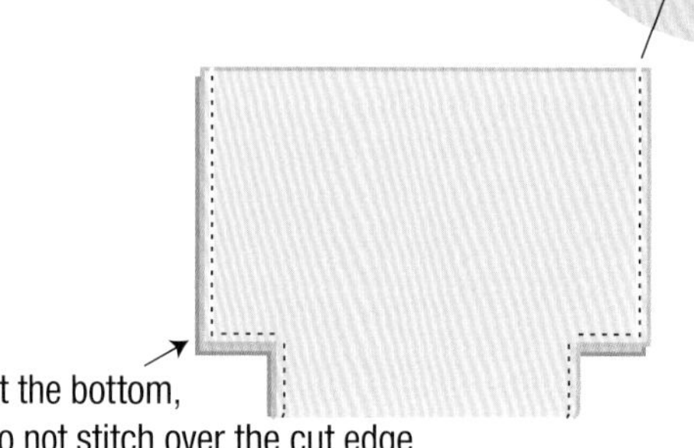

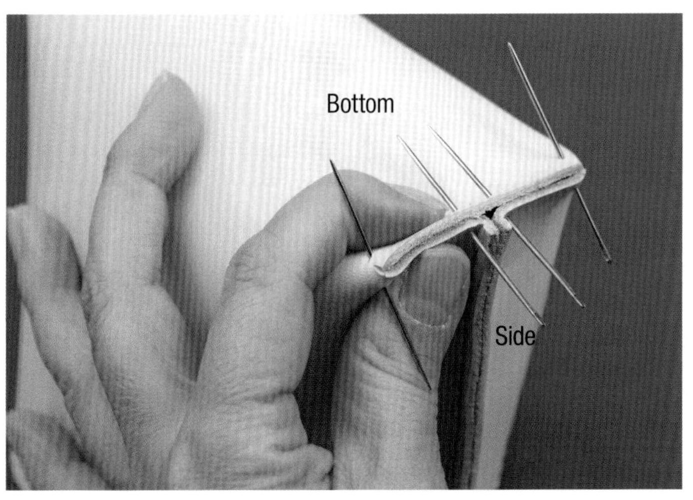

3 Fold the bottom leather by pinching and align the marked holes using a needle. Then glue the bottom to the side.

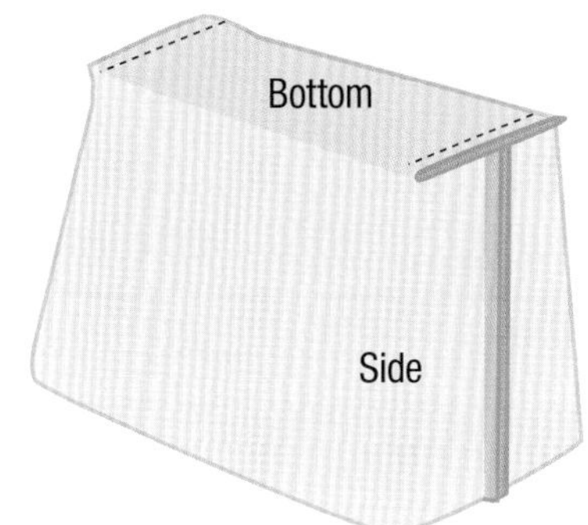

4 Stitch the bottom. Different colored thread is used to make the instructions easier to understand.

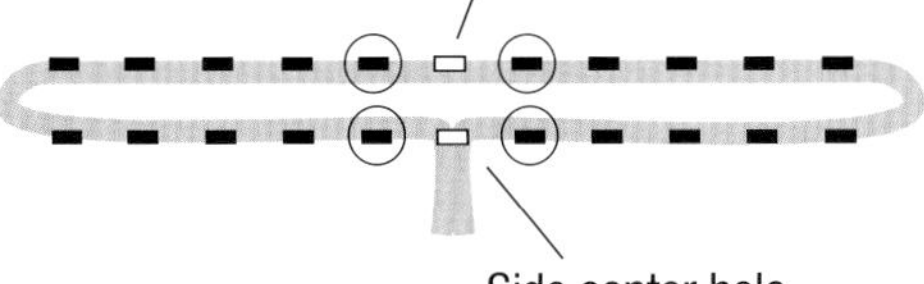

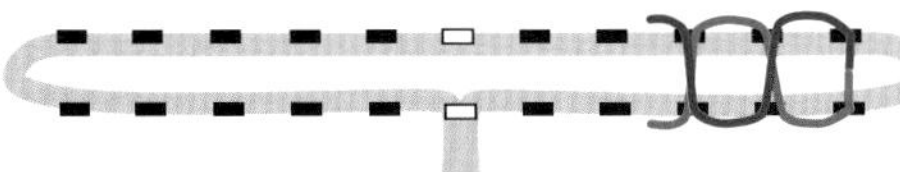

Finished bottom

5 Dispose of the thread either by tying it inside the item or cutting it off at the bottom.

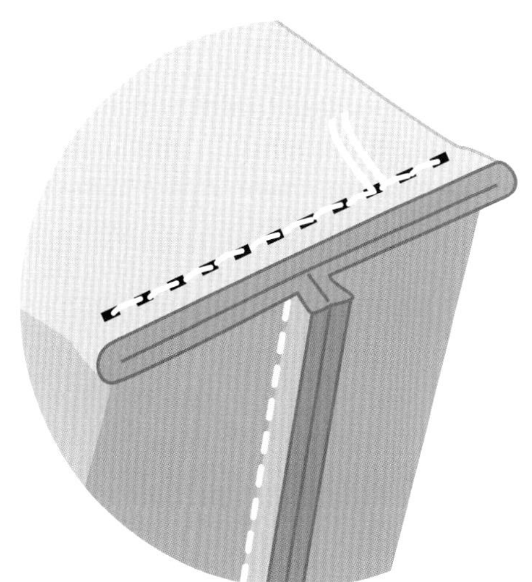

6 Burnish the seam edges. Refer to page 43.

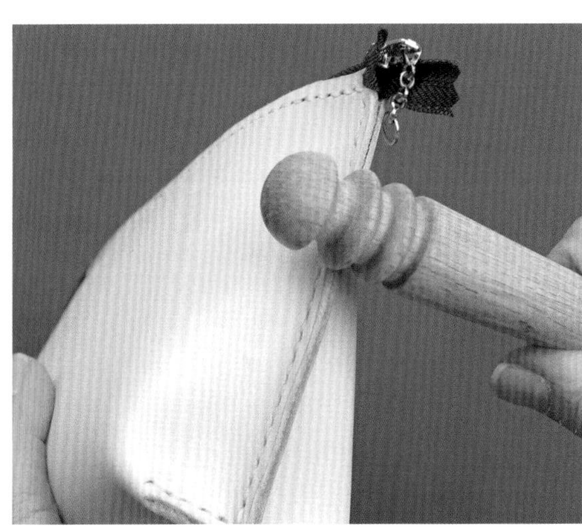

cutting pattern

Instructions P. 86

A Tote Bag Using a Single Sheet of Leather

This is a sturdy tote bag that uses the same structure as the zipper pouch using a single sheet of leather (see P. 80), but it is different in size.

detail

how to make

A Tote Bag Using a Single Sheet of Leather

1 Punch the stitching holes and cut the leather according to the pattern for the bag, the pocket, and the straps. Burnish the flesh-side of the leather and the edges.

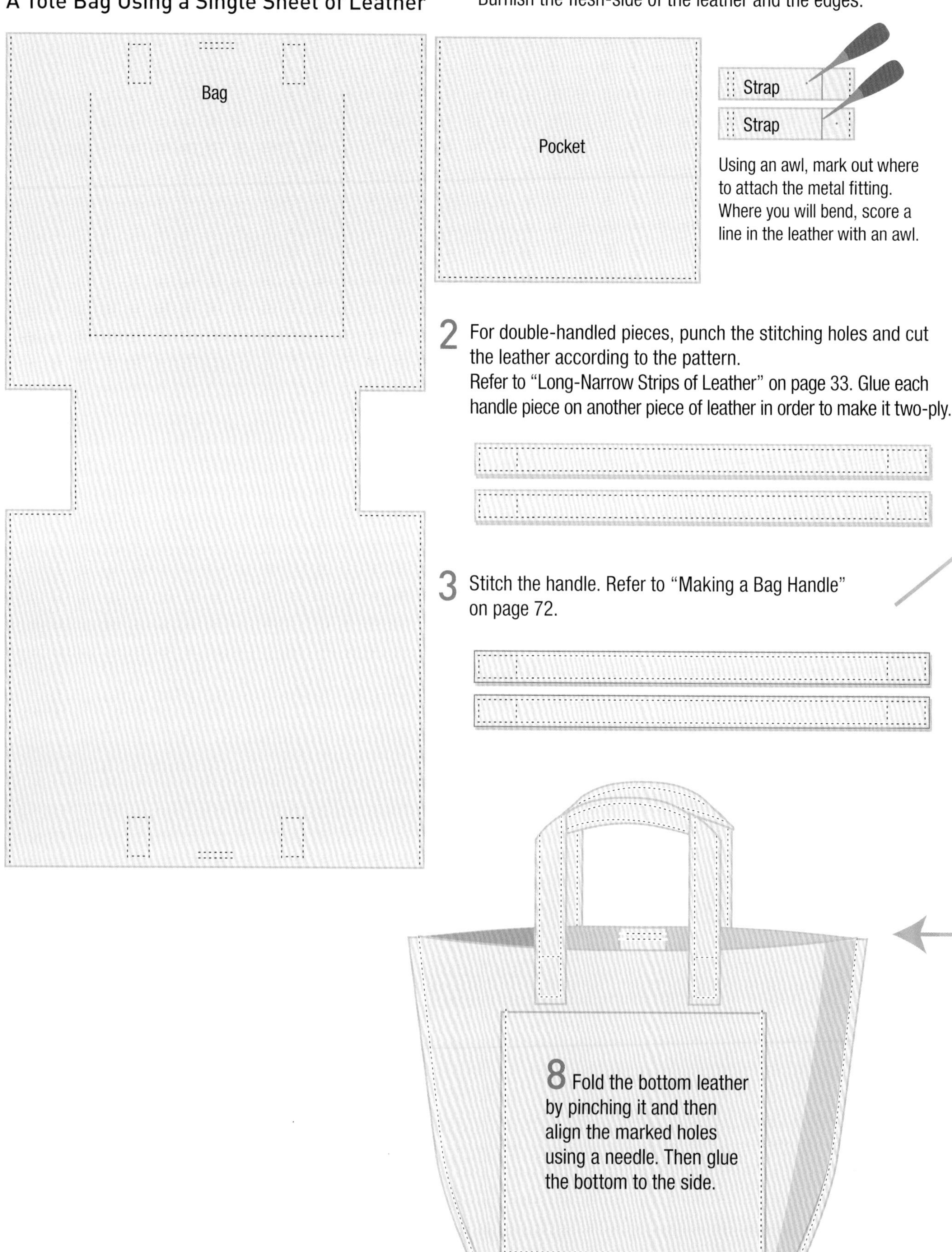

Using an awl, mark out where to attach the metal fitting. Where you will bend, score a line in the leather with an awl.

2 For double-handled pieces, punch the stitching holes and cut the leather according to the pattern.
Refer to "Long-Narrow Strips of Leather" on page 33. Glue each handle piece on another piece of leather in order to make it two-ply.

3 Stitch the handle. Refer to "Making a Bag Handle" on page 72.

8 Fold the bottom leather by pinching it and then align the marked holes using a needle. Then glue the bottom to the side.

4 Place the pocket on the bag piece by aligning the marks and then glue the bottom and the side.
Place a piece of paper in between the leather and apply glue along the seam allowance. Then glue on the pocket while aligning the stitching holes.
Then sew.

5 Attach the "magnetic snap" on the strap's grain-side facing up. Press the prongs of the snap against the grain-side to make an impression. Then score the impression with a utility knife.

Slide the washer over the prongs, then bend the prongs. Strike with a wooden mallet to flatten.
Fold the strap along the scored line.
Force a lacing needle through the stitching hole and then sew the leather.

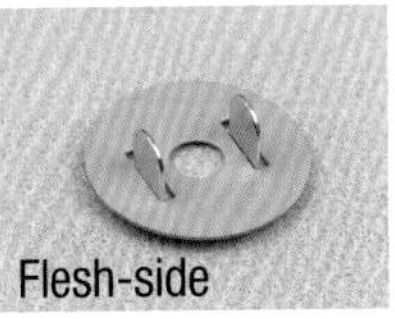

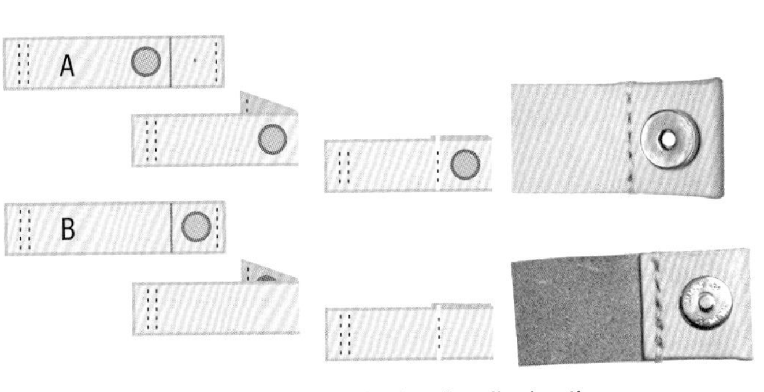

Glue the strap onto the opening of the bag by aligning the marks. Then sew.

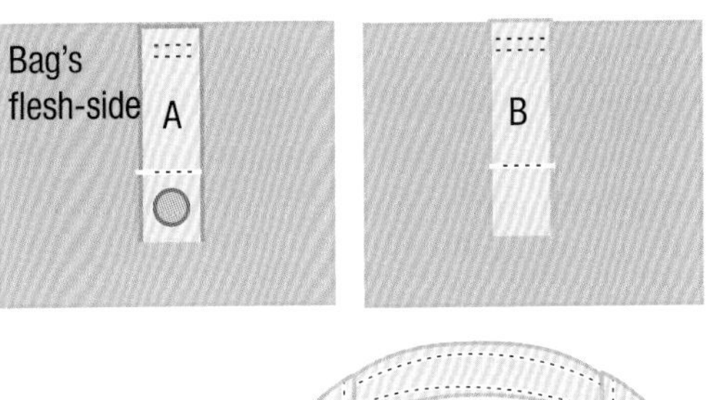

7 Fold the bag piece. Put a piece of paper in between the leather, align the seam allowance at the mark on each side and glue. Then sew.
Refer to "Gluing on a Large Sheet of Leather" on page 76, "Making a Bag Using a Single Sheet of Leather" on page 82.

6 Align the handle with the bag's stitching hole and glue, then sew.

cutting pattern

Instructions P. 92

A Shoulder Bag Using a Single Sheet of Leather

This shoulder bag is made by attaching a flap and a strap to a bag that was made from a single sheet of leather.

detail

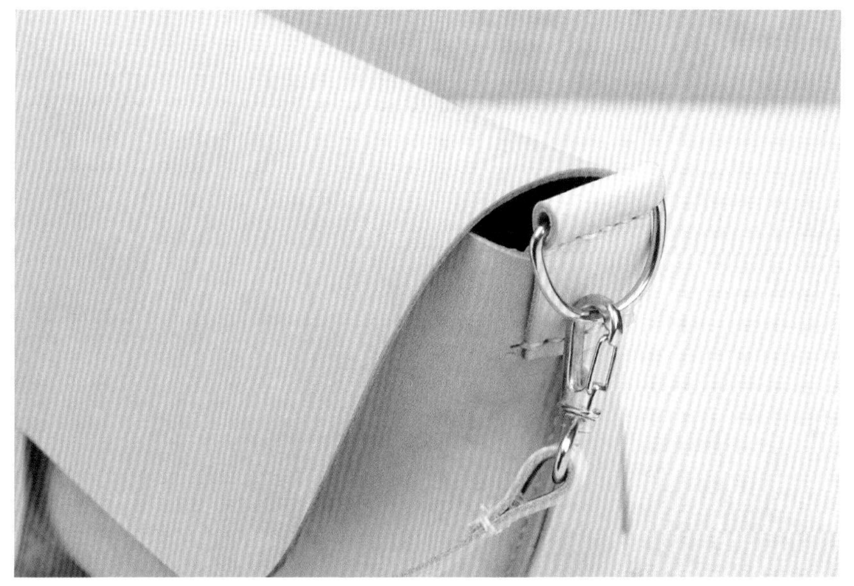

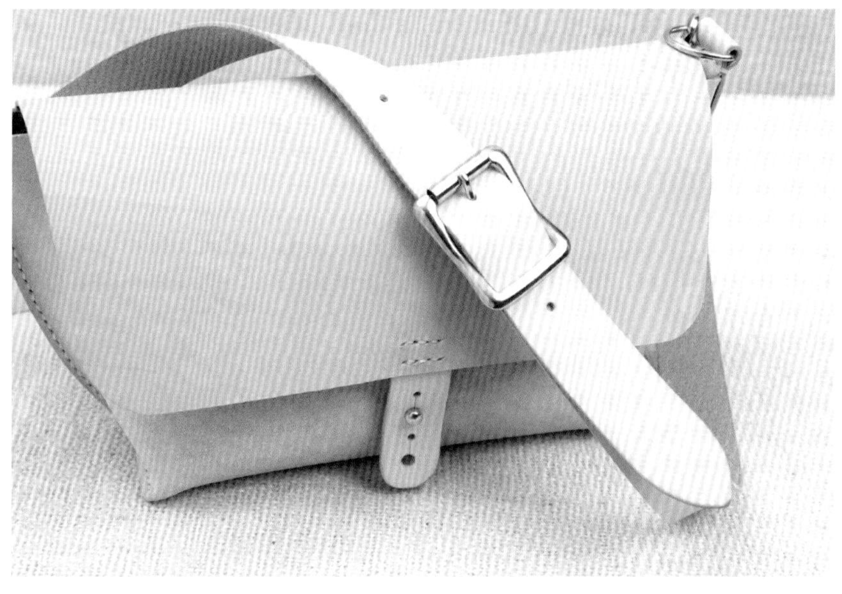

Making a Shoulder Strap

This section explains how to make a buckled shoulder strap and how to attach it to a bag. The length of the strap varies for each person. Please decide on the length by referring to a bag you already have. Long-narrow strips of leather for making straps and belts are commercially available. When you cut your own leather for a strap, be sure to use a piece that is not easily stretched. Then burnish the flesh-side and the edges. The instructions given here use 30 mm (1 1/4 in.) wide metal fittings. Accordingly the strap is made of 30 mm (1 1/4 in.) wide leather.

[The Structure of the Strap]

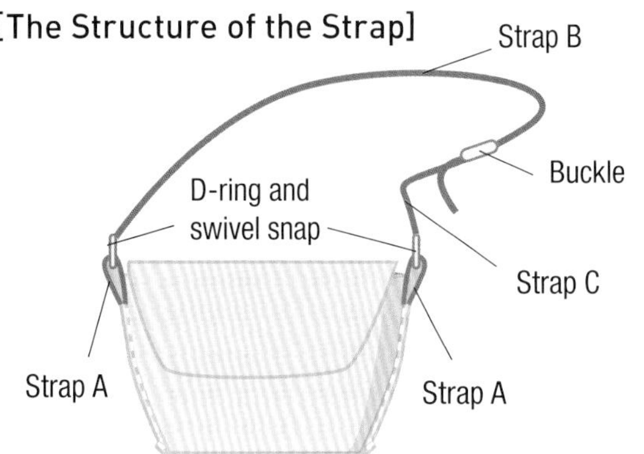

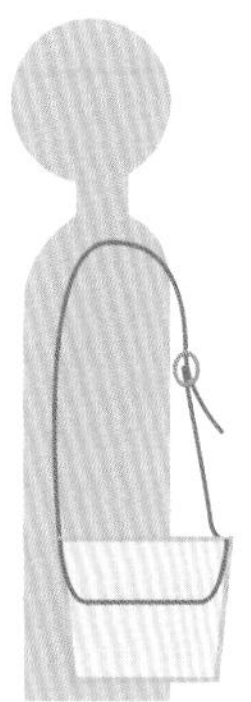

In order to make sure the buckle does not rest on your shoulder, you should attach the buckle about 1/3 of the strap's total length above the D-ring. Just adjust the length of each strap accordingly.

[About Metal Fittings]

Use a buckle, swivel-snap, and D-ring that have the same width on their labels. Although, the actual width might vary slightly from what is printed on certain labels due to the particular design of the fitting. Once you have purchased the metal fittings, confirm their sizing and adjust the width of your straps accordingly.

Buckle

Swivel-snap

D-ring

[Strap A] Attaching a D-ring and sewing the leather on a bag

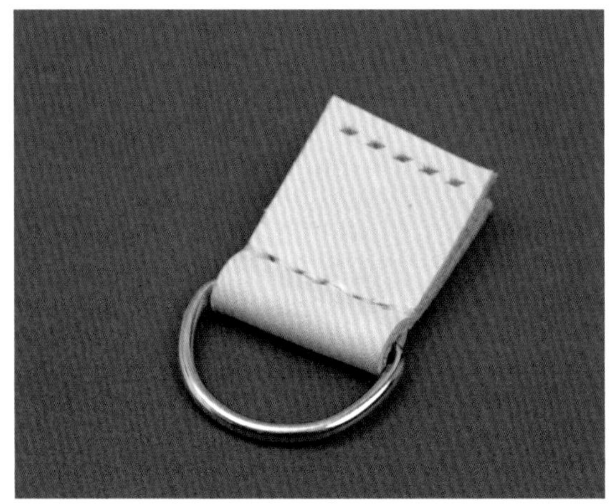

Put the D-ring through the leather and fold the leather back. Sew the leather while aligning the stitching holes.

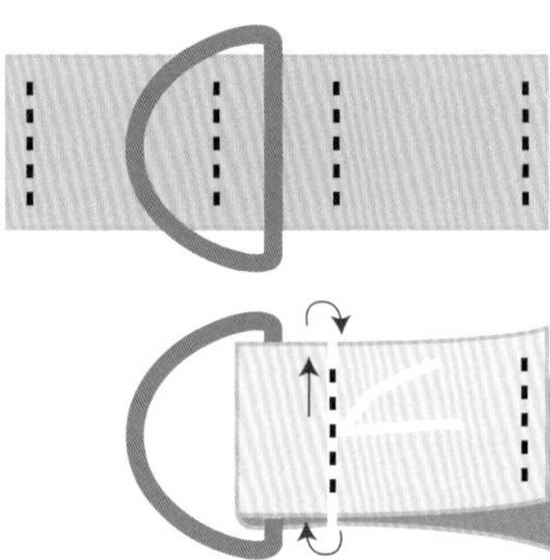

Put the needle through the hole located at the center of the strap and leave a tail of thread. Then start a running stitch. Sew the leather so the last stitch is at the center. Then dispose of the thread ends.

[Strap B]

Attach the swivel-snap on one end and punch adjustor holes on the other.

1 Cut the tip of the leather diagonally and then punch adjustor holes.

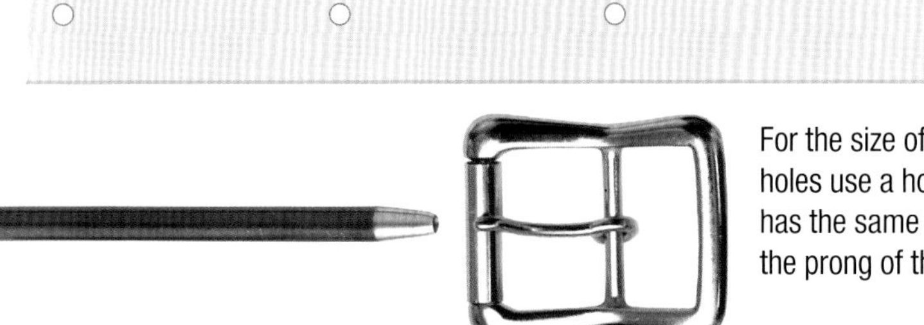

For the size of the adjustor holes use a hole punch that has the same diameter as the prong of the buckle.

2 Attach the swivel-snap on the opposite end. Attach the swivel-snap and fold the leather back, like you did with the D-ring.

[Strap C]

Attach the buckle and D-ring.

1 Punch two holes, as shown in the figure, for the buckle prong.

2 Cut out the leather with a box-cutter to connect the two holes.

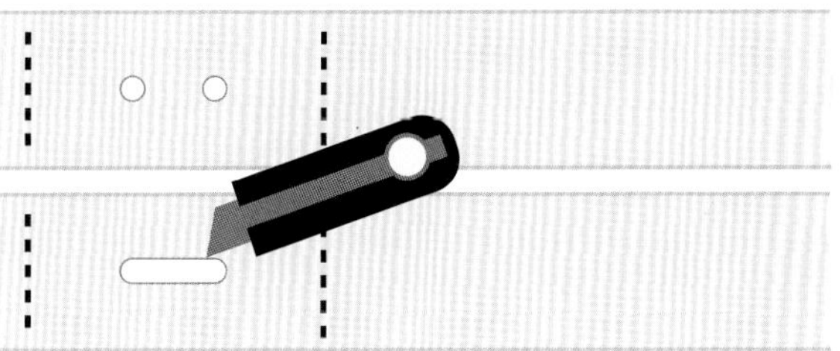

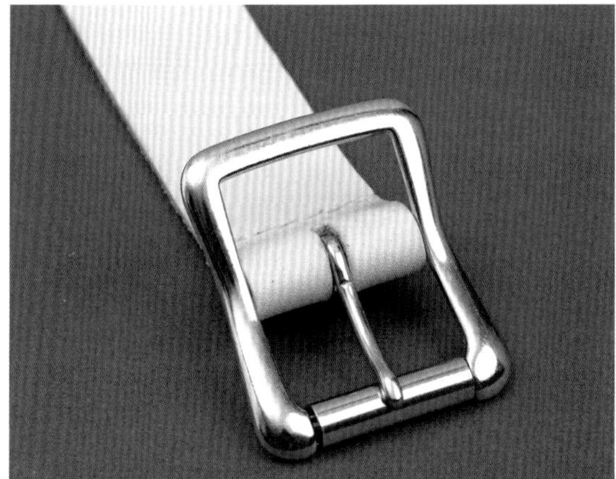

3 Put the prong of the buckle through the hole and fold the leather back. The hole may be too tight, depending on the design of the buckle. Make fine adjustments accordingly.

4 Sew the leather in the same manner as the D-ring to secure the buckle.

how to make

A Shoulder Bag Using a Single Sheet of Leather

1 Punch stitching holes and cut out the leather according to the pattern for all of the items, except the strap. For the strap, cut out the leather and punch the stitching holes according to the pattern while referring to "Making a Shoulder Strap" on page 90. Then burnish the flesh-side and the edges.

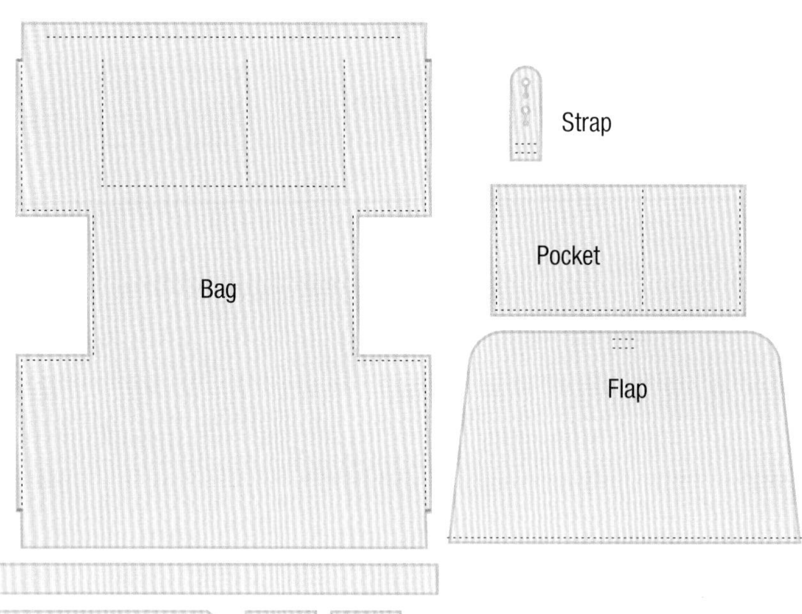

2 Place a strap piece, flesh-side up, on the flesh-side of the flap and glue them while aligning the marks. Then sew.

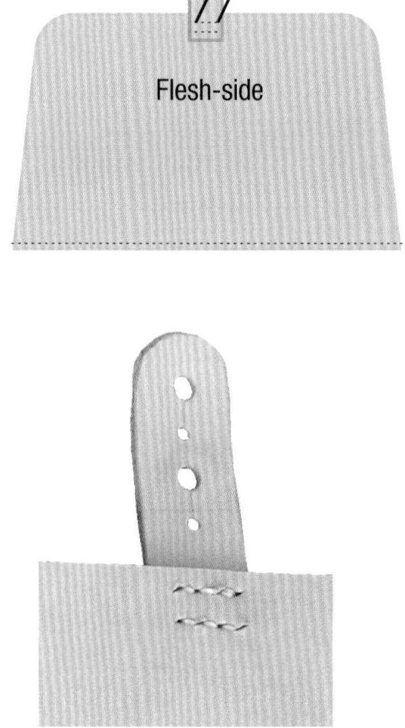

3 Glue the flap piece on the bag piece while aligning them. Make fine adjustments to align the position of the holes every few stitches by using an awl. Sew the leather.

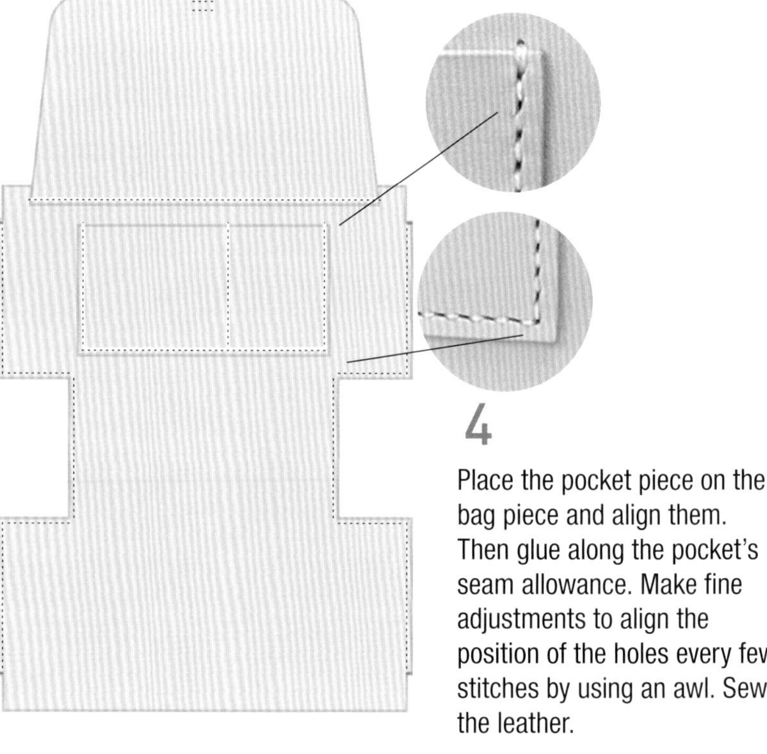

4 Place the pocket piece on the bag piece and align them. Then glue along the pocket's seam allowance. Make fine adjustments to align the position of the holes every few stitches by using an awl. Sew the leather.

5

Fold the bag piece and align each marked position on the seam allowance. Then glue the side and sew. Refer to "Making a Bag Using a Single Sheet of Leather" on page 82.

6

Glue the bottom onto the side by pinching the bottom and folding the leather to align the stitching holes with a needle. Then sew.

7

Align the edges where a gap remains and then sew.

8

Make the parts for the strap.
Put strap A (with the D-ring attached) on the bag. Glue strap A on the bag by aligning the stitching holes and then sew.

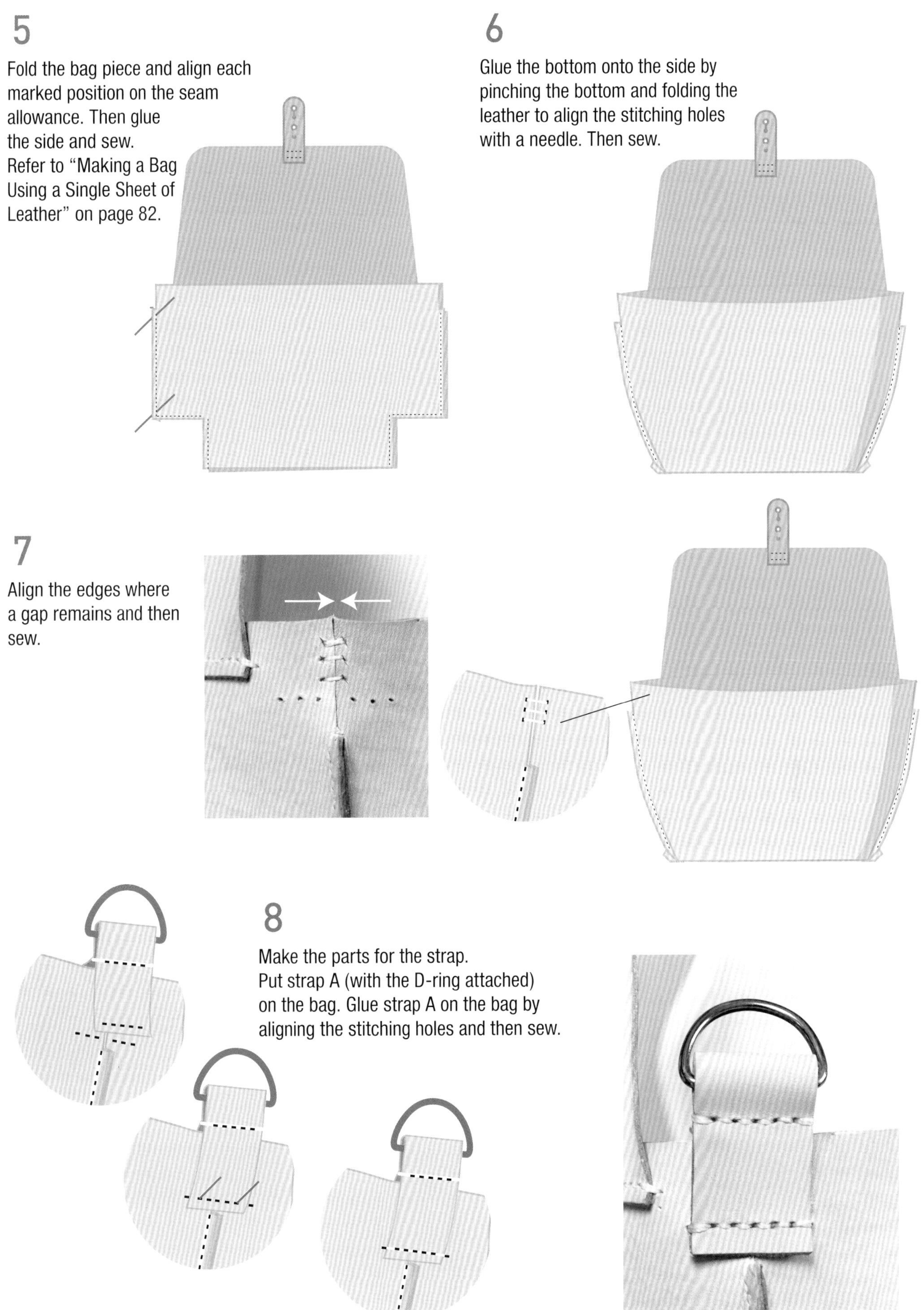

cutting pattern

A Bag with a Zipper Using a Single Sheet of Leather

This bag is made out of one sheet of leather. Since the leather portion with the zipper attached is sewn on the bag's opening, the leather will make a unique curve along the side-seam.

how to make

The method for making the bag in this project is the same as for the tote bag on page 84.

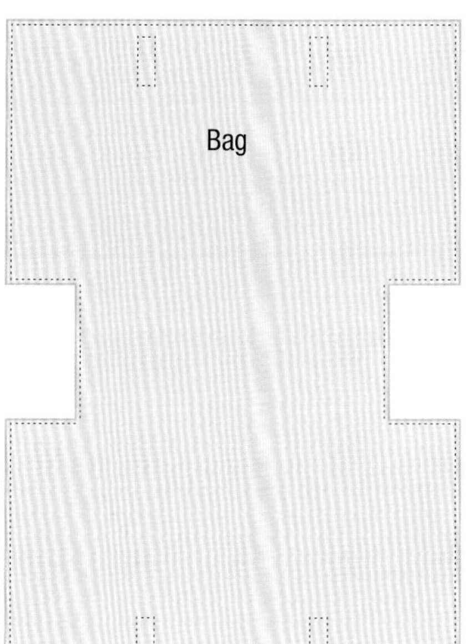

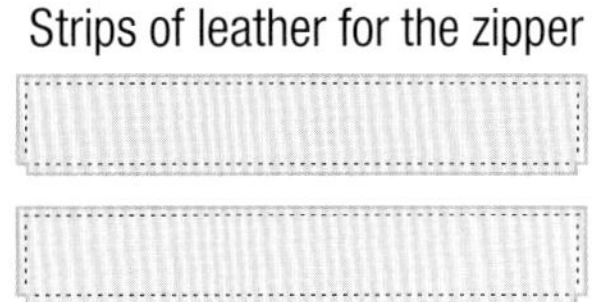

1 Punch the stitching holes and cut out the leather according to the pattern for both the bag and the zipper strips.
Burnish the flesh-side and the edges of the leather strips.

2 For the two strips of leather for the handle, punch the stitching holes and cut according to the pattern. Refer to "Long-Narrow Strips of Leather" on page 33. Glue the leather strips on another piece of leather to make it two-ply.

3 Attach the handle and sew the bag. Refer to "A Tote Bag Using a Single Sheet of Leather" on page 84 (do not attach a pocket or strap) and "Making a Bag Using a Single Sheet of Leather" on page 82.

4 Glue a zipper on the leather strips and then sew. Refer to "Sewing on a Zipper" on page 61.

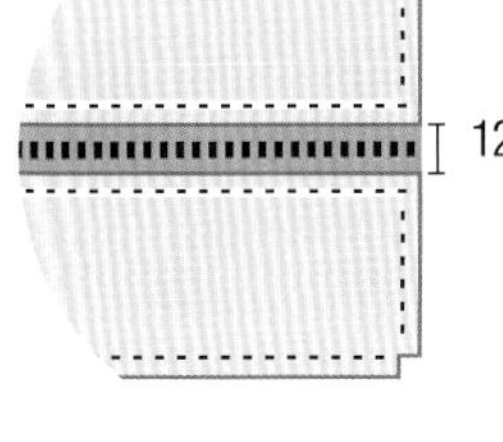

5 Glue the zipper strips onto the bag's top while aligning the marked stitching holes. Temporarily secure the leather with threads and then make fine adjustments to align the holes every few stitches using an awl. Refer to "Gluing on a Large Sheet of Leather" on page 76.

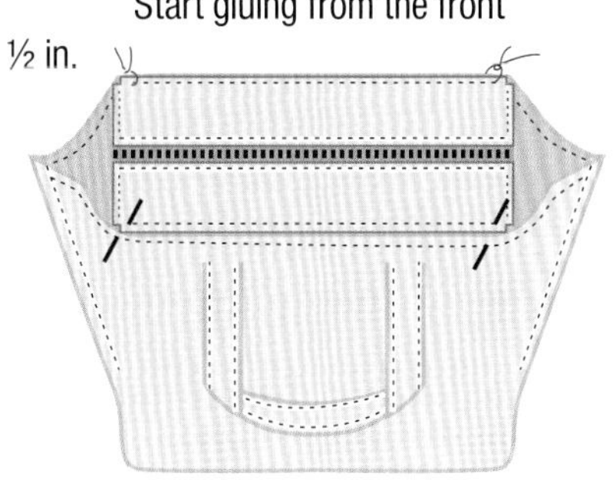

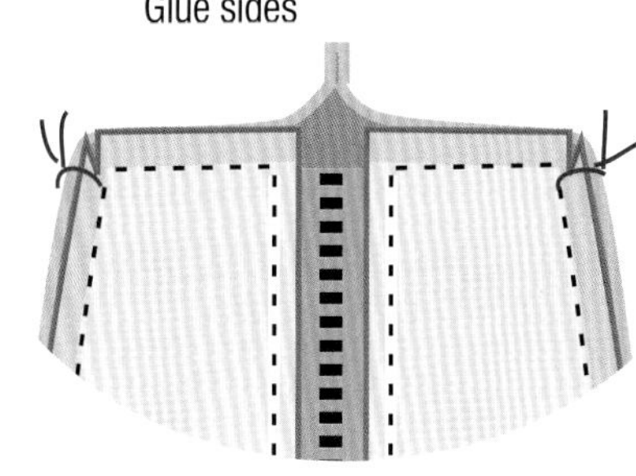

detail

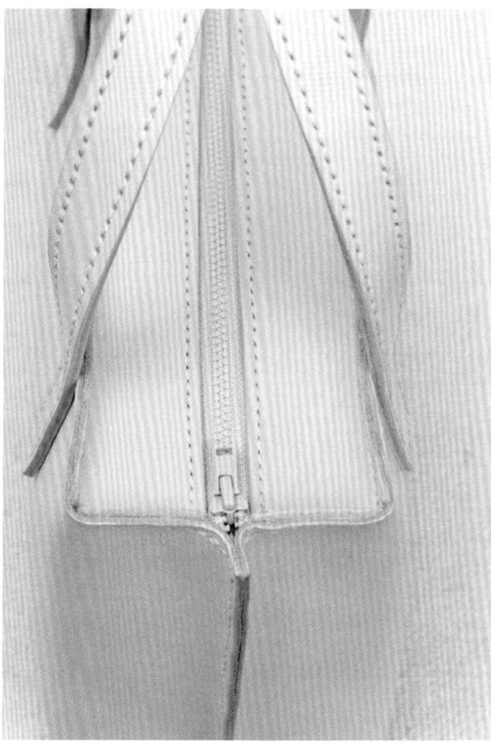

6 Sew the leather. Make sure to stitch the marked holes on each side together.

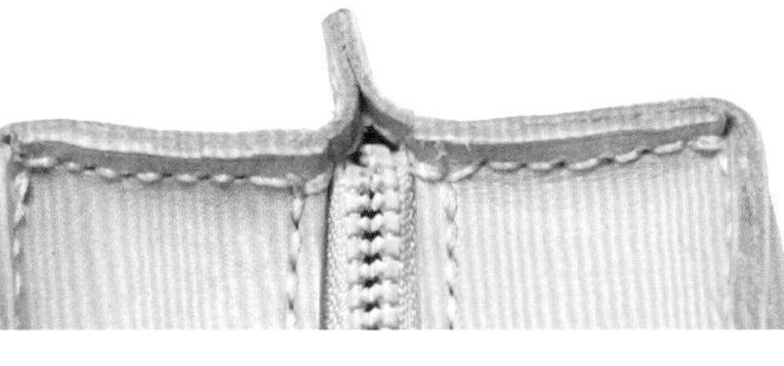

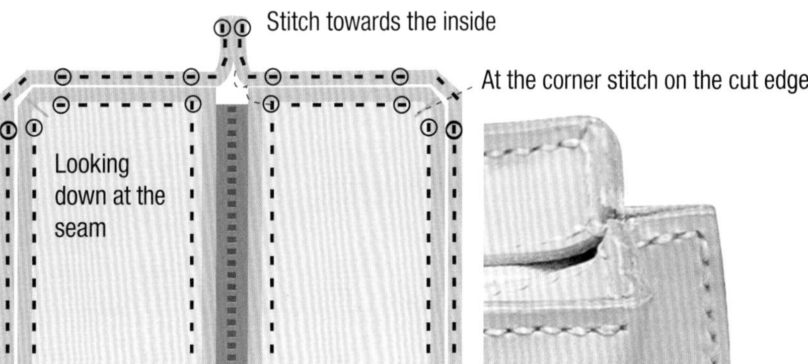

cutting pattern

A Bag with Darts

Adding darts makes a simple bag quite cute.

how to make

1 Punch the stitching holes and cut the leather according to the pattern. Burnish the flesh-side and the edges of the leather.

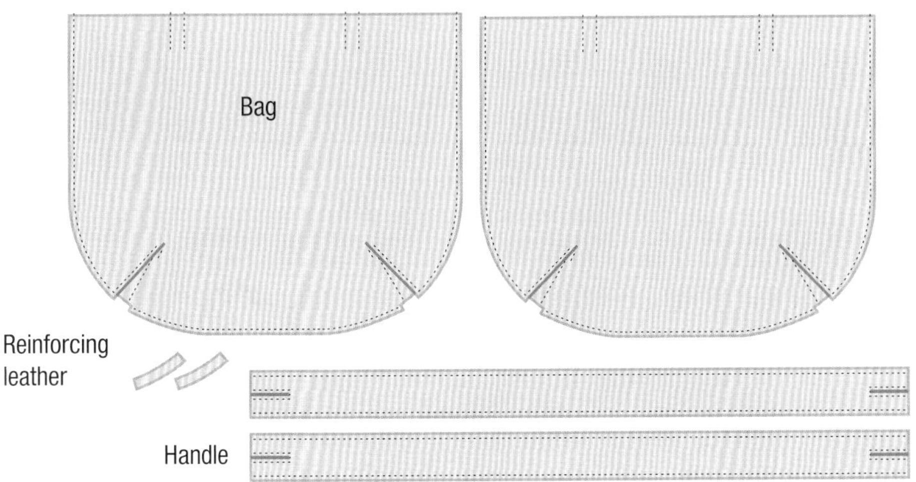

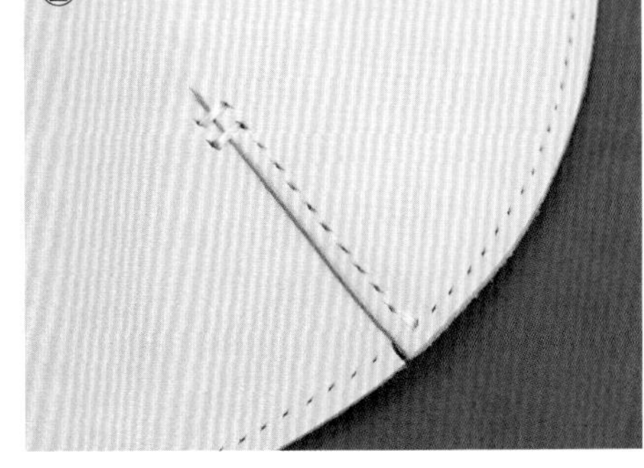

2 Refer to the photos on right: ① Align the stitching holes and glue dart, ② sew the leather, ③ & ④ glue reinforcing leather on the bag's flesh-side. Then pierce a lacing needle through the stitching holes, into the reinforcing leather, from the front-side.

3 Fold the strap and sew the leather to just before where it will be attached to the bag. Refer to "Making a Bag Handle" on page 72.

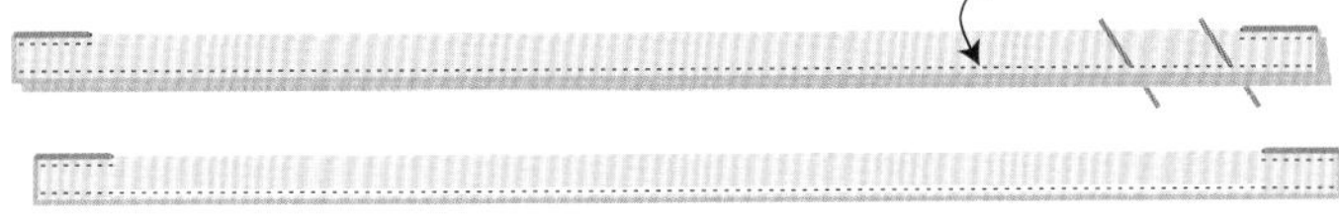

4 Open the end of the handle and then insert the bag so that the handle's seams face outward. Align the stitching holes, glue the handle on the bag, and then sew.

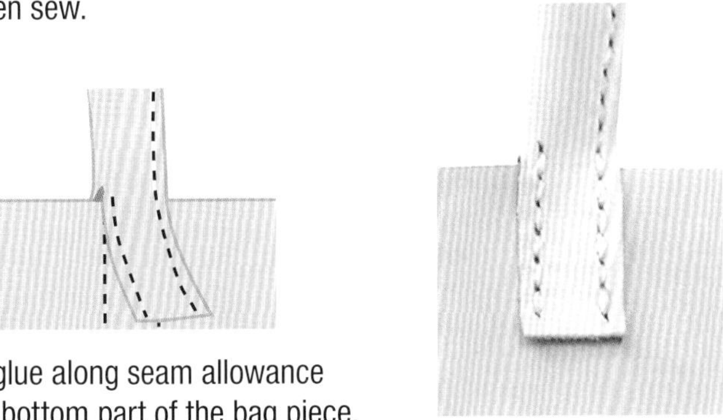

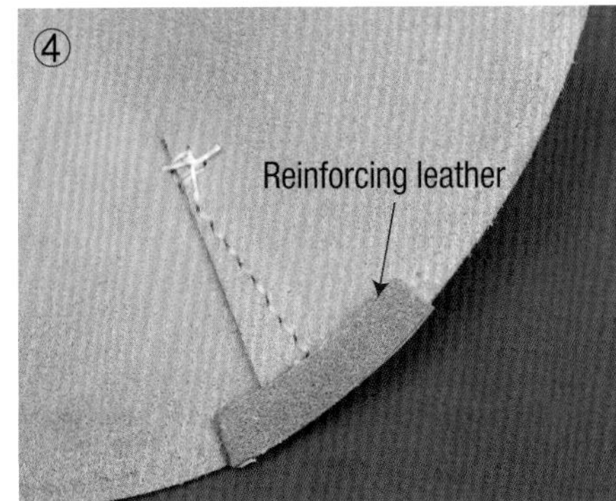

5 Apply glue along seam allowance on the bottom part of the bag piece. Put the two bag pieces together, both flesh-sides facing inward, while putting a piece of paper between them to prevent gluing another area unintentionally. Glue the leather while aligning the position of the stitching holes. Next, glue the sides (in a similar fashion to the bottom) one at a time.

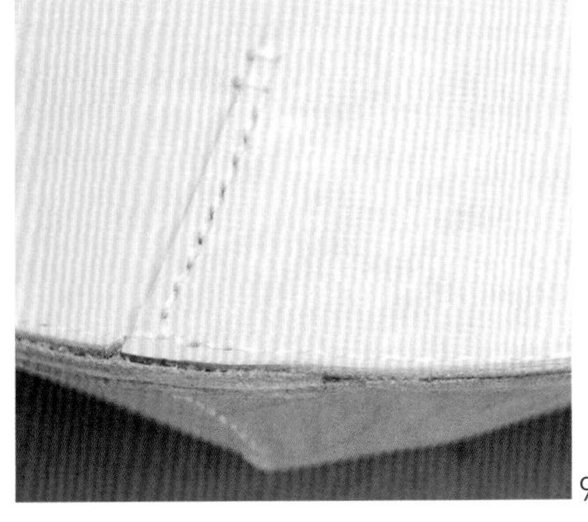

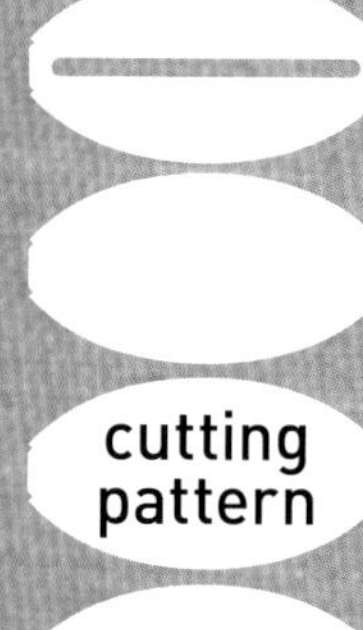

A Ball-shaped Bag

A rugby ball-like bag made using four oval shaped pieces sewn together.

detail

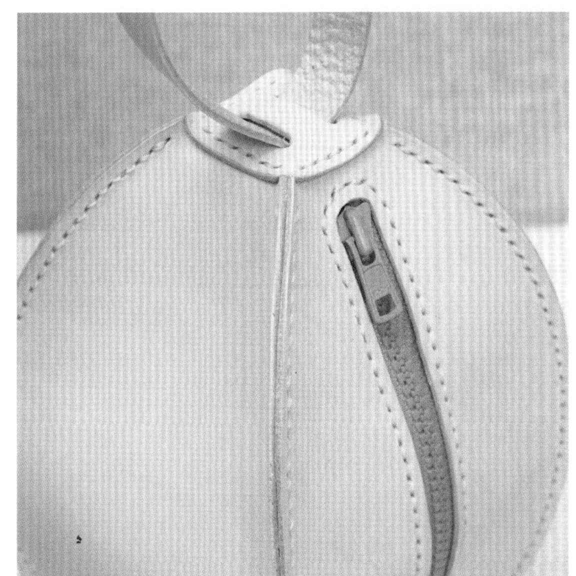

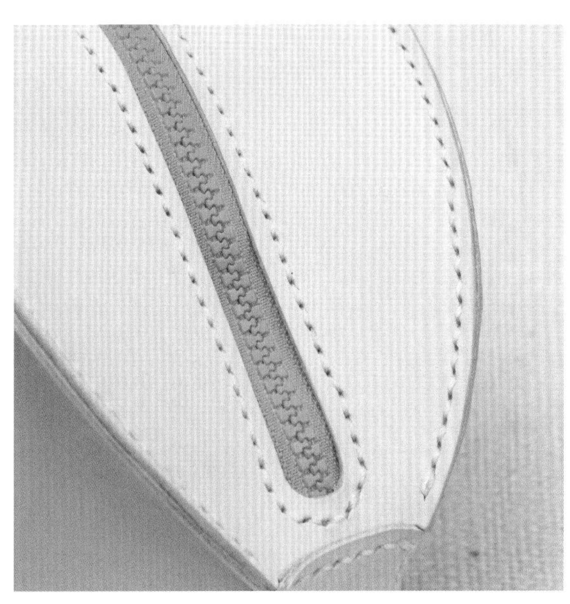

how to make

A Ball-shaped Bag

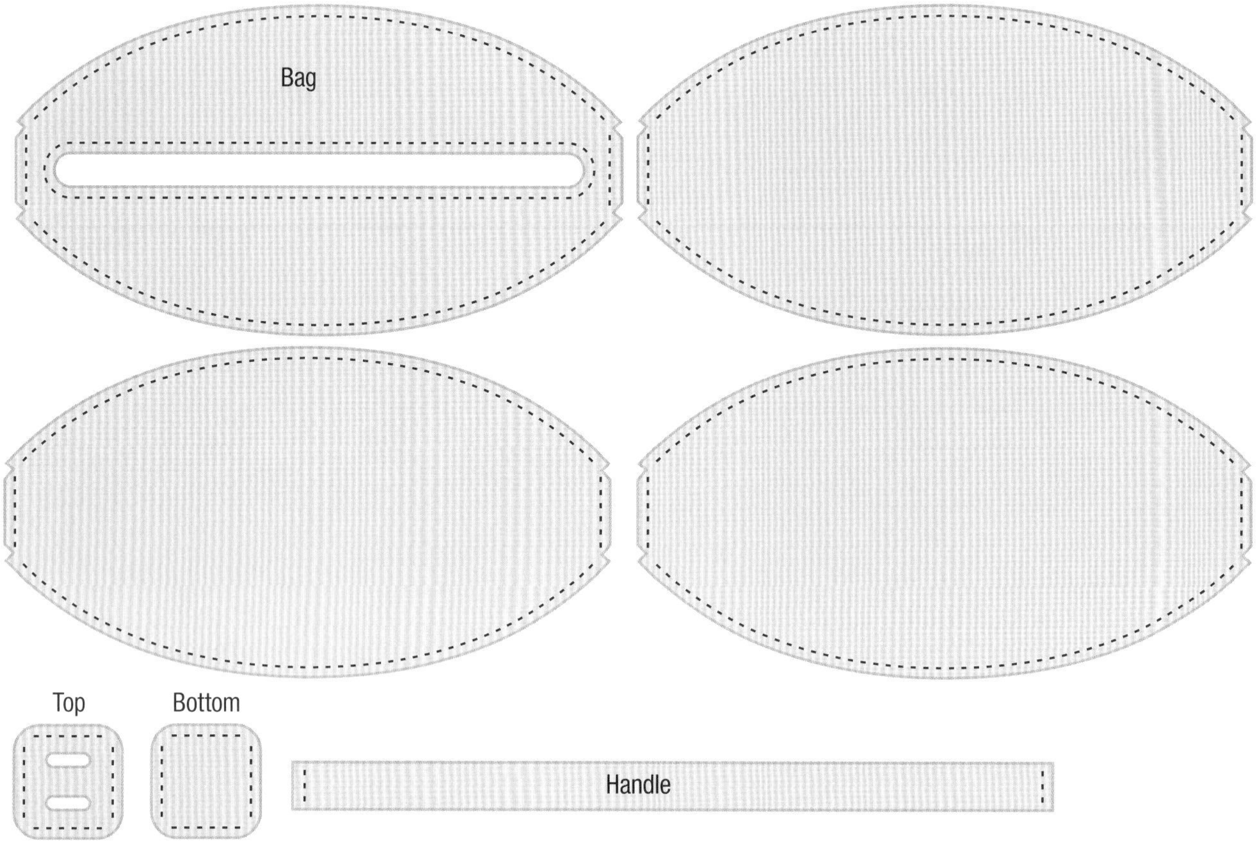

Bag

Top

Bottom

Handle

1 Punch the stitching holes and cut out the leather according to the pattern. Burnish the flesh-side and the edges of the leather.

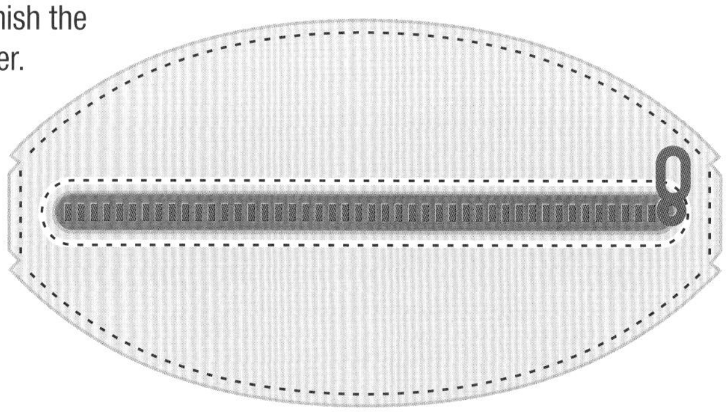

2 Refer to “Sewing on a Zipper” on page 61.

3 Put the handle through to the top piece and sew it on.

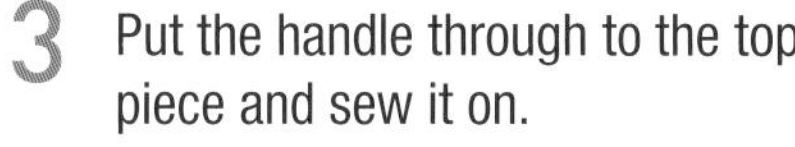

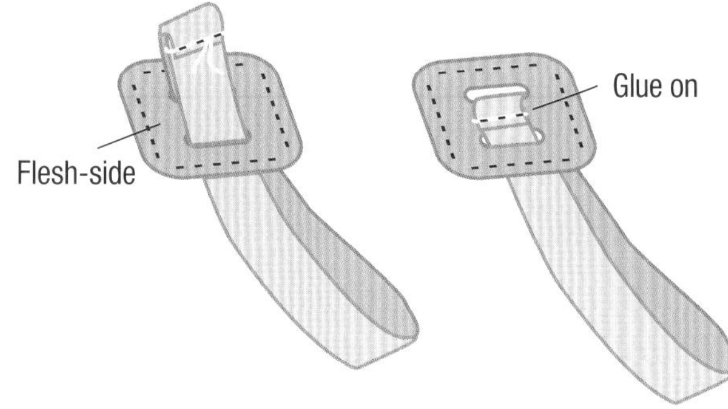

4 As in the figure shown below, glue each pair of bag pieces while aligning the marked stitching holes. While making fine adjustments every few stitches with an awl, sew the leather.

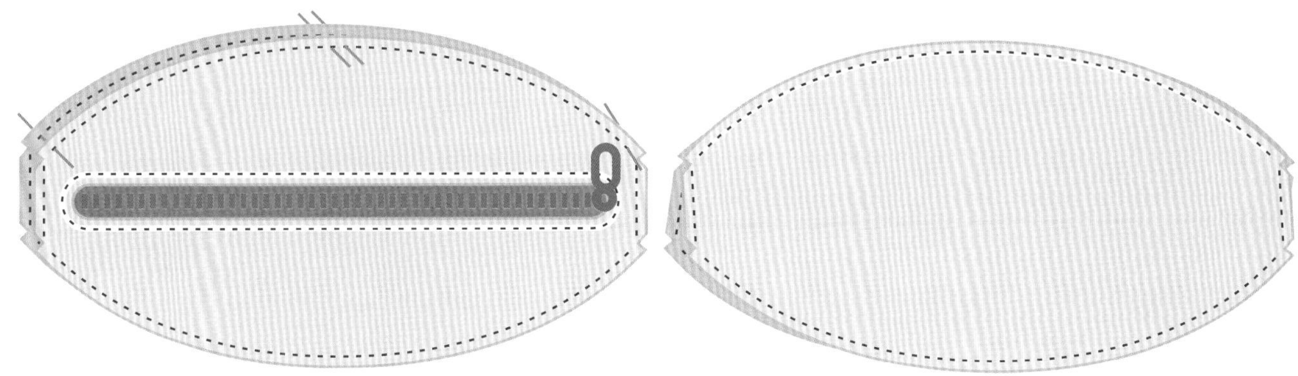

5 Glue just one side of each of the paired pieces together while aligning the marked stitching holes. Then make fine adjustments every few stitches with an awl. Sew the leather along the seam.

Leave one side unstitched in order to make stitching the top and bottom pieces easier.

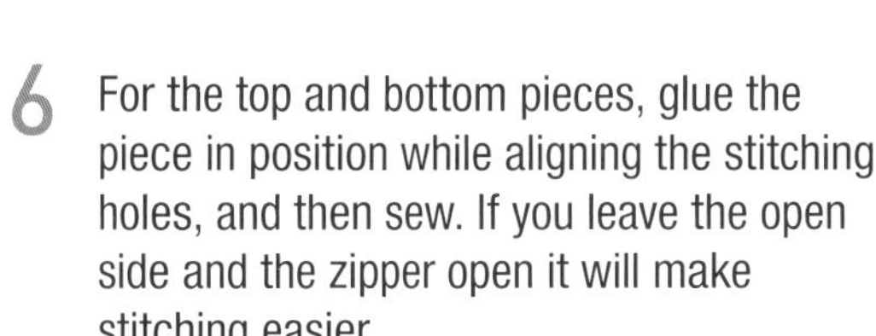

6 For the top and bottom pieces, glue the piece in position while aligning the stitching holes, and then sew. If you leave the open side and the zipper open it will make stitching easier.

7 For the unsewn side, glue the edges together while aligning the stitching holes, and then sew.

cutting pattern

Instructions P. 104

A Belt Pouch

A small-sized bag to hang on a belt. The design of the metal fittings varies a great deal, so just choose one that you like.

detail

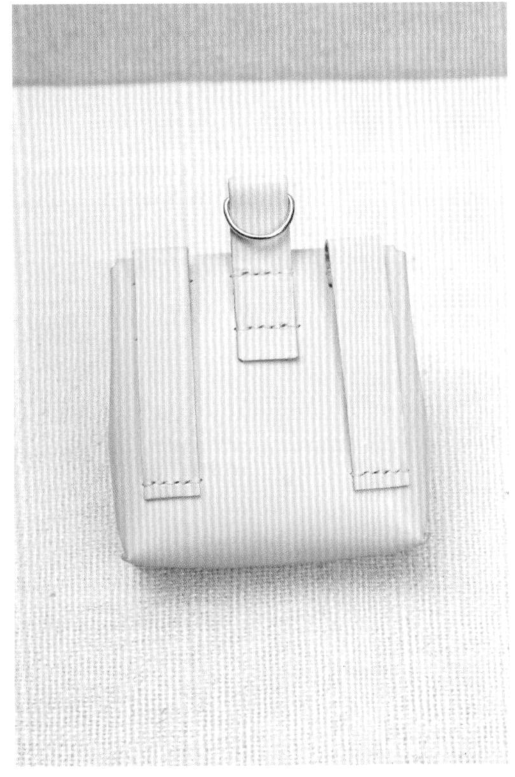

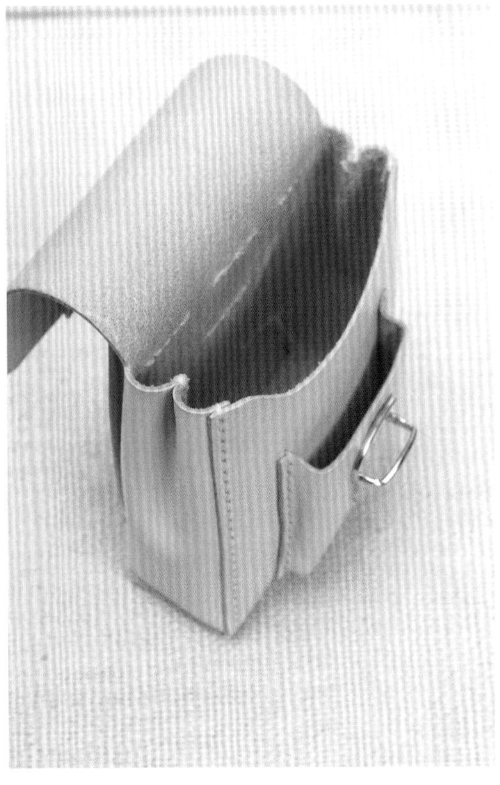

how to make

A Belt Pouch

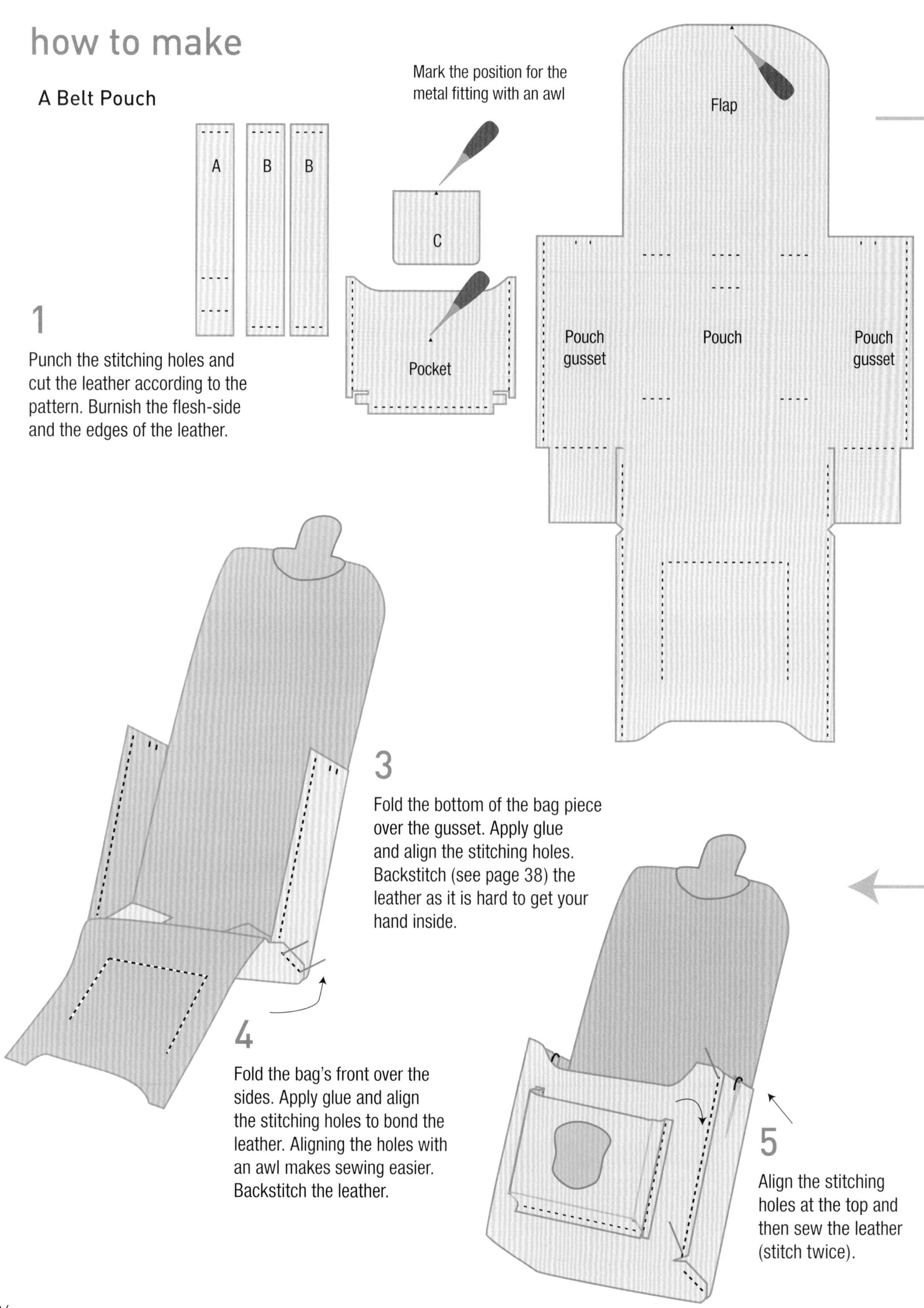

1

Punch the stitching holes and cut the leather according to the pattern. Burnish the flesh-side and the edges of the leather.

3

Fold the bottom of the bag piece over the gusset. Apply glue and align the stitching holes. Backstitch (see page 38) the leather as it is hard to get your hand inside.

4

Fold the bag's front over the sides. Apply glue and align the stitching holes to bond the leather. Aligning the holes with an awl makes sewing easier. Backstitch the leather.

5

Align the stitching holes at the top and then sew the leather (stitch twice).

2 Attach metal fittings and other parts. Glue them while aligning the stitching holes.

C

Apply glue along the edge of the marked side and then glue C on the flap piece (while aligning the marks).

Attach the center of the metal fitting at the center of the mark. (The method for attaching the tack differs depending on type. Please refer to the metal fitting's instructions)

This metal fitting is attached after making slits in the leather.

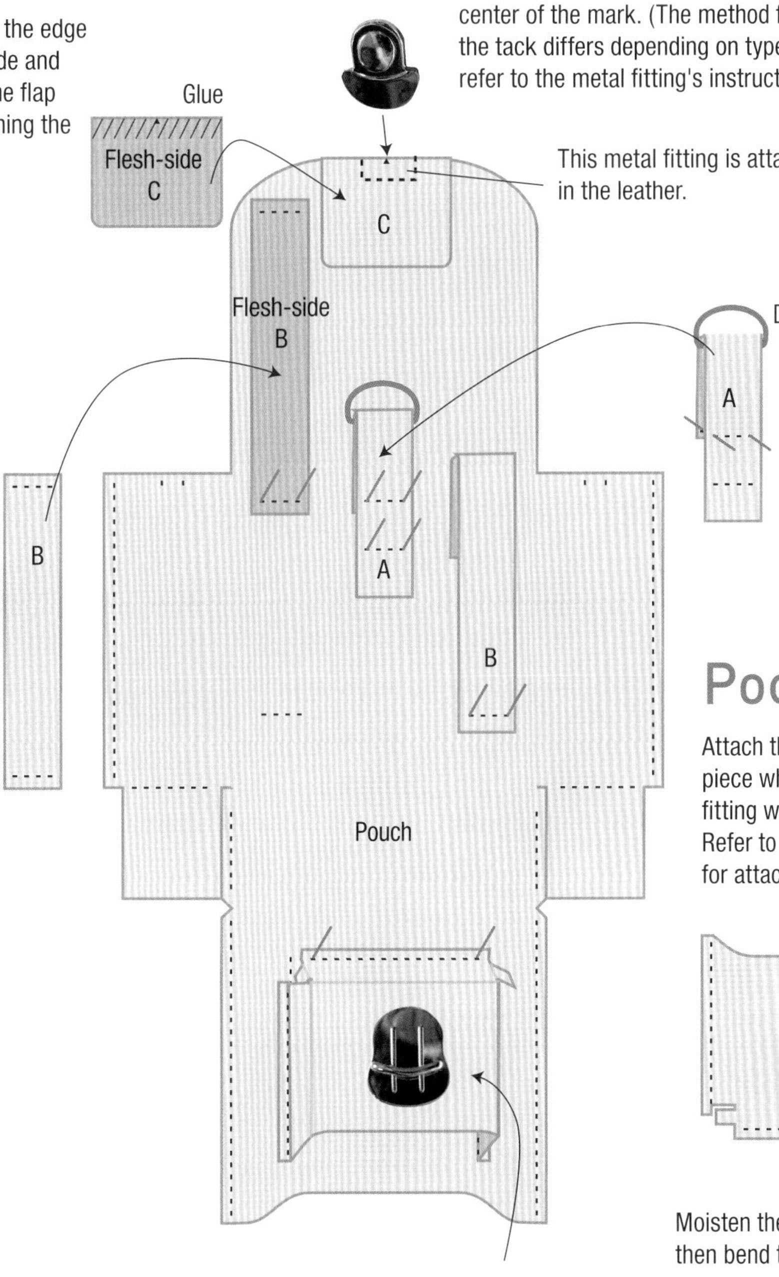

A

Put A through the D-ring and glue the leather while aligning the stitching holes. Then, glue A on the pouch piece while aligning the stitching holes and sew.

B

Place B on the pouch piece with the flesh-side facing up. Glue it while aligning the stitching holes and then sew.

Fold B so the other stitching holes align with ones on the pouch piece, glue, and then sew.

Pocket

Attach the metal fitting on the pocket piece while aligning the center of the fitting with the mark on the pocket. Refer to "magnetic snap" on page 87 for attaching directions.

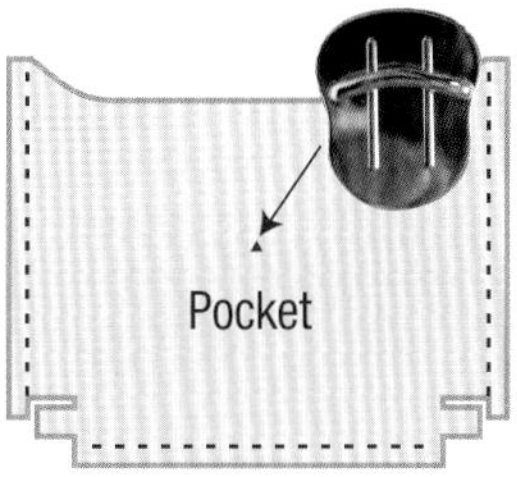

Moisten the edges with a sponge and then bend the edge as if folding.

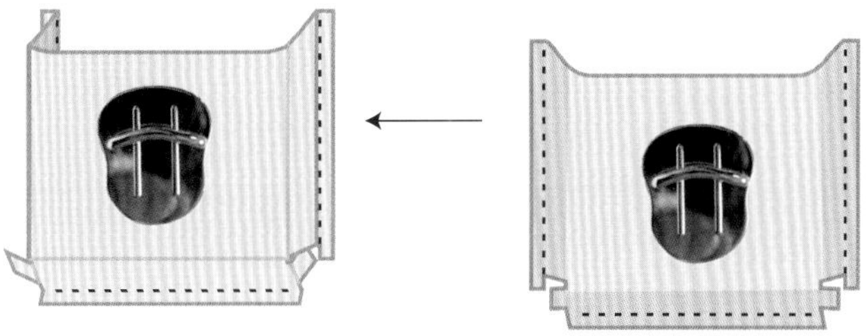

After it has dried, apply glue along the seam allowance. First the bottom and then the gusset. Glue this onto the pouch piece while aligning the marked stitching holes and then sew.

cutting pattern

A Small Oval-shaped Bottom Bag

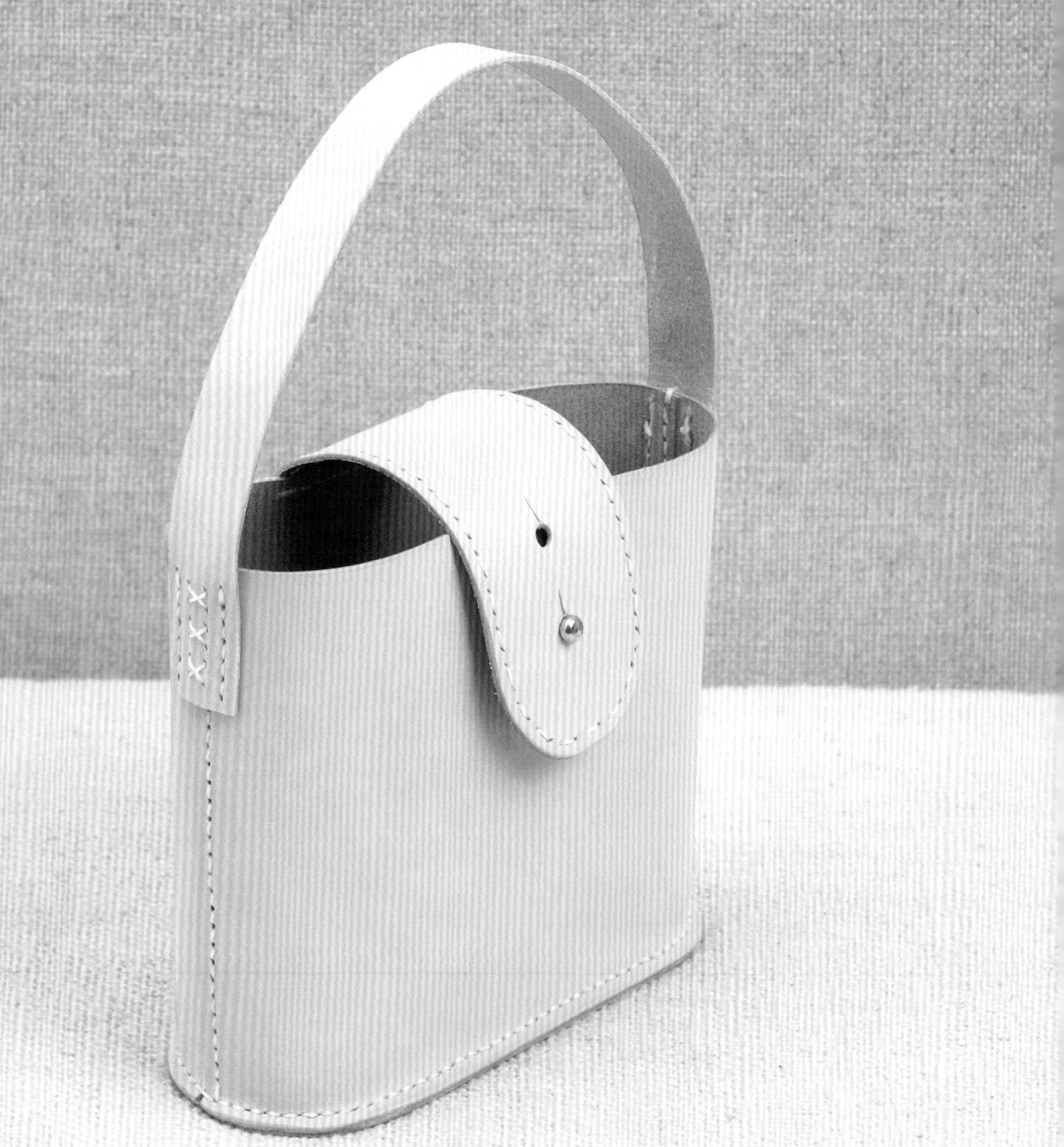

A small bag that can carry your everyday necessities.

how to make

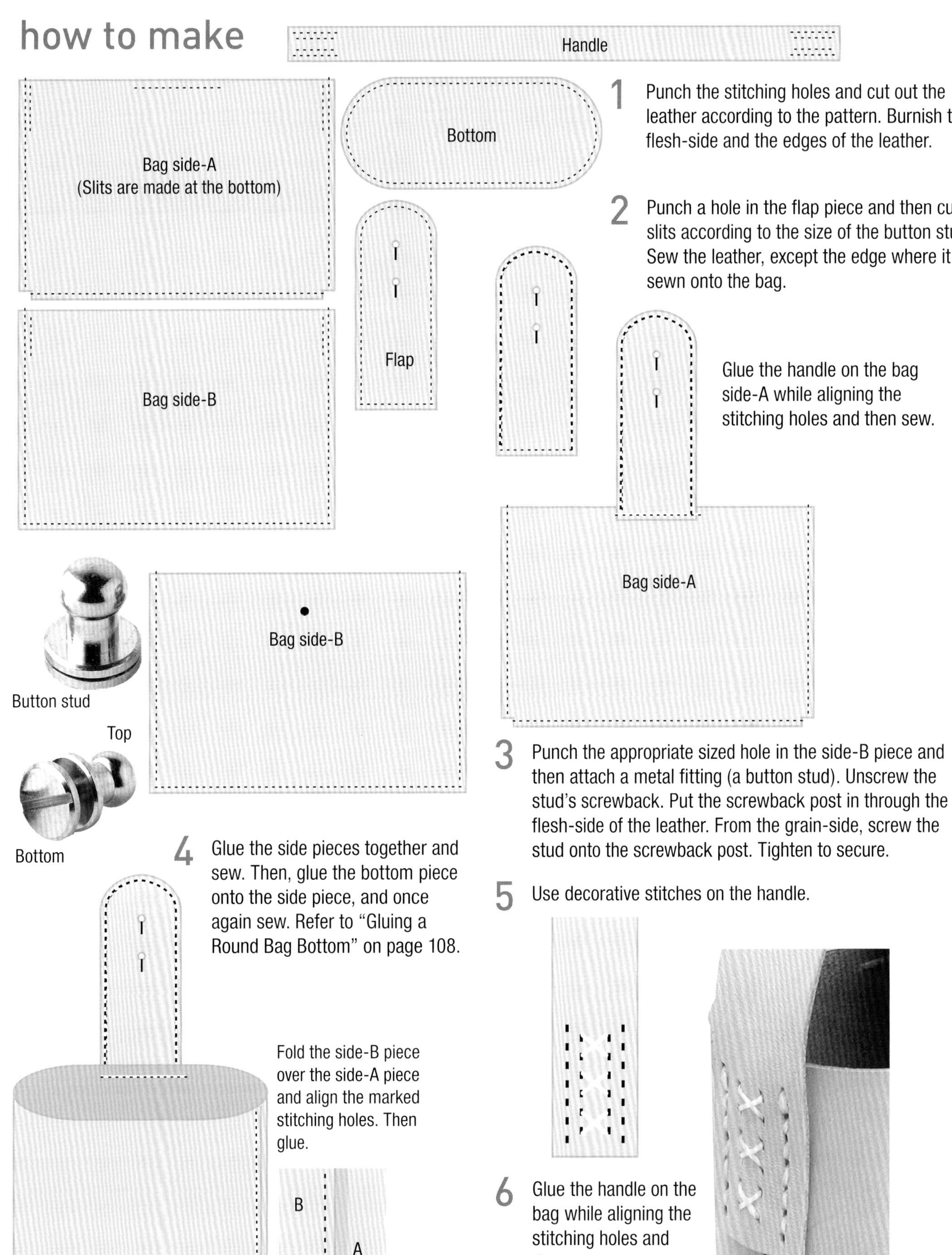

1 Punch the stitching holes and cut out the leather according to the pattern. Burnish the flesh-side and the edges of the leather.

2 Punch a hole in the flap piece and then cut slits according to the size of the button stud. Sew the leather, except the edge where it is sewn onto the bag.

Glue the handle on the bag side-A while aligning the stitching holes and then sew.

3 Punch the appropriate sized hole in the side-B piece and then attach a metal fitting (a button stud). Unscrew the stud's screwback. Put the screwback post in through the flesh-side of the leather. From the grain-side, screw the stud onto the screwback post. Tighten to secure.

4 Glue the side pieces together and sew. Then, glue the bottom piece onto the side piece, and once again sew. Refer to "Gluing a Round Bag Bottom" on page 108.

Fold the side-B piece over the side-A piece and align the marked stitching holes. Then glue.

5 Use decorative stitches on the handle.

6 Glue the handle on the bag while aligning the stitching holes and then sew.

Gluing a Round Bag Bottom

For items that have round bottoms, first moisten the circumference of either the item or the bottom and then bend accordingly to shape. Then glue.

[Glue by Bending Circumference]

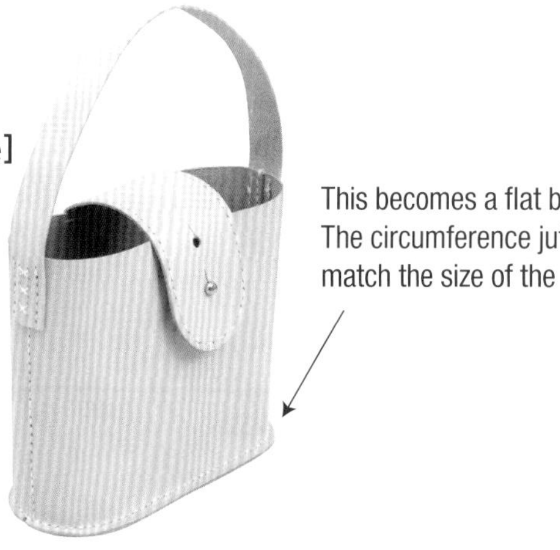

This becomes a flat bottom. The circumference juts out to match the size of the bottom.

1 Sew side pieces together.
★ The flap is excluded from this illustration to facilitate instruction.

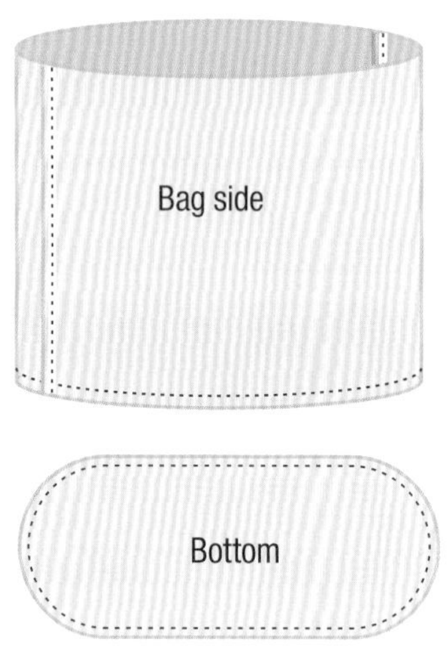

2 Bend slightly inside of the seam allowance along the circumference. Refer to "Gluing on a Large Sheet of Leather: Bend by Moistening" on page 76.

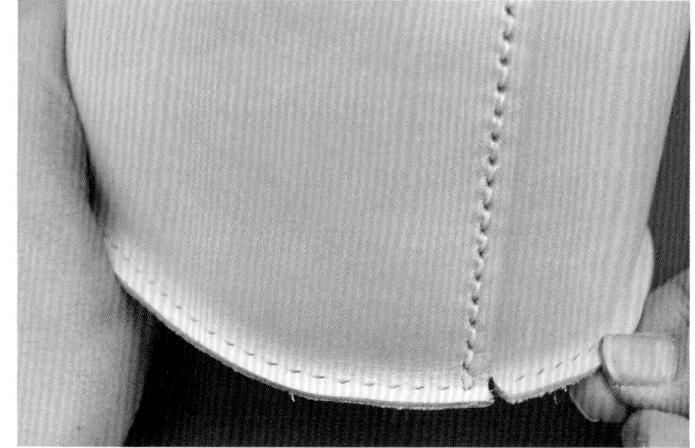

3 Apply glue along seam allowance. Glue bottom on while aligning the marked stitching holes and placing a piece of paper in between. Refer to "Gluing on a Large Sheet of Leather: Bend by Moistening" on page 76.

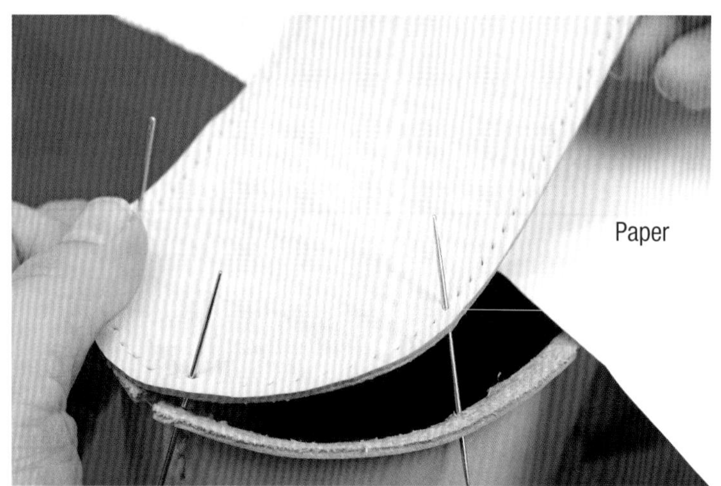

Paper

★ The stitching holes easily fall out of position when sewing round bottoms. Therefore, when dealing with large sized bags, carry out the gluing process after first securing the leather temporarily with thread (as shown on the facing page).

[Glue by Bending Bottom]

The bag's sides are perpendicular. Bend along the bottom piece's seam allowance.

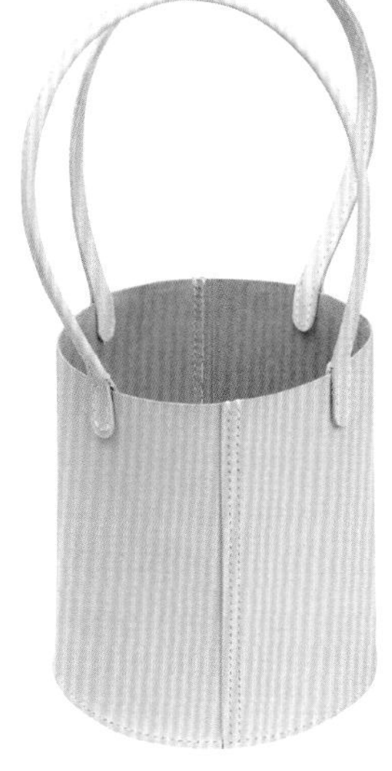

By attaching a cord over the opening of the bag (as shown on the left), a bucket shape is made. The bag on the right has seams on both the left and right.

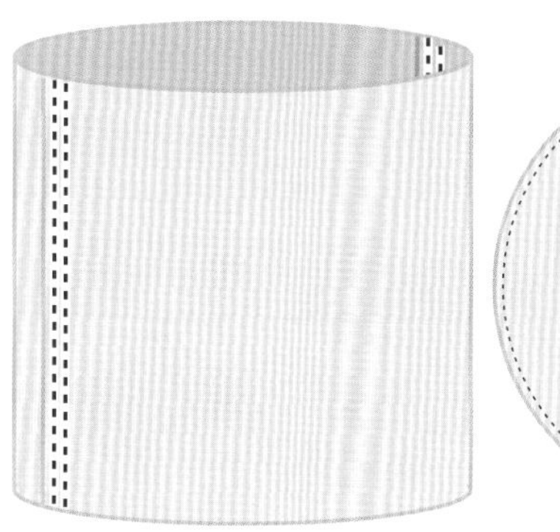

1 Sew the side pieces together.
★ For ease of instruction, the handle and other items are excluded.

2 Bend slightly inside of the seam allowance along the bottom piece. Refer to "Gluing on a Large Sheet of Leather: Bend by Moistening" on page 76.

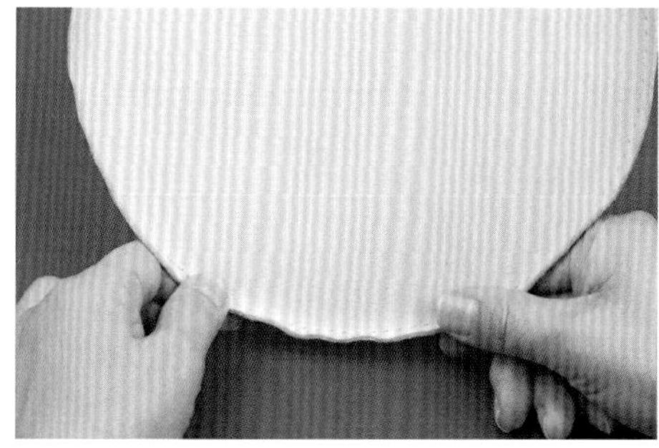

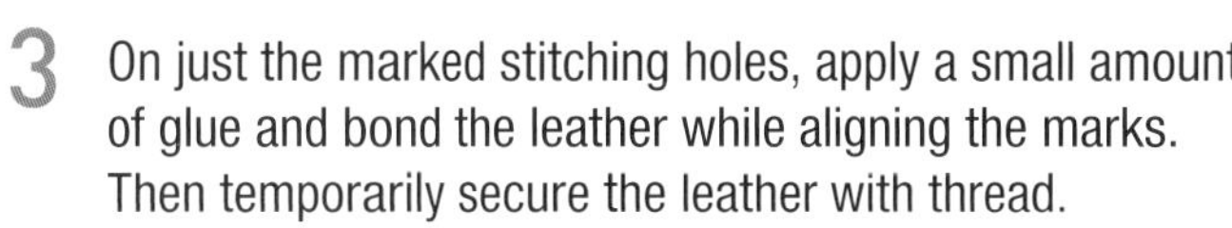

3 On just the marked stitching holes, apply a small amount of glue and bond the leather while aligning the marks. Then temporarily secure the leather with thread.

4 Glue each section, divided by thread, separately. Apply glue along the seam allowance. Put a piece of paper between the leather and continue to glue while aligning the stitching holes.

cutting pattern

A Cylindrical-shaped Bag

Moistening the leather enables you to manipulate its shape freely. This bag is made by bending the bottom circle of the bag and gluing it to the side piece.

how to make

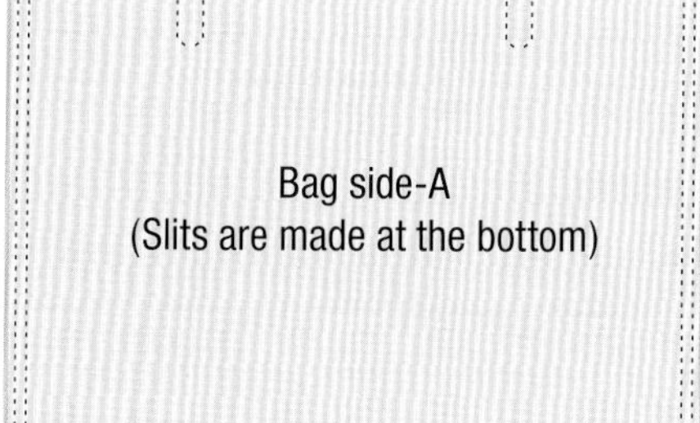

Bag side-B

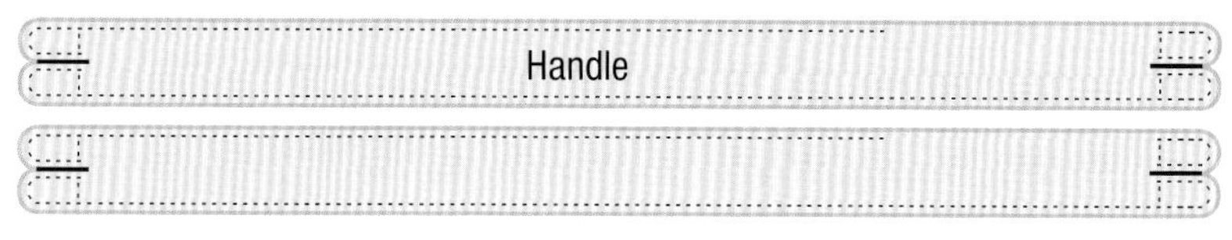

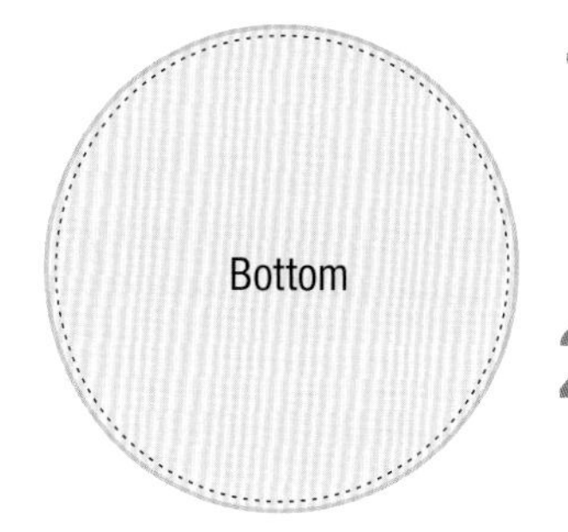

1 Punch the stitching holes and cut out the leather according to the pattern. Burnish the flesh-side and the edges of the leather.

2 Make the handles and then open both ends and clasp the bag with them.
Glue the handles on the bag while aligning the stitching holes. Then sew. Refer to "Making a Bag Handle" on page 72.

3 Glue the bag's side pieces together and then sew.

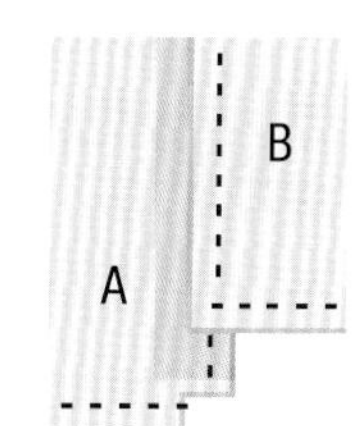

Place side-B over side-A and align the marked stitching holes. Then glue.

4 Glue on the bottom piece. Refer to "Gluing a Round Bag Bottom" on page 108. Sew the leather.

detail

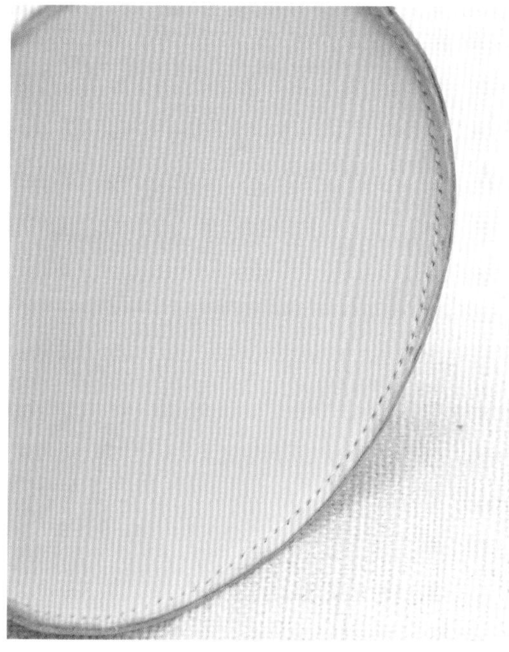

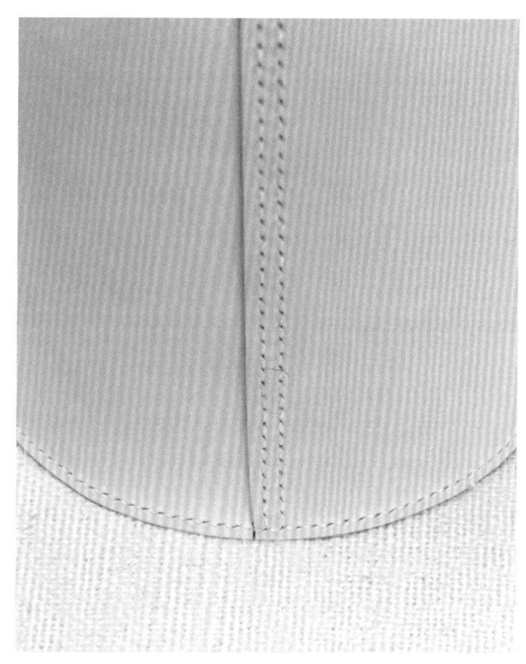

cutting pattern

A Bucket-shaped Bag

An attached button accentuates this bucket-shaped bag. Even though the handle length and attached accessories are different, this bag shares the pattern and production method with the cylindrical-shaped bag on page 110.
A round leather cord is used to fasten the bag's opening.

how to make

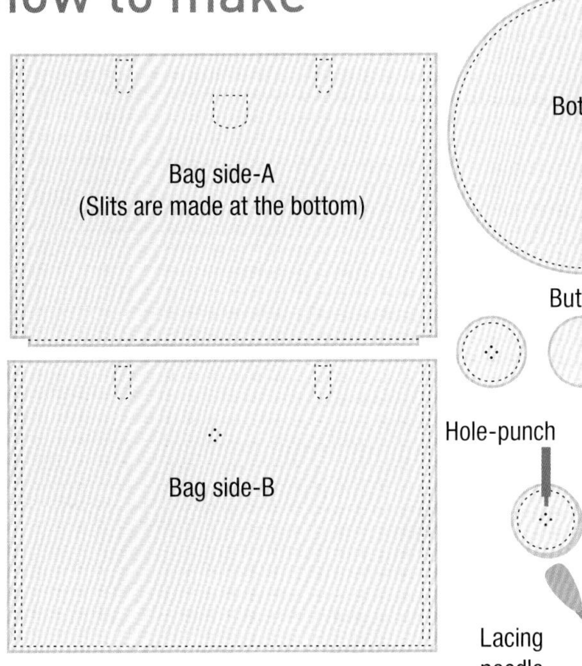

Bottom

Handle

1 Punch the stitching holes and cut out the leather according to the pattern.
Burnish the flesh-side and the edges of the leather.

Button

Cord tag

Hole-punch

Lacing needle

2 For the button glue two large circular pieces of leather together with the flesh-sides facing each other. Then punch holes.
Pierce a lacing needle through the stitching holes to the back piece of leather.
Punch holes through a small circular piece of leather.
For the cord tag, punch out two separate holes and then cut out the leather between the two holes with a utility knife.

3 Put a leather cord through the cord tag and fold the leather in half. Glue the folded leather while aligning the stitching holes.
Glue the cord tag onto side-A while aligning the stitching holes. Then sew it on.

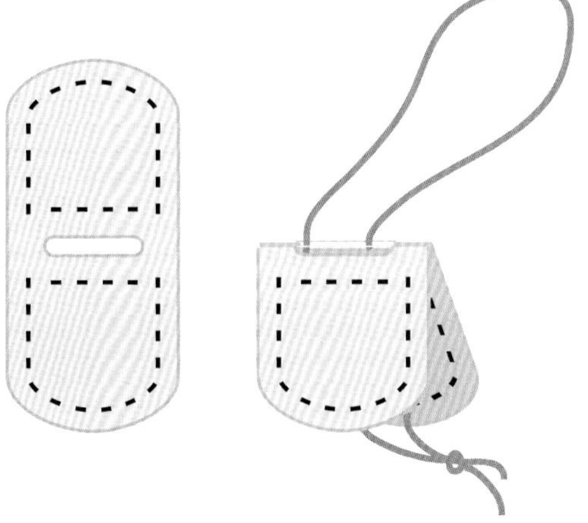

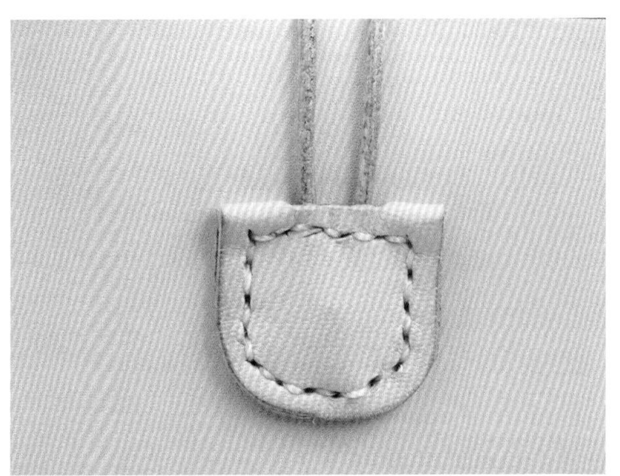

4 Put the large button on the small one and sew them on side-B right away.

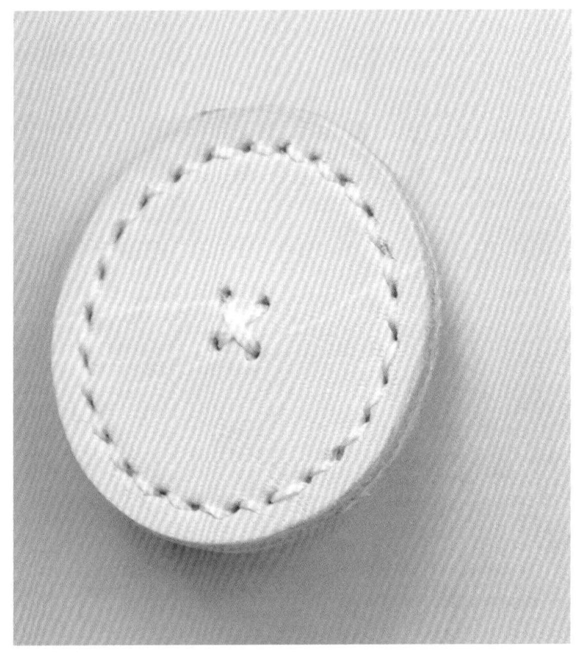

5 Make the handle. Open both ends of the handle and clasp them around the bag.
Glue the handle on the bag while aligning the stitching holes, and then sew it on.
Refer to “Making a Bag Handle” on page 72.
Sew the side pieces together, then the bottom.
Refer to “A Cylindrical-shaped Bag” on page 111 and “Gluing a Round Bag Bottom” on page 108.

cutting pattern

A Two-gored Leather Travel Bag

This is a simple, two-gored leather bag. Since the seam is long and curved it tends to shift out of position easily. Be careful that doesn't happen.

how to make

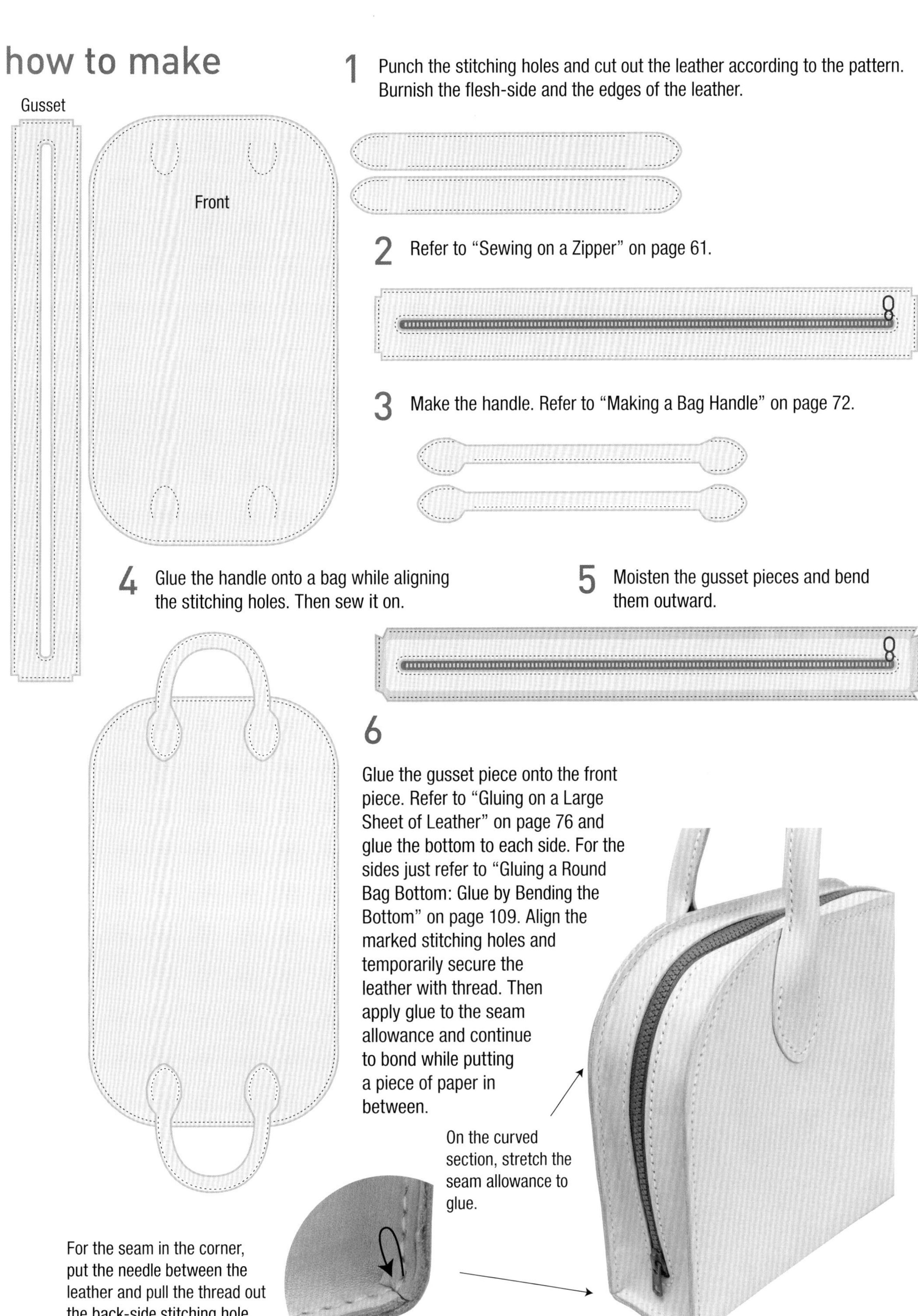

1 Punch the stitching holes and cut out the leather according to the pattern. Burnish the flesh-side and the edges of the leather.

2 Refer to “Sewing on a Zipper” on page 61.

3 Make the handle. Refer to “Making a Bag Handle” on page 72.

4 Glue the handle onto a bag while aligning the stitching holes. Then sew it on.

5 Moisten the gusset pieces and bend them outward.

6

Glue the gusset piece onto the front piece. Refer to “Gluing on a Large Sheet of Leather” on page 76 and glue the bottom to each side. For the sides just refer to “Gluing a Round Bag Bottom: Glue by Bending the Bottom” on page 109. Align the marked stitching holes and temporarily secure the leather with thread. Then apply glue to the seam allowance and continue to bond while putting a piece of paper in between.

On the curved section, stretch the seam allowance to glue.

For the seam in the corner, put the needle between the leather and pull the thread out the back-side stitching hole.

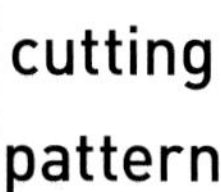

cutting pattern

Instructions P. 118

A Curved Bottom Shoulder Bag

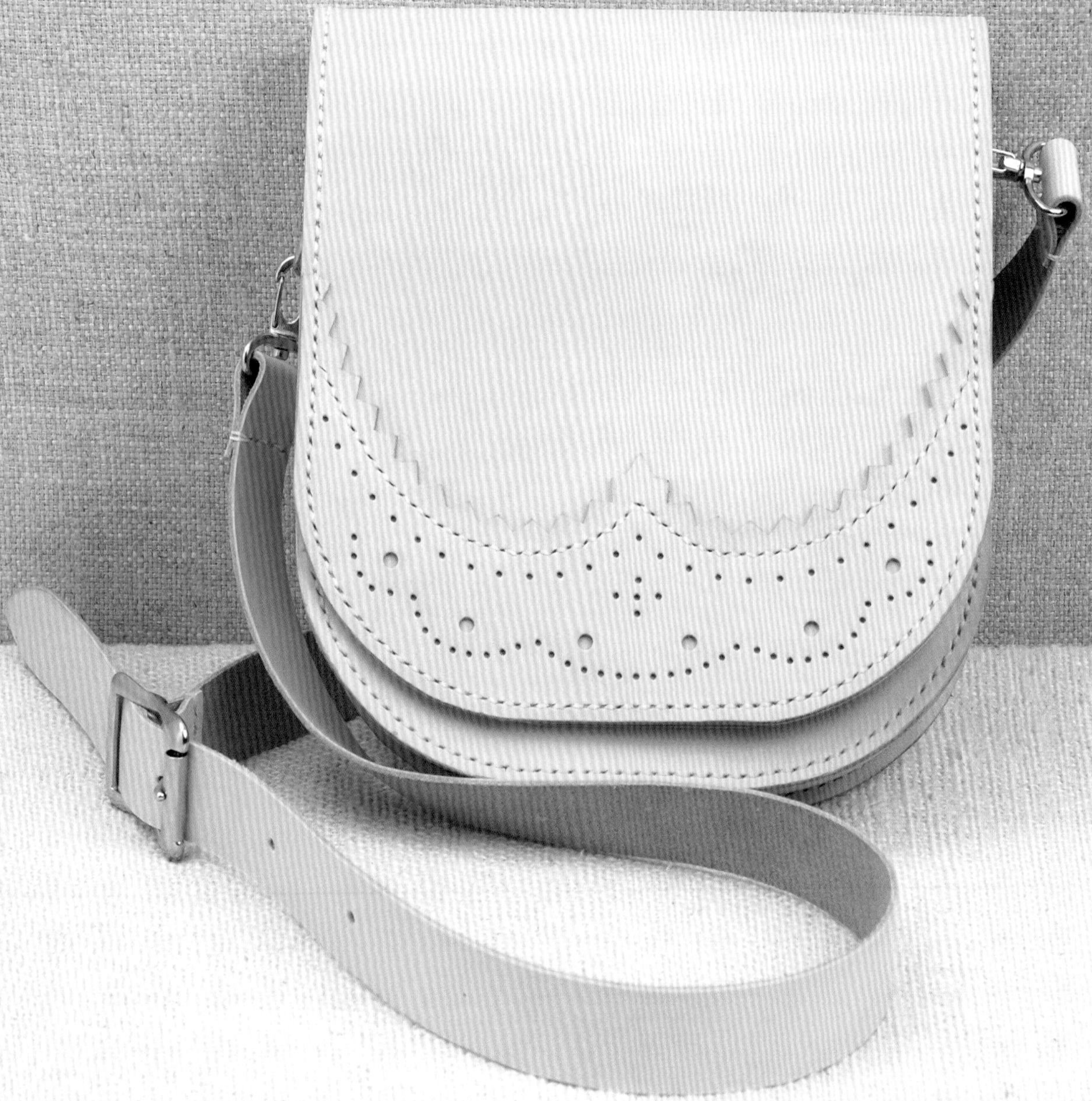

The decoration on the flap is just patterned punch holes. The strap is the same as that found on page 88.

detail

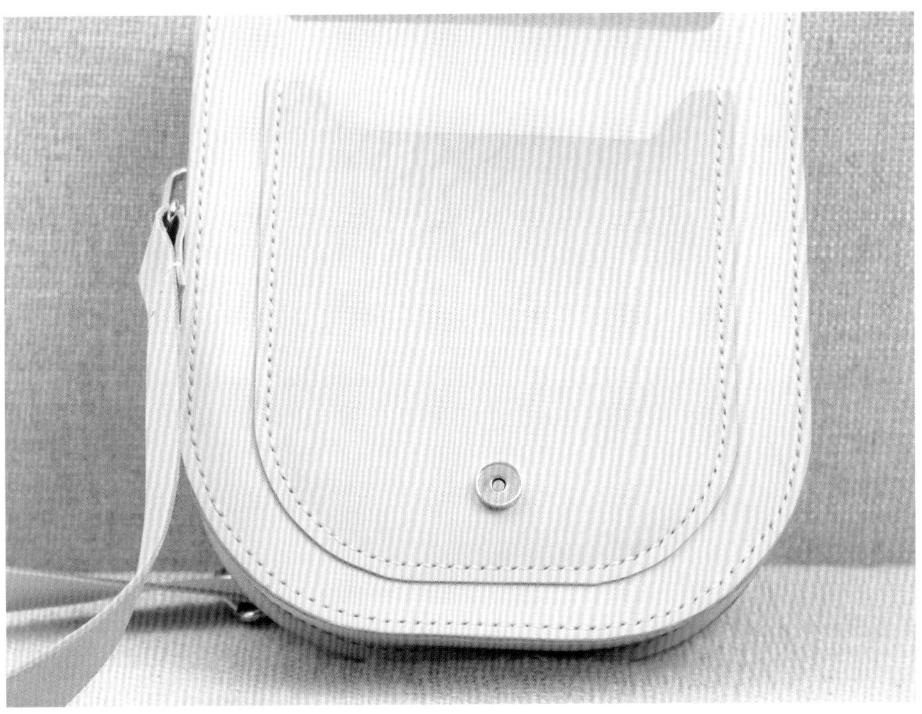

how to make

A Curved Bottom Shoulder Bag

1 Punch the stitching holes and cut out the leather according to the pattern. Burnish the flesh-side and the edges of the leather.

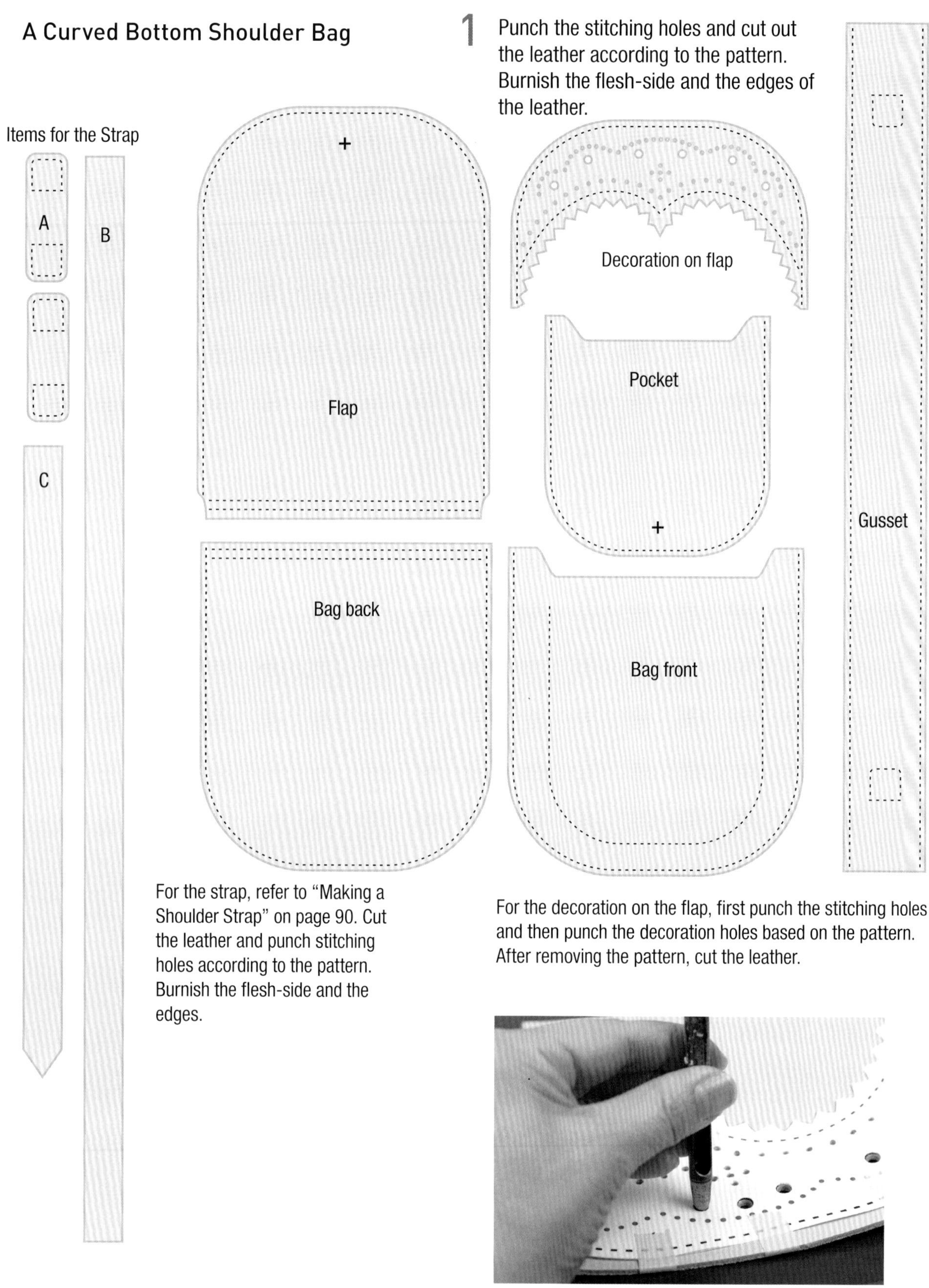

For the strap, refer to "Making a Shoulder Strap" on page 90. Cut the leather and punch stitching holes according to the pattern. Burnish the flesh-side and the edges.

For the decoration on the flap, first punch the stitching holes and then punch the decoration holes based on the pattern. After removing the pattern, cut the leather.

2 Attach a magnetic snap on the pocket and flap piece. See page 87.

3 Glue each item on the bag piece while aligning the marked stitching holes. Use an awl to make fine adjustments to align the holes every few stitches as you sew.

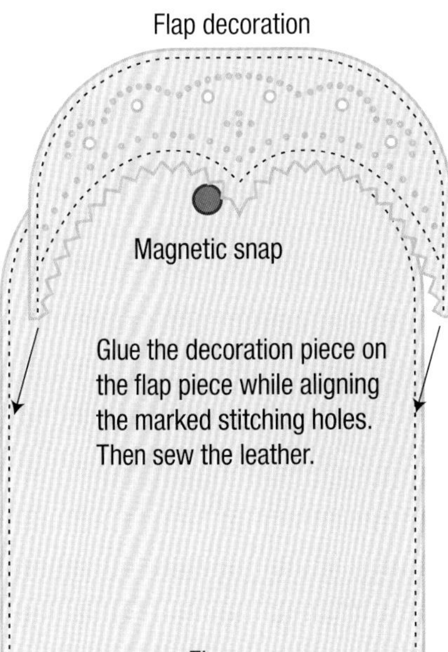

Flap

Glue the pocket piece on the front piece while aligning the marked stitching holes. Then sew the leather.

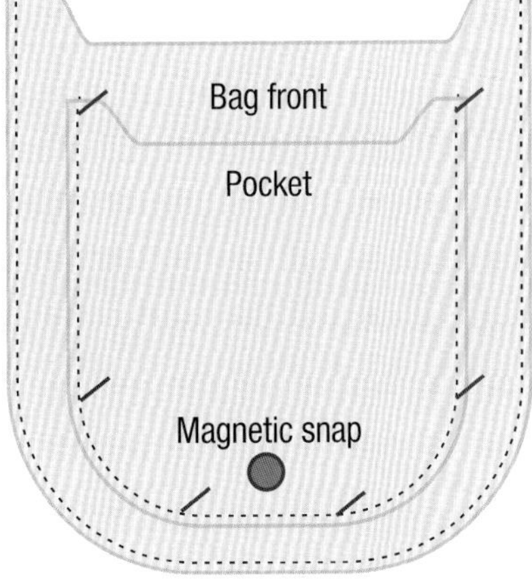

Put the D-ring on strap item A. Fold the strap back to glue while aligning the marked stitching holes. Then sew.

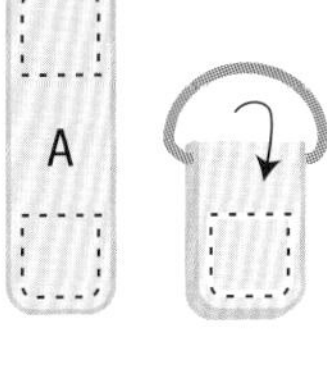

Glue strap item A (D-ring attached) on the gusset piece while aligning the marked stitching holes. Then sew the leather.

Gusset

Bag back

4 Moisten the gusset piece and then bend the seam allowance outward. Glue the gusset piece onto the bag piece while aligning the marked stitching holes. Temporarily secure the leather with thread. Glue the bottom part of the bag first, then glue each side. Refer to "Gluing on a Large Sheet of Leather: Bend by Moistening" on page 76. Sew the leather.

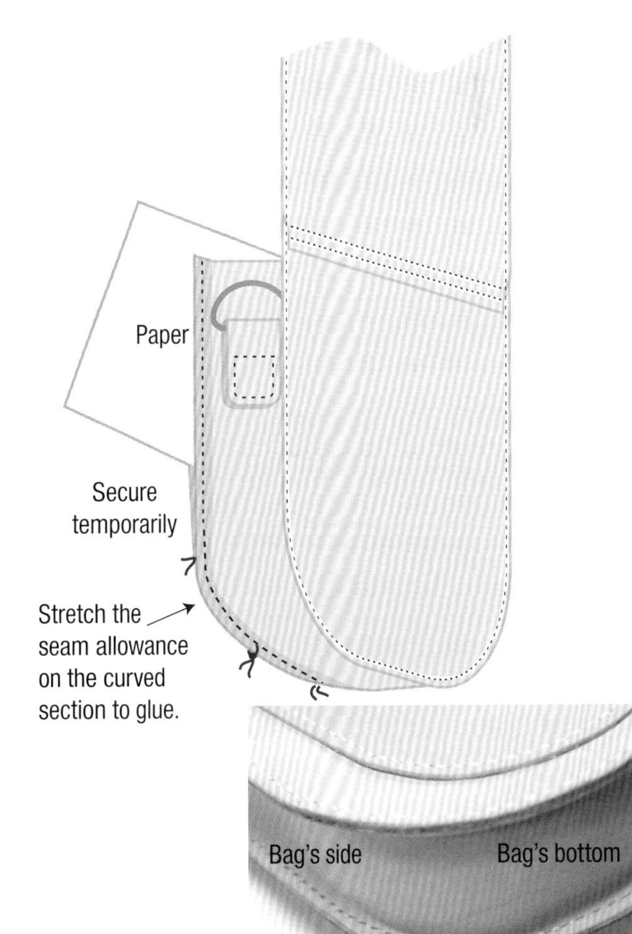

cutting pattern

Instructions
P. 122

A Tool Bag

Though there are abundant pockets and partitions, they only use a single sheet of leather that is bent or folded.

detail

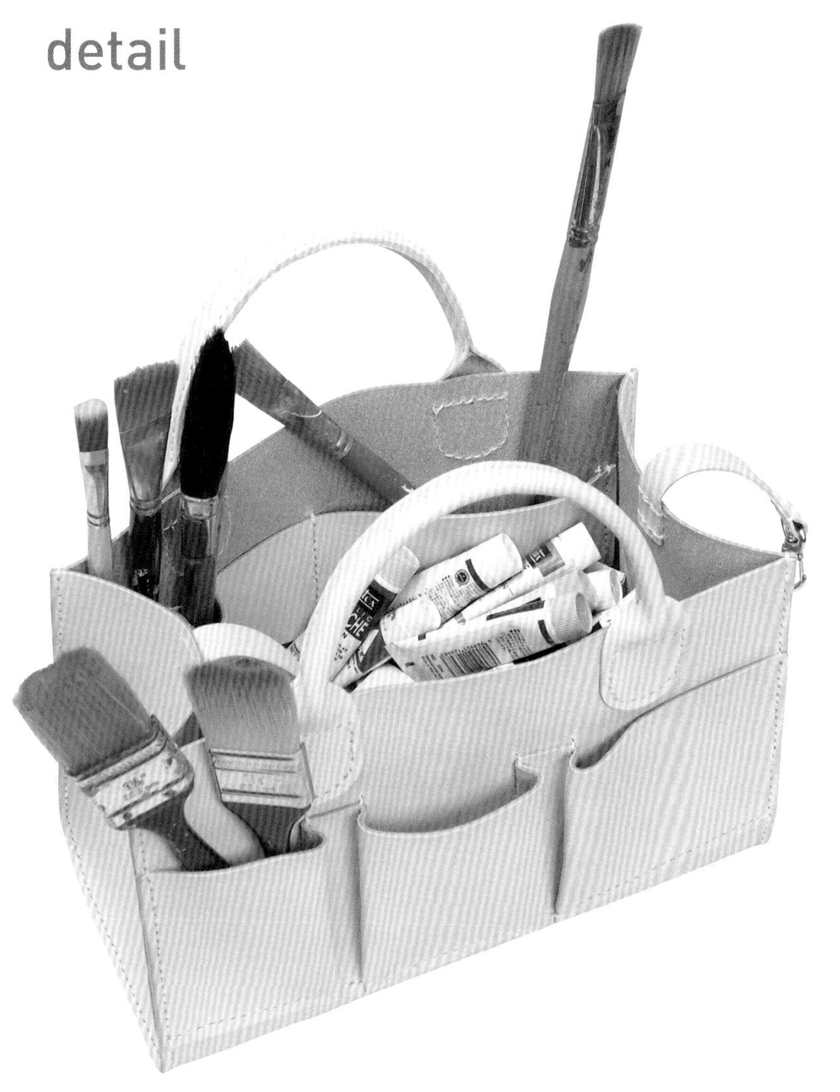

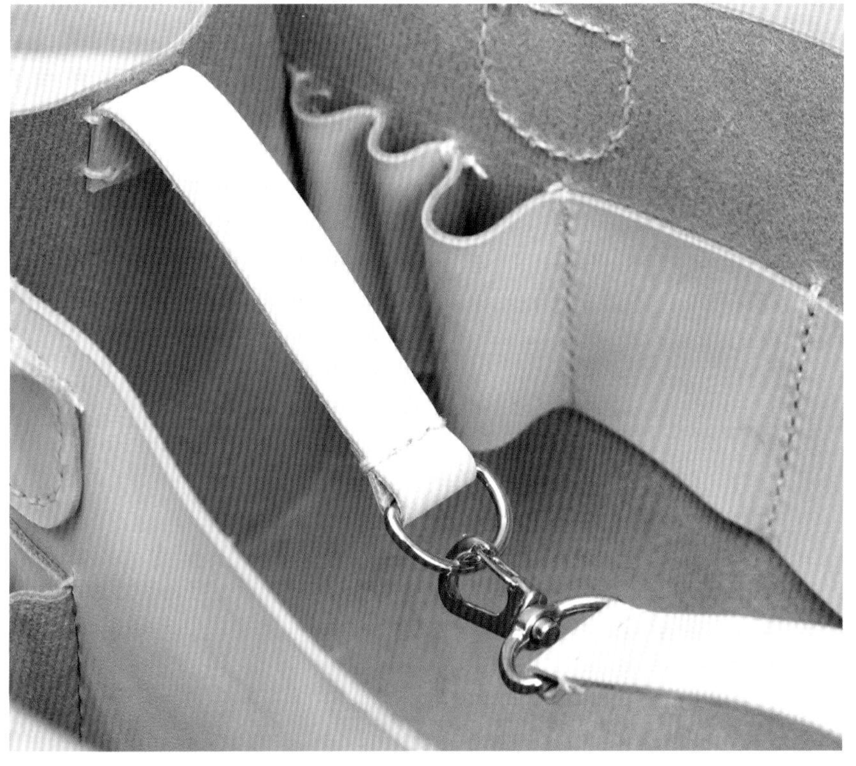

how to make

A Tool Bag

1 Punch the stitching holes and cut out the leather according to the pattern. Burnish the flesh-side and the edges of the leather.

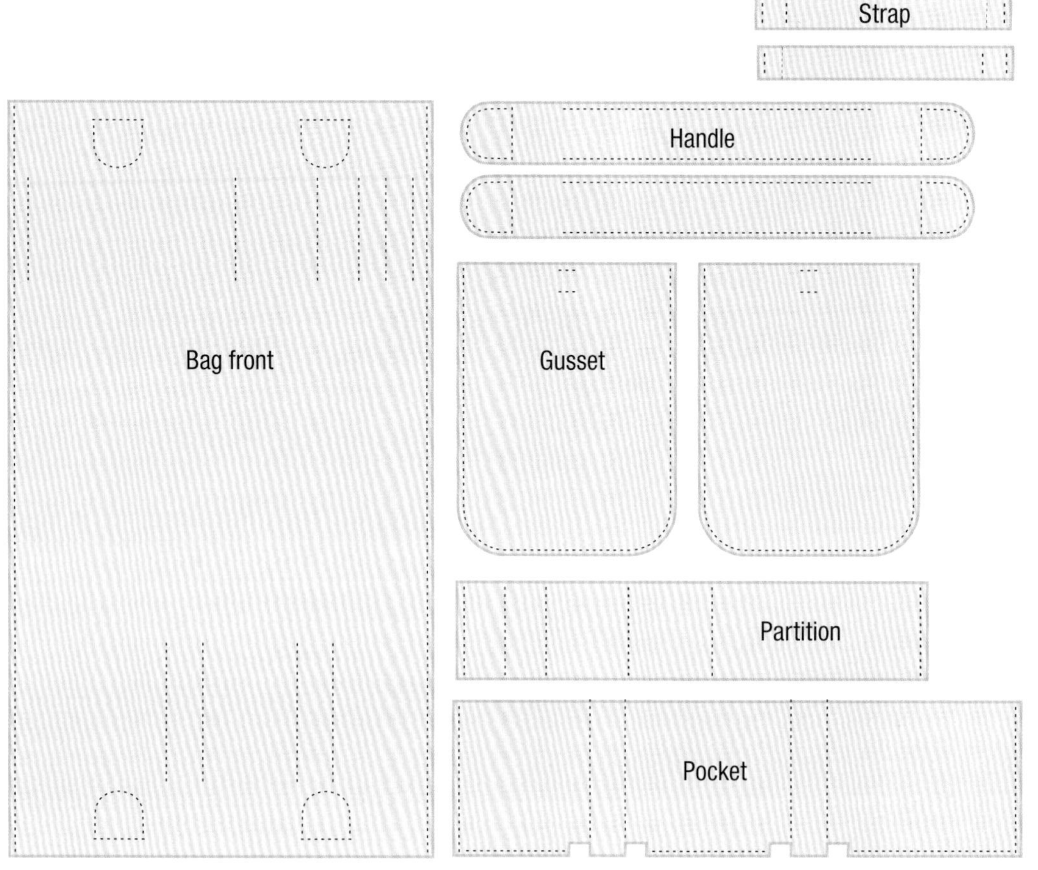

2 Put the metal fitting through the strap piece and then fold the strap piece. Align the stitching holes and sew. Refer to "Making a Shoulder Strap" on page 90.

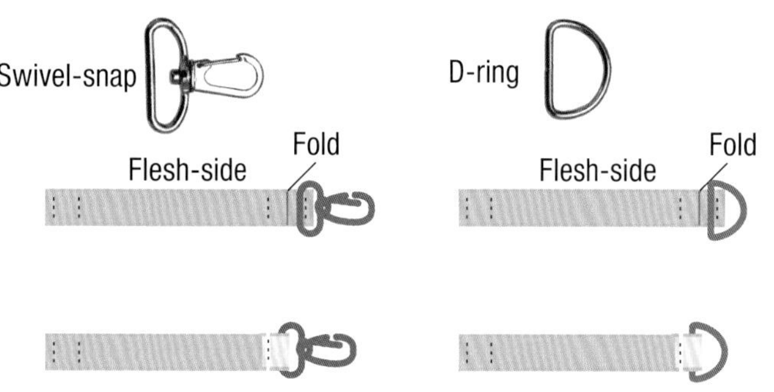

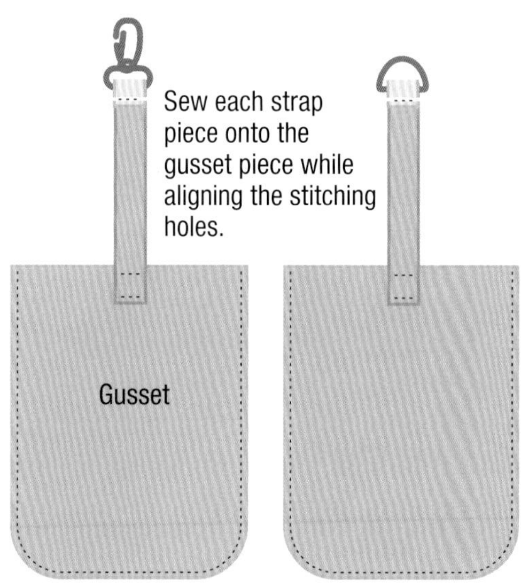

3 Place a cord in the middle of the handle piece and fold the leather around it. Align the stitching holes, and then glue and sew. Refer to "Making a Bag Handle" on page 72.

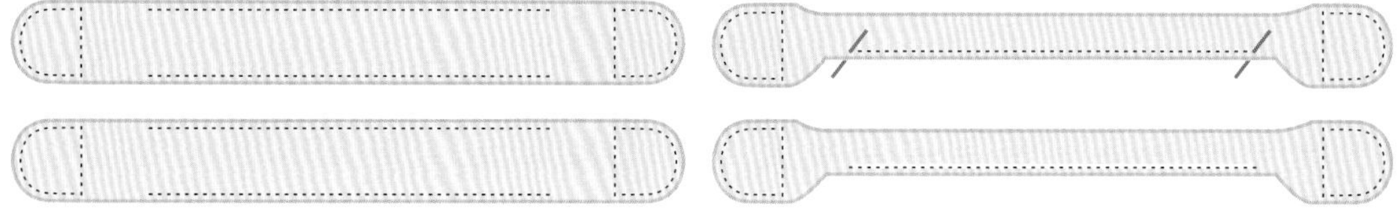

4 Moisten the pocket piece and bend in order to lightly mark it.

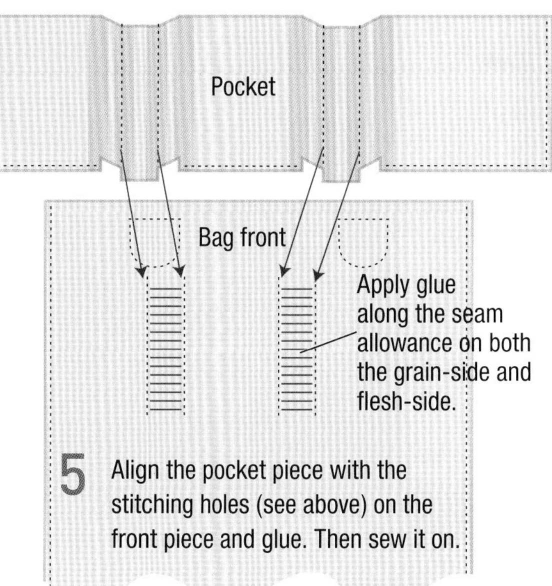

5 Align the pocket piece with the stitching holes (see above) on the front piece and glue. Then sew it on.

6 Moisten the bent part and then hold it down firmly.

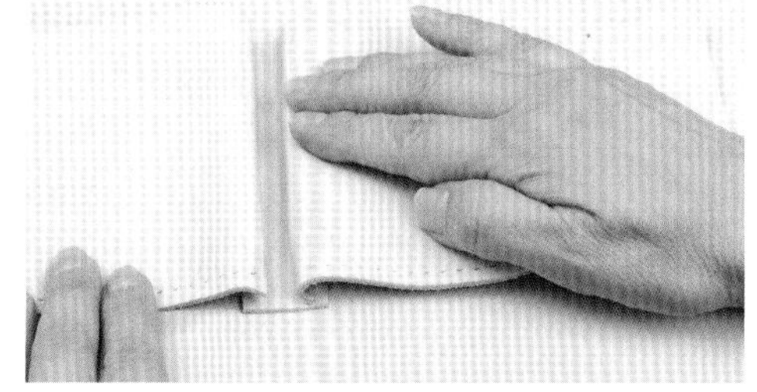

7 After the moistened area has dried, glue down the bottom seam allowance of the pocket piece. Pierce a lacing needle through each stitching hole on the pocket piece through to bag's front piece.

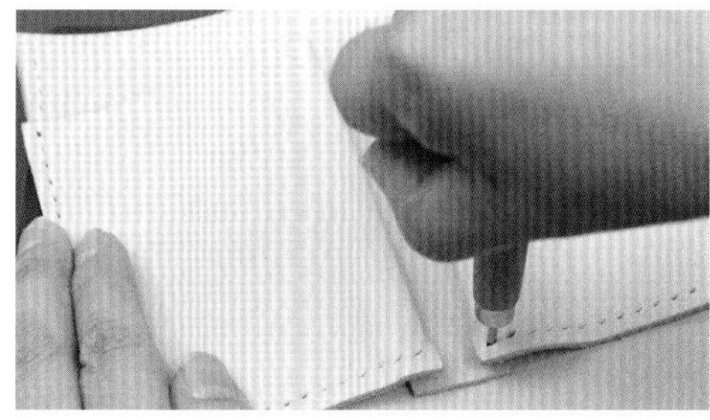

8 Sew along the pierced holes.

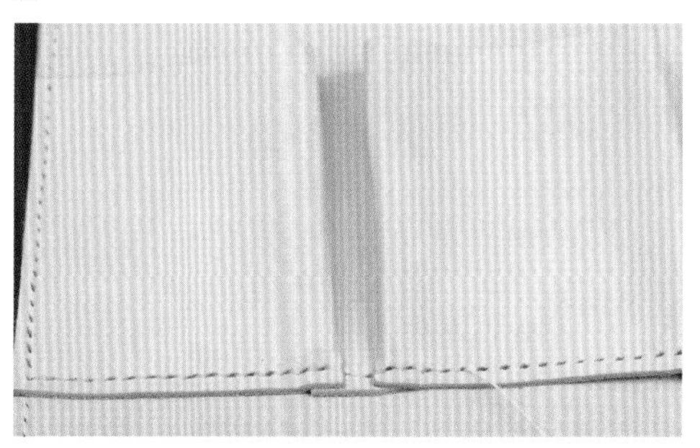

9 Glue the partition piece onto the opposite side of the pocket piece (the flesh side) while aligning the marked stitching holes. Then sew the leather.

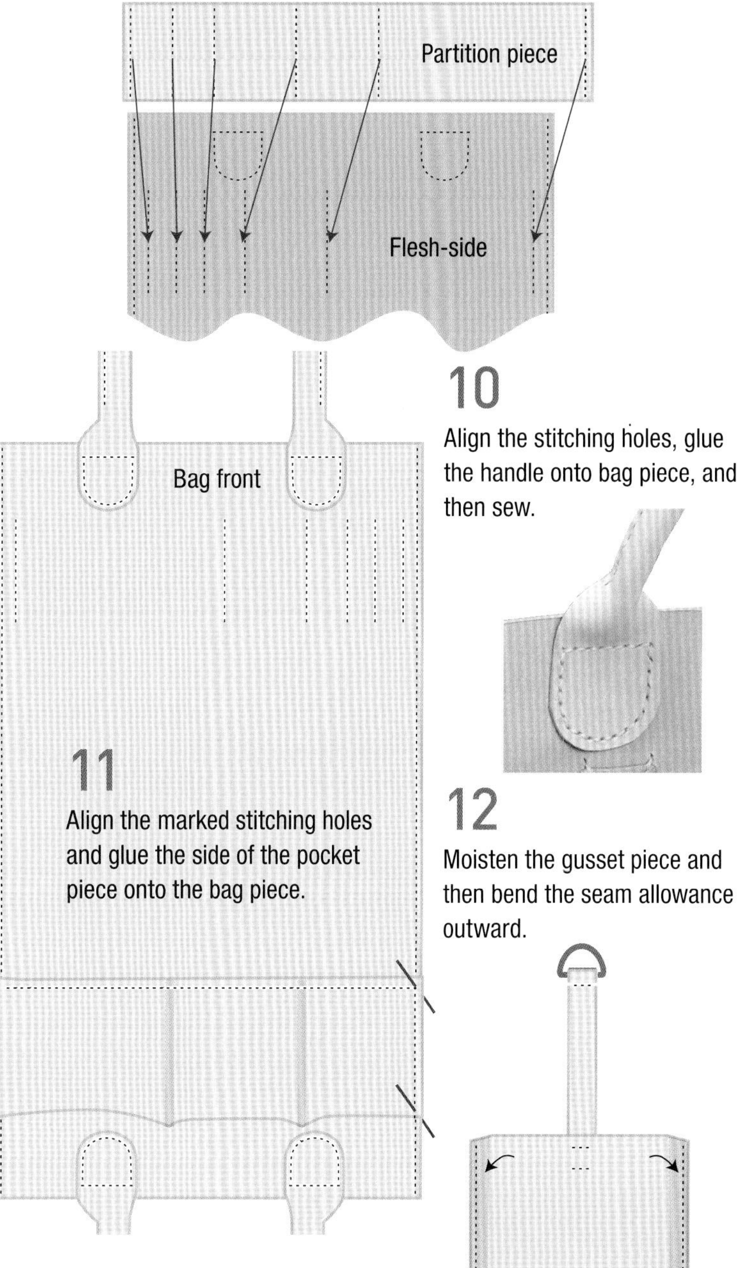

11 Align the marked stitching holes and glue the side of the pocket piece onto the bag piece.

10 Align the stitching holes, glue the handle onto bag piece, and then sew.

12 Moisten the gusset piece and then bend the seam allowance outward.

13 Align the marked stitching holes and secure the leather temporarily with thread while gluing the bottom side of the gusset piece onto the bag piece. Next, glue each side of the gusset onto the bag piece while putting a piece of paper between the two pieces. Refer to “Gluing on a Large Sheet of Leather” on page 76. Sew the leather.

Sew side of pocket piece together with the side of the gusset piece

Glue bottom first

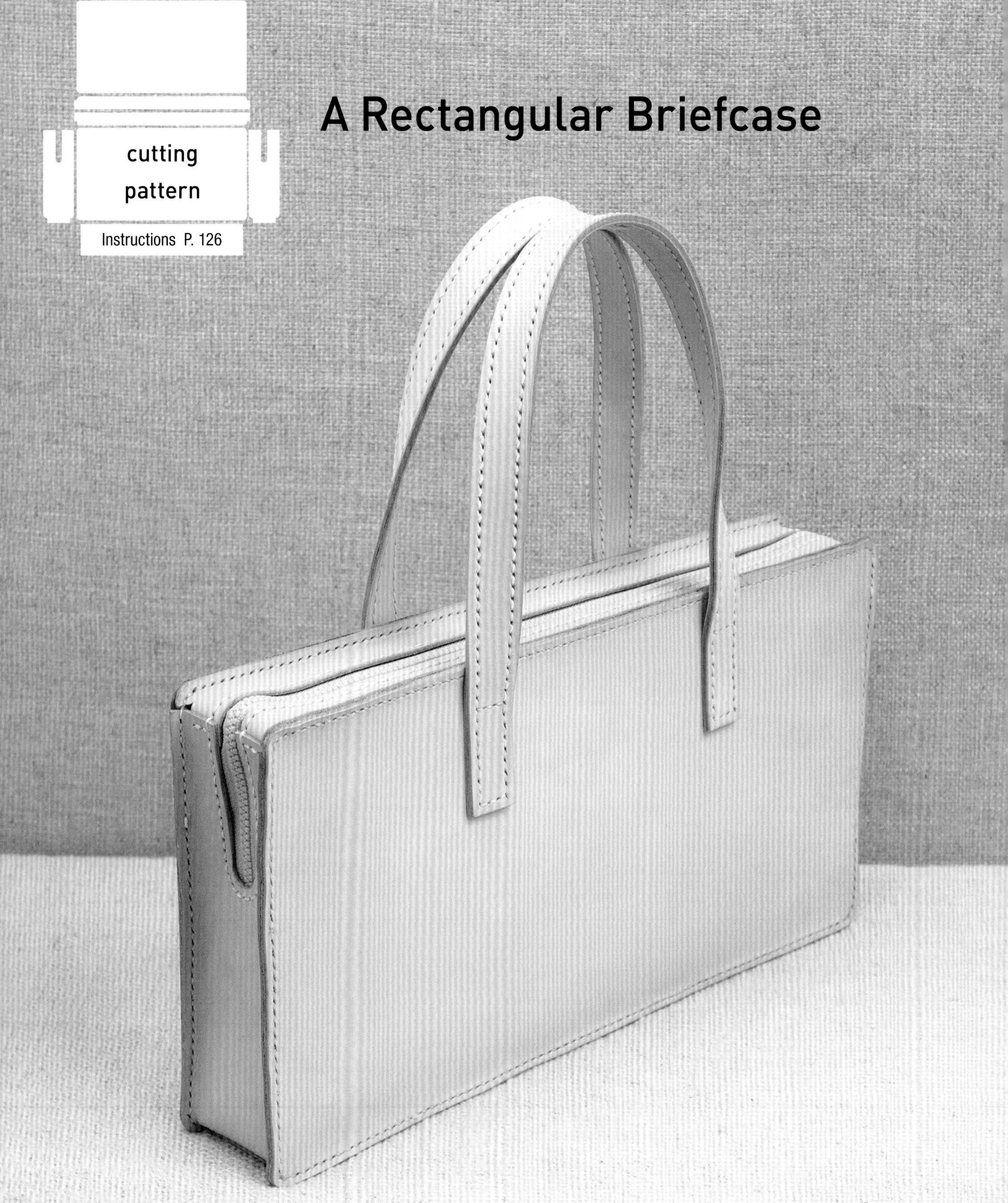

A Rectangular Briefcase

This is a briefcase that has gussets on four sides. Put the gusset pieces together first and then glue them onto the main piece.

detail

Making a Four-sided Gusset Bag

This type of bag is made by stitching four gusset pieces and encasing that in the two main pieces. In this section, instructions are given for the fabrication of a "rectangular bag." "Briefcase" also uses the same method, only the size is different, so please refer to this section for the briefcase.

how to make

A Rectangular Bag (P. 124)

A Briefcase (P. 130)

1 Punch the stitching holes and cut out the leather according to the pattern. Burnish the flesh-side and the edges of the leather.

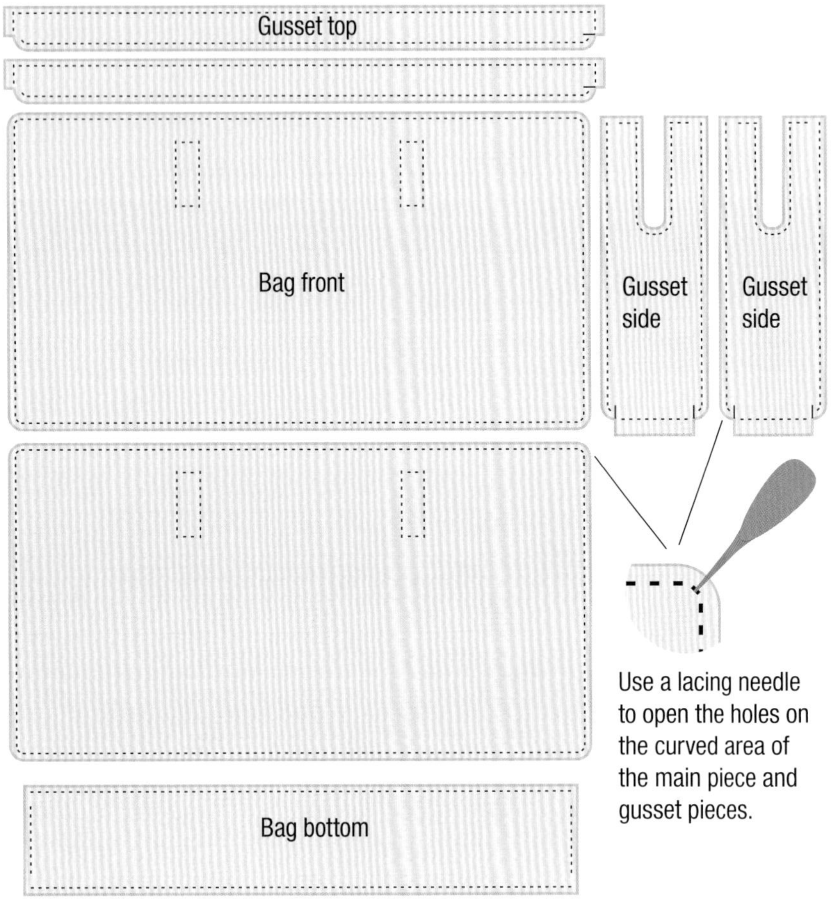

Gusset top

Bag front

Gusset side

Gusset side

Bag bottom

Handle

Use a lacing needle to open the holes on the curved area of the main piece and gusset pieces.

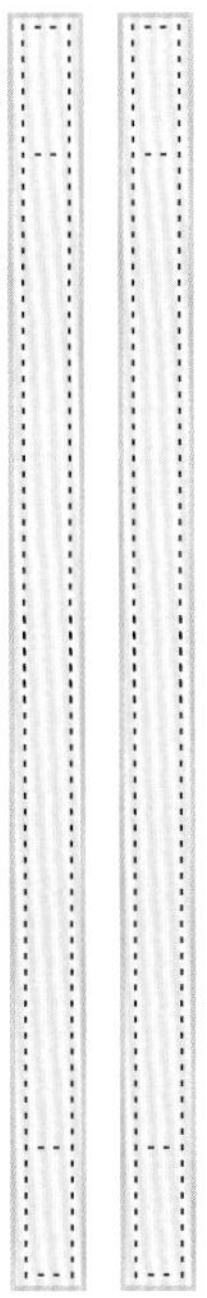

2 Punch stitching holes and cut out the leather for making two handle pieces according to the pattern. Refer to "Long-Narrow Strips of Leather" on page 33. Glue each handle piece on a separate leather strip to make it two-ply. Refer to "Making a Bag Handle" on page 72.

3 Stitch each handle onto the main piece. Refer to "Making a Bag Handle" on page 72. Glue each handle onto the main piece while aligning the stitching holes. Then stitch.

4 As seen in the figures below, glue the gusset pieces one by one while aligning the marked stitching holes. Then stitch.

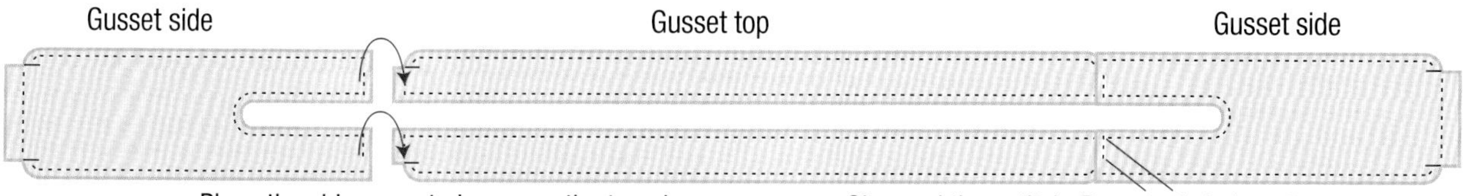

Gusset side

Gusset top

Gusset side

Place the side gusset piece over the top piece

Glue and then stitch. Do not stitch the edge.

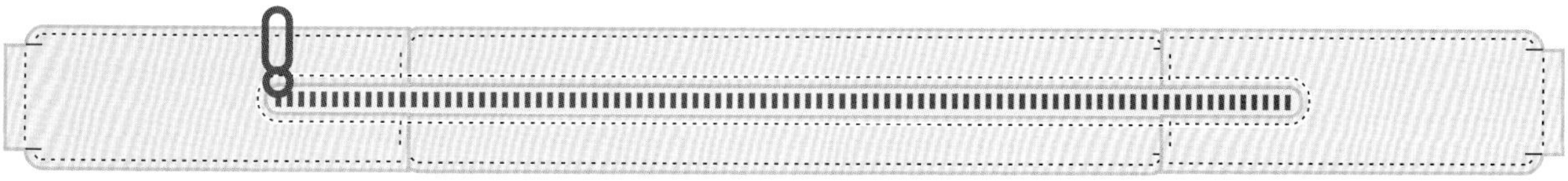

Glue on a zipper and then sew it.

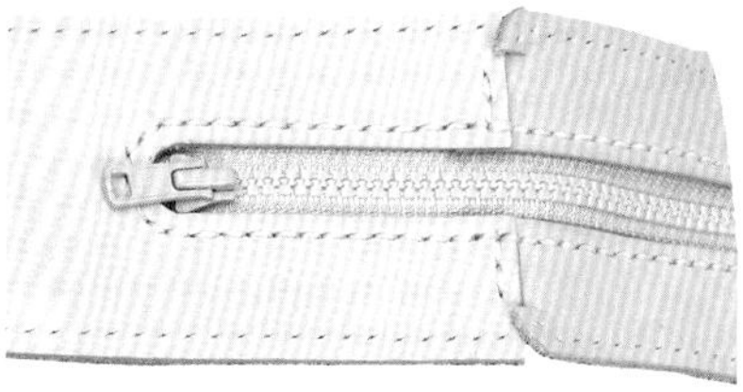

Glue the edge of the zipper onto the flesh-side. Cut remnants of leather according to the size of the zipper tape end that you want to cover. Then glue the piece of leather onto the zipper tape end.

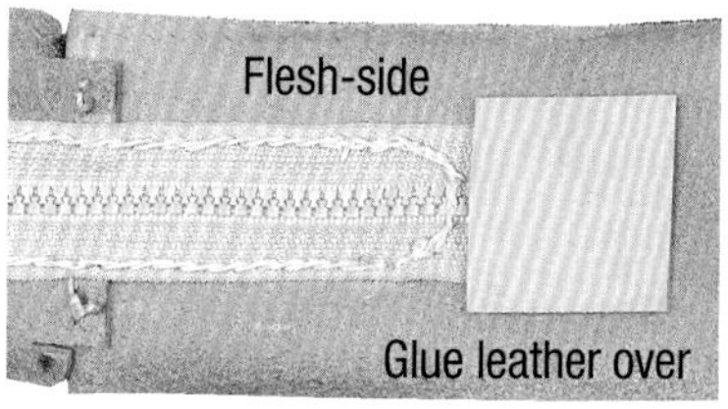

Flesh-side

Glue leather over

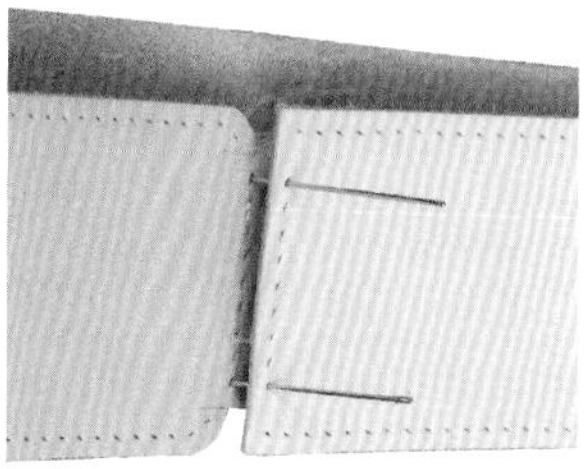

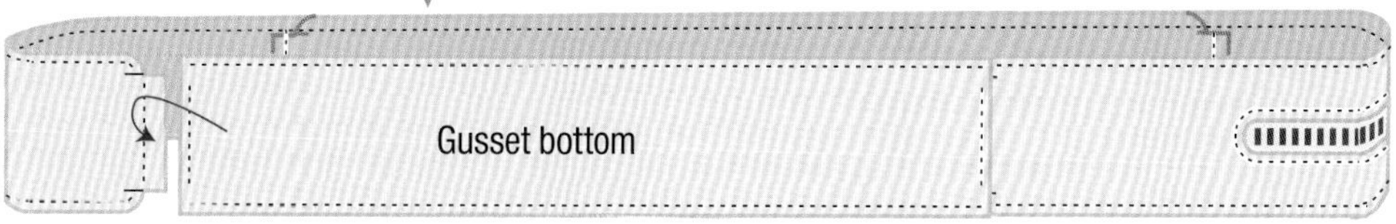

Overlap bottom-side gusset with the side gusset and then glue and stitch.

5 Moisten the circumference of the combined gusset piece and bend the circumference outward. Refer to "Gluing on a Large Sheet of Leather" on page 76.

Moisten

Bend slightly inside of seam allowance

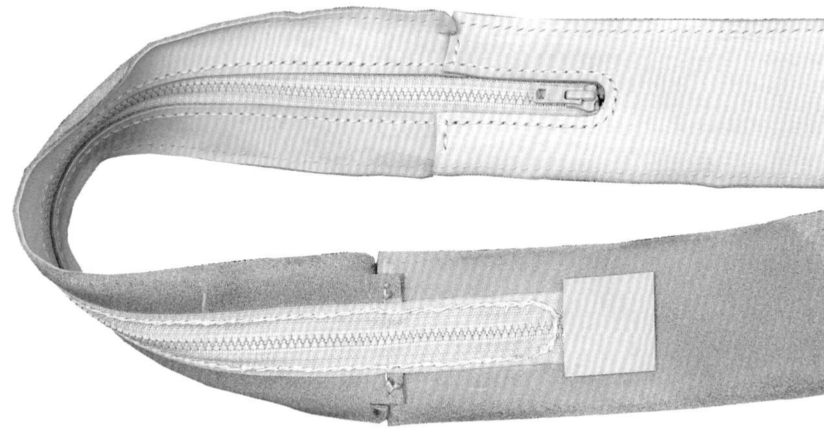

6 Join front piece and top piece while aligning the marked stitching holes and temporarily secure with thread.
Put a piece of paper in between and glue the pieces together while aligning the stitching holes every few stitches. Refer to "Gluing on a Large Sheet of Leather" on page 76.

[Pattern]

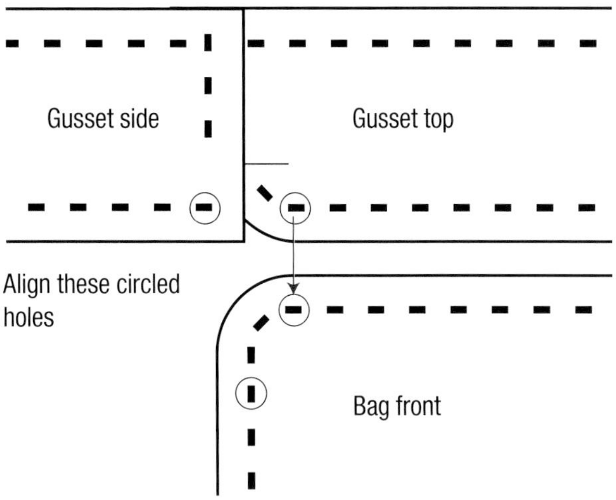

Gusset side
Gusset top
Align these circled holes
Bag front

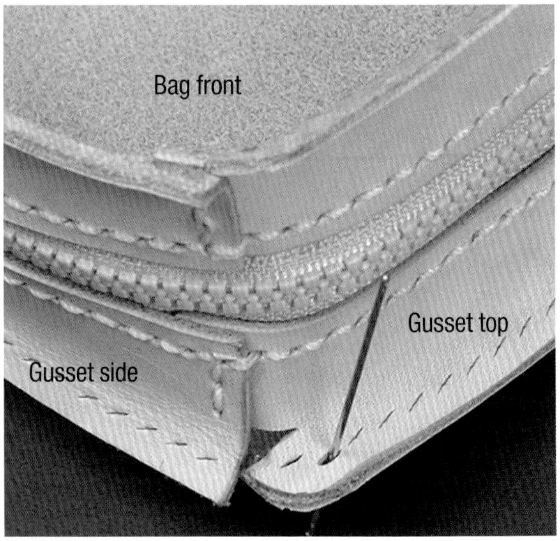

Bag front
Gusset top
Gusset side

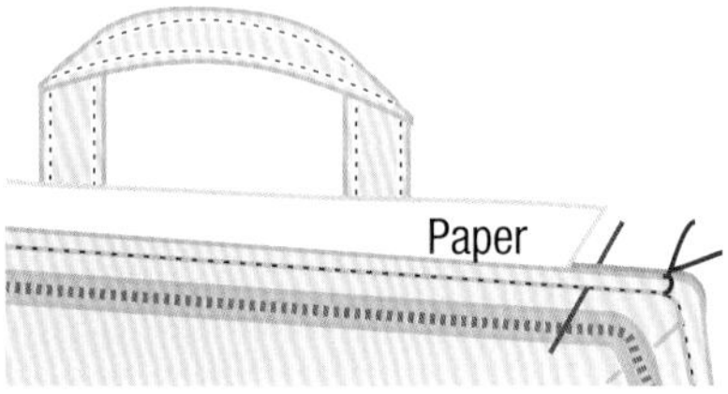

Paper

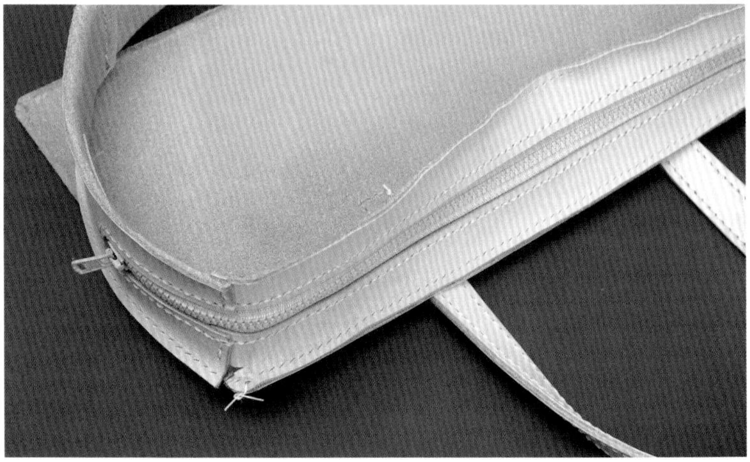

The bag's front and top gusset bonded together

7 Glue front piece and gusset piece in the same manner as in step 6.

[Pattern]

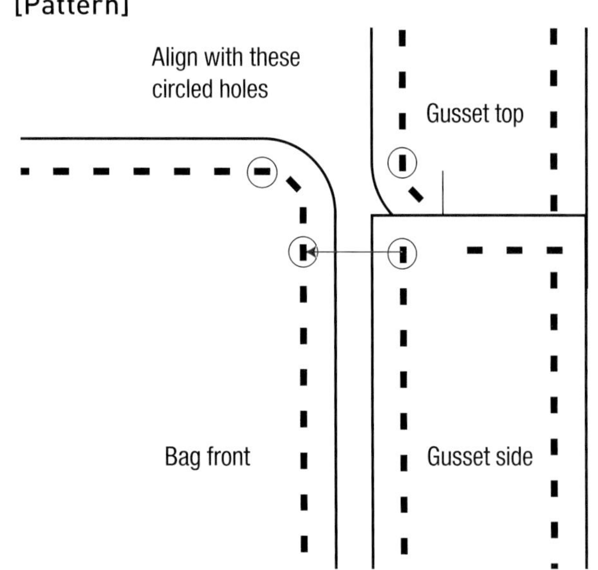

8 Same as step 6, glue front piece and gusset.

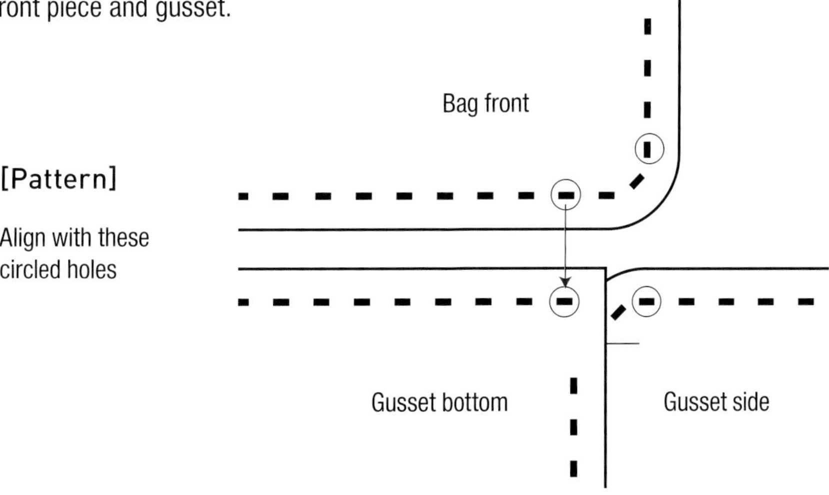

9 Do the same for the opposite side of the bag.

Finished stitching

10 Moisten the leather and adjust the shape of the bag.

11 File uneven seam allowances to adjust and then burnish the edges.

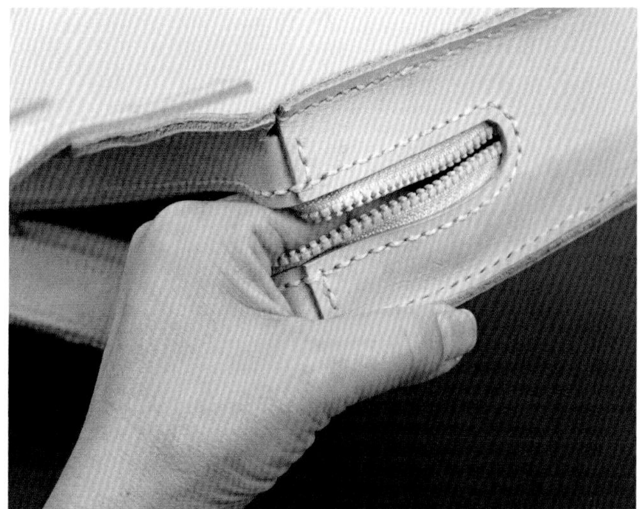

cutting pattern

Instructions P. 126

A Briefcase

This bag shares the same structure as the rectangular briefcase, but the size and design of the handle are different.

How to Alter Patterns

The basic design of a bag is basically decided by the manner of attaching the front piece and gusset. Using one basic form, you can alter the pattern and change the design of the handle to make bags that have different designs and uses. Feel free to try to make you own original bag! For changing handles, just refer to "Changing a Bag Handle" on page 71.

[Alterations That Do Not Affect the Seam]

Altering areas that do not have a seam, such as single piece pouches or bags, is easiest.

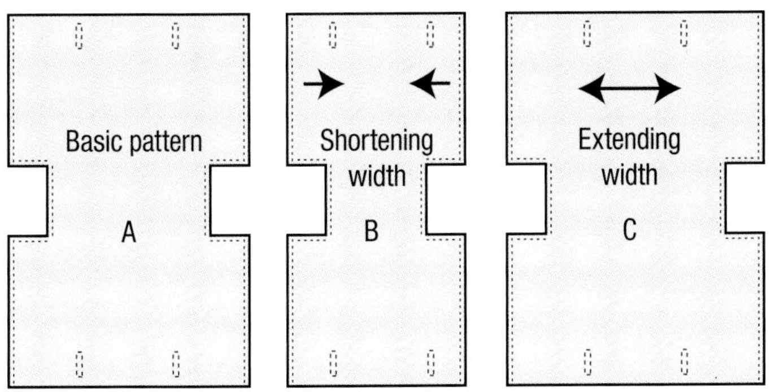

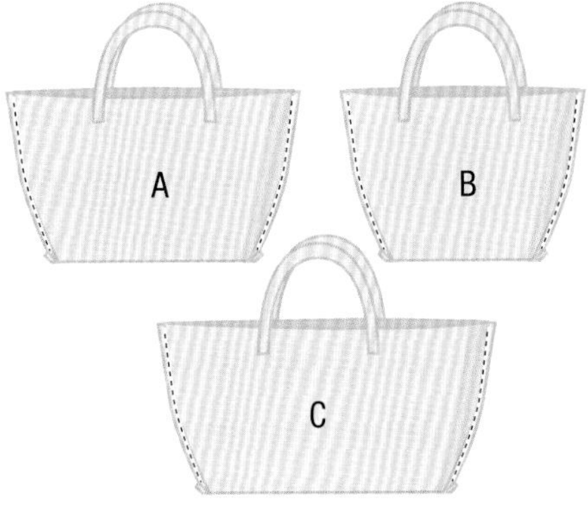

Do not make big changes to the handle's position. If the change is drastic, it could make holding the bag uncomfortable.

Altering Pattern

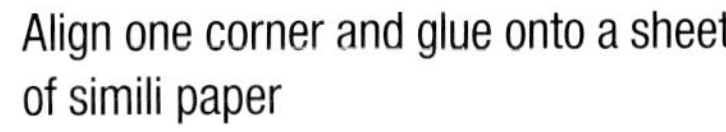

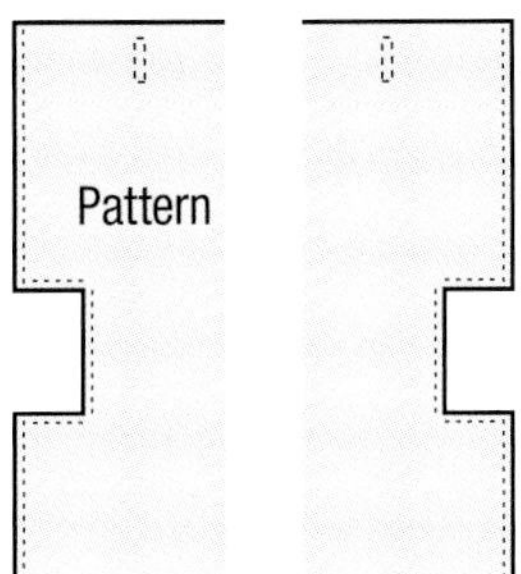

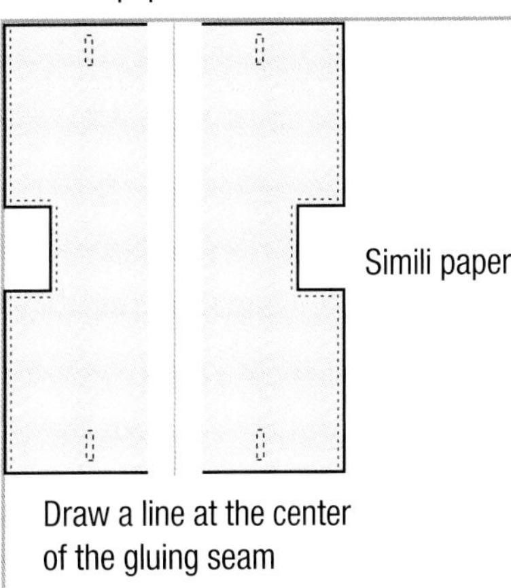

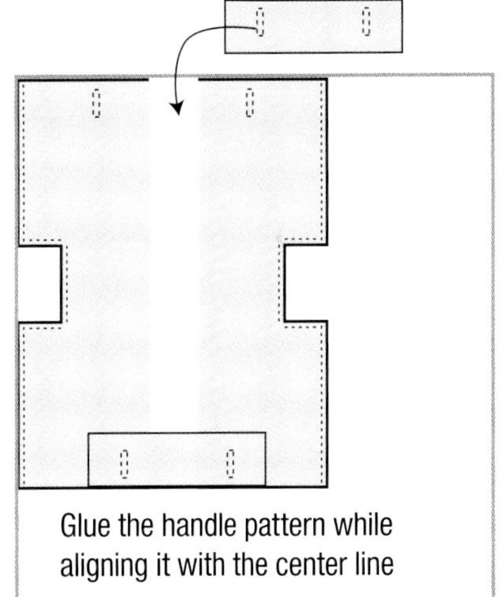

[When Alterations Affect Seams]

When changing the size of the area where stitching holes are located, just adjust the interval of the stitching holes when cutting the pattern.

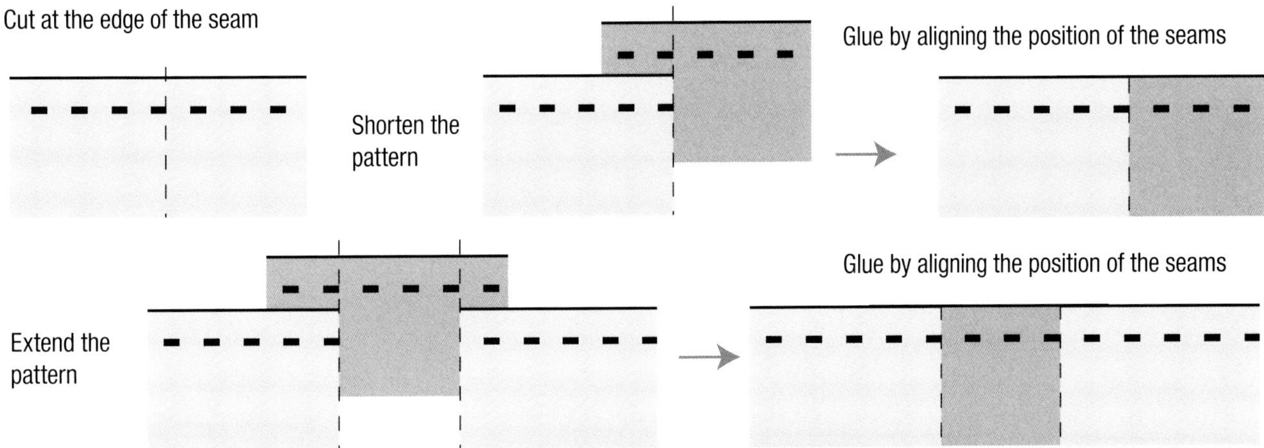

Methods of Altering Patterns

The figures are drawn without handles and accessories.

[Needle Case P. 44]

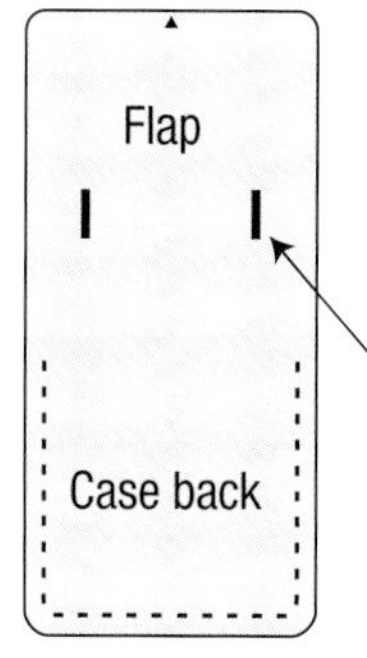

This needle case is for shorter needles. When you are making a case for longer needles, extend the length of the flap part on the back-side of the case according to the size of the needles. After attaching the metal fittings, confirm the folding position of the flap part, and then alter the stitching position of the handle.

[A Journal Cover P.54]

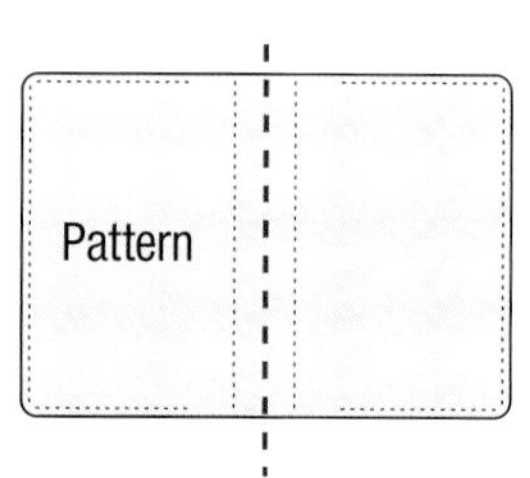

This is for a journal that has a spine width of approximately 10 mm (3/8 in.). When using a journal with a different spine width, cut the pattern at the center and adjust the width accordingly.

[A Three-gored Bag P. 74·78]

Alter front piece width

Since there is no seam, cut the front piece pattern, make changes, and then glue it back together.

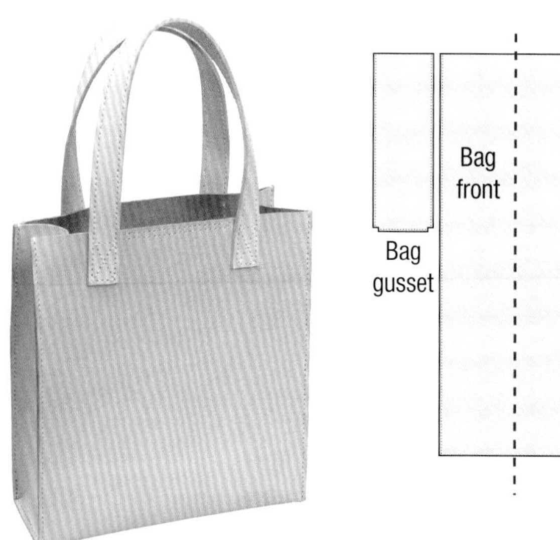

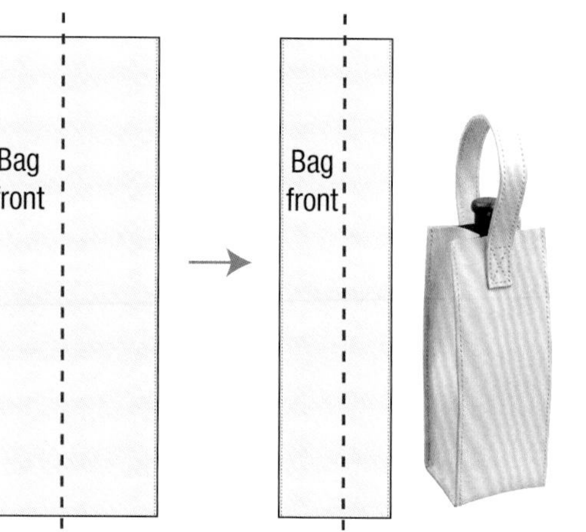

Though the size is slightly different, the finished image is somewhat like the one on the left.

Altering height Adjust the height of the gusset and front piece by cutting, while referring to "When Alterations Affect Seams" on page 131, and glue together.

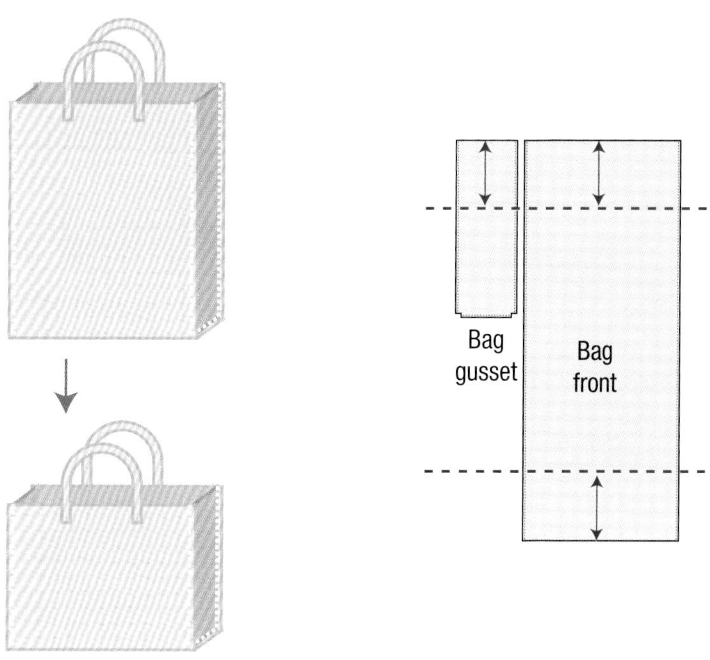

[Bag Using a Single Sheet of Leather P. 80, 84, 88, 94]

Alter height using the same method.

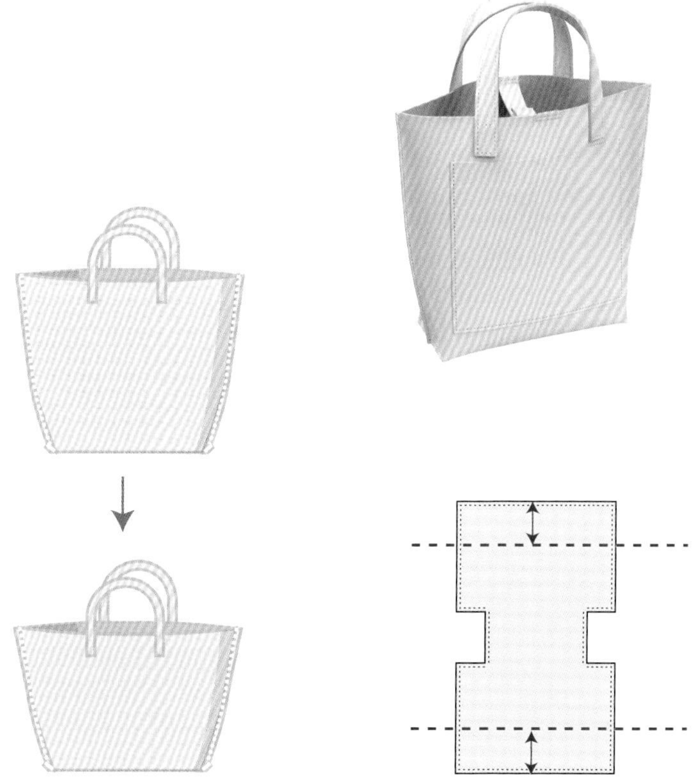

Alter Width

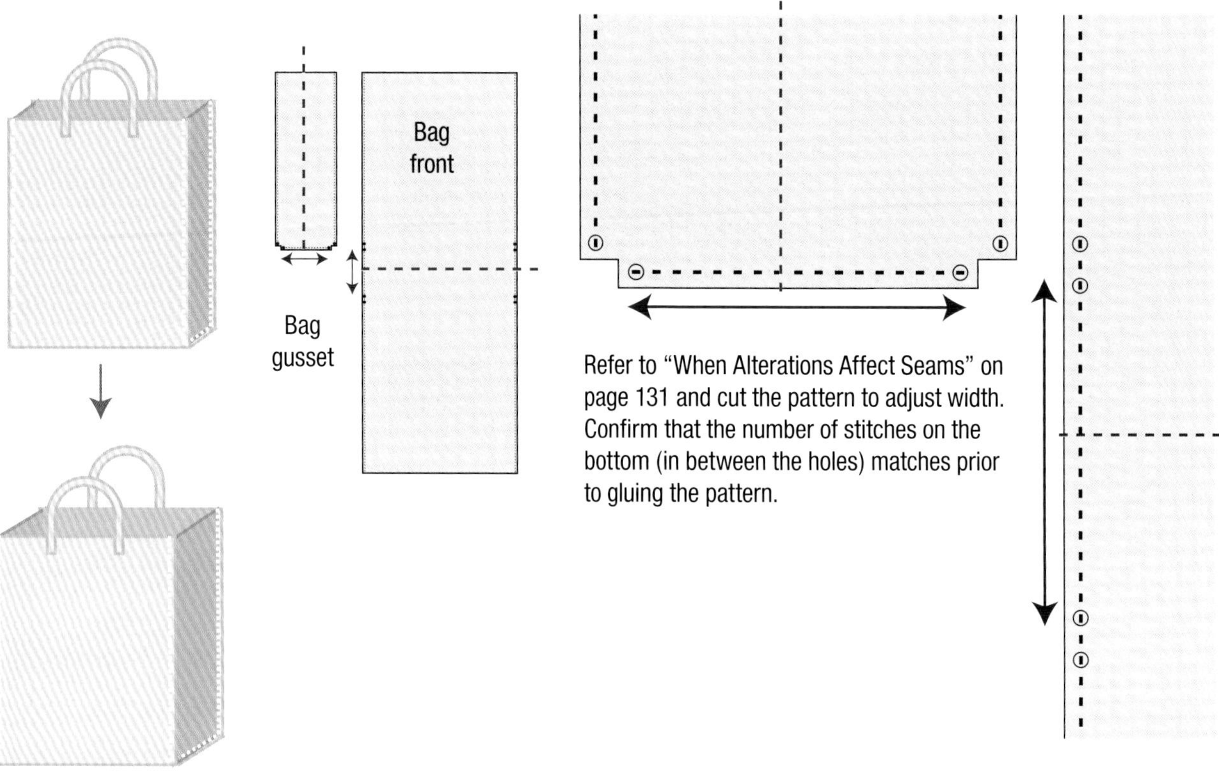

Refer to "When Alterations Affect Seams" on page 131 and cut the pattern to adjust width. Confirm that the number of stitches on the bottom (in between the holes) matches prior to gluing the pattern.

[A Rectangular Briefcase·A Briefcase P. 124·130]

Altering Height

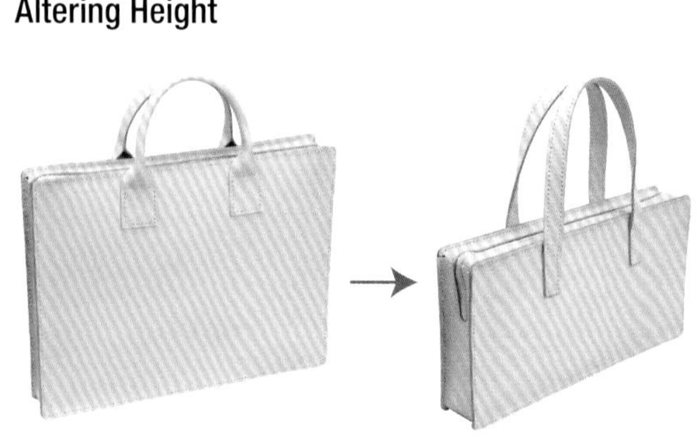

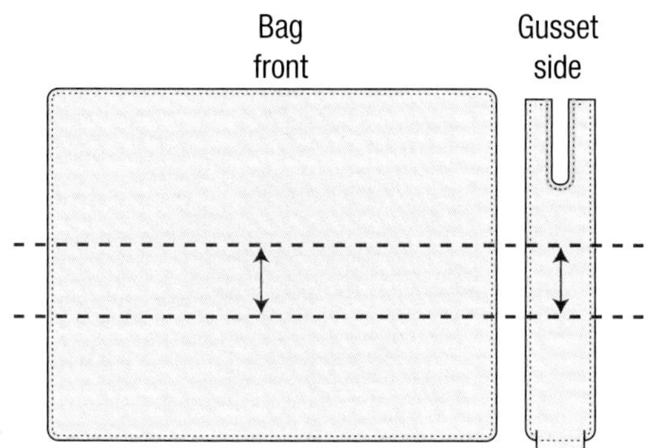

Adjust height of front and gusset patterns and then cut the adjusted patterns. Glue the pattern while aligning the intervals of the stitching holes.

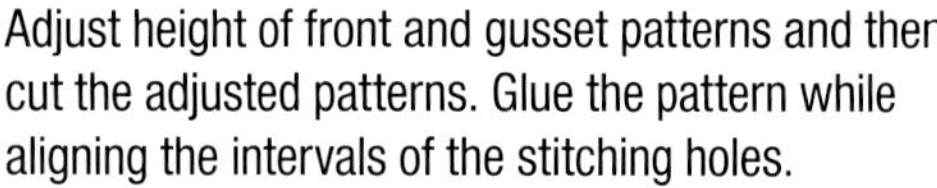

[A Two-gored Travel Bag P. 114]

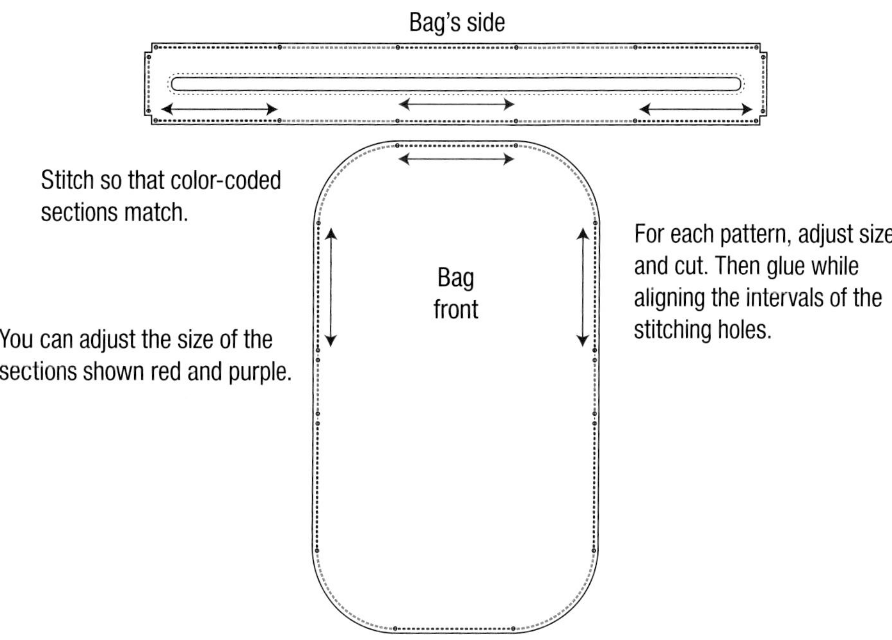

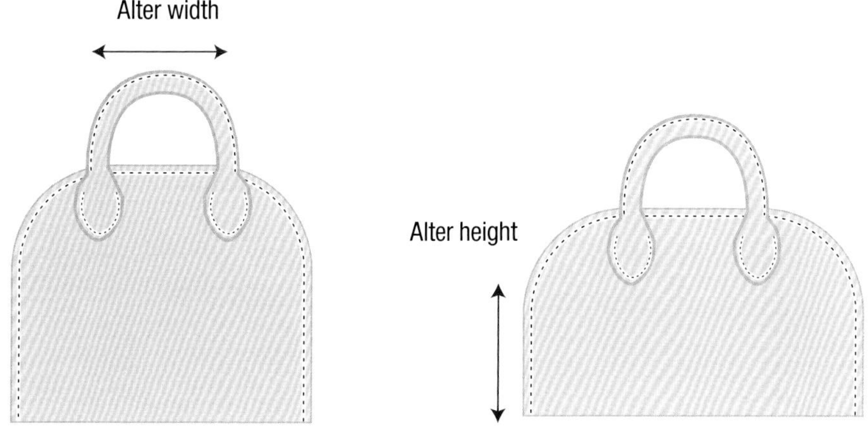

Adjusting Stitching Holes

Once in a while, even though you think that you made sure to align the stitching holes for gluing, you may notice that the number of holes doesn't match. Please use the following method to adjust the stitching holes. The finished shape won't be perfect right away, especially if you can't completely peel off the glued area prior to adjusting. The finished shape is just warped. Moisten the leather so it will stretch and allow the shape to adjust.

[Peeling Off Glued Area]

In order to peel off glued areas, while not stretching the leather, force an awl into a gap in the glued edge.

①: Force the awl in at an angle
②: Pry open the stitched holes

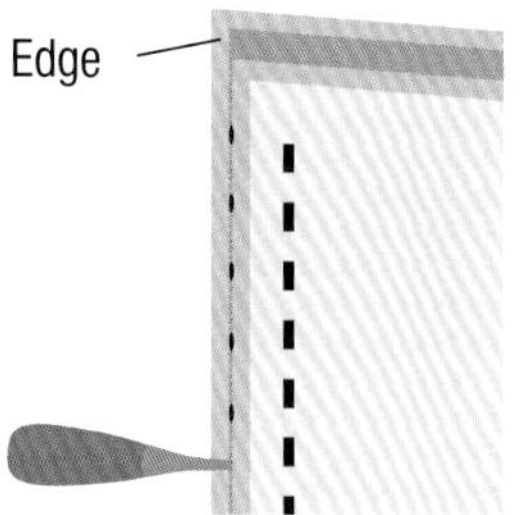

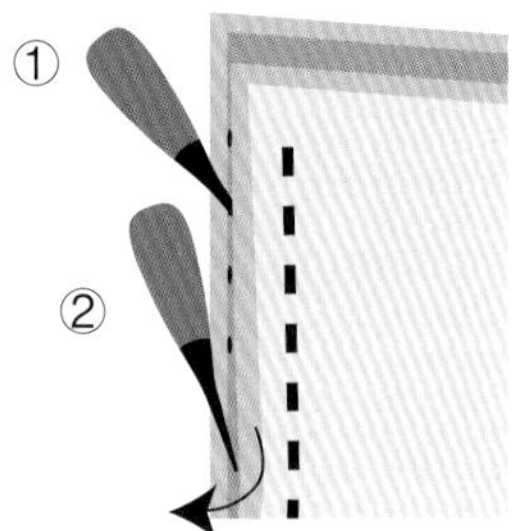

[When Openings Do Not Align]

When cutting the leather to adjust the alignment is not possible for some reason:

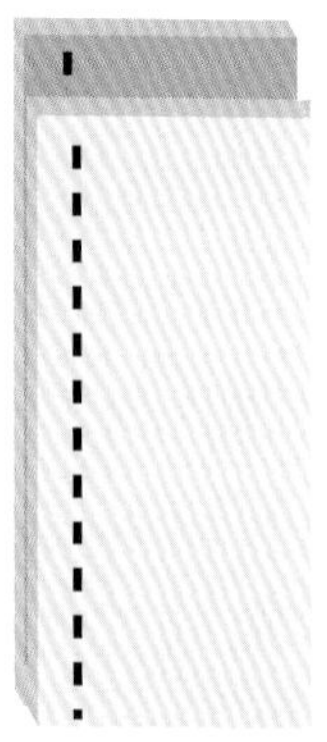

1 Peel off the glued seam allowance about 10 cm (approx. 4 in.) away from an opening.

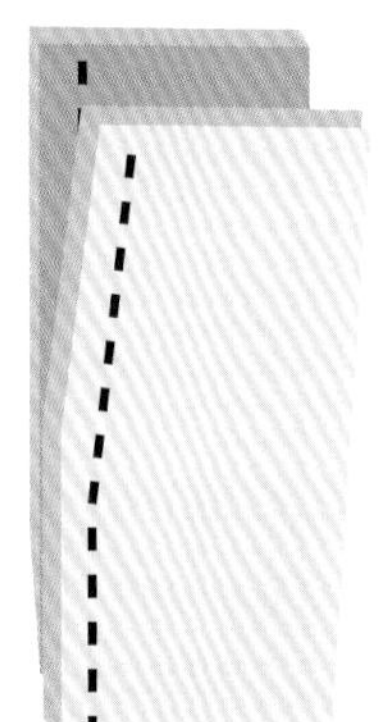

2 Pull the shorter leather so it aligns with the longer.

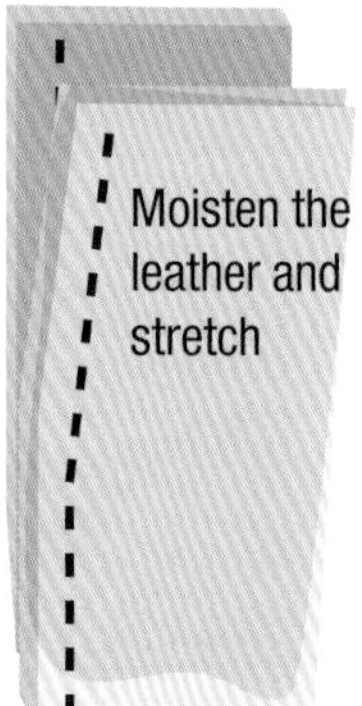

3 After the moistened leather has dried, add one hole by piercing a lacing needle through the leather.

4 Stop stitching a few holes before the added hole. Then start stitching from an opening while aligning the holes with an awl.

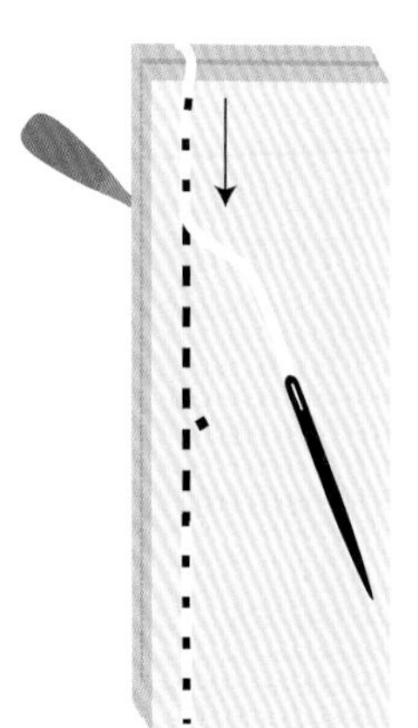

5 Open the joined seam and apply glue. Then bond it securely.

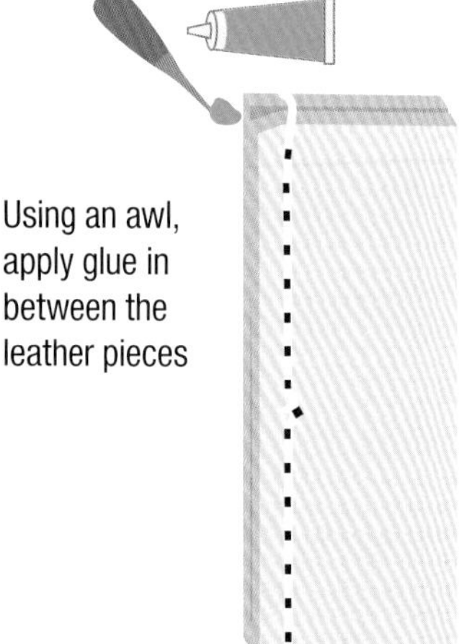

[Stitch Does Not Align at Middle]

Similar to adjusting an opening, moisten the leather to stretch, and then add a hole and sew.

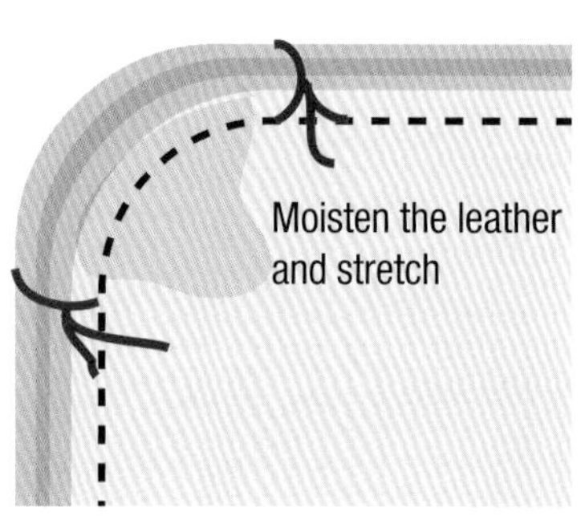

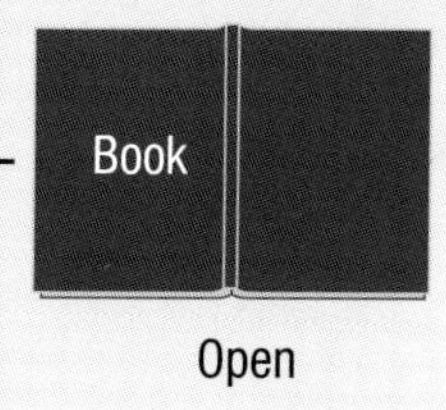

0  20

When photocopied at 160% scale, the gauge is 20 cm ($\frac{7}{8}$ in.) long.

Chapter 4

Patterns

These are the patterns with stitching-hole marks used in chapter 2 and 3.

- If unspecified, produce only one pattern per diagram.
- Since the pattern is scaled-down, only produce the final pattern after photocopying 160% scale on A3 (ledger) size paper.
- Make photocopies of the patterns by firmly opening the pages. This will prevent the patterns from becoming distorted.
- On enlarged photocopies, make sure that the gauge beside the pattern is actually 20 cm ($7\frac{7}{8}$ in.) in length.
- The finished size for each project is only approximated. It is slightly different from the pattern size.
- After enlarging to 160% scale, the metal fittings become close to actual size.

Contents [Pattern Pages]

 In chapter 4 the page number is printed inside of each page to make photocopying the pattern easier.

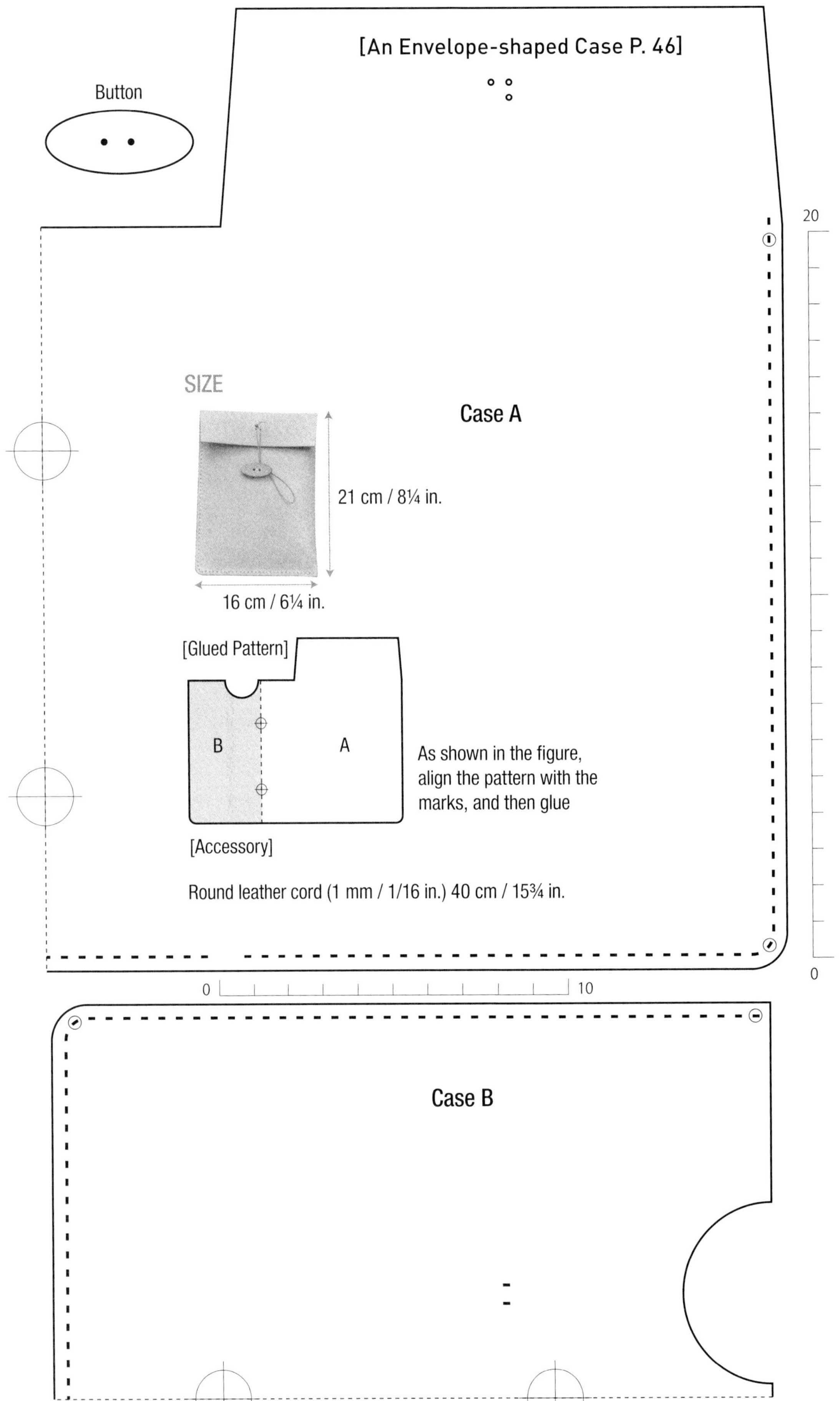
[An Envelope-shaped Case P. 46]
Button
SIZE
Case A
21 cm / 8¼ in.
16 cm / 6¼ in.
[Glued Pattern]
B
A
As shown in the figure, align the pattern with the marks, and then glue
[Accessory]
Round leather cord (1 mm / 1/16 in.) 40 cm / 15¾ in.
20
0
0
10
Case B

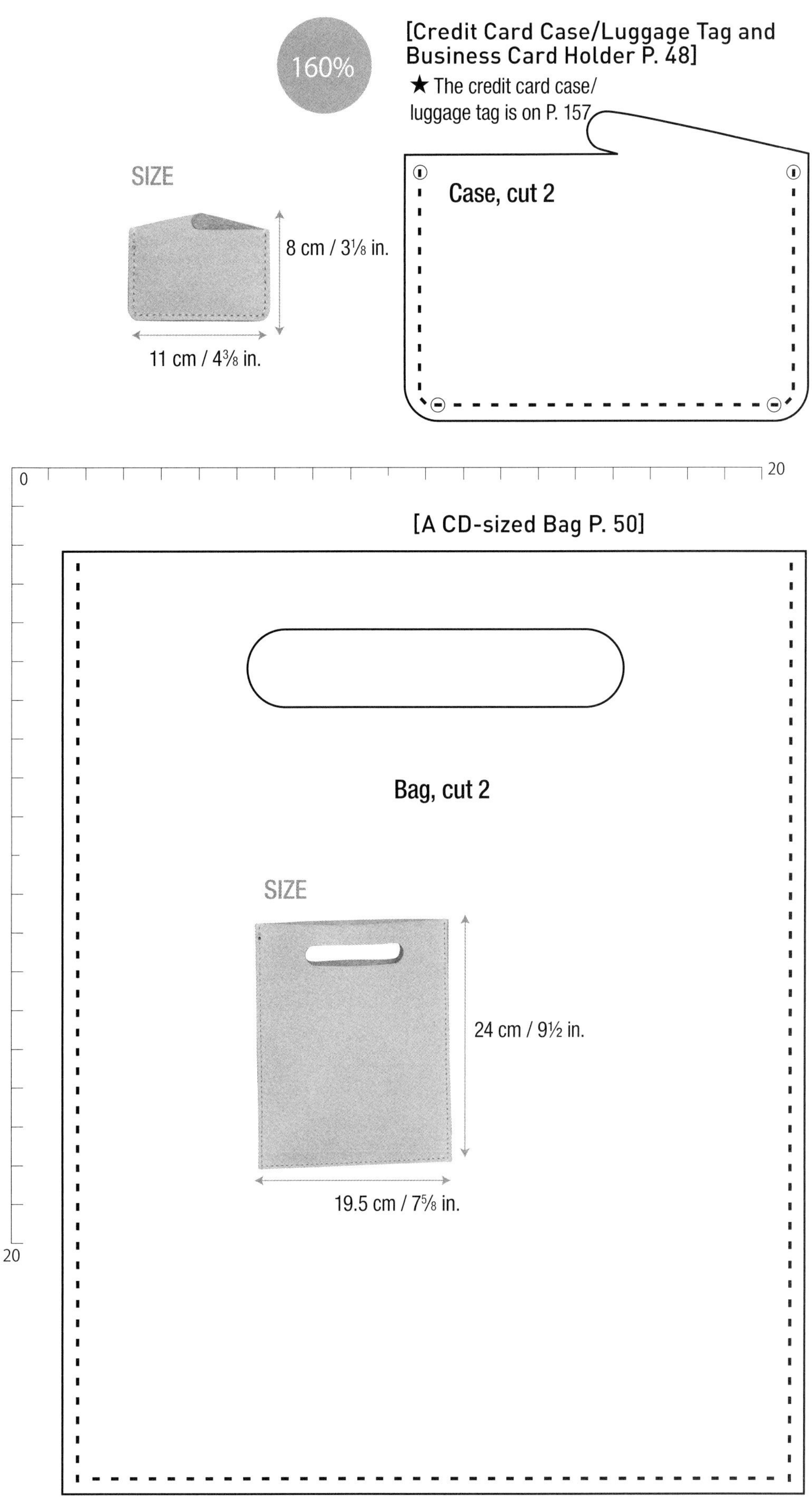
160%
[Credit Card Case/Luggage Tag and Business Card Holder P. 48]
★ The credit card case/ luggage tag is on P. 157
SIZE
8 cm / 3⅛ in.
11 cm / 4⅜ in.
Case, cut 2
0
20
[A CD-sized Bag P. 50]
Bag, cut 2
SIZE
24 cm / 9½ in.
19.5 cm / 7⅝ in.
20

160%

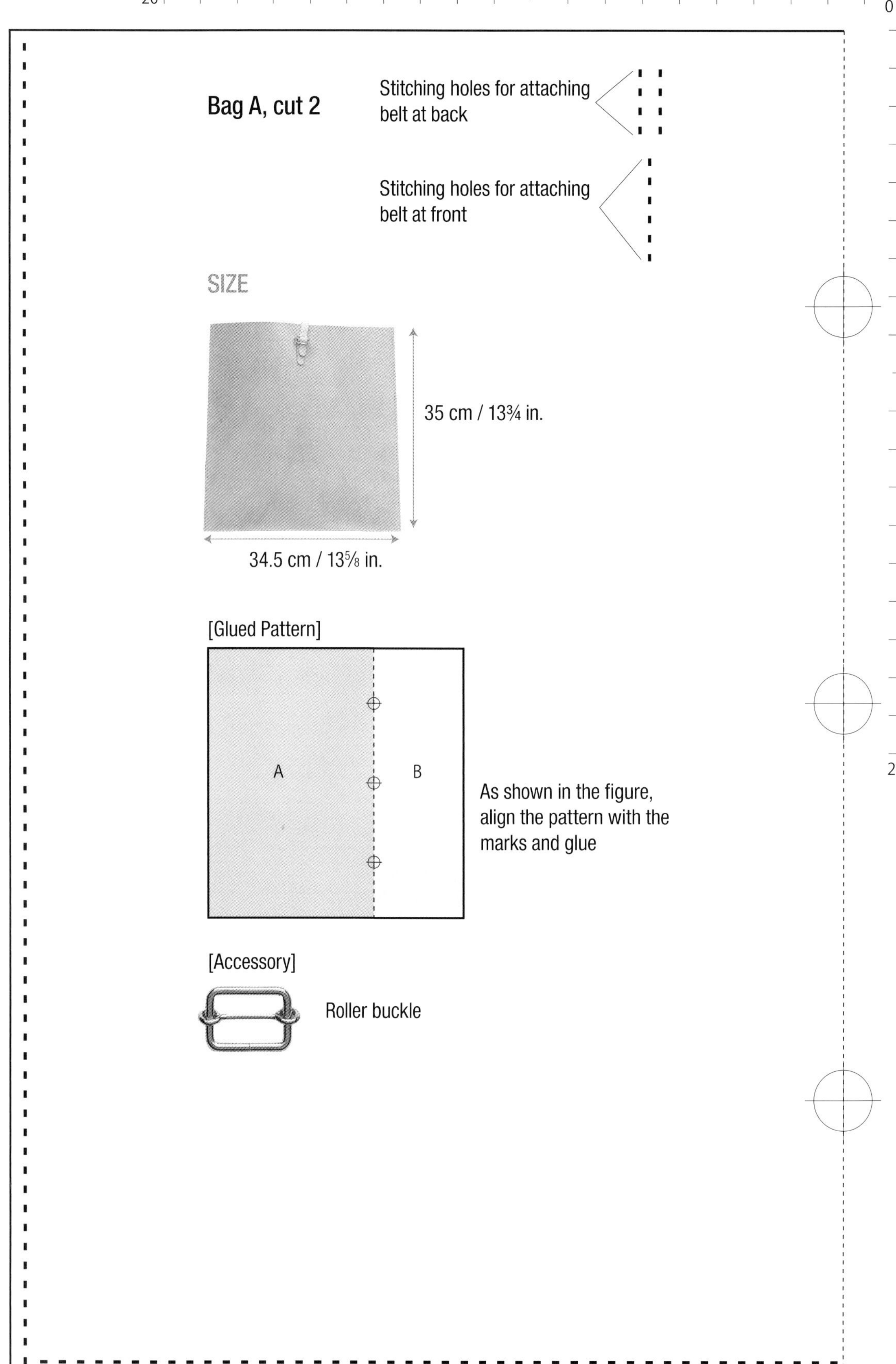
20
0
20
Bag A, cut 2
Stitching holes for attaching belt at back
Stitching holes for attaching belt at front
SIZE
35 cm / 13¾ in.
34.5 cm / 13⅝ in.
[Glued Pattern]
A
B
As shown in the figure, align the pattern with the marks and glue
[Accessory]
Roller buckle

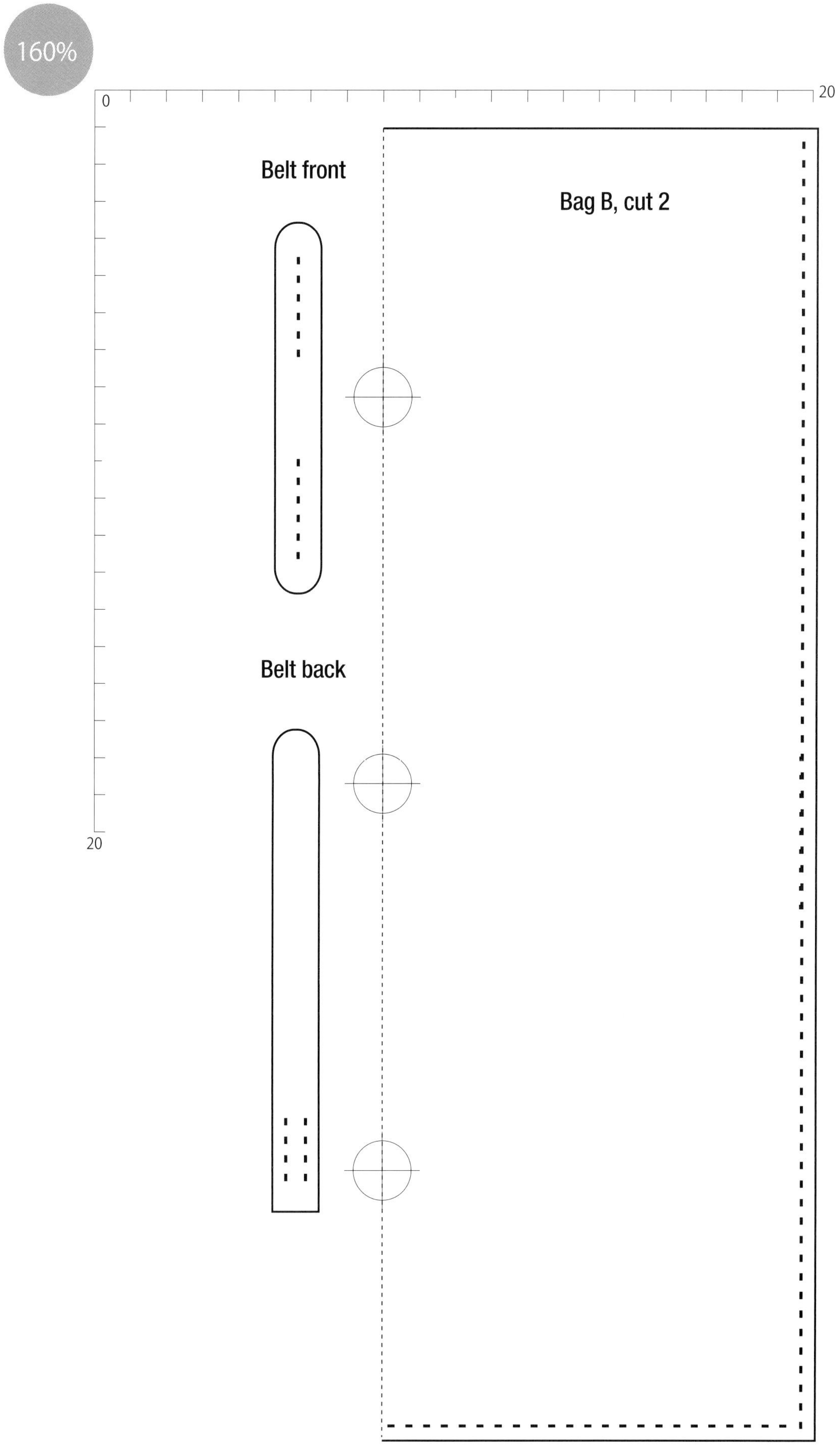
160%
0
20
20
Belt front
Bag B, cut 2
Belt back

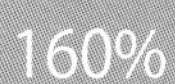

[A Journal Cover P. 54]

160%

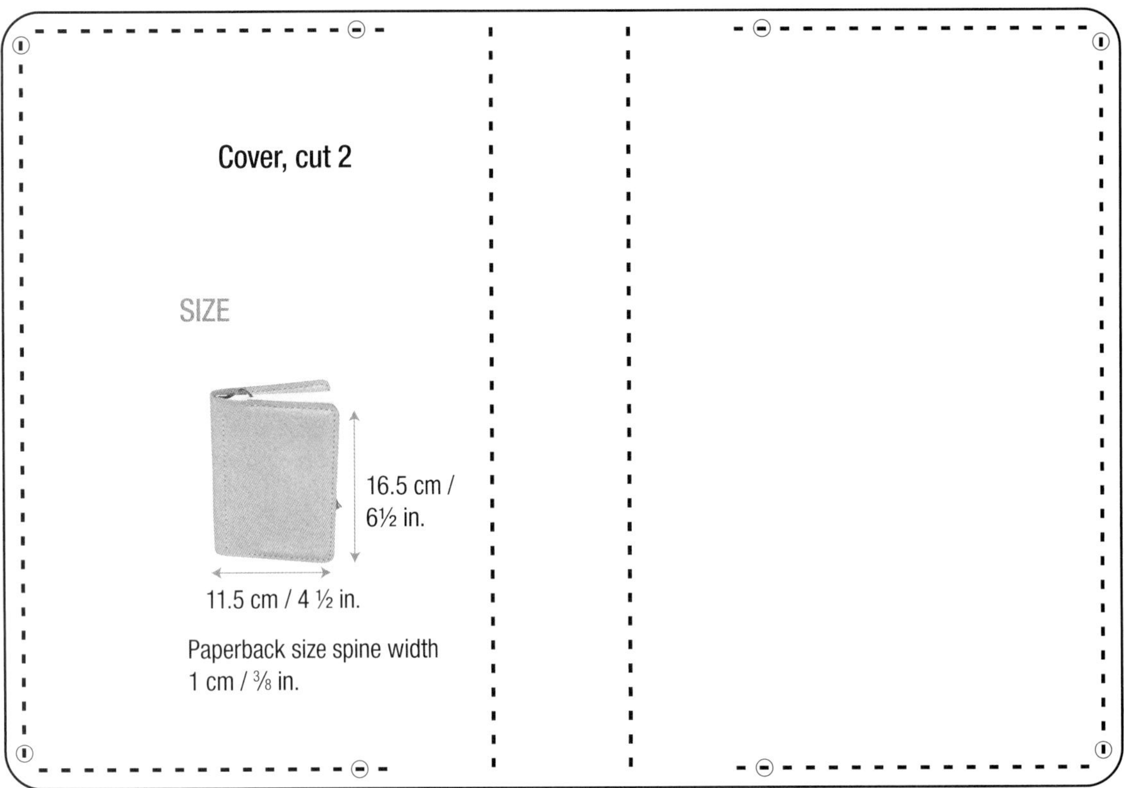

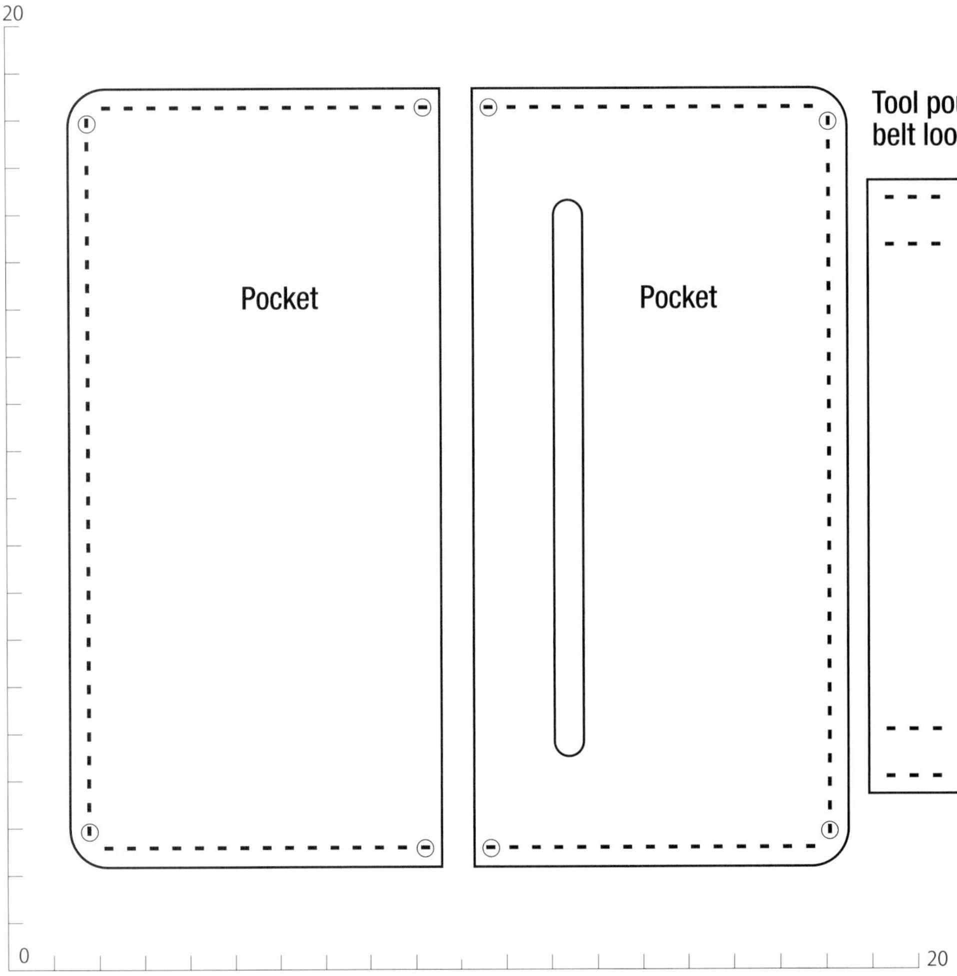

20

Pocket

Pocket

Tool pouch belt loop, cut 2

0

20

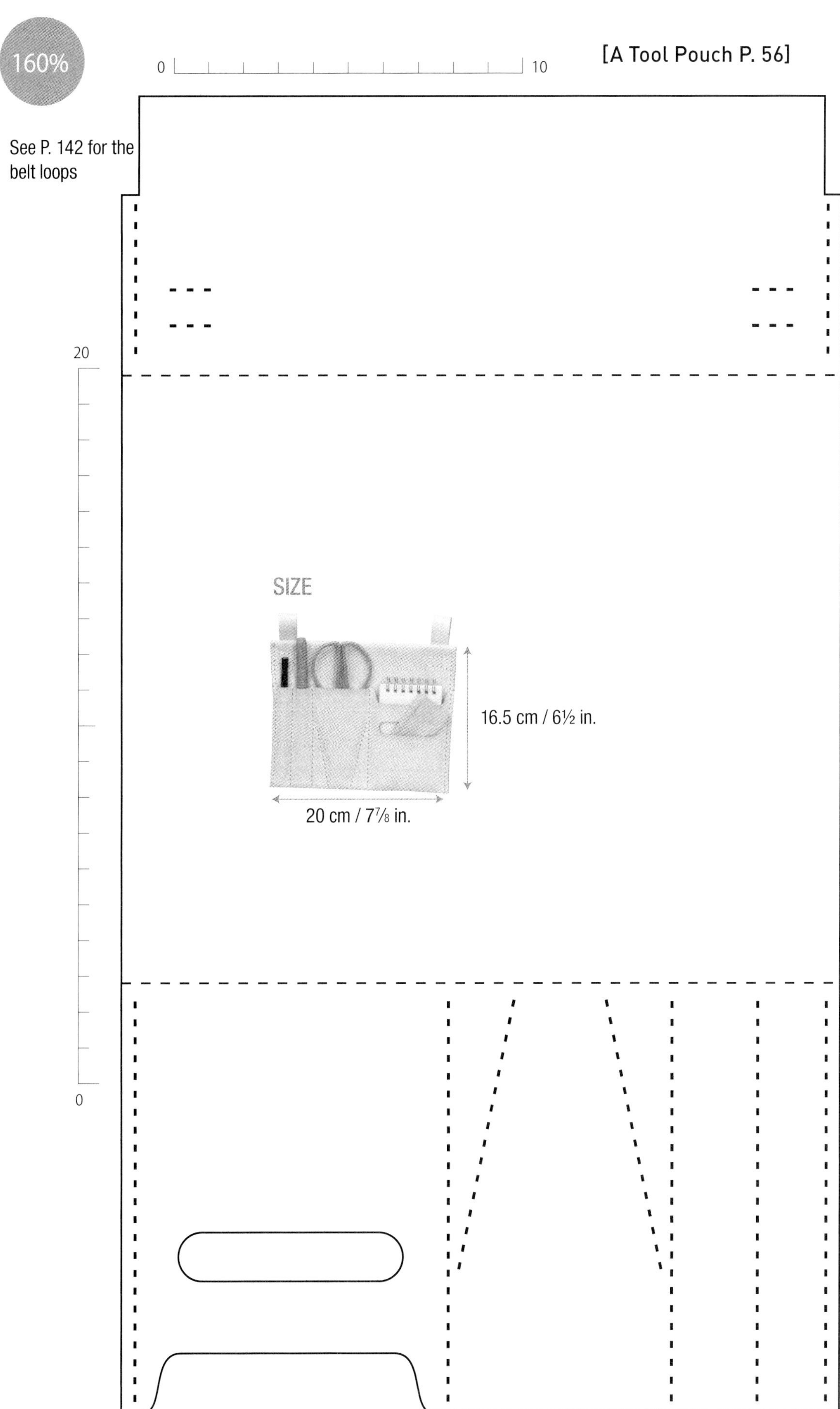
160%
0
10
See P. 142 for the belt loops
20
0
SIZE
16.5 cm / 6½ in.
20 cm / 7⅞ in.

[A Pen Case with a Zipper P. 60]

160%

SIZE
7 cm / 2¾ in.
21 cm / 8¼ in.

[Accessory]

Zipper
18.5 cm / 7¼ in.

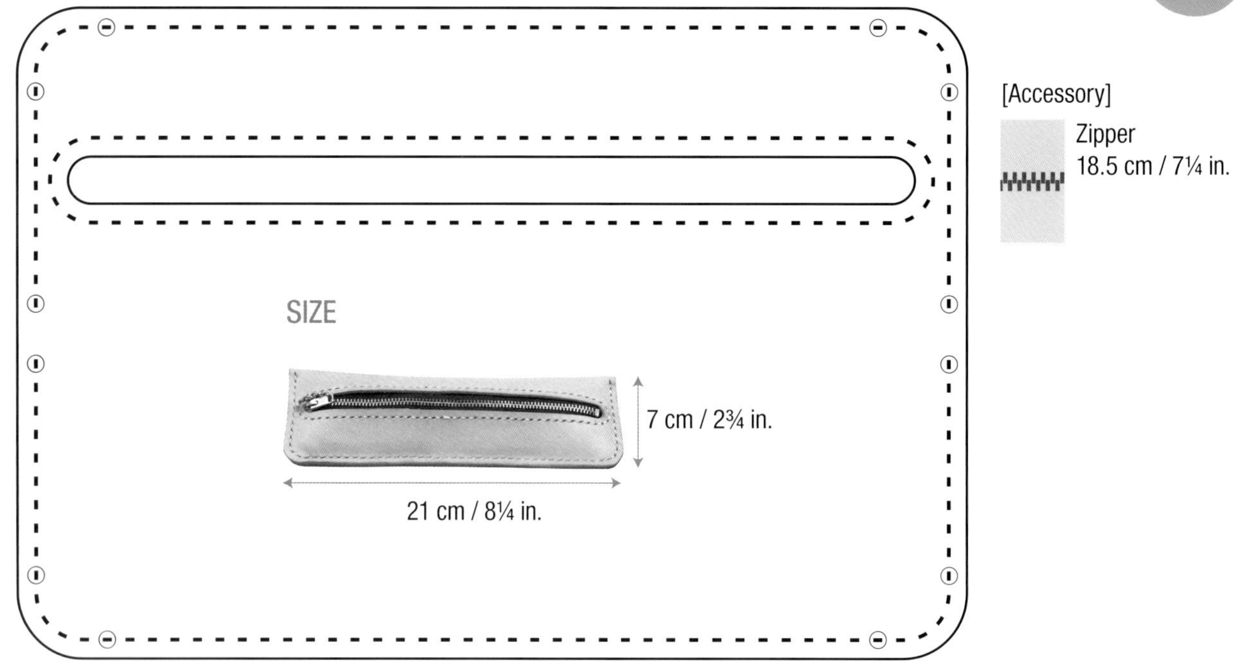

[A Flat Case P. 64]

★ See P. 146 for triangular and quadrilateral shaped items

SIZE

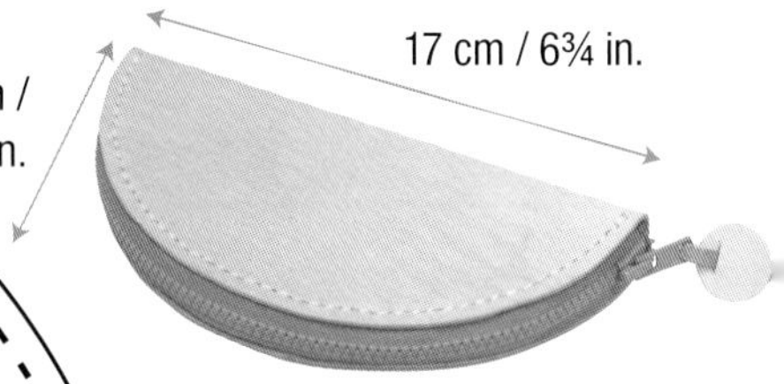

17 cm / 6¾ in.
9 cm / 3½ in.

20
Fold line
Fold line
Case
Zipper tag
Reinforcing leather to be glued inside
0
20

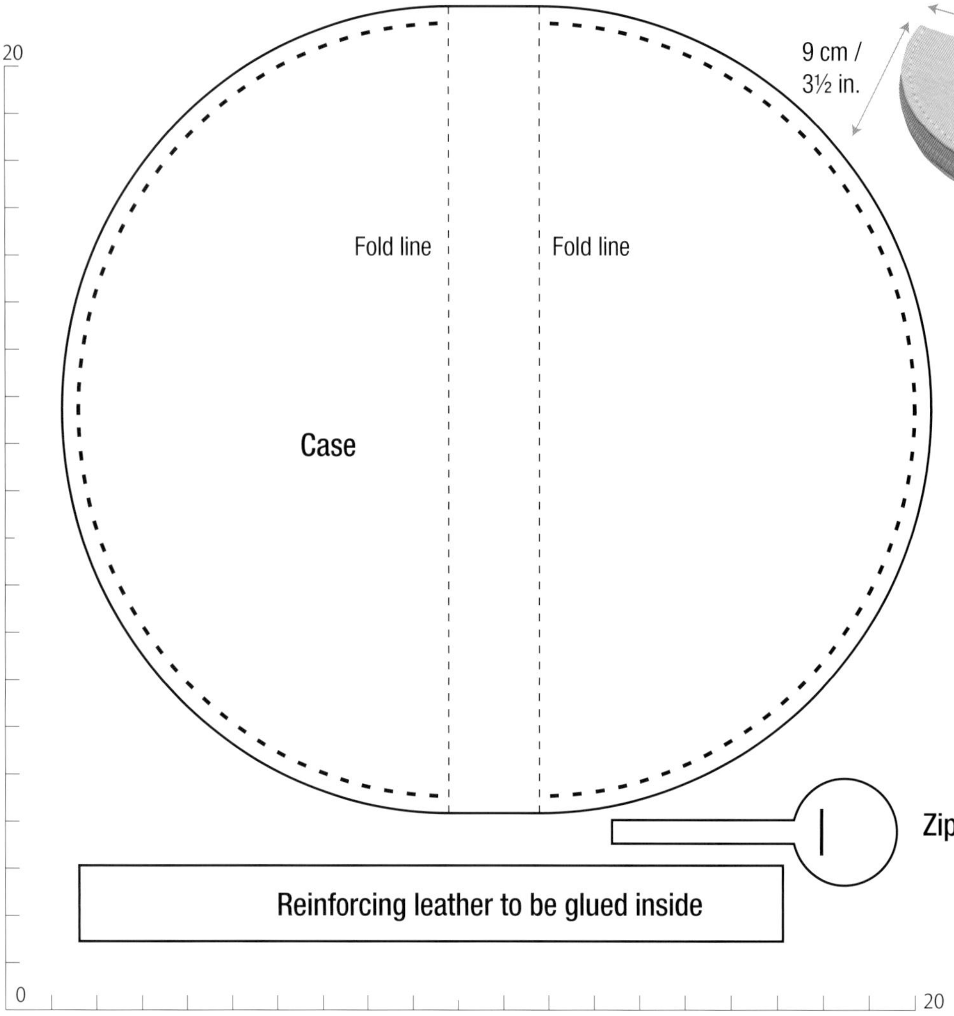

[Accessory]

Zipper
30 cm / 11¾ in.

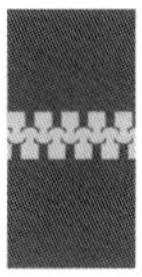

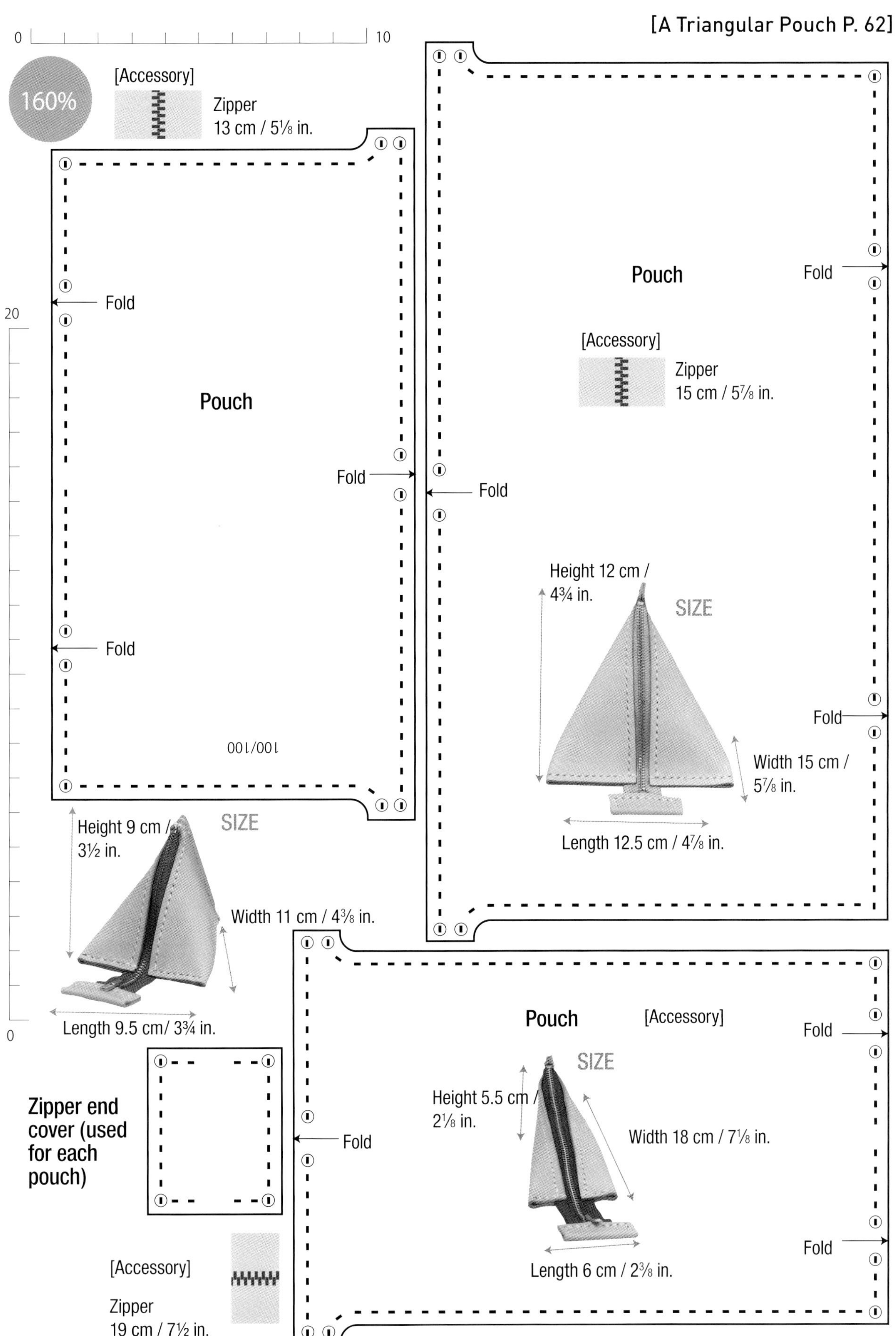
0
10
160%
[Accessory]
Zipper
13 cm / 5⅛ in.
Pouch
Fold
Fold
Fold
100/100
Height 9 cm / 3½ in.
SIZE
Width 11 cm / 4⅜ in.
Length 9.5 cm/ 3¾ in.
20
0
Pouch
Fold
[Accessory]
Zipper
15 cm / 5⅞ in.
Fold
Height 12 cm / 4¾ in.
SIZE
Fold
Width 15 cm / 5⅞ in.
Length 12.5 cm / 4⅞ in.
Pouch
[Accessory]
Fold
SIZE
Height 5.5 cm / 2⅛ in.
Width 18 cm / 7⅛ in.
Fold
Fold
Length 6 cm / 2⅜ in.
Zipper end cover (used for each pouch)
[Accessory]
Zipper
19 cm / 7½ in.

[Flat Cases P. 64]

★ See P. 144 for a round shaped case

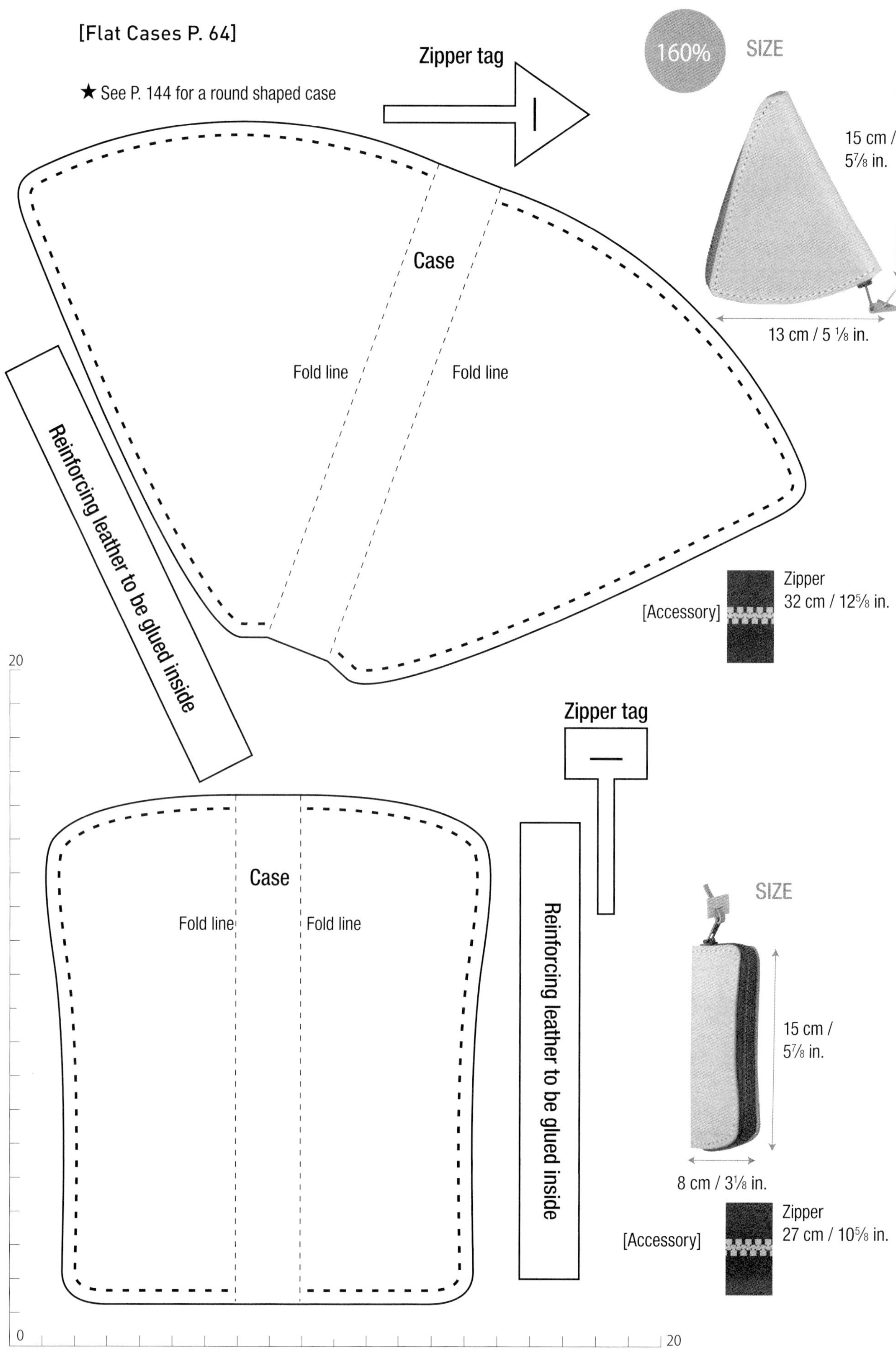

160%

[A Three-gored Tall Bag P. 74]

Handle

[Glued Pattern]

Bag front, cut 2

[Glued Pattern] Make 2 photocopies and glue them together while aligning the marks

Bag side, cut 2

Make 2 photocopies and glue them together while aligning the marks

20

SIZE

28 cm / 11 in.

15 cm / 5⅞ in.

11 cm / 4⅜ in.

0

20

[A Three-gored Tote Bag P. 78]

See P. 171 for the handle pattern

160%

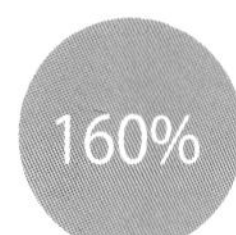

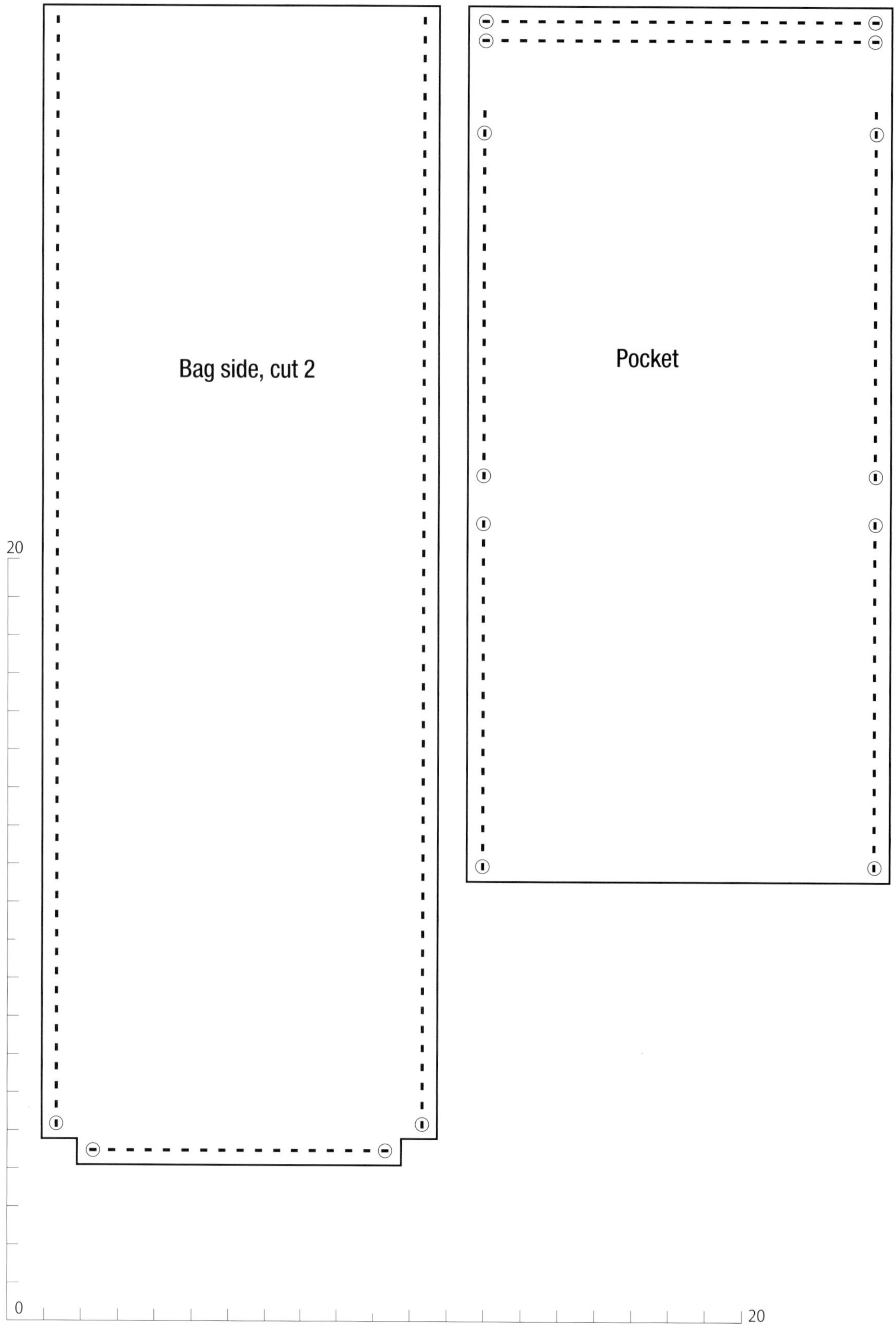
Bag side, cut 2
Pocket
20
0
20

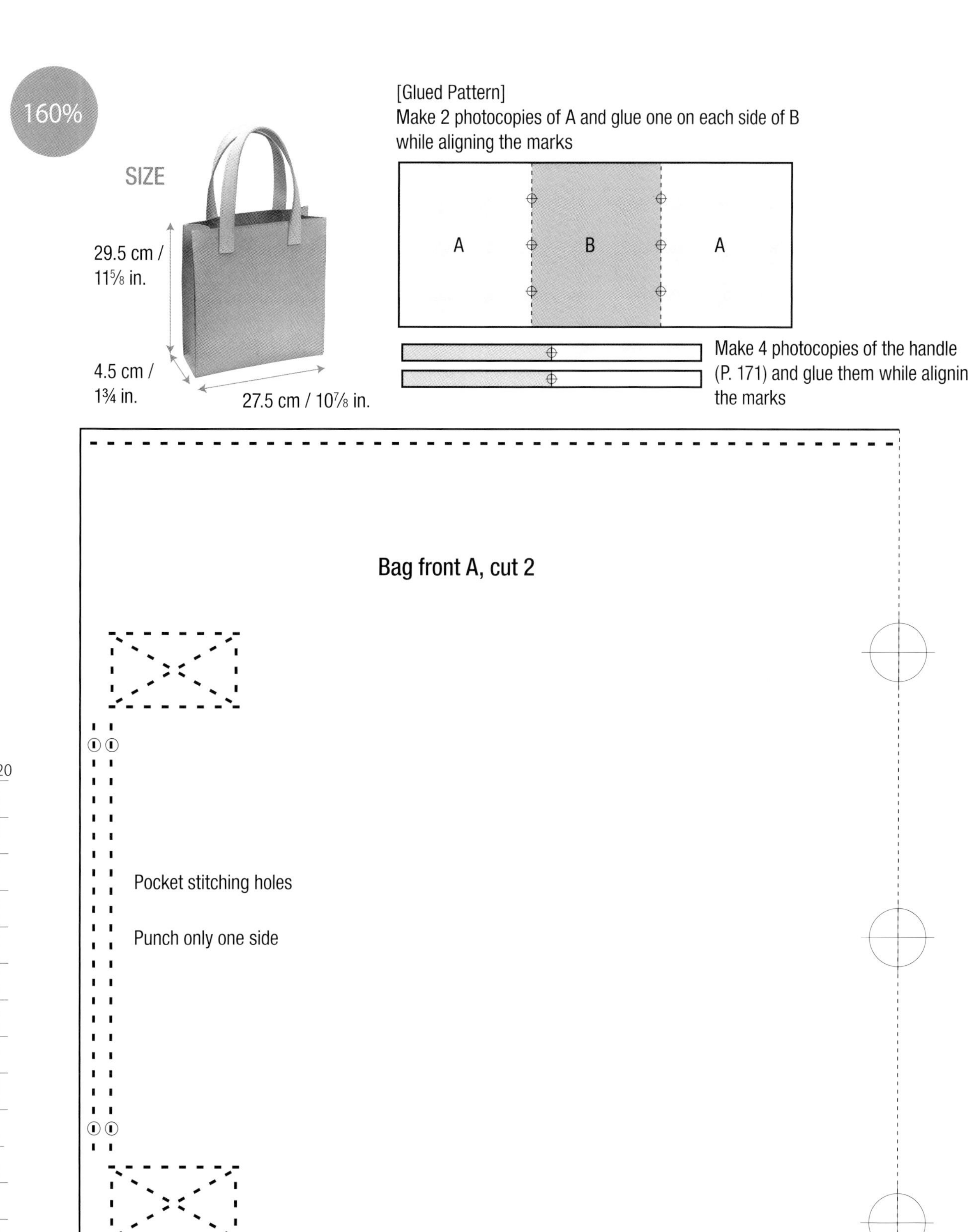
160%
SIZE
29.5 cm /
11⅝ in.
4.5 cm /
1¾ in.
27.5 cm / 10⅞ in.
[Glued Pattern]
Make 2 photocopies of A and glue one on each side of B
while aligning the marks
A
B
A
Make 4 photocopies of the handle
(P. 171) and glue them while aligning
the marks
Bag front A, cut 2
Pocket stitching holes
Punch only one side
20
0
20

160%

[A Zipper Pouch Using a Single Sheet of Leather P. 80]

SIZE

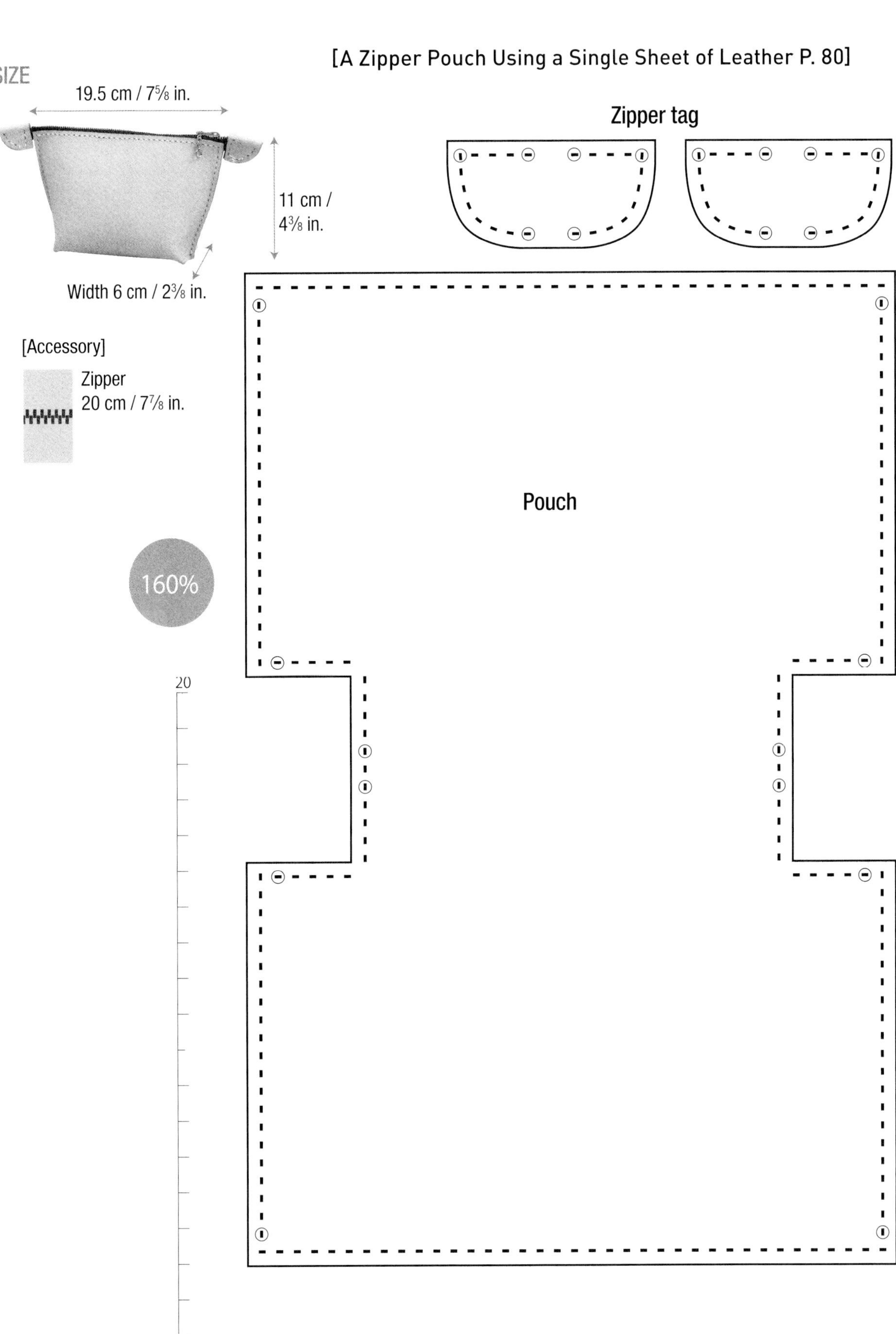

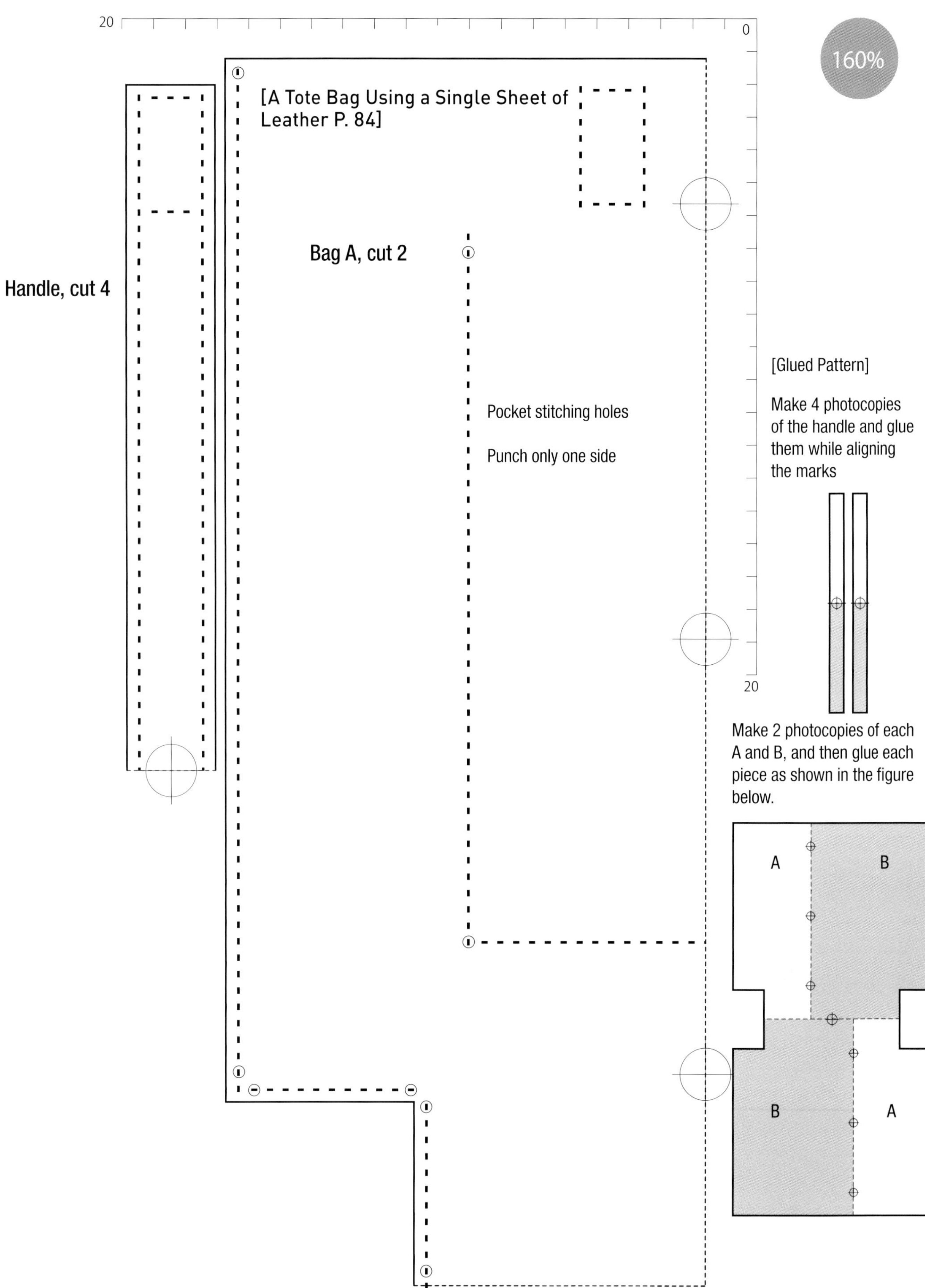

20
0
20
160%
[A Tote Bag Using a Single Sheet of Leather P. 84]
Bag A, cut 2
Handle, cut 4
Pocket stitching holes
Punch only one side
[Glued Pattern]
Make 4 photocopies of the handle and glue them while aligning the marks
Make 2 photocopies of each A and B, and then glue each piece as shown in the figure below.
A
B
B
A

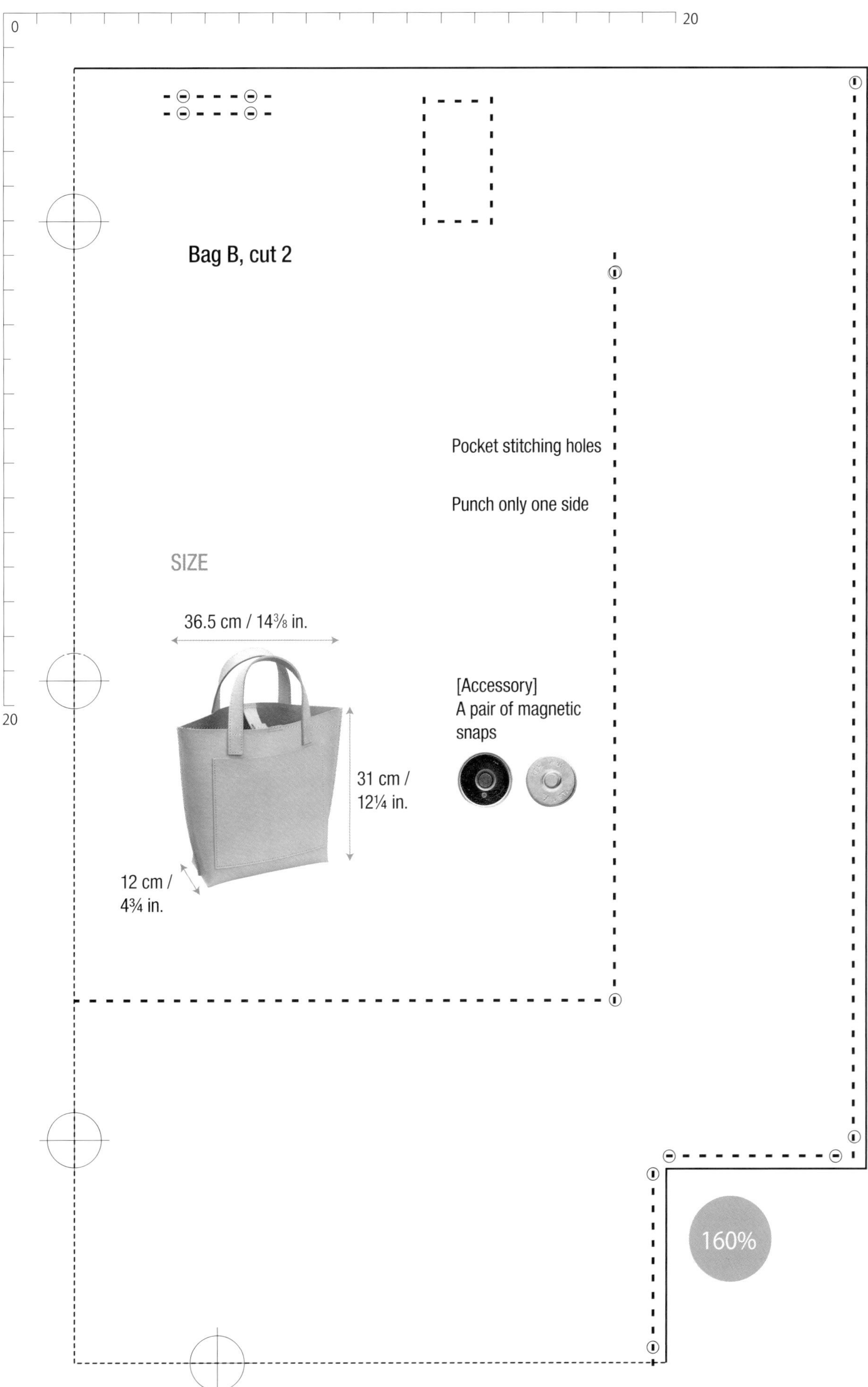
0
20
20
Bag B, cut 2
Pocket stitching holes
Punch only one side
SIZE
36.5 cm / 14⅜ in.
31 cm / 12¼ in.
12 cm / 4¾ in.
[Accessory]
A pair of magnetic snaps
160%

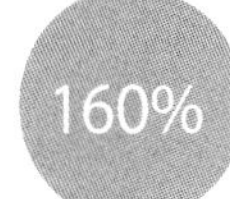

[A Tote Bag Using a Single Sheet of Leather P. 84]

160%

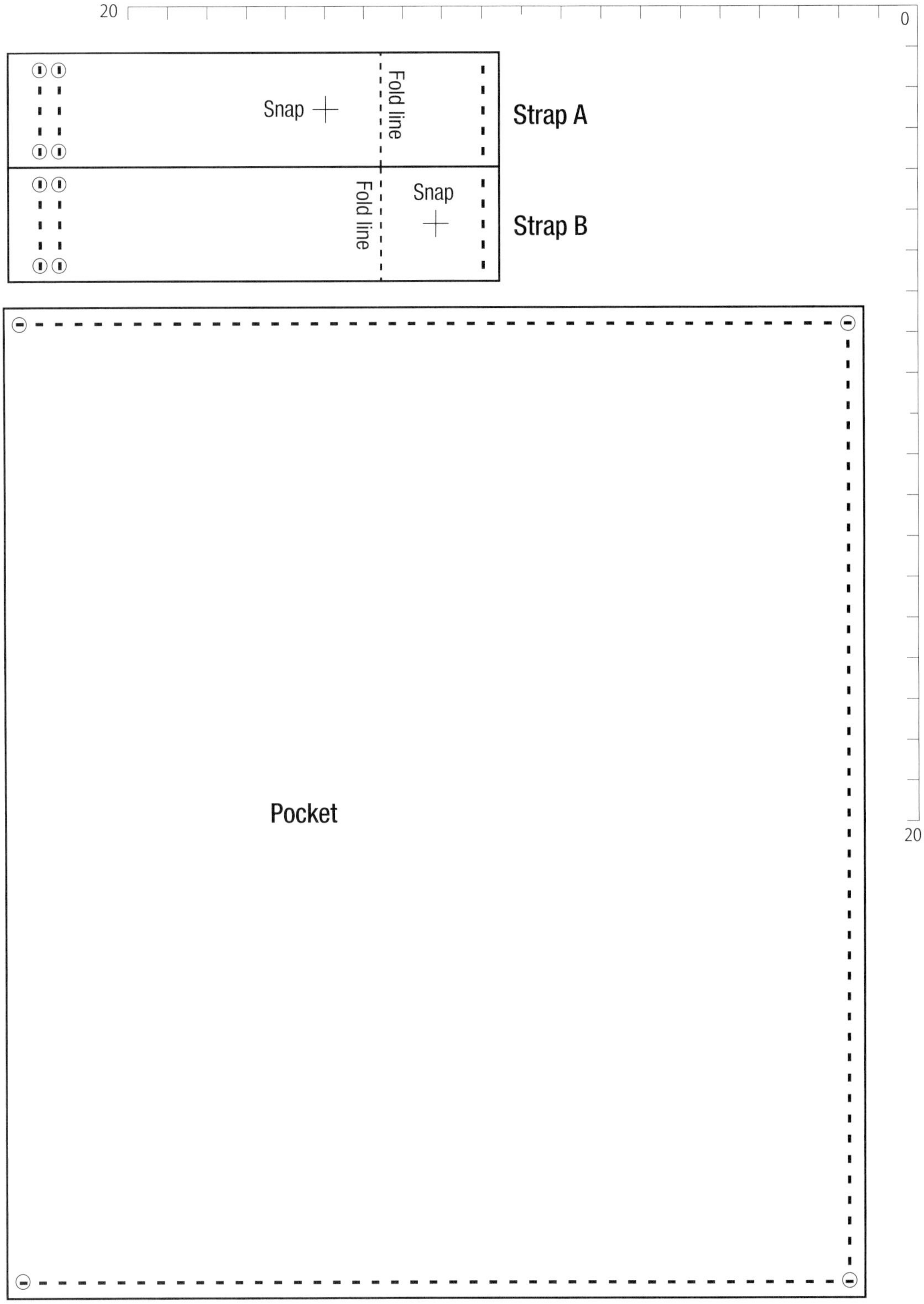
20
0
20
Snap
Fold line
Strap A
Fold line
Snap
Strap B
Pocket

160%

[A Shoulder Bag Using a Single Sheet of Leather P. 88]

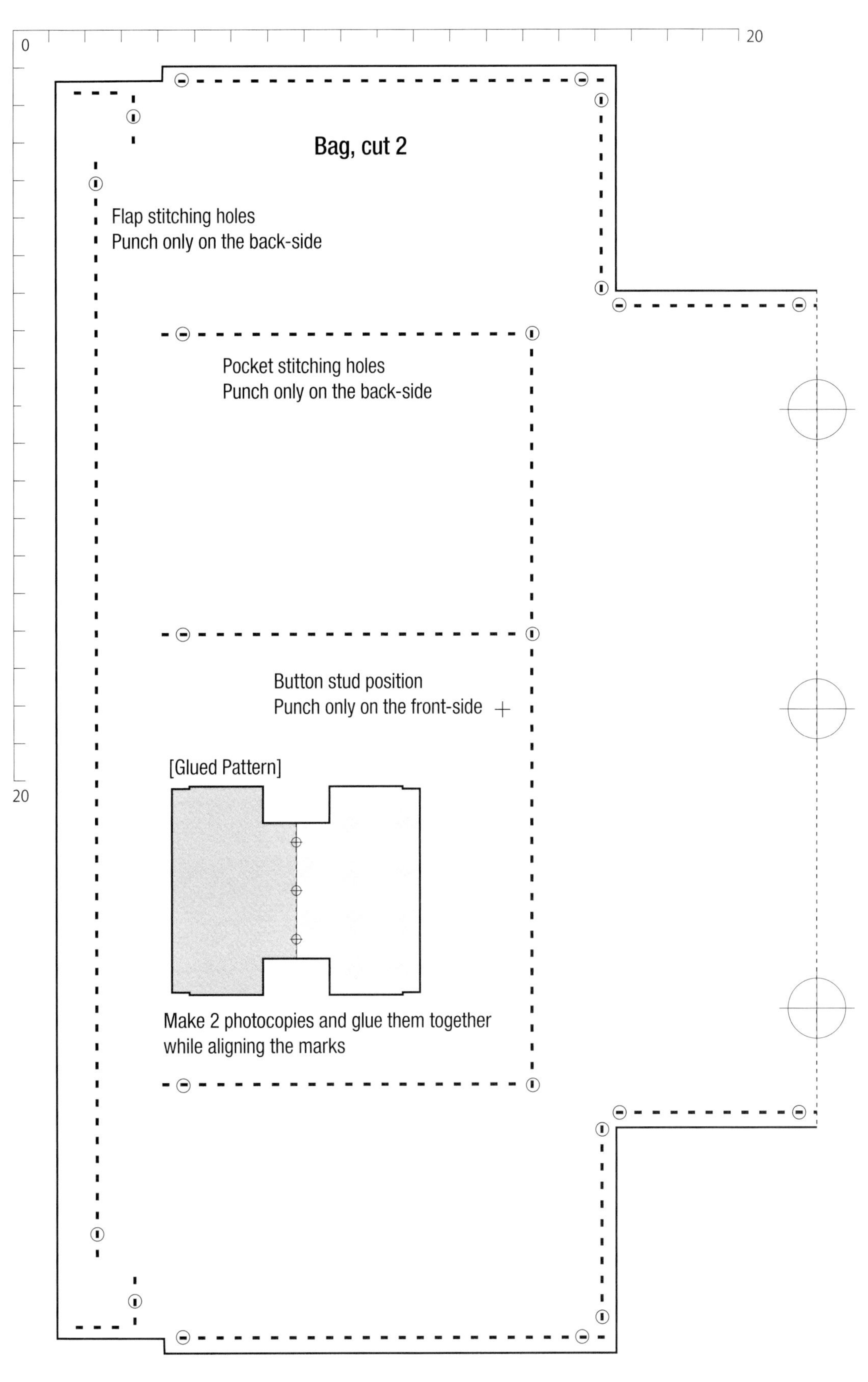

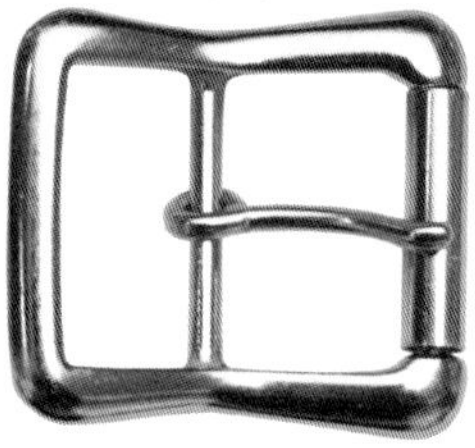

[Glued Pattern]
Attach patterns to leather that is cut to the necessary dimensions with masking tape. Then, punch stitching holes and mark it.

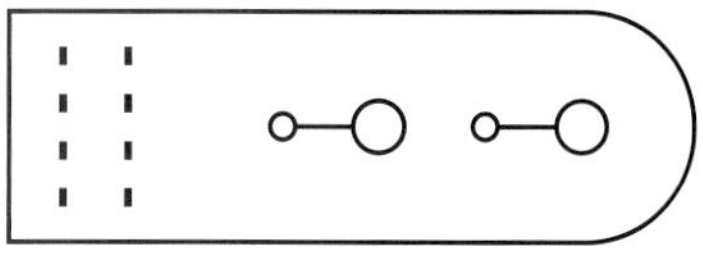

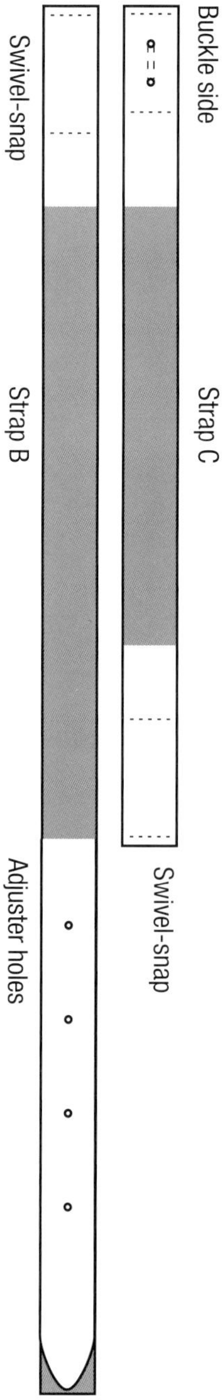

[Strap]

Straps B and C are commonly used for shoulder bags using single sheets of leather (P. 88) and for curved bottom shoulder bags (P. 116).

Strap B: Adjuster holes - side

Swivel-snap

Strap B

Adjuster holes

Buckle side

Strap C

Swivel-snap

SIZE

16 cm / 6¼ in.

30 cm / 11¾ in.

Width 11 cm / 4⅜ in.

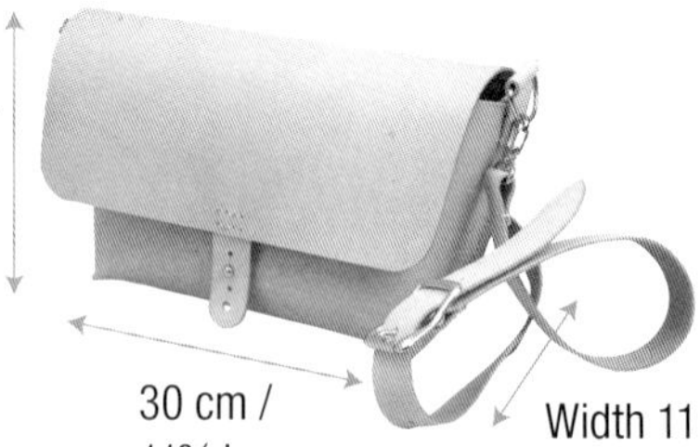

Flap

[Accessory]

Button stud

D-ring: 2

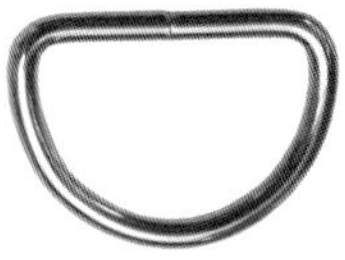

Swivel-snap: 2

Buckle

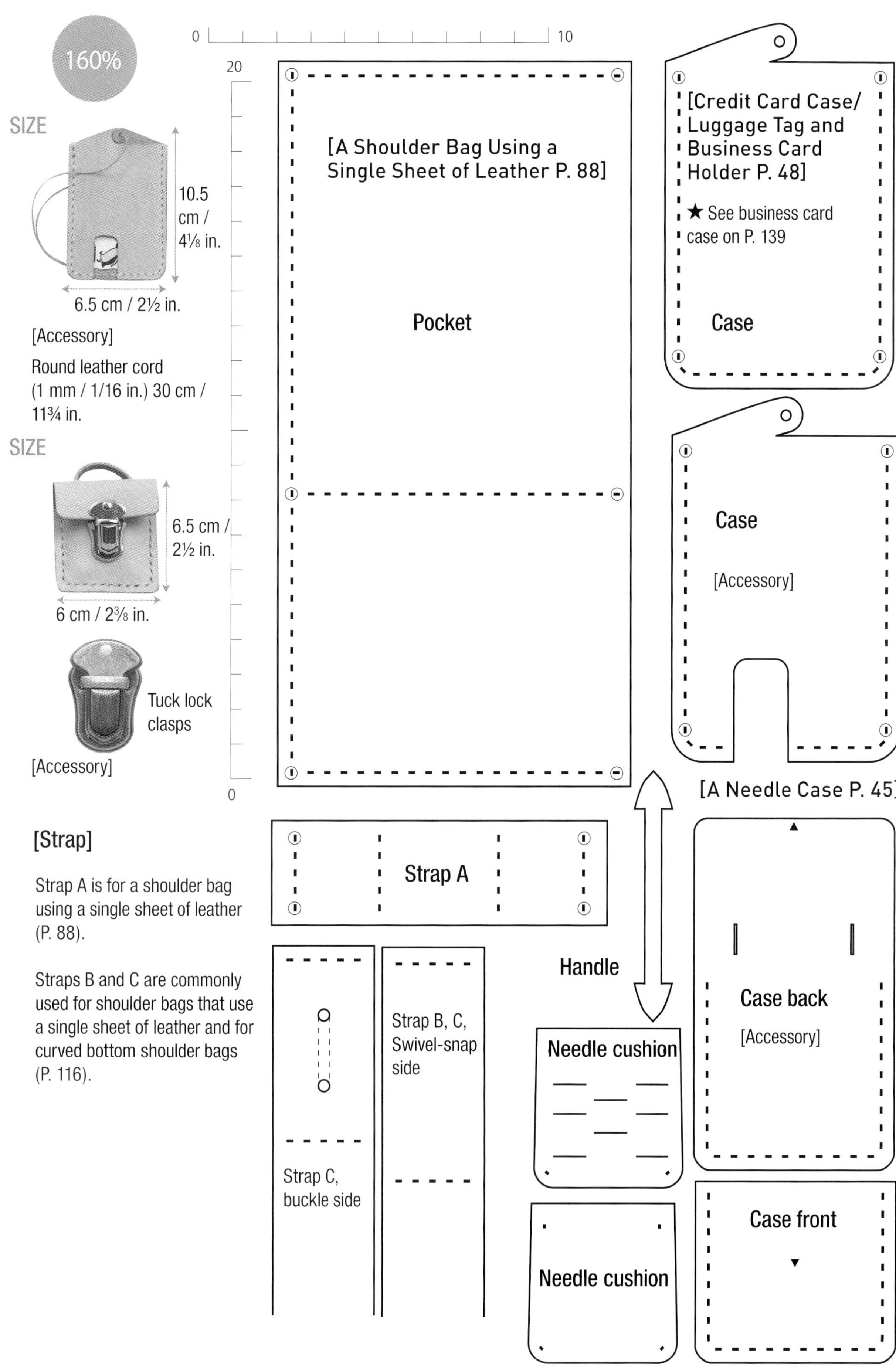
160%
0
10
20
0
SIZE
10.5 cm / 4⅛ in.
6.5 cm / 2½ in.
[Accessory]
Round leather cord (1 mm / 1/16 in.) 30 cm / 11¾ in.
SIZE
6.5 cm / 2½ in.
6 cm / 2⅜ in.
Tuck lock clasps
[Accessory]
[A Shoulder Bag Using a Single Sheet of Leather P. 88]
Pocket
[Credit Card Case/ Luggage Tag and Business Card Holder P. 48]
★ See business card case on P. 139
Case
Case
[Accessory]
[A Needle Case P. 45]
[Strap]
Strap A is for a shoulder bag using a single sheet of leather (P. 88).
Straps B and C are commonly used for shoulder bags that use a single sheet of leather and for curved bottom shoulder bags (P. 116).
Strap A
Handle
Strap C, buckle side
Strap B, C, Swivel-snap side
Needle cushion
Needle cushion
Case back
[Accessory]
Case front

[A Bag with a Zipper Using a Single Sheet of Leather P. 94]

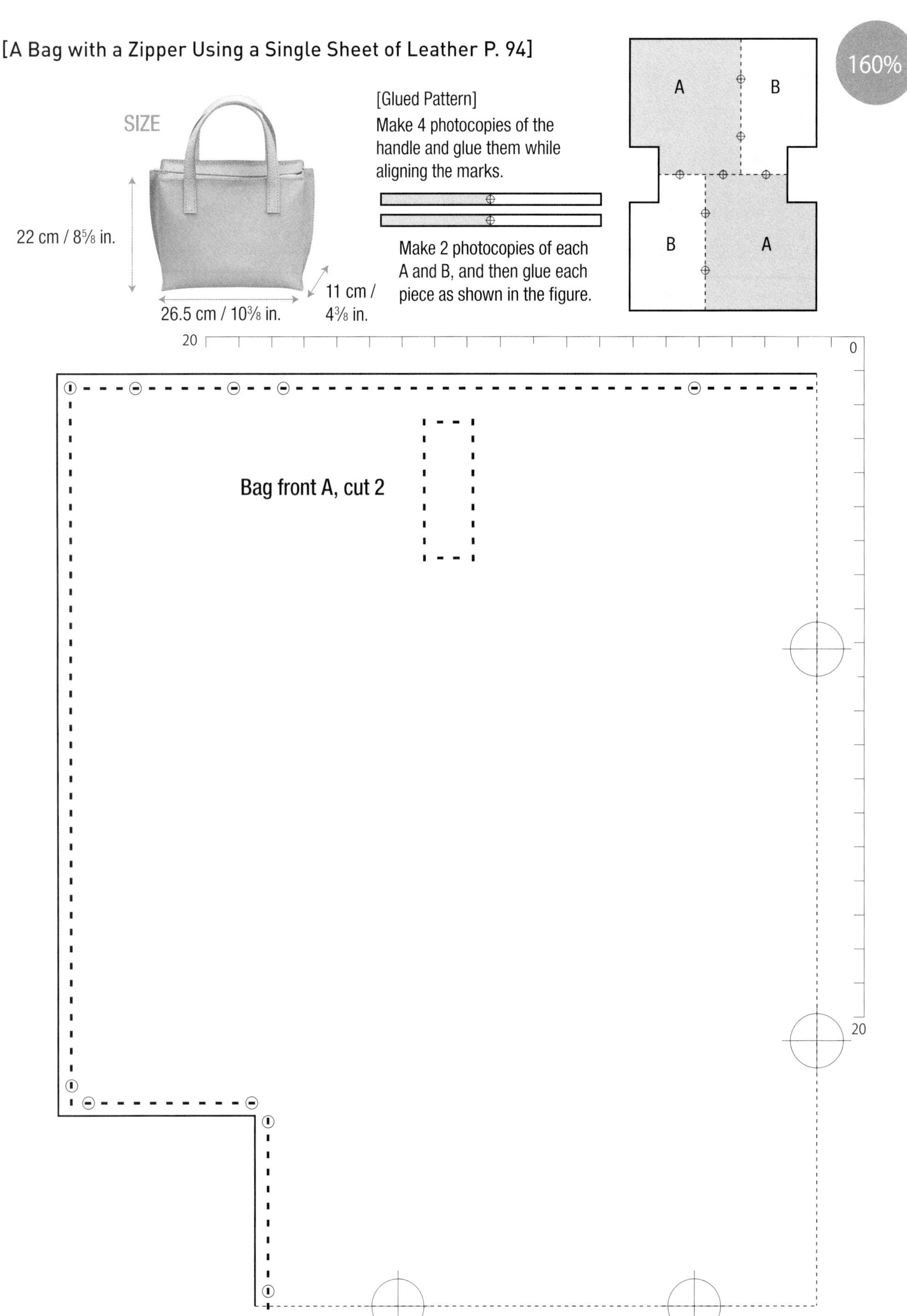

160%

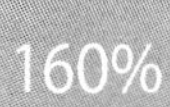

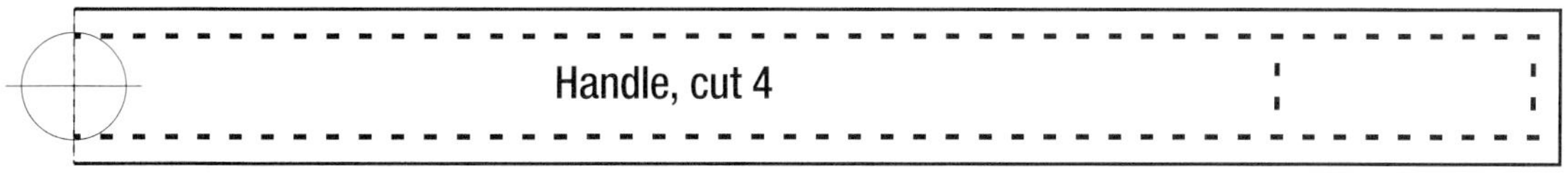

Handle, cut 4

[Accessory]

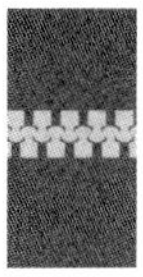

Zipper
26 cm / 10¼ in.

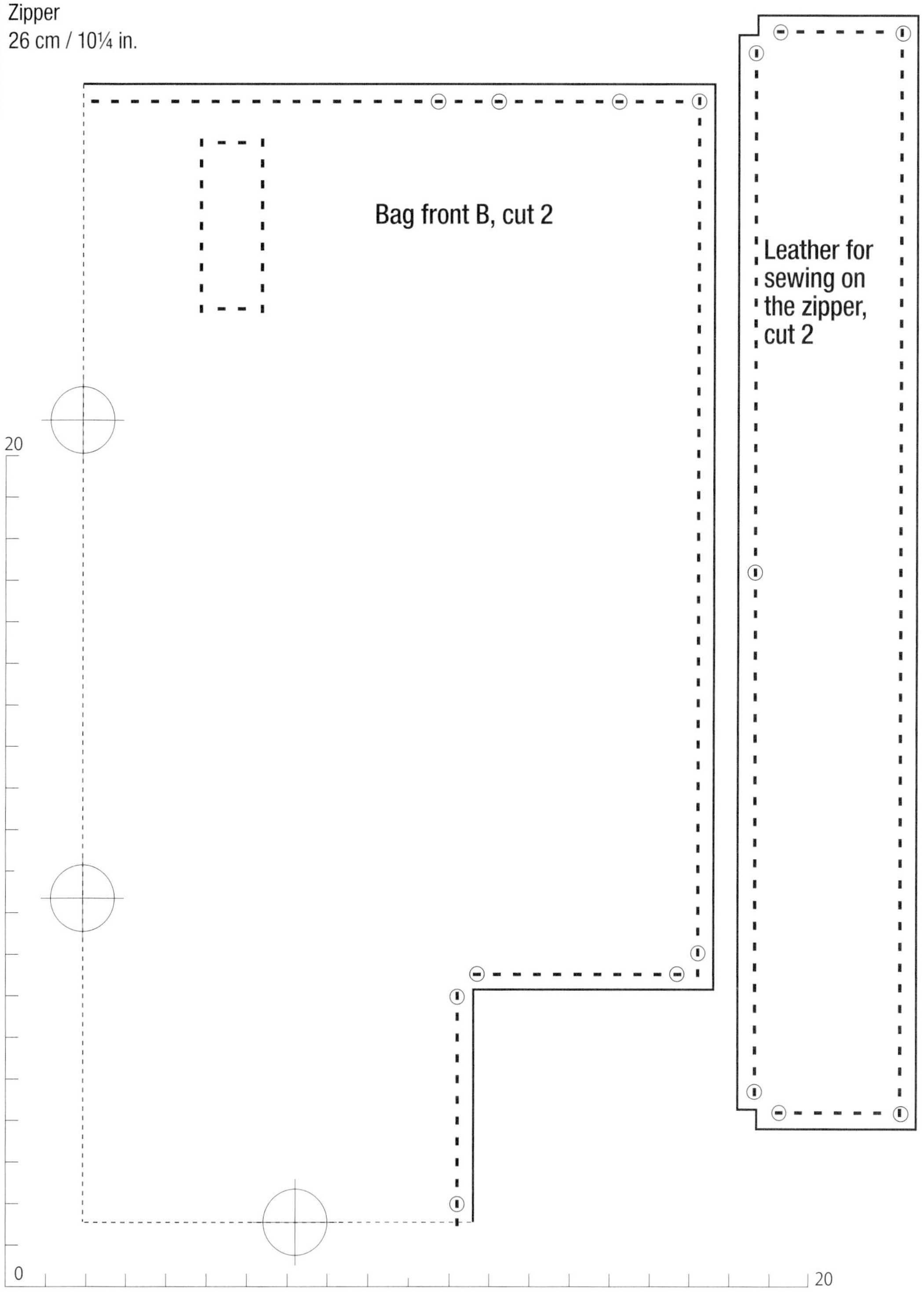

Bag front B, cut 2
Leather for sewing on the zipper, cut 2
20
0
20

160%

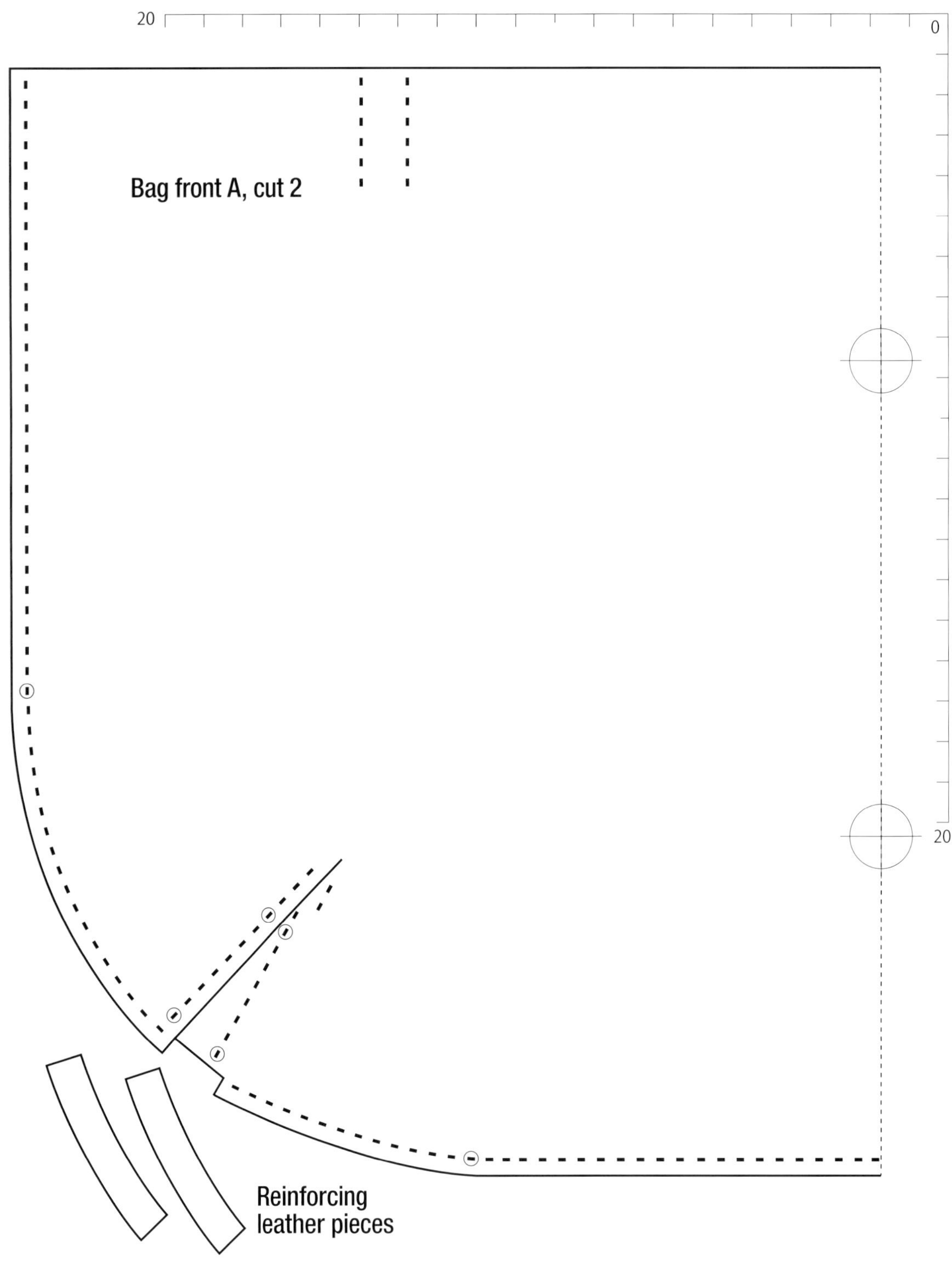

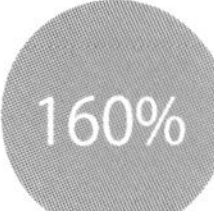

160%

[Glued Pattern]

A
B

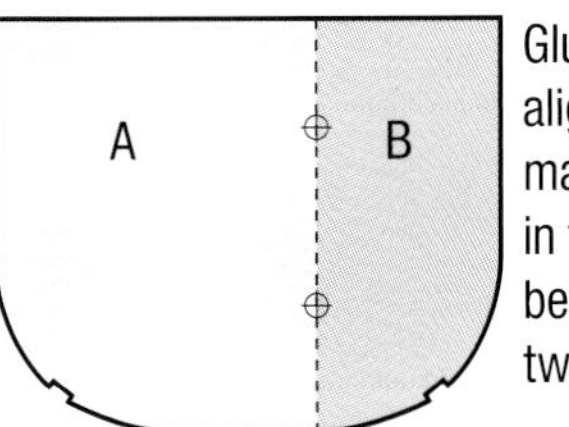

Glue while aligning the marks as shown in the figure below. Make two.

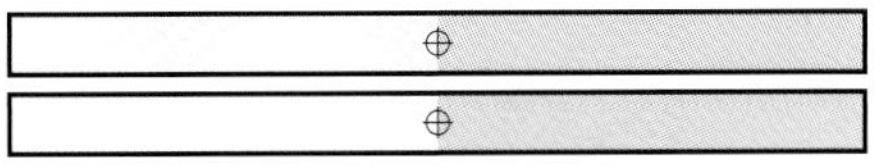

Make 4 photocopies of the handle and glue them while aligning the marks

SIZE

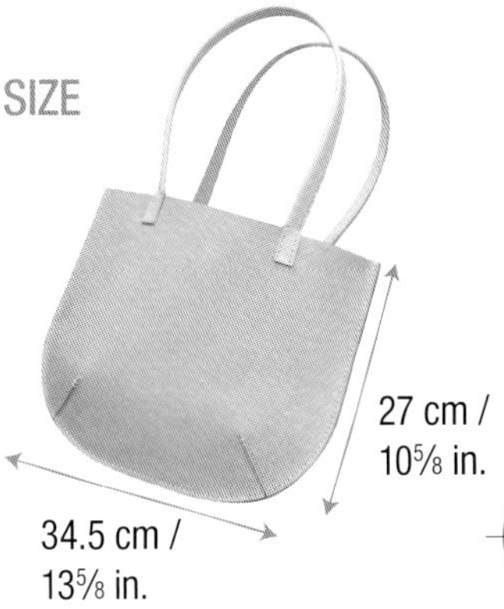

27 cm /
10⅝ in.
34.5 cm /
13⅝ in.

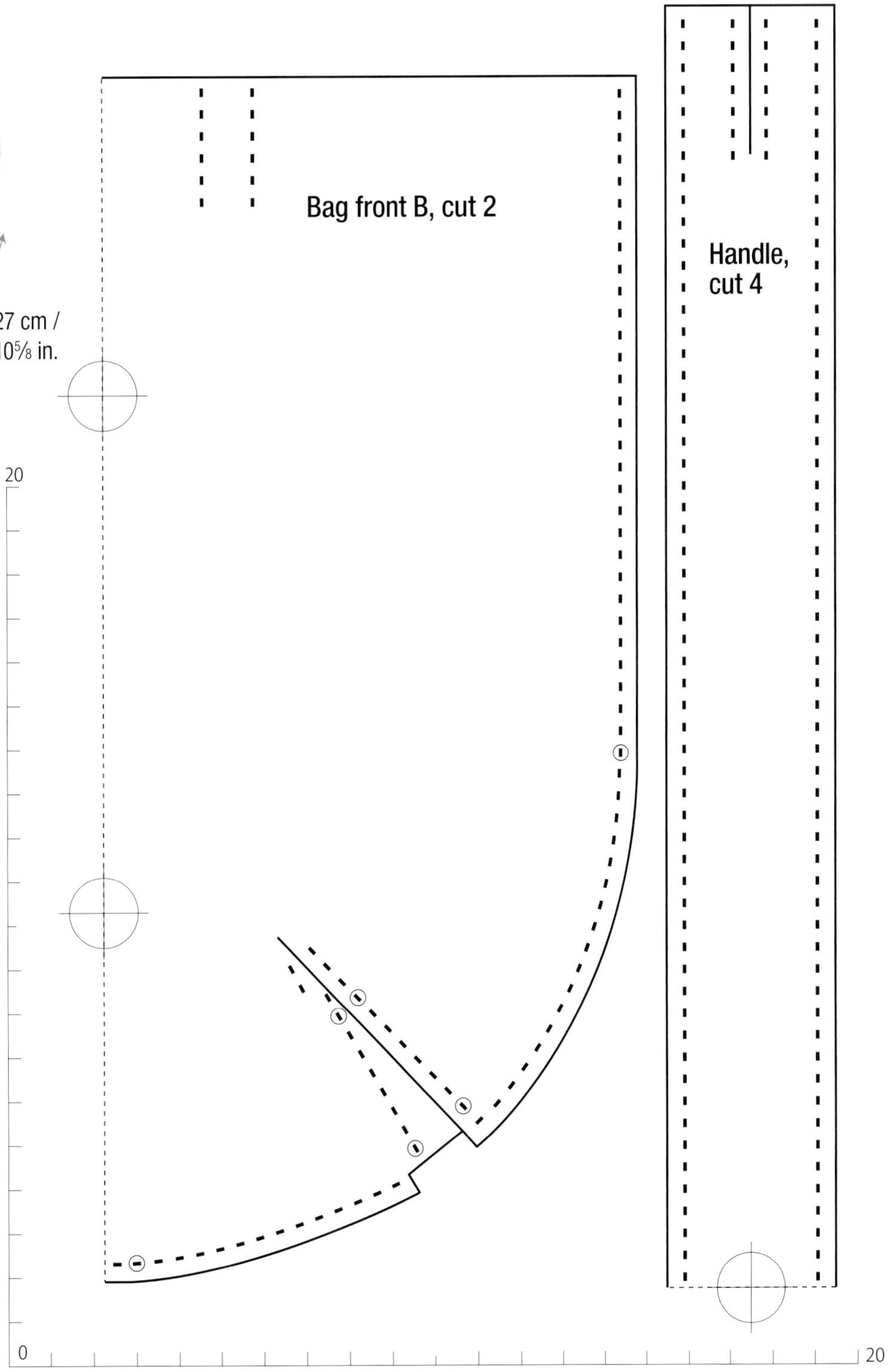

Bag front B, cut 2
Handle,
cut 4
20
0
20

[A Belt Pouch P. 102]

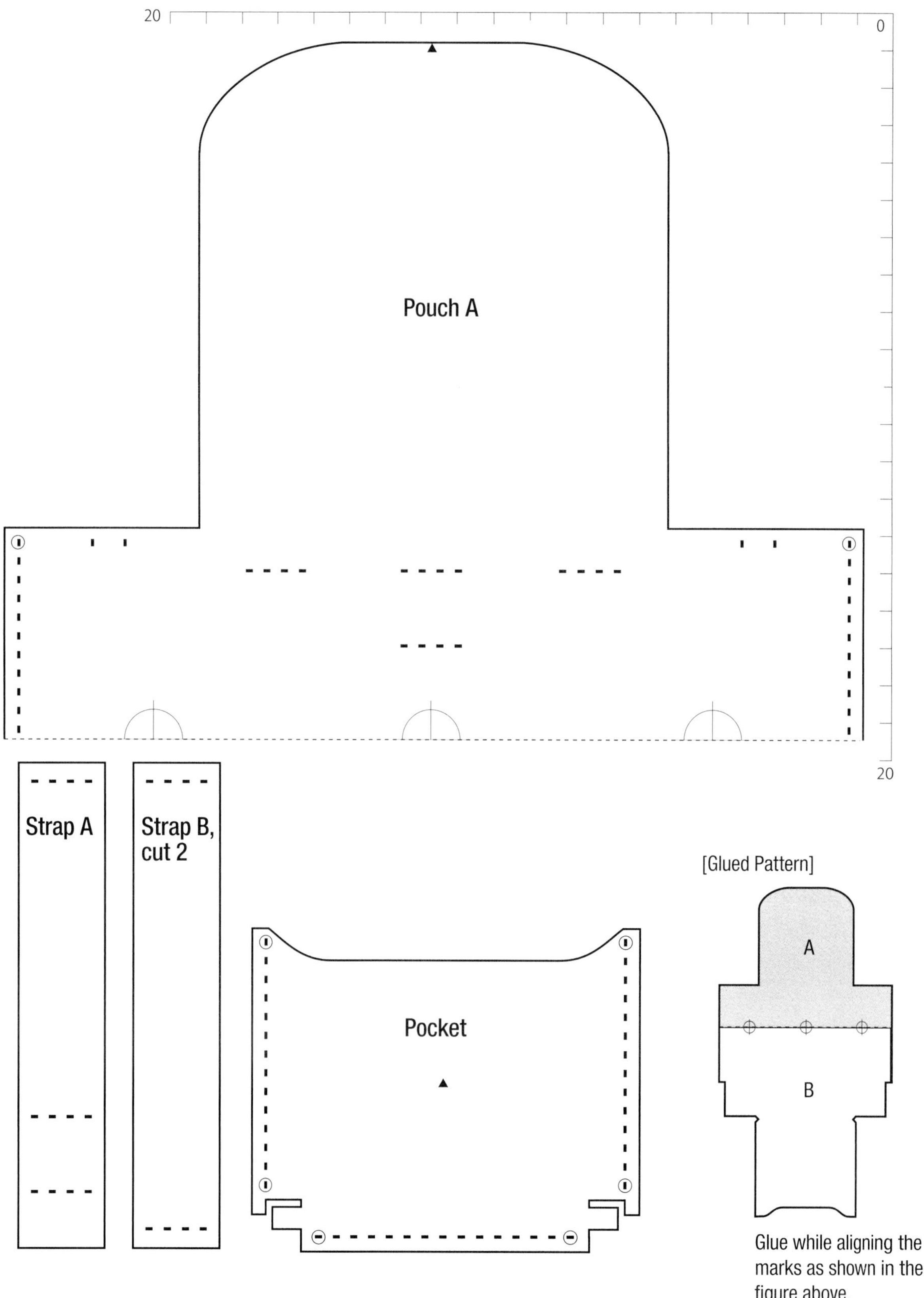

Glue while aligning the marks as shown in the figure above.

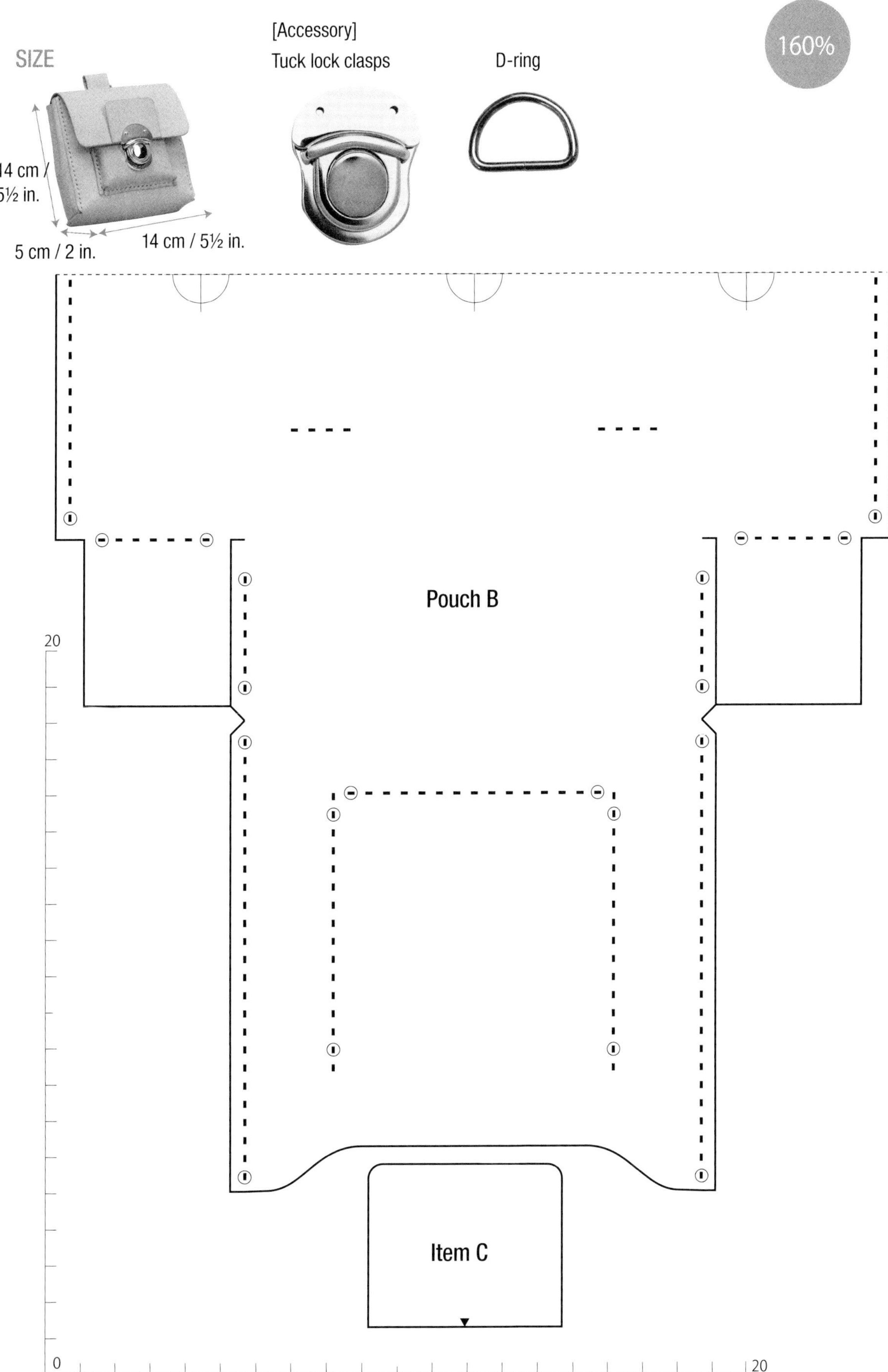
SIZE
14 cm / 5½ in.
5 cm / 2 in.
14 cm / 5½ in.
[Accessory]
Tuck lock clasps
D-ring
160%
Pouch B
Item C
20
0
20

[A Ball-shaped Bag P. 98]

★ See P. 165 for the handle

160%

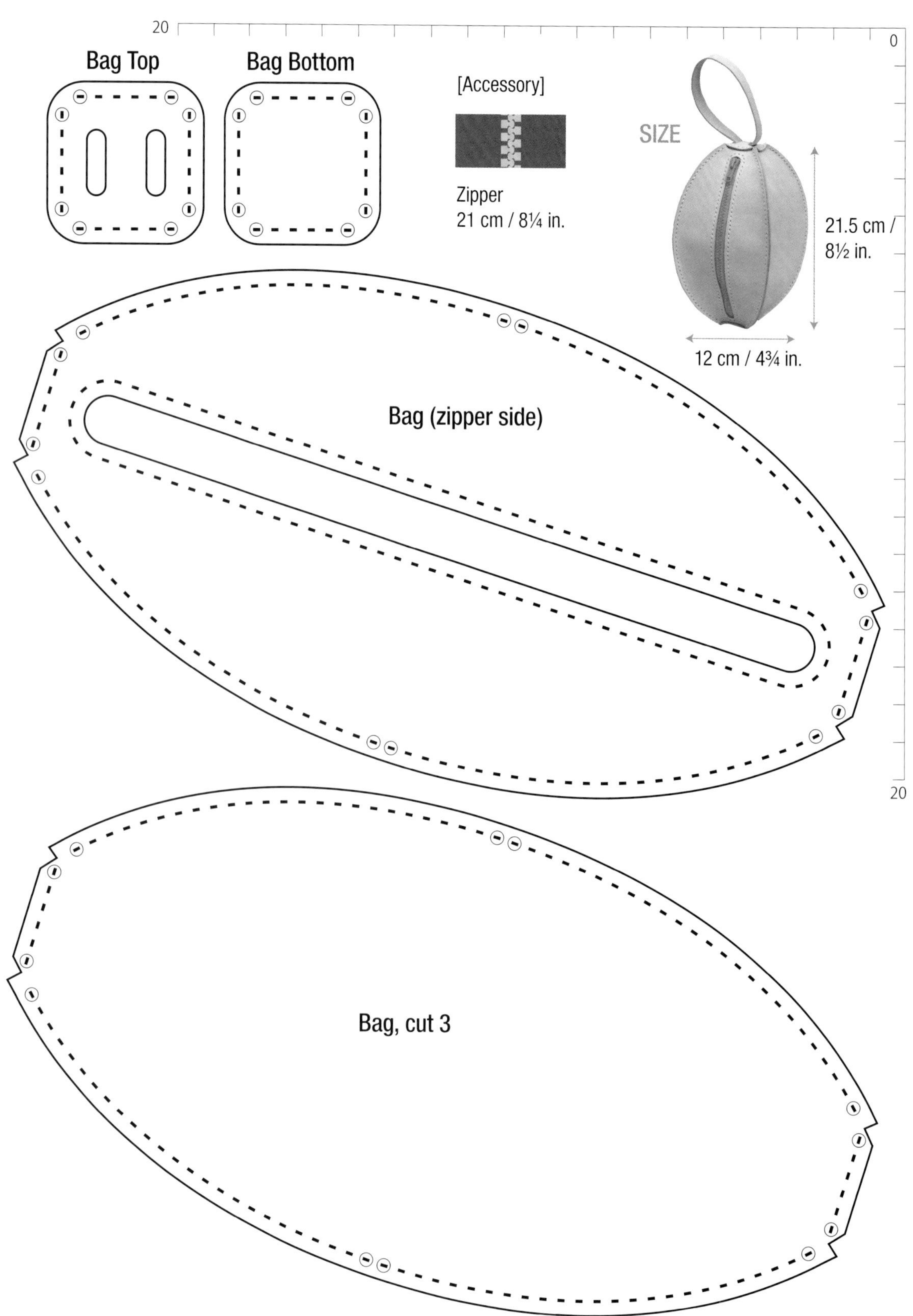

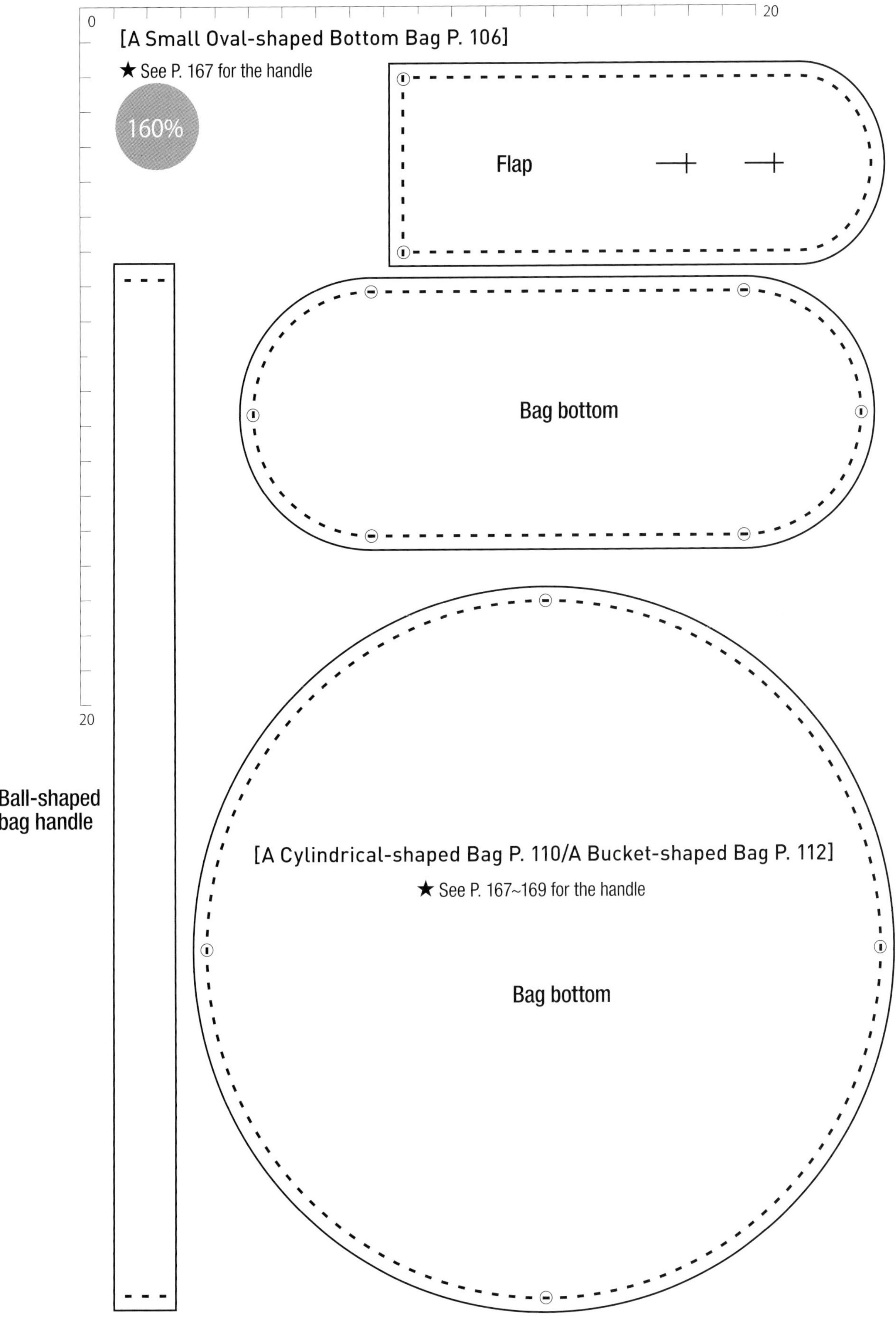
0
20
20
[A Small Oval-shaped Bottom Bag P. 106]
★ See P. 167 for the handle
160%
Flap
Bag bottom
Ball-shaped
bag handle
[A Cylindrical-shaped Bag P. 110/A Bucket-shaped Bag P. 112]
★ See P. 167~169 for the handle
Bag bottom

[A Small Oval-shaped Bottom Bag P. 106]

SIZE

15 cm / 5⅞ in.

8 cm / 3⅛ in.

18.5 cm / 7¼ in.

160%

[Accessory]

Button stud

20

0

Bag A
(cut slits at bottom)

20

Bag B

[A Small Oval-shaped Bottom Bag P. 106]

[A Cylindrical-shaped Bag P. 110]

[A Bucket-shaped Bag P. 112]

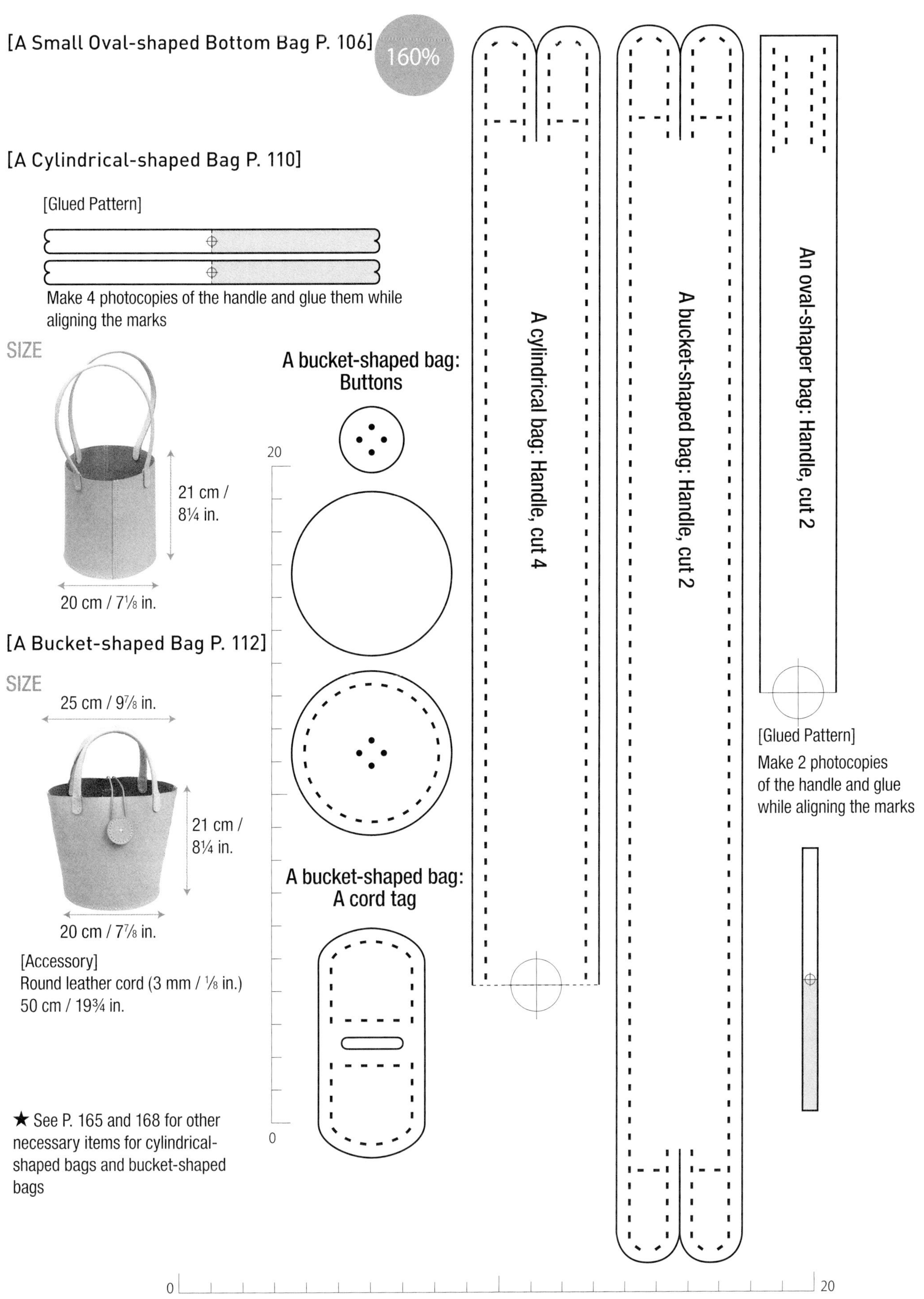

[A Cylindrical-shaped Bag P. 110/A Bucket-shaped Bag P. 112]

★ See P. 167 for the handle and other items

20

0

20

Bag B

160%

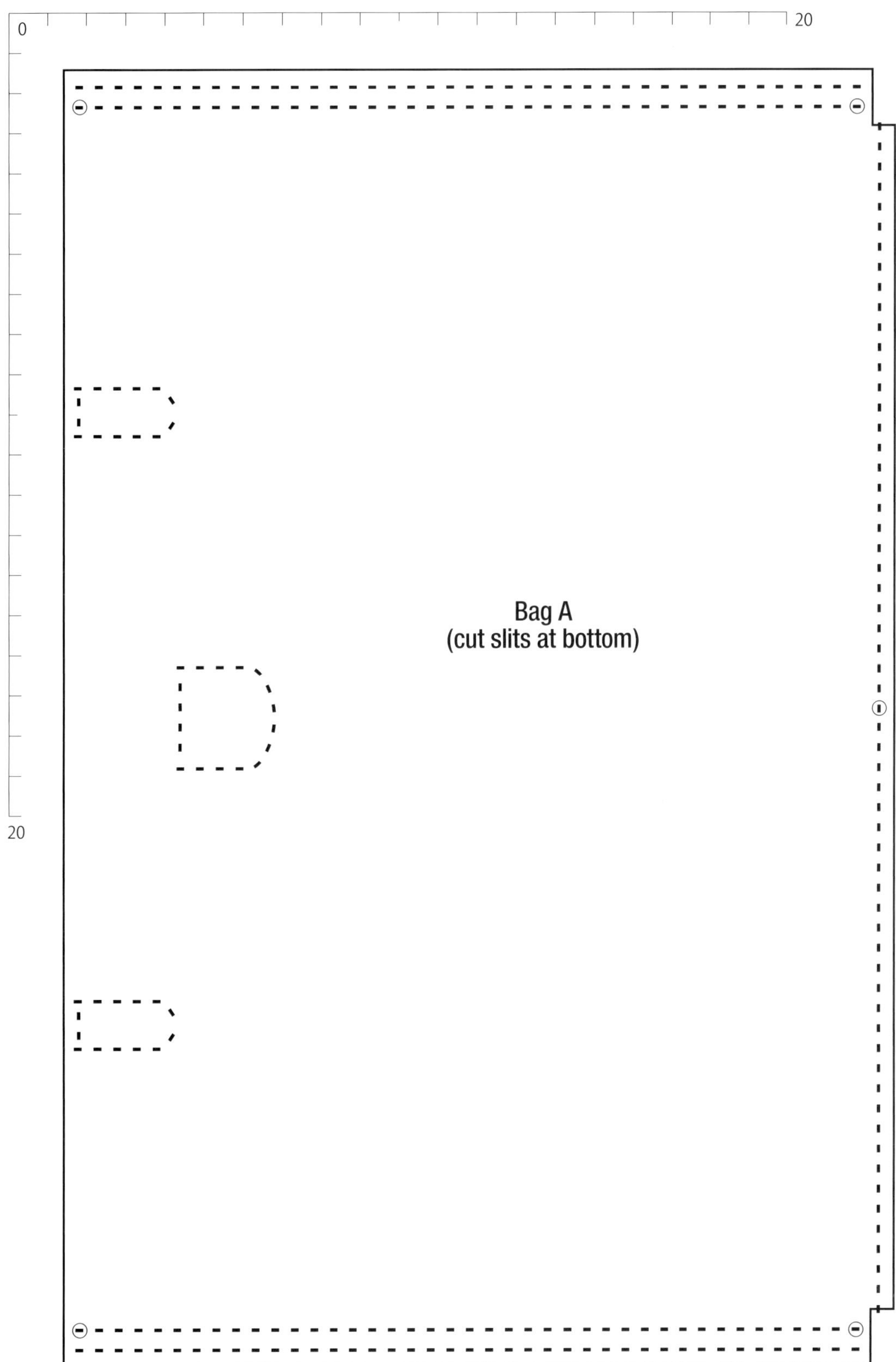

[A Two-gored Leather Travel Bag P. 114]

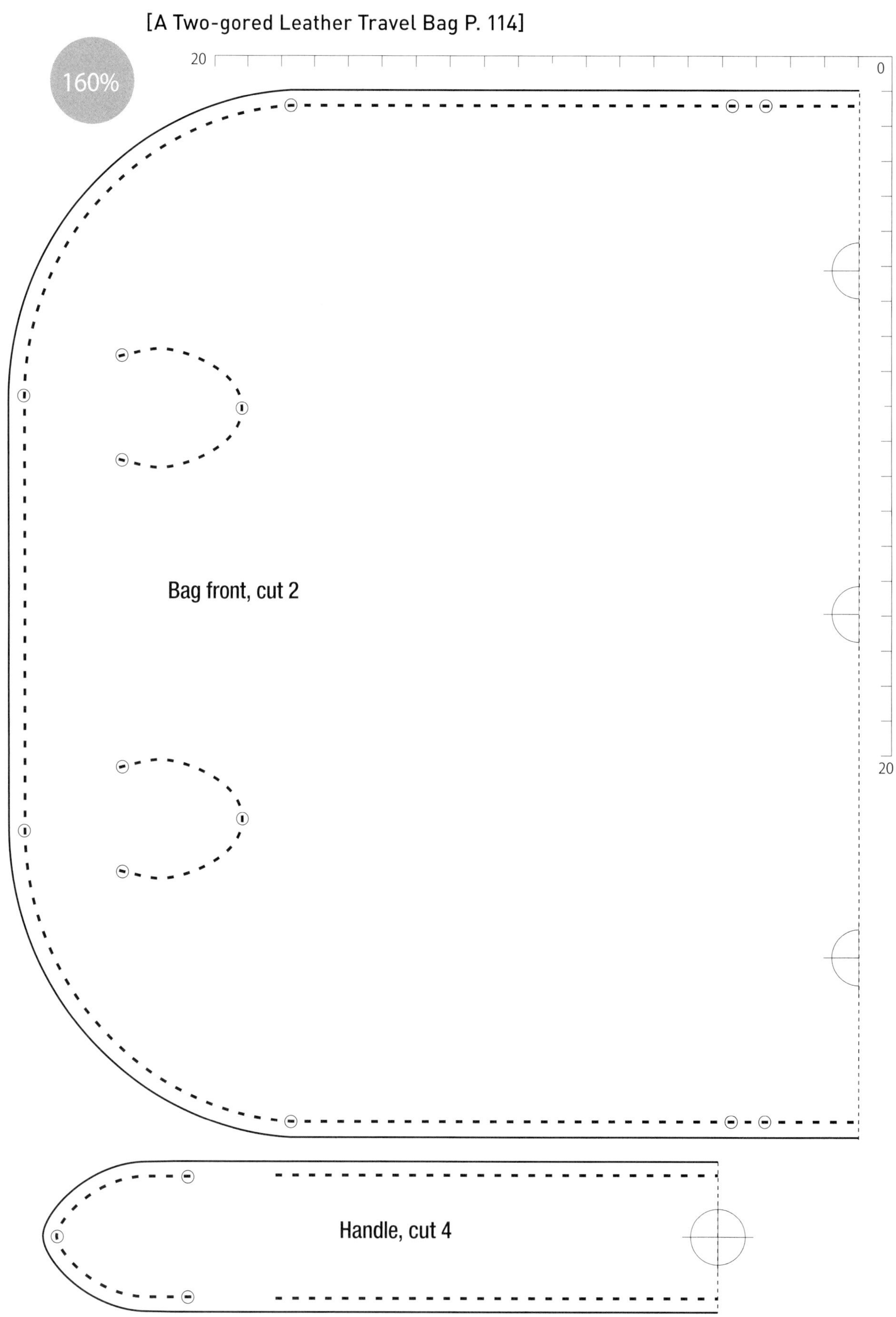

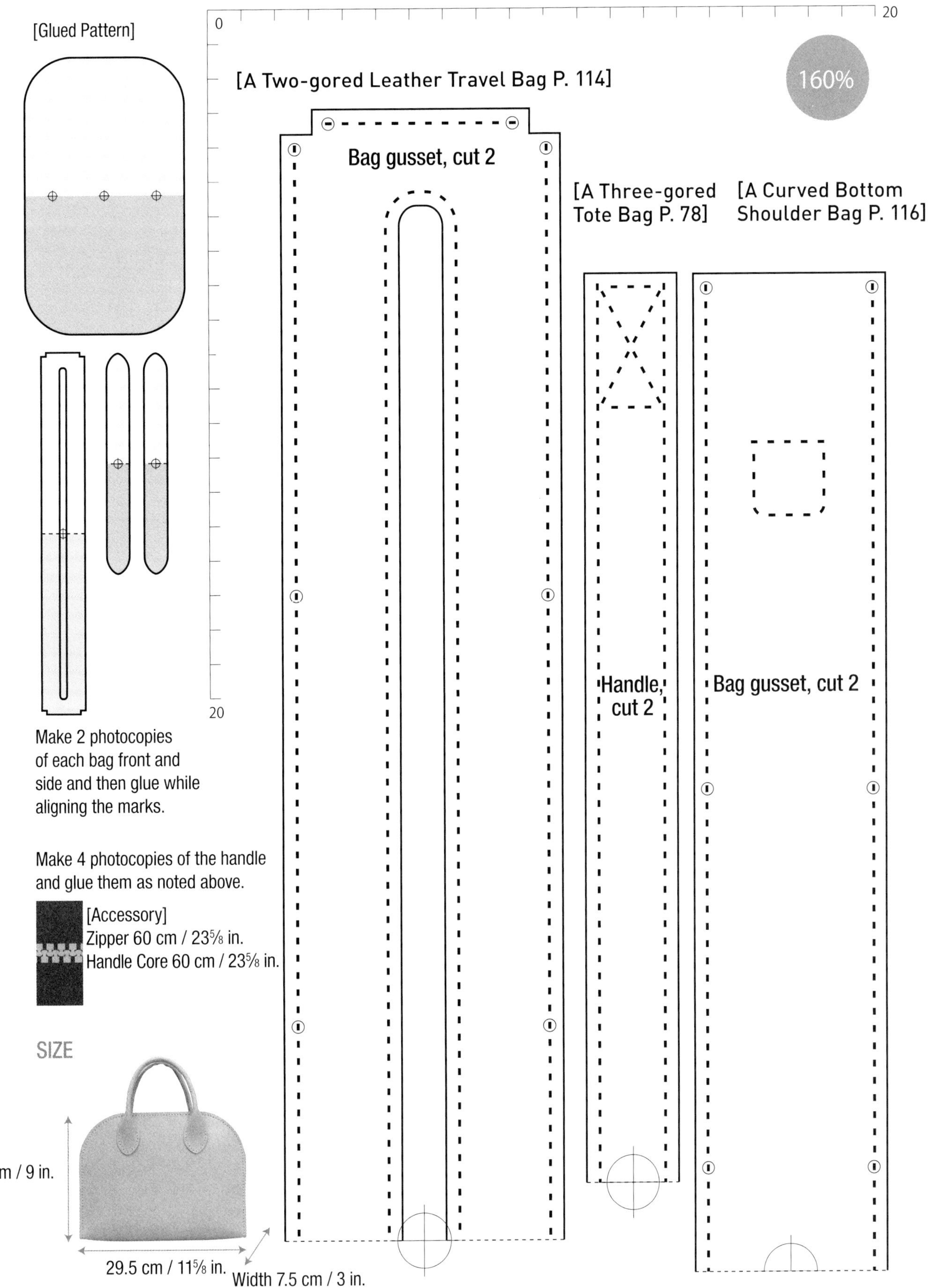

Make 2 photocopies of each bag front and side and then glue while aligning the marks.

Make 4 photocopies of the handle and glue them as noted above.

[Accessory]
Zipper 60 cm / 23⅝ in.
Handle Core 60 cm / 23⅝ in.

SIZE

[A Curved Bottom Shoulder Bag P. 116]

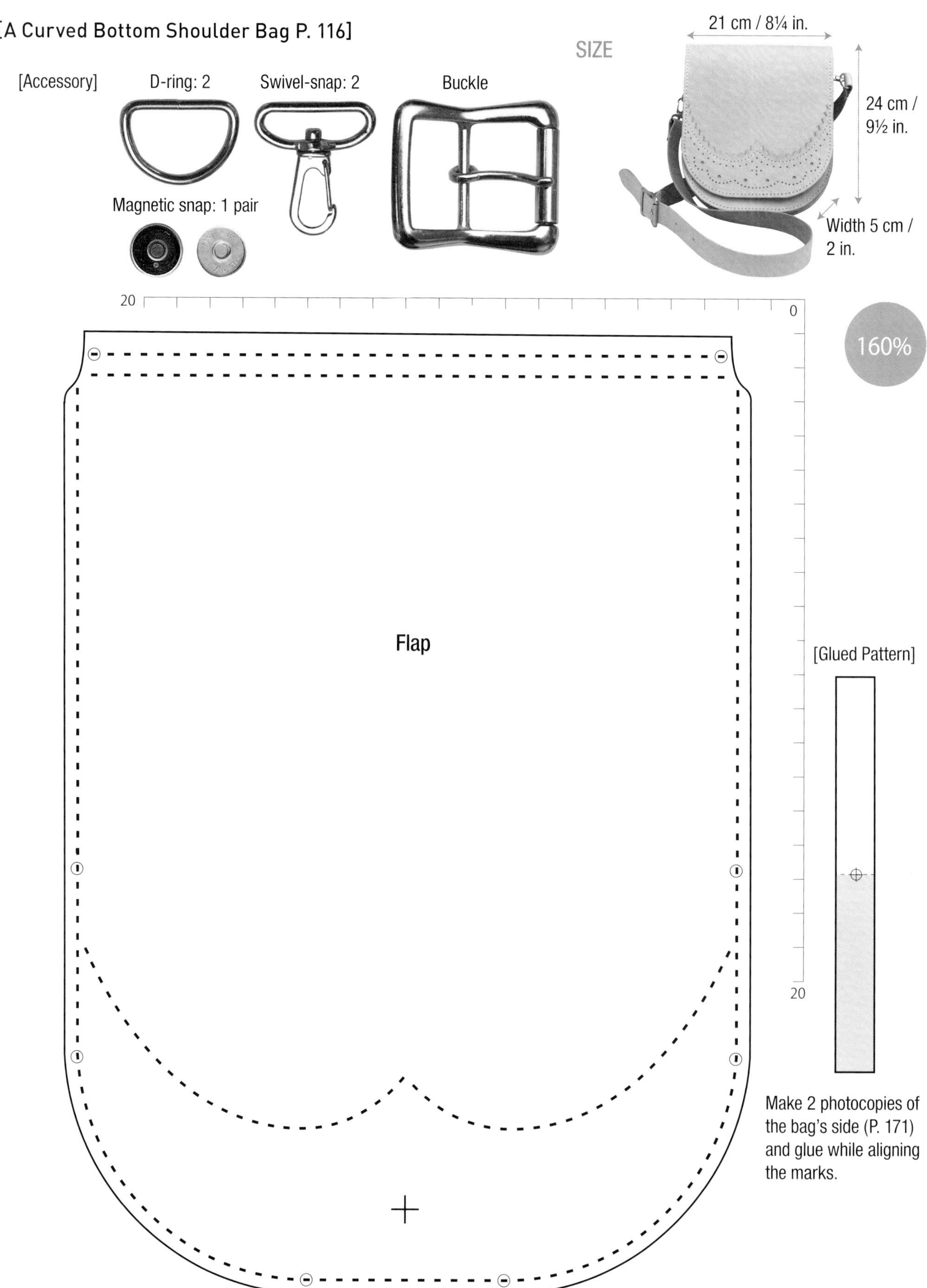

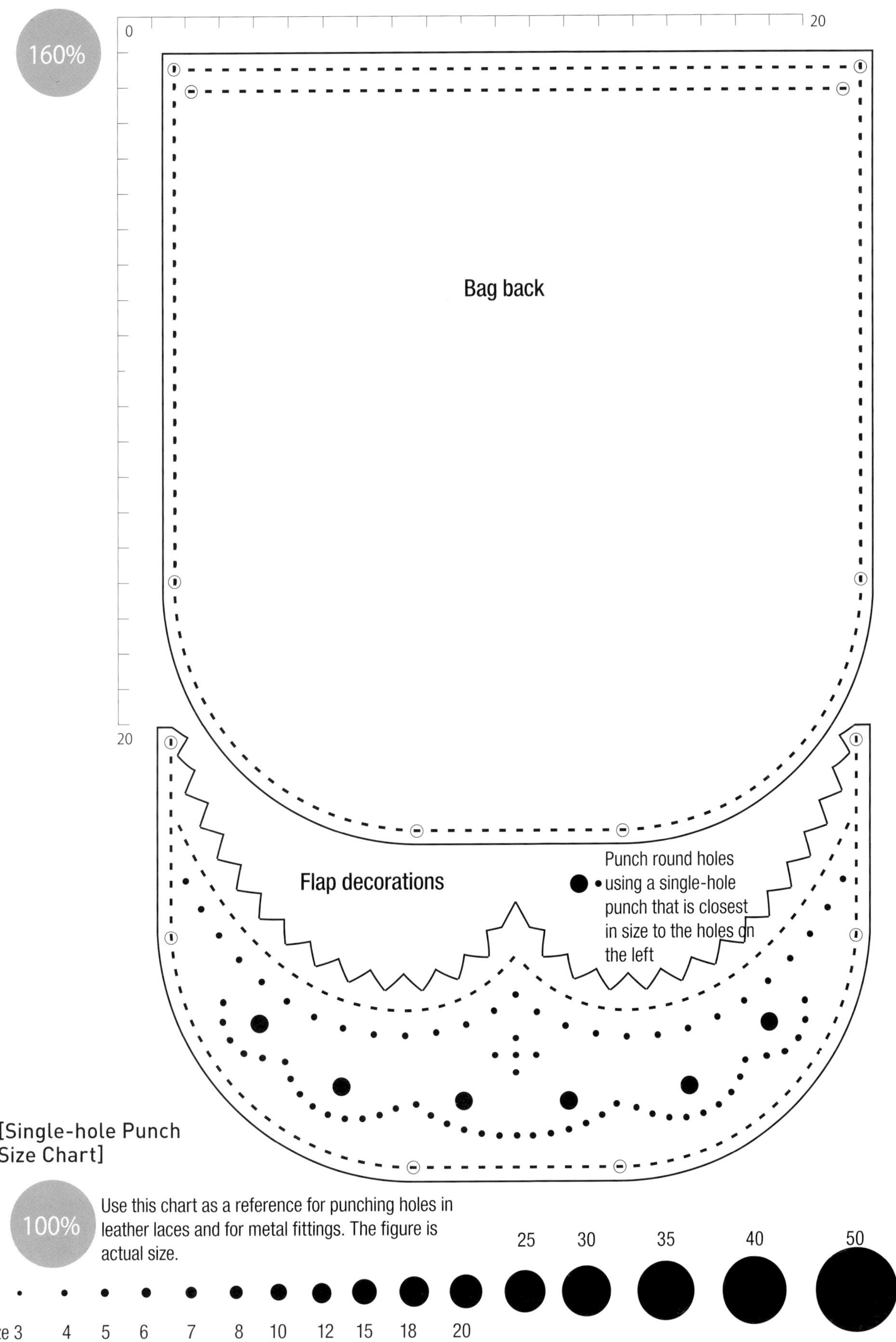
160%
0
20
20
Bag back
Flap decorations
Punch round holes using a single-hole punch that is closest in size to the holes on the left
[Single-hole Punch Size Chart]
100%
Use this chart as a reference for punching holes in leather laces and for metal fittings. The figure is actual size.
25 30 35 40 50
Size 3 4 5 6 7 8 10 12 15 18 20

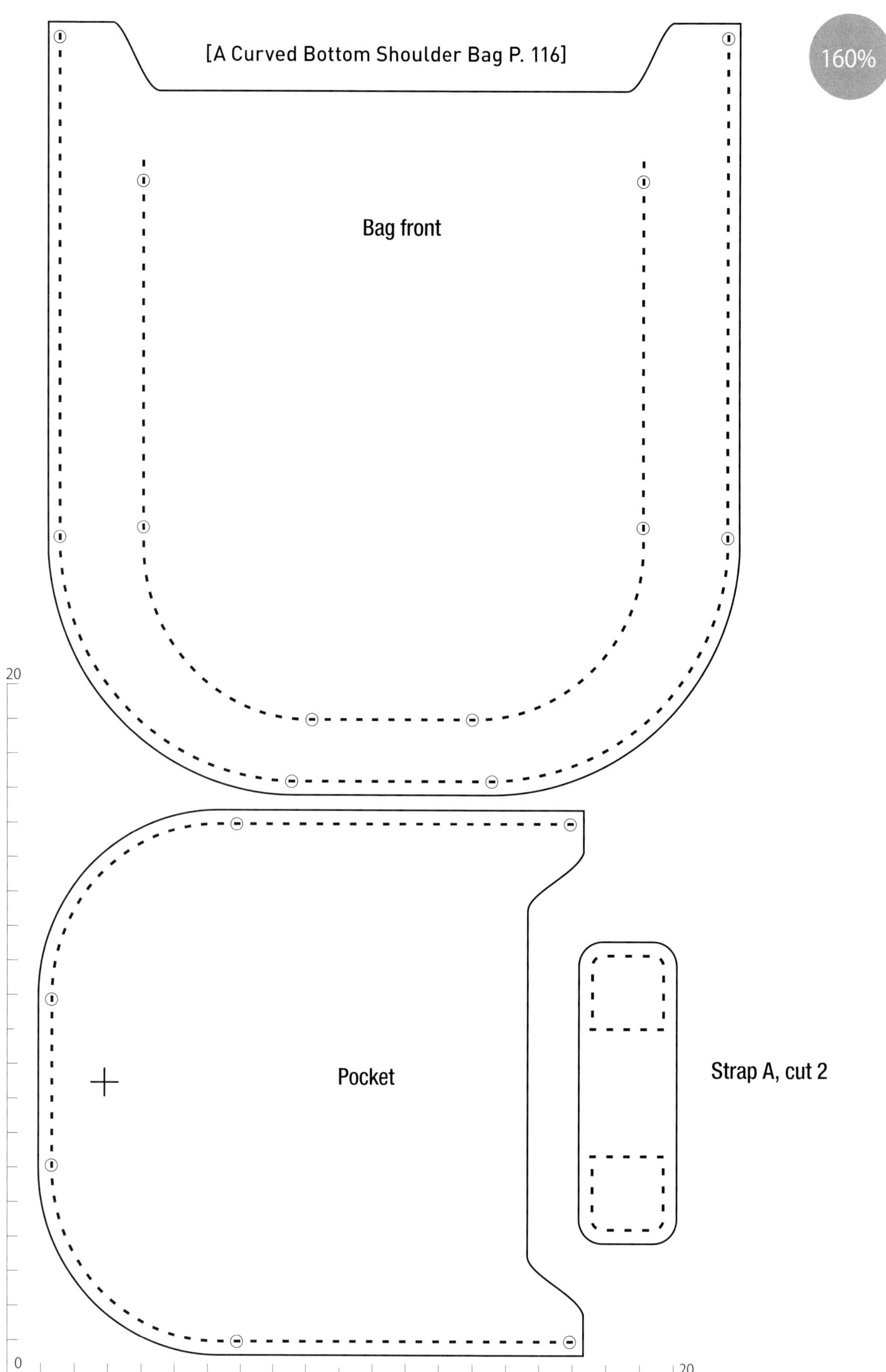

[A Curved Bottom Shoulder Bag P. 116]
160%
Bag front
Pocket
Strap A, cut 2
20
0
20

160%

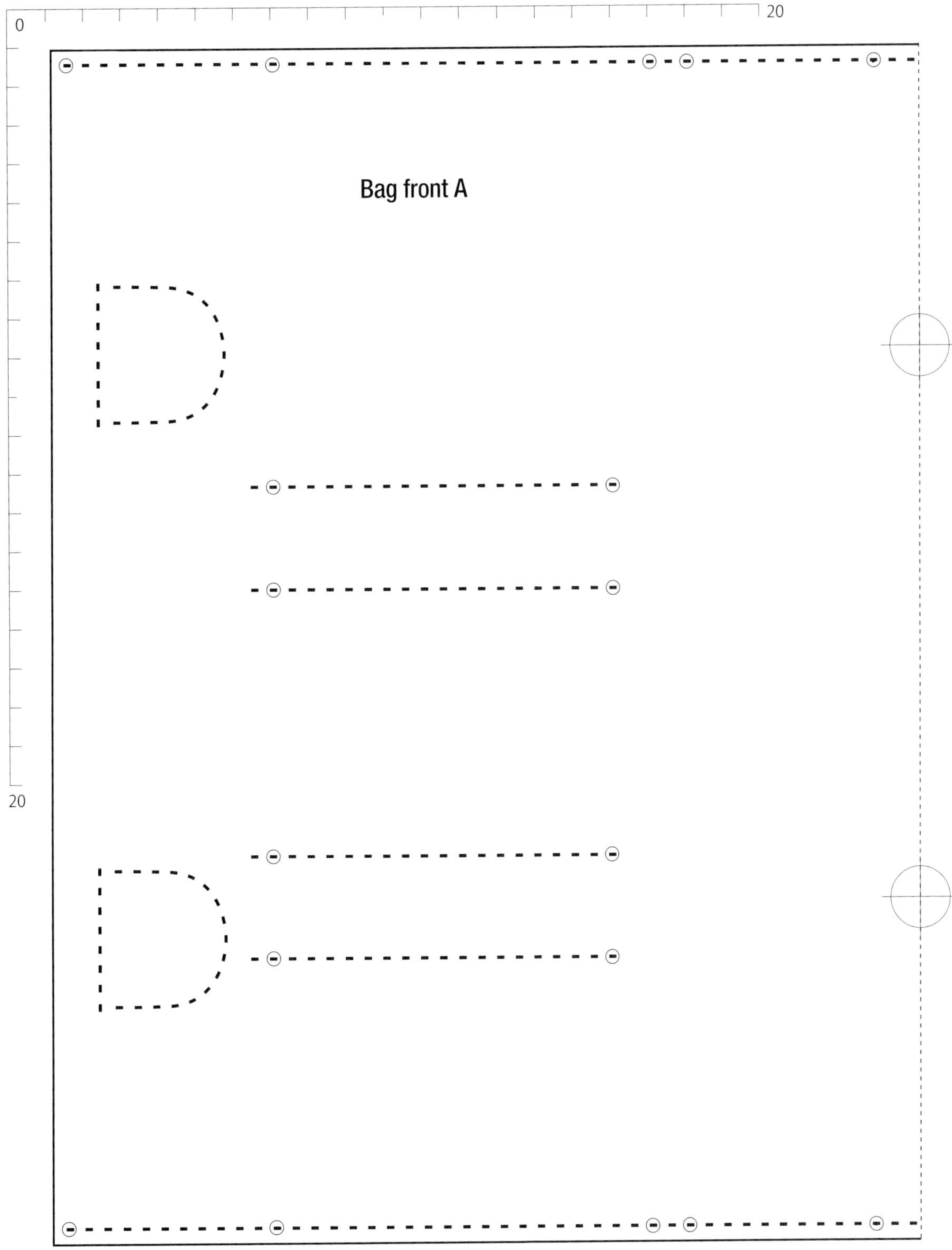

160%

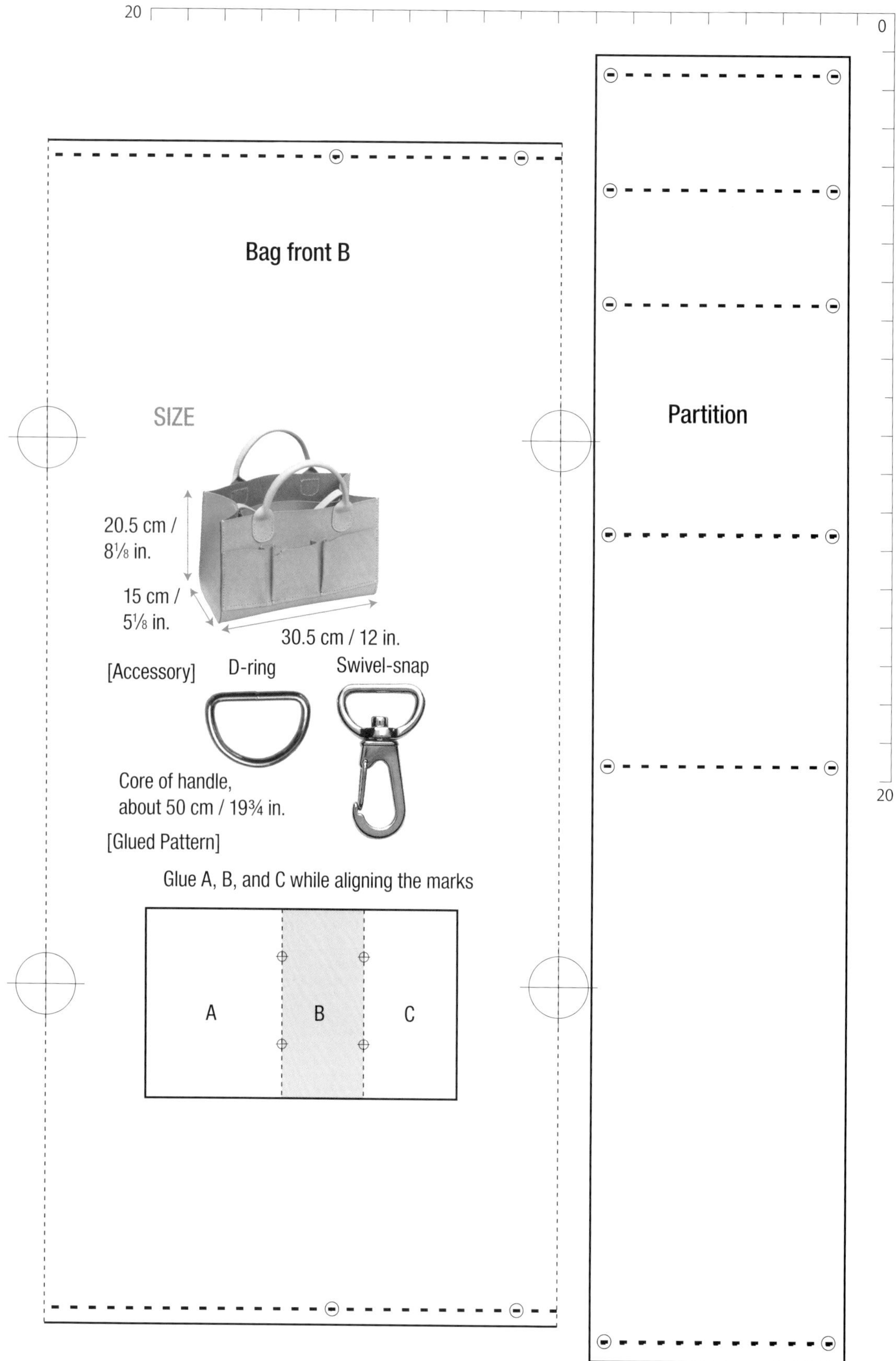
20
0
20
Bag front B
Partition
SIZE
20.5 cm / 8⅛ in.
15 cm / 5⅛ in.
30.5 cm / 12 in.
[Accessory]
D-ring
Swivel-snap
Core of handle, about 50 cm / 19¾ in.
[Glued Pattern]
Glue A, B, and C while aligning the marks
A
B
C

160%

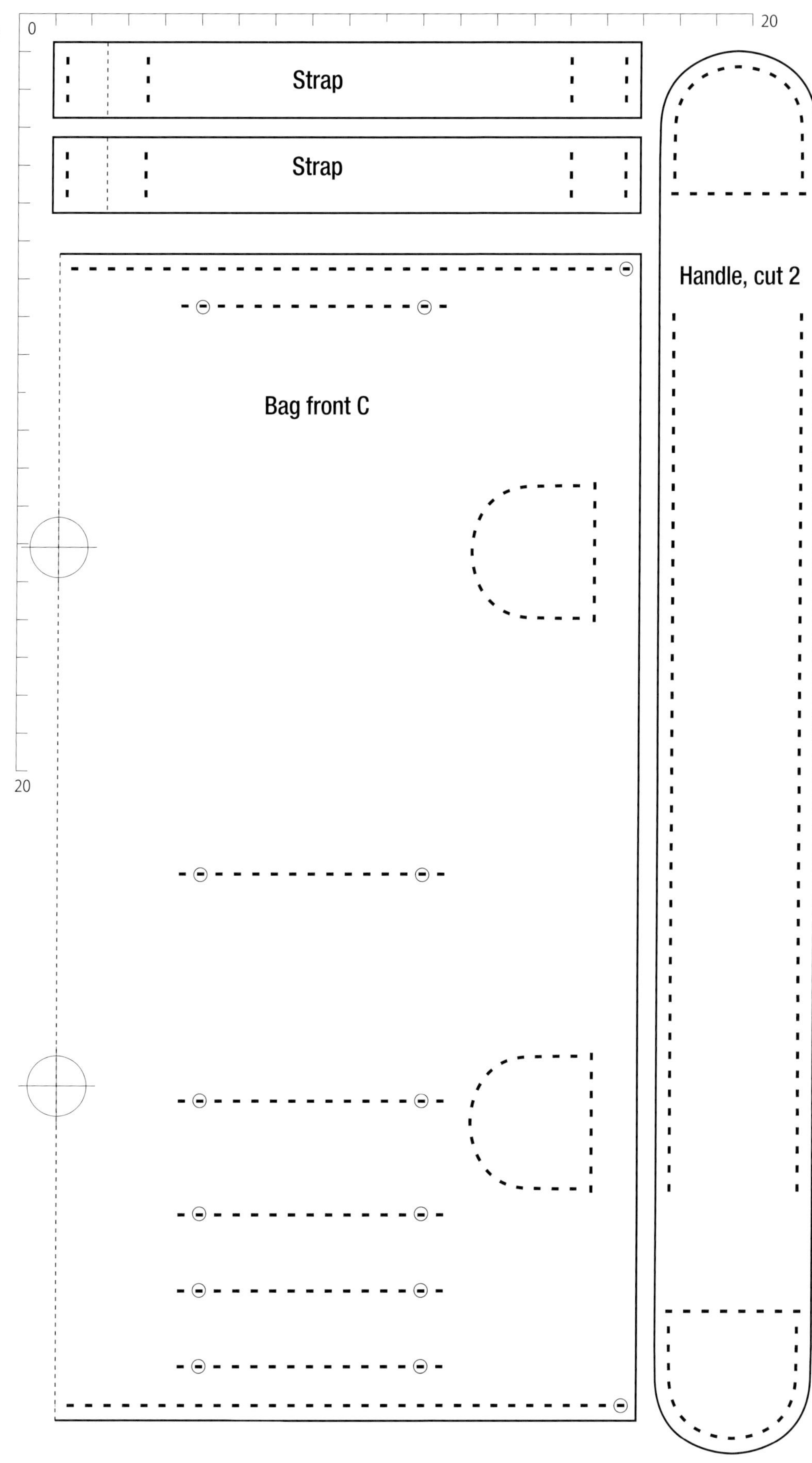

[A Tool Bag P. 120]

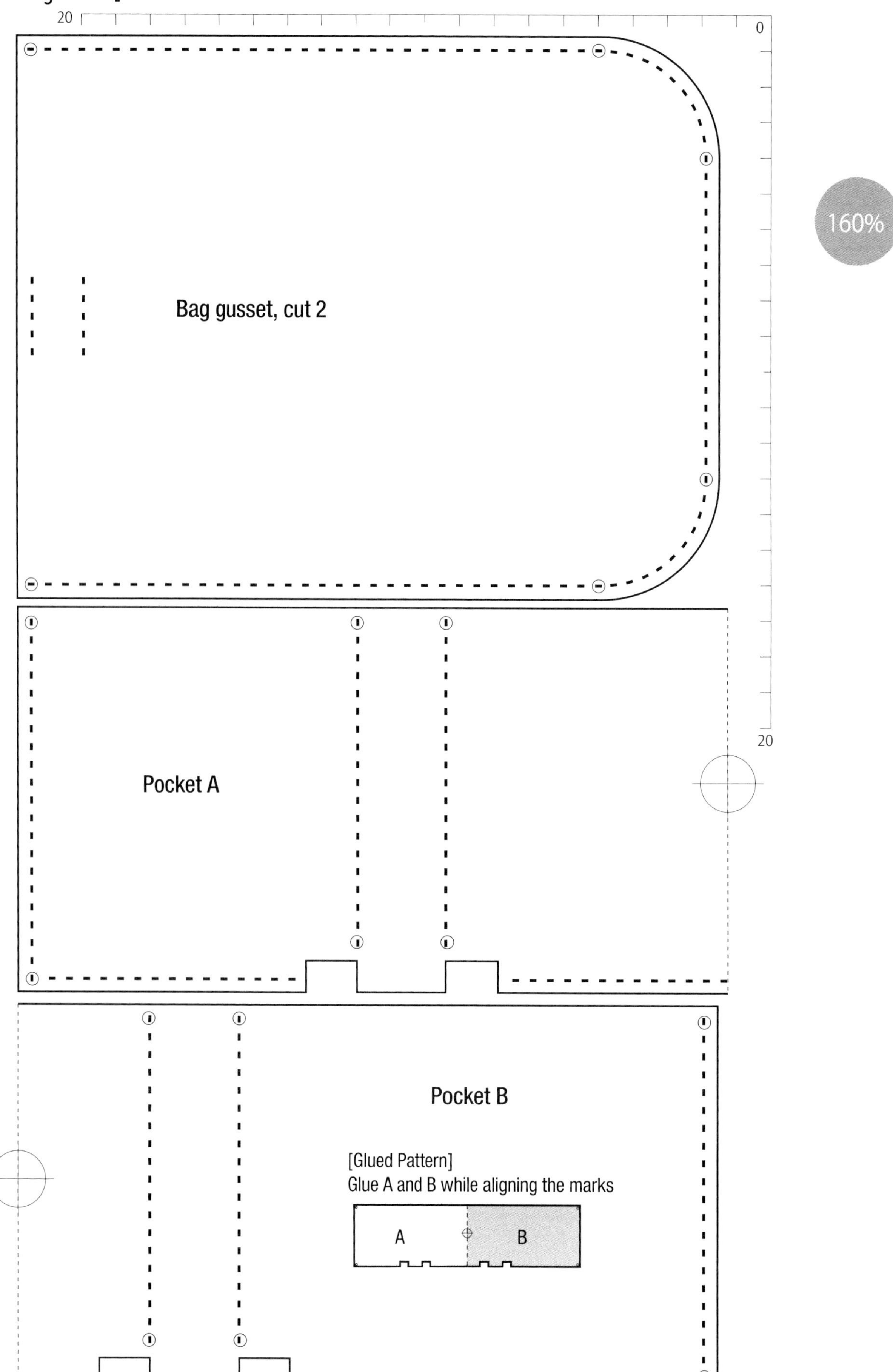

0

20

20

160%

Punch a hole in the corner using a lacing needle

Punch a hole in the corner using a lacing needle

[A Rectangular Briefcase P. 124]

Bag front, cut 2

Punch a hole in the corner using a lacing needle

Punch a hole in the corner using a lacing needle

[A Rectangular Briefcase P. 124]

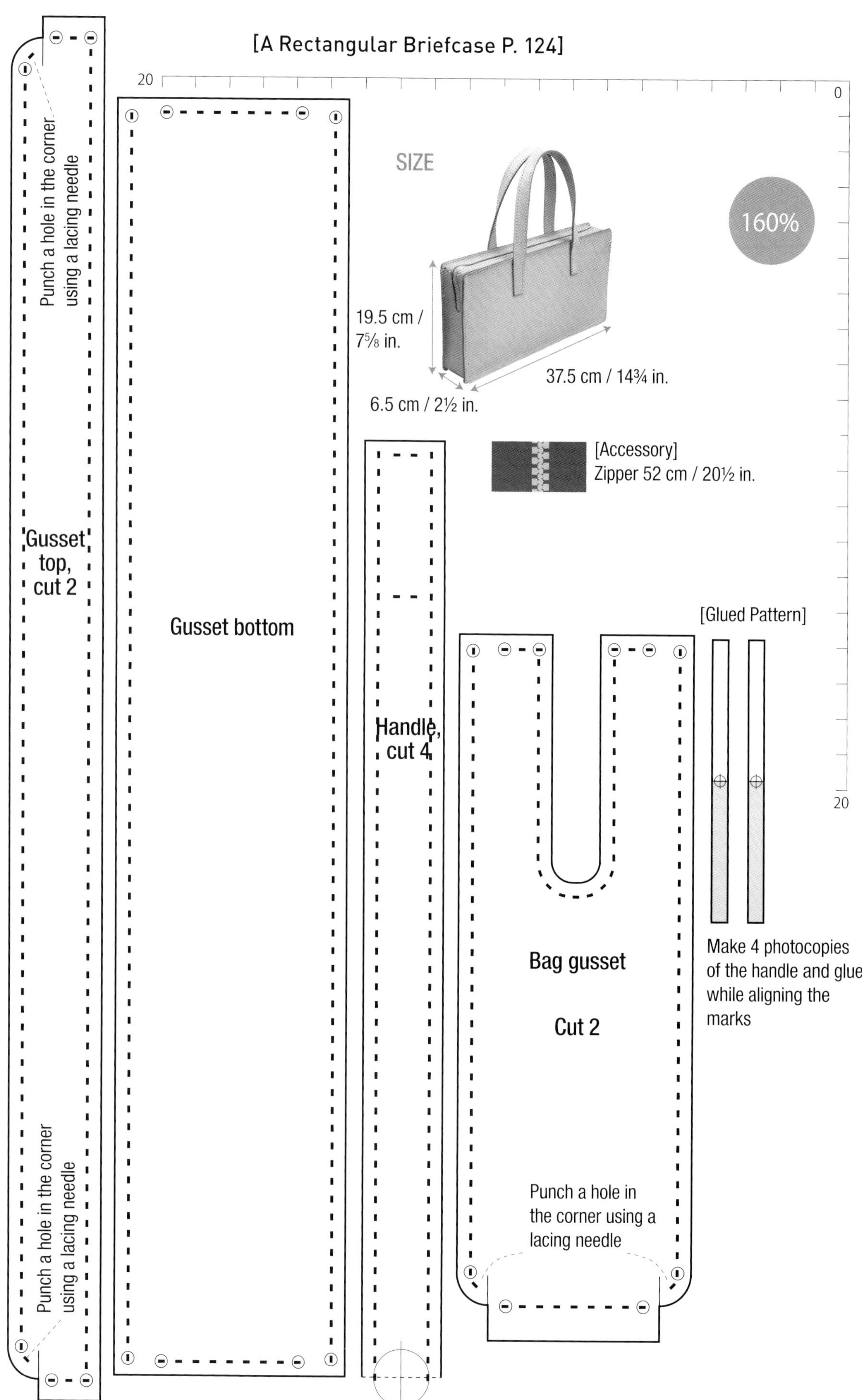

160%

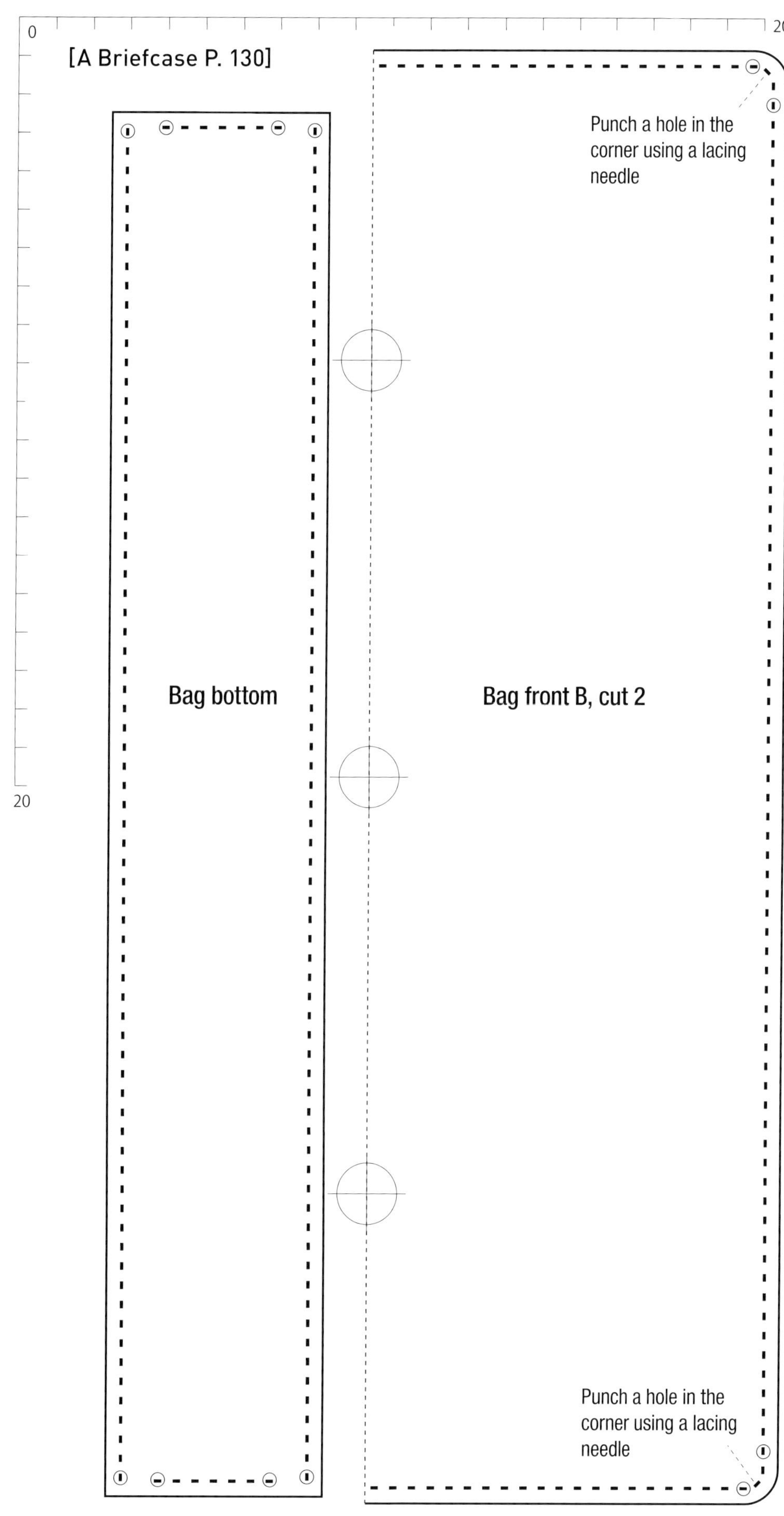
0
20
20
[A Briefcase P. 130]
Bag bottom
Bag front B, cut 2
Punch a hole in the corner using a lacing needle
Punch a hole in the corner using a lacing needle

[A Briefcase P. 130]

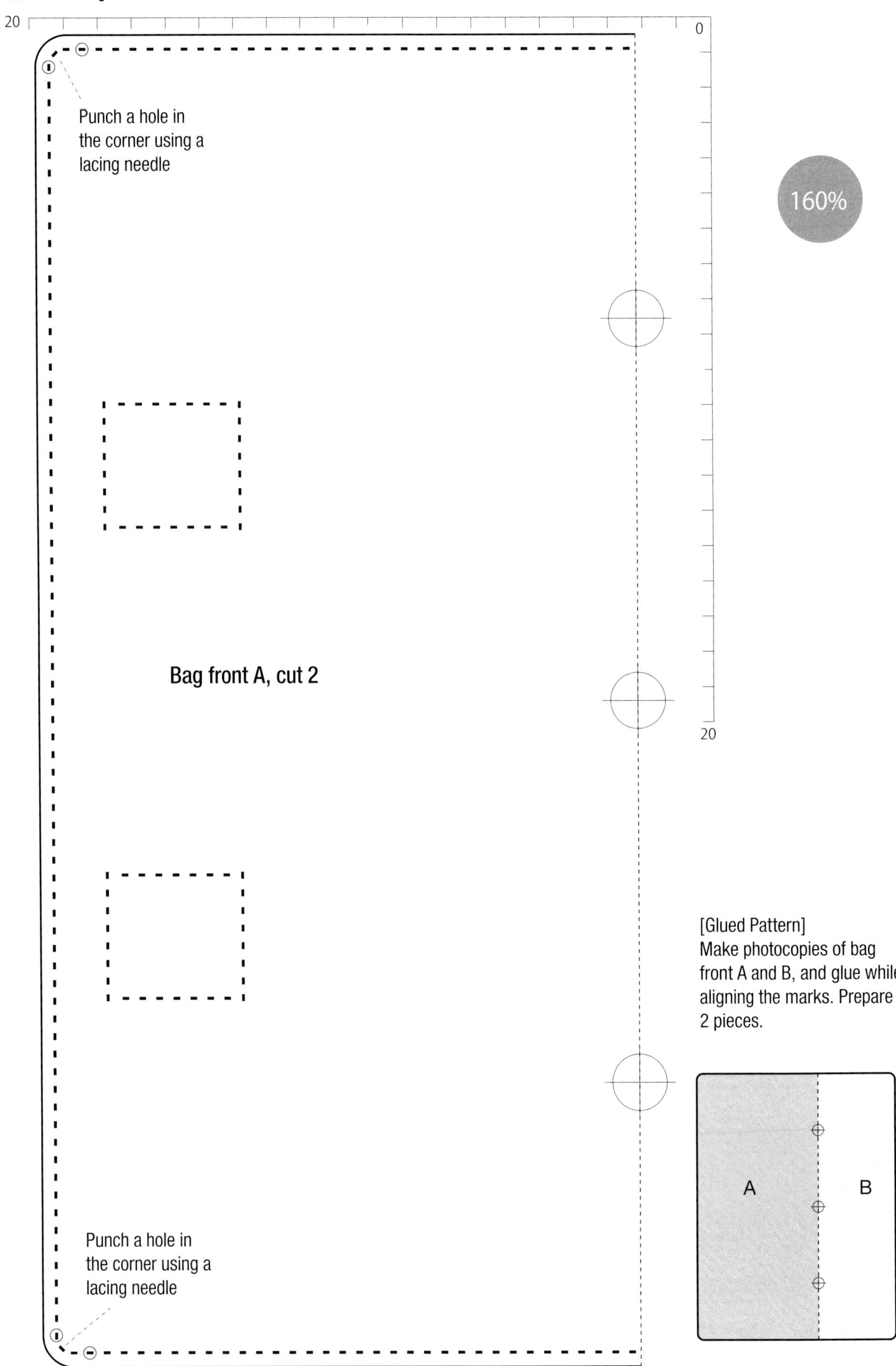

[Glued Pattern]
Make photocopies of bag front A and B, and glue while aligning the marks. Prepare 2 pieces.

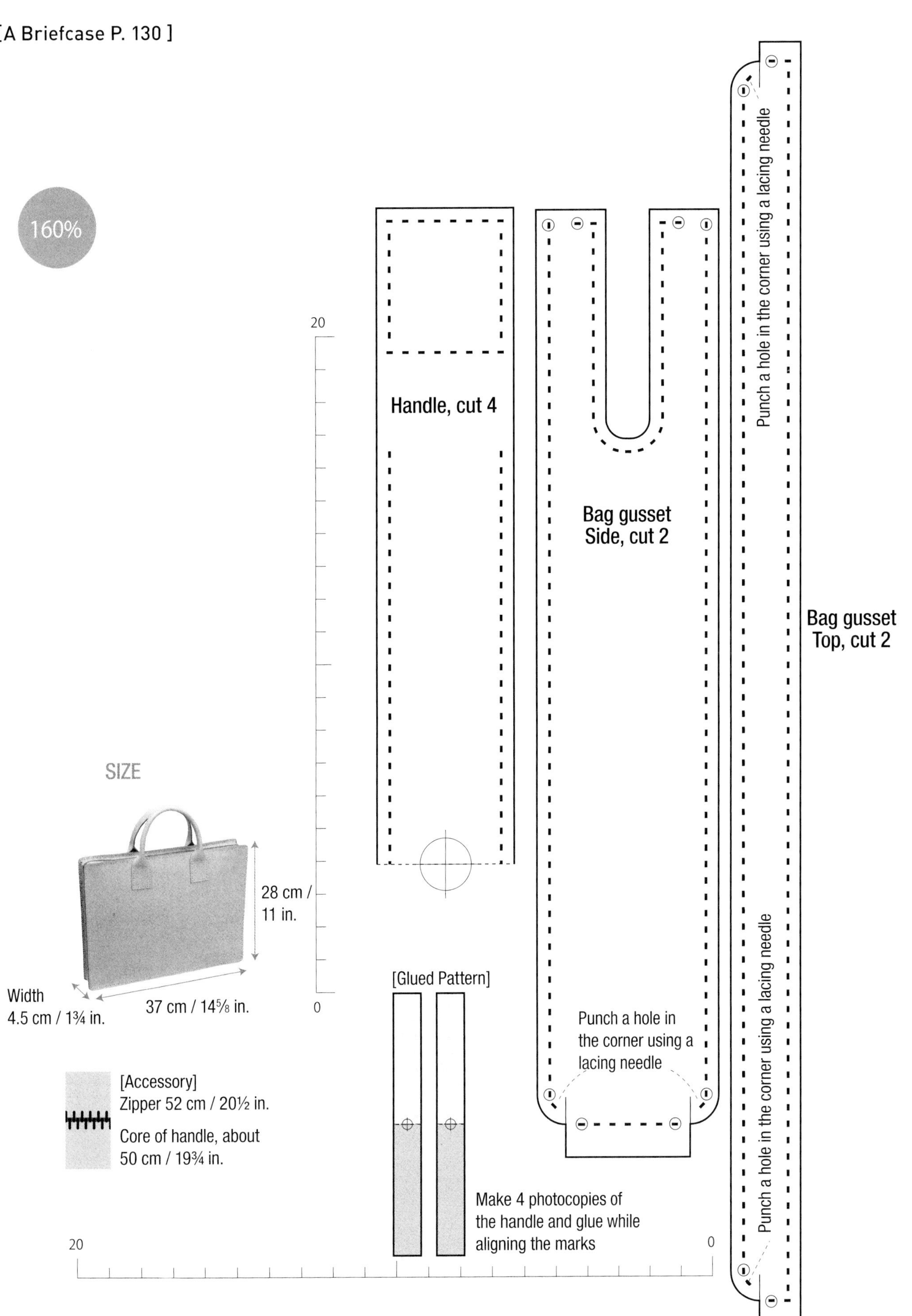

160%
20
Handle, cut 4
Bag gusset
Side, cut 2
Punch a hole in the corner using a lacing needle
Bag gusset
Top, cut 2
SIZE
28 cm / 11 in.
Width 4.5 cm / 1¾ in.
37 cm / 14⅝ in.
0
[Glued Pattern]
Punch a hole in the corner using a lacing needle
Punch a hole in the corner using a lacing needle
[Accessory]
Zipper 52 cm / 20½ in.
Core of handle, about 50 cm / 19¾ in.
Make 4 photocopies of the handle and glue while aligning the marks
20
0

Author Profile

Pigpong: Yoko Ganaha-Piggy Tsujioka

Pigpong is Yoko Ganaha and Piggy Tsujioka's arts and craft production unit.
Product planning, book design, illustration, dye, creating objects, displays, etc.
Pigpong delivers unique projects full of originality.

Tanned Leather Hand-Made Bags
Handy Patterns with Marked Stitching Holes for Hand-stitching Included
by PIGPONG (Yoko Ganaha, Piggy Tsujioka)

First designed and published in Japan in 2014 by Graphic-sha Publishing Co., Ltd.

English edition published in the United States of America in 2018 by Schiffer Publishing, Ltd.

Published by Schiffer Publishing, Ltd.
4880 Lower Valley Road
Atglen, PA 19310
Phone: (610) 593-1777; Fax: (610) 593-2002
E-mail: Info@schifferbooks.com
www.schifferbooks.com

ISBN 978-0-7643-5612-4
Library of Congress Control Number: 2018934619

First English Edition: September 2018

Printed in China
10 9 8 7 6 5 4 3 2 1

Original creative staff

Photos:	Tadashi Ikeda
Book design:	Yoko Ganaha
Editorial collaboration:	Hisako Rokkaku, Mitsue Kobayashi
Editing:	Naoko Yamamoto (Graphic-sha Publishing Co., Ltd.)

English edition

English translation:	Kevin Wilson
English edition layout:	Shinichi Ishioka
Editing:	Peggy Kellar (Schiffer Publishing, Ltd.)
Production and management:	Kumiko Sakamoto (Graphic-sha Publishing Co., Ltd.)